I0752989

HISTORIC PHOTOS OF
LOUISIANA

Text and Captions by Dean M. Shapiro

TURNER
PUBLISHING COMPANY

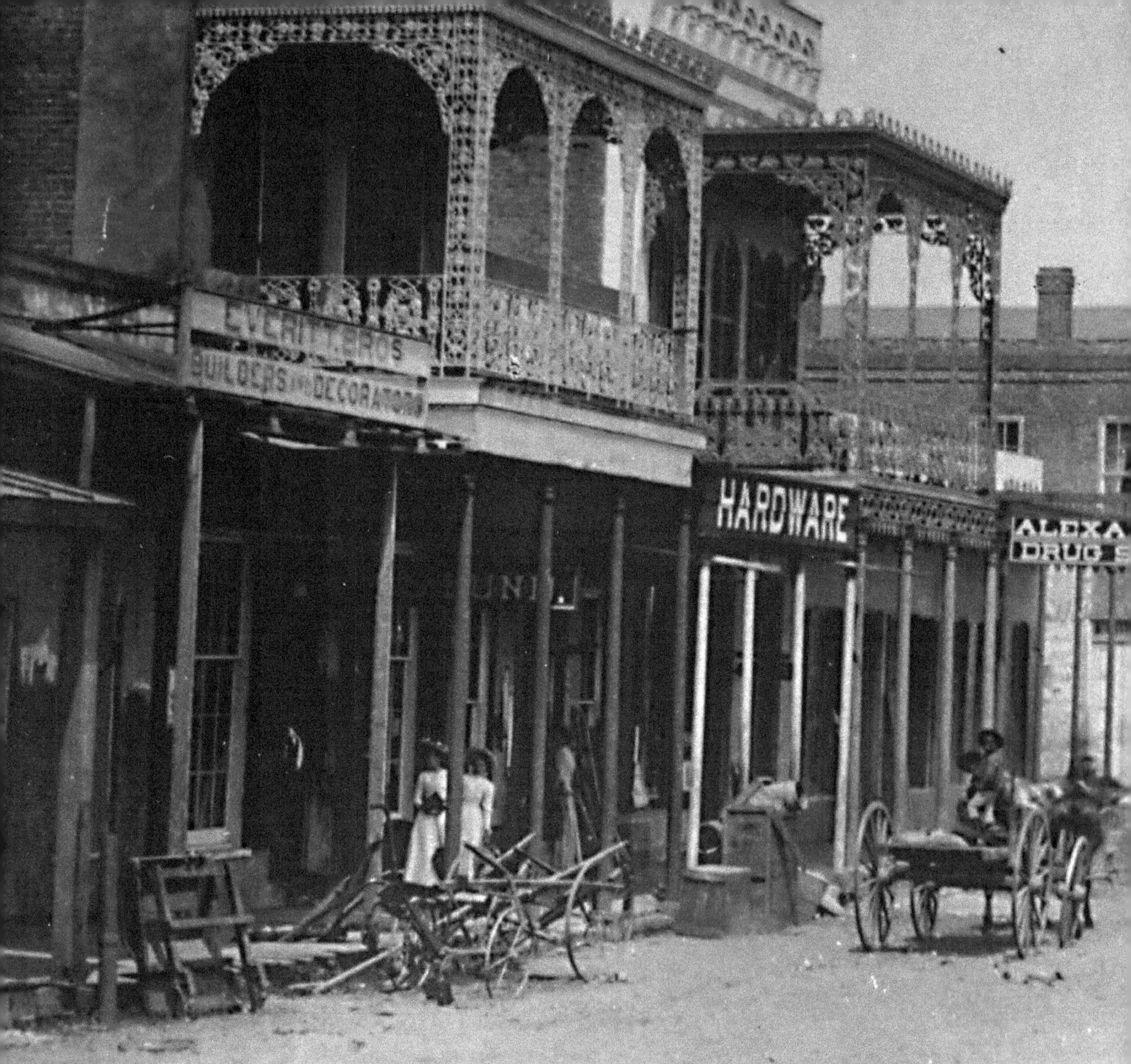

Front Street in Alexandria is seen in this 1891 image. The iron lace–styled balconies on two of the buildings resemble those of the New Orleans French Quarter and attest to the city's diverse cultural heritage. Located in the center of the state on the Red River, Alexandria is the hub of the state's "Cross Currents" section—a transitional region between the predominantly French Cajun southern parishes and the more typically Anglo-Saxon parishes of north Louisiana.

HISTORIC PHOTOS OF LOUISIANA

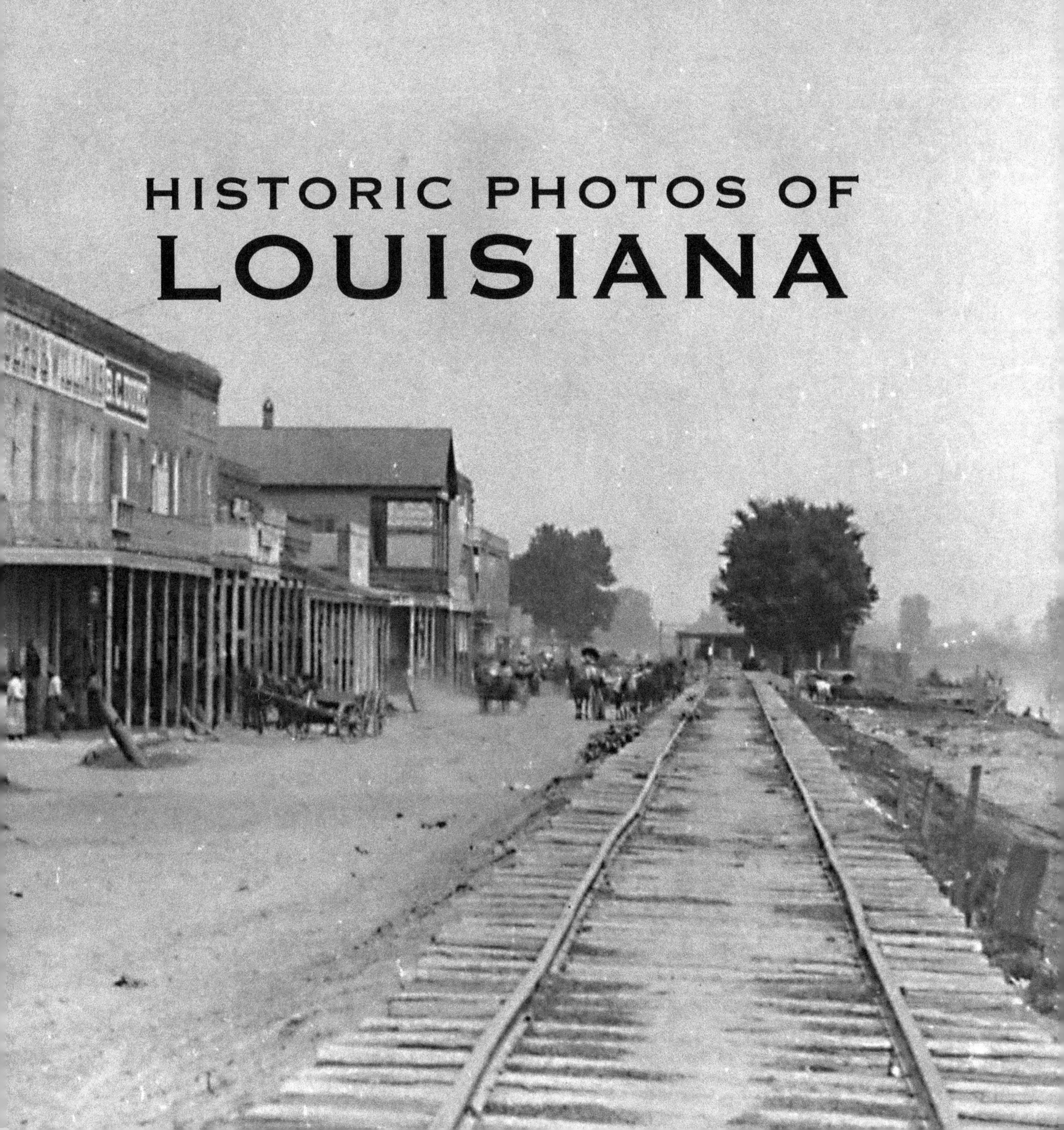

Turner Publishing Company
4507 Charlotte Avenue • Suite 100
Nashville, Tennessee 37209
(615) 255-2665

www.turnerpublishing.com

Historic Photos of Louisiana

Library of Congress Control Number: 2009933008

ISBN: 978-1-59652-557-3

Printed in the United States of America

ISBN: 978-1-68442-103-9 (hc)

10 11 12 13 14 15 16—0 9 8 7 6 5 4 3 2 1

Contents

St. Paul's Episcopal Church on Camp Street, New Orleans, is seen in this photograph taken between 1890 and 1901. At left is the white marble statue honoring Margaret Haughery, who founded an orphanage, nursed yellow fever victims, and performed other philanthropic acts in the nineteenth century. When St. Paul's was razed in the 1950s to make way for a new bridge over the Mississippi River, many of its furnishings were moved to the church's new location.

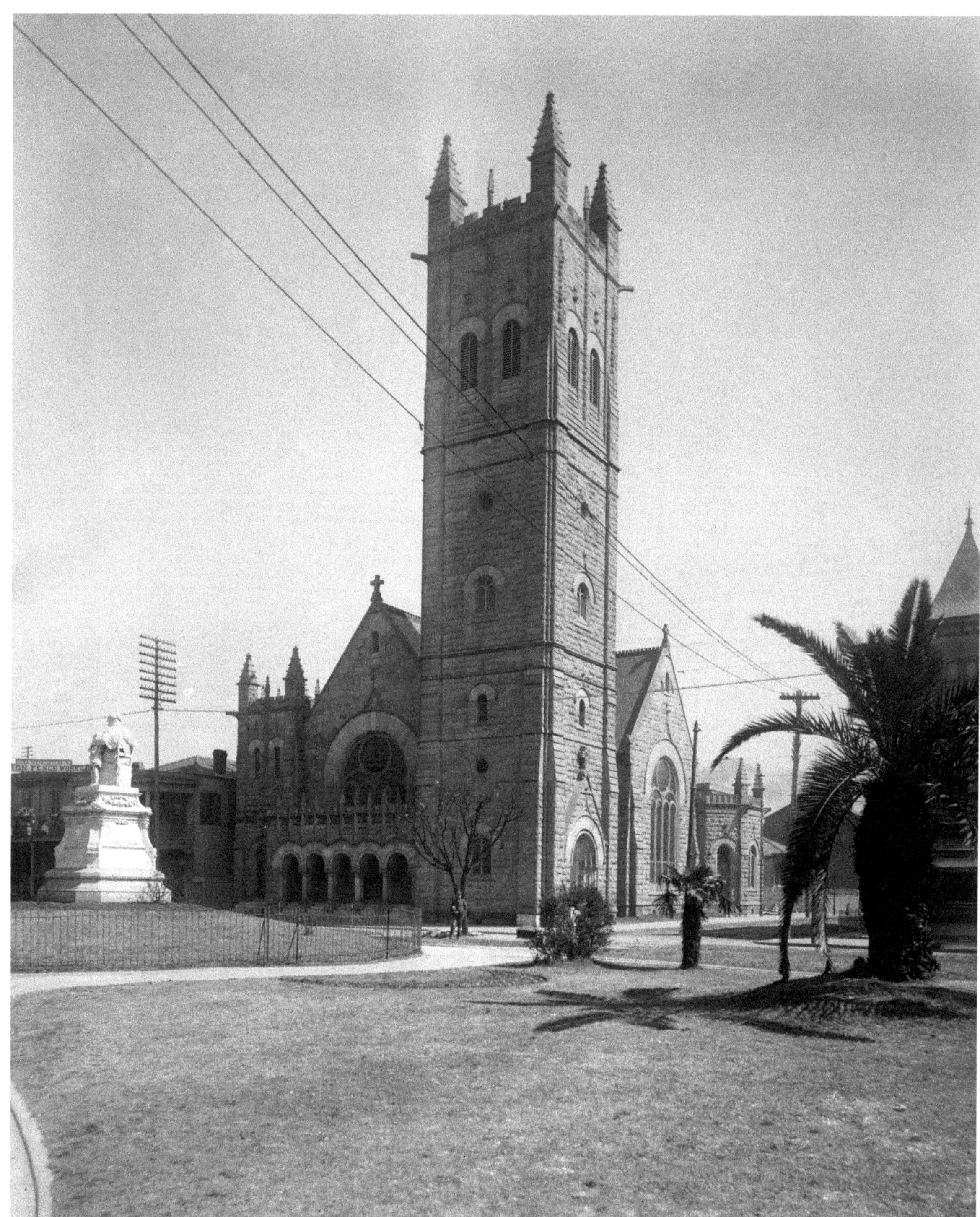

Acknowledgments

The author would like to acknowledge the contributions of the following individuals for their valuable assistance in completing this book:

Michael McCalip of Turner Publishing Company for his work in preparing the project and selecting the photos to be included.

The United States Library of Congress and the Louisiana State Library for the images seen on these pages.

Arthur Hardy, publisher of *Arthur Hardy's Mardi Gras Guide,* for helping identify the Mardi Gras photos in this book.

Greg Lambousy, Elizabeth Sherwood, and Sarah-Elizabeth Gundlach of the Louisiana State Museum for helping to identify several photos of old New Orleans.

My daughter Heather, who helped in the research, and my son Jonathan, for building me a new computer that enabled me to work much faster and more efficiently.

With the exception of touching up imperfections that have accrued with the passage of time and cropping where necessary, no changes have been made. The focus and clarity of many images is limited by the technology and the ability of the photographer at the time they were taken.

Preface

For the past 300 years—from its earliest remote settlements to the present time—Louisiana has been one of the most fascinating and culturally diverse locales on the North American continent. And one of the least-known-about until relatively recent years. With sizable sections of the state largely inaccessible until well into the twentieth century, much of Louisiana grew up in an isolation that allowed it to nurture an indigenous culture unlike anywhere else in the United States.

However, the state's strategic location at the southern end of the most important waterway on the continent virtually guaranteed that it would grow and develop into a crossroads of cultures and a center of commerce. From the roots of the tiny, precariously situated outpost near the mouth of the Mississippi River named La Nouvelle Orléans by its French founders, a great city would emerge and become a bone of contention between three European powers and a newly developing American nation. And with the waves of various nationalities that swept in from Europe, Africa, the West Indies, and elsewhere in the New World, a veritable gumbo of cultures would give New Orleans and Louisiana a unique, multi-dimensional flavor.

Natchitoches, founded in 1714, gave France a foothold in the northwestern quadrant of its recently claimed territory, while New Orleans, founded four years later, gave the French an anchor in the southern region from which to move goods and people to and from the mother country. French-speaking Acadian exiles (nicknamed Cajuns) from the British-conquered eastern provinces of Canada found their way to the remote bayous of southern Louisiana in the mid to late eighteenth century. They settled into lives of fishing, trapping, and light farming where conditions permitted. Other nationalities followed closely behind them. Among them were the Spanish who took control of the territory in the 1760s, Germans who tilled the rich alluvial soil along the lower reaches of the river, and free people of color who made their way from the Caribbean into the port of New Orleans and pursued vocations available to them at the time. Intermarriage between these groups and those of French descent resulted in a distinct Creole class that, for many years, dominated a large segment of New Orleans society.

By the time Louisiana passed into American hands, thanks to the Louisiana Purchase (which was signed in New Orleans in 1803), the stage was already set for the varied crosscurrents of culture to begin interacting and creating a new dynamic that stood out in contrast with the rest of a largely homogeneous nation. A multiplicity of languages, customs, cuisines, forms of entertainment, and artistic and architectural styles merged into a whole whose parts were distinct from one another yet were inextricably interrelated.

Religion played a leading role in the growth, development, and melding of Louisiana, both before statehood in 1812 and afterward. Catholic church jurisdictional divisions known as "parishes" later came to define the boundaries of geographical entities termed "counties" nearly everywhere else in the United States. Churches were the focal points of whole communities, spiritually as well as socially. Large-scale festivals like Mardi Gras in New Orleans and its surrounding areas have their roots in religious traditions. In the predominantly Baptist parishes of northern Louisiana, a strong work ethic helped that region to grow and prosper as well.

The twentieth century brought great changes to Louisiana, although more slowly to some regions of the state than others. The discovery of oil in northwestern Louisiana accelerated the pace of modernization there. No sooner did those reserves begin to run dry than large undersea oil deposits were discovered and tapped in the Gulf of Mexico, helping the state's southern region to enjoy its own measure of prosperity. Concurrent with the oil boom in the Gulf, the isolation of the bayou country finally came to an end. Roads and power lines brought modern conveniences to those who, for centuries, had been self-sufficient and insular. New Orleans developed into a great import-export hub for international trade. With tourism, music of all genres, and haute cuisine adding to the mix, Louisiana began playing host to millions of curious visitors of all nationalities.

In the pages that follow, the growth and development of Louisiana can be seen pictorially—almost grudgingly at times—from the 1860s to the 1960s. Unlike most other states, Louisiana was not especially eager to give up its old ways, its customs, and its priceless architectural inventory. And as time has proven in many cases, it didn't have to. Many of the old buildings seen in this book still stand. Many of the old customs still prevail. Many of the old traditions are still observed. The new coexists with the old. These are among the unique characteristics that make Louisiana such an intriguing place to this day.

—Dean M. Shapiro

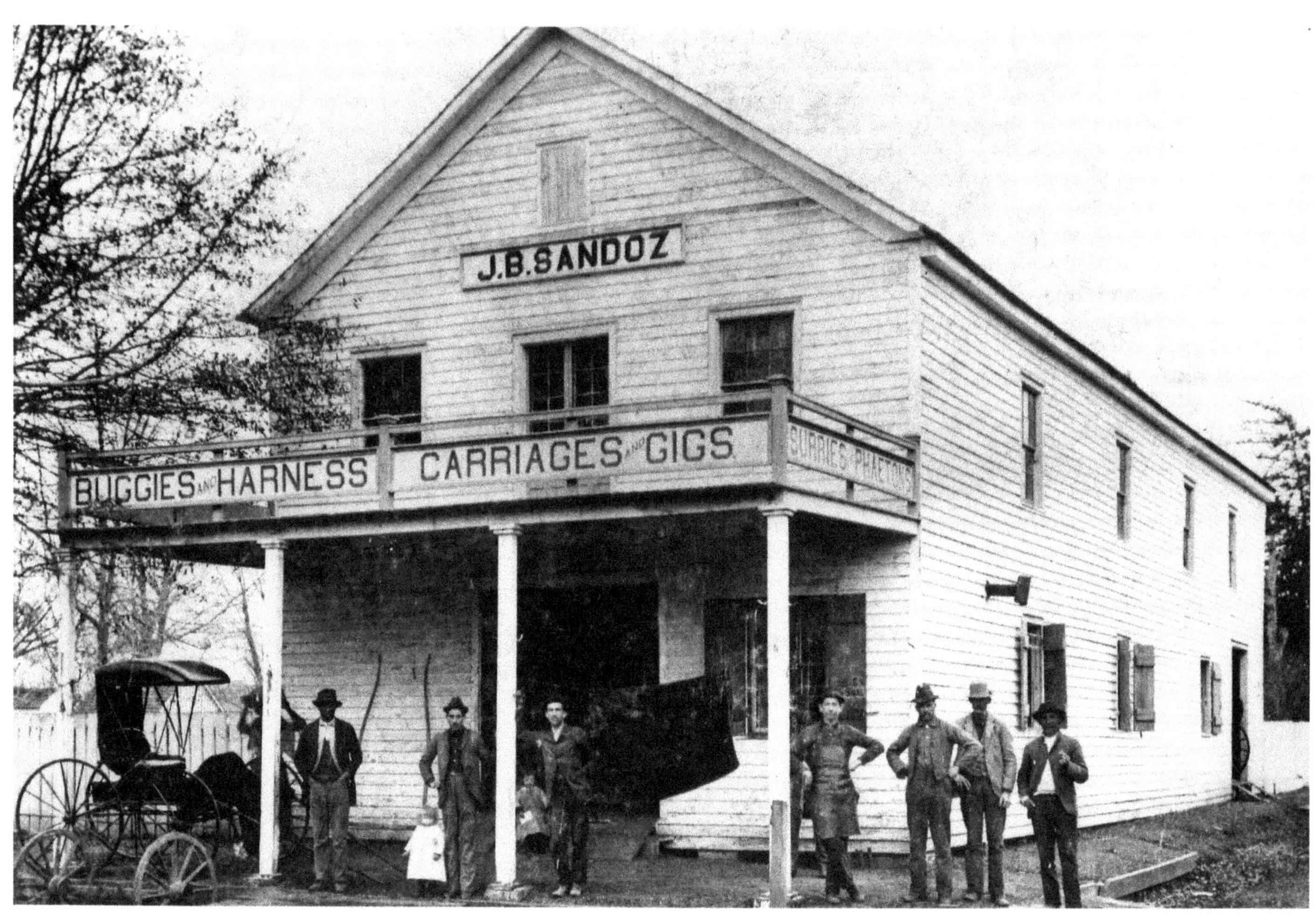

In this 1893 photograph taken in the town of Opelousas, a group of men stand around the front of the J. B. Sandoz store, which specialized in horse-drawn carriages and accessories. The parish seat of St. Landry Parish, Opelousas was founded in 1720 and is the third-oldest city in the state, after Natchitoches and New Orleans. Today it is the home of three large festivals, the Original Southwest Louisiana Zydeco Festival, the Yambilee Festival, and the Opelousas Spice and Music Festival.

Reconstruction and Return to Normality (1865–1899)

When the guns of the Civil War fell silent and the Reconstruction Era began, life began returning to normal in New Orleans and the rest of Louisiana. Having surrendered early in the conflict, New Orleans, Baton Rouge, and other cities along the Mississippi and in the interior were largely spared the devastation brought down upon other areas of the South where the fighting was more intense.

New Orleans immediately resumed its importance as a leading port city and commerce once again flowed into the docks and markets there. The city's cultural, social, and religious life returned to normal as well. Mardi Gras parades hit the streets again after a four-year hiatus. New construction abounded, commodity prices were stabilized, electrified railways connected outlying neighborhoods with the bustling downtown, and prosperity was enjoyed by many.

Elsewhere in the state life returned to normal as well. Smaller towns and rural villages were connected by railroads and improved roadways. New and improved ways of transporting goods to market were devised. Machines began replacing human labor as the method of harvesting crops on a large scale.

A newly enfranchised segment of the population, the former slaves, contributed significantly to the postwar growth of the state's economy and social life. Although emancipated from the forced drudgery of their former existences, most of them chose to stay on where they were, continuing to work the land as small farmers and sharecroppers. For a brief time they enjoyed unprecedented political power, but by the end of the nineteenth century, many of their newly gained rights had been compromised by "separate but equal" Jim Crow laws resulting from a Supreme Court decision on a New Orleans test case.

As the twentieth century dawned, Louisiana stood poised on the threshold of a new era of technology and industrialization that would bring about great changes in the lives and lifestyles of the state's largely rural population. New discoveries were about to be made that would forever alter the landscape and introduce an insular populace to the intricacies of the modern world. Despite the changes that were coming, most Louisianians stubbornly clung to their treasured past and preserved a priceless heritage that can be appreciated to the present day.

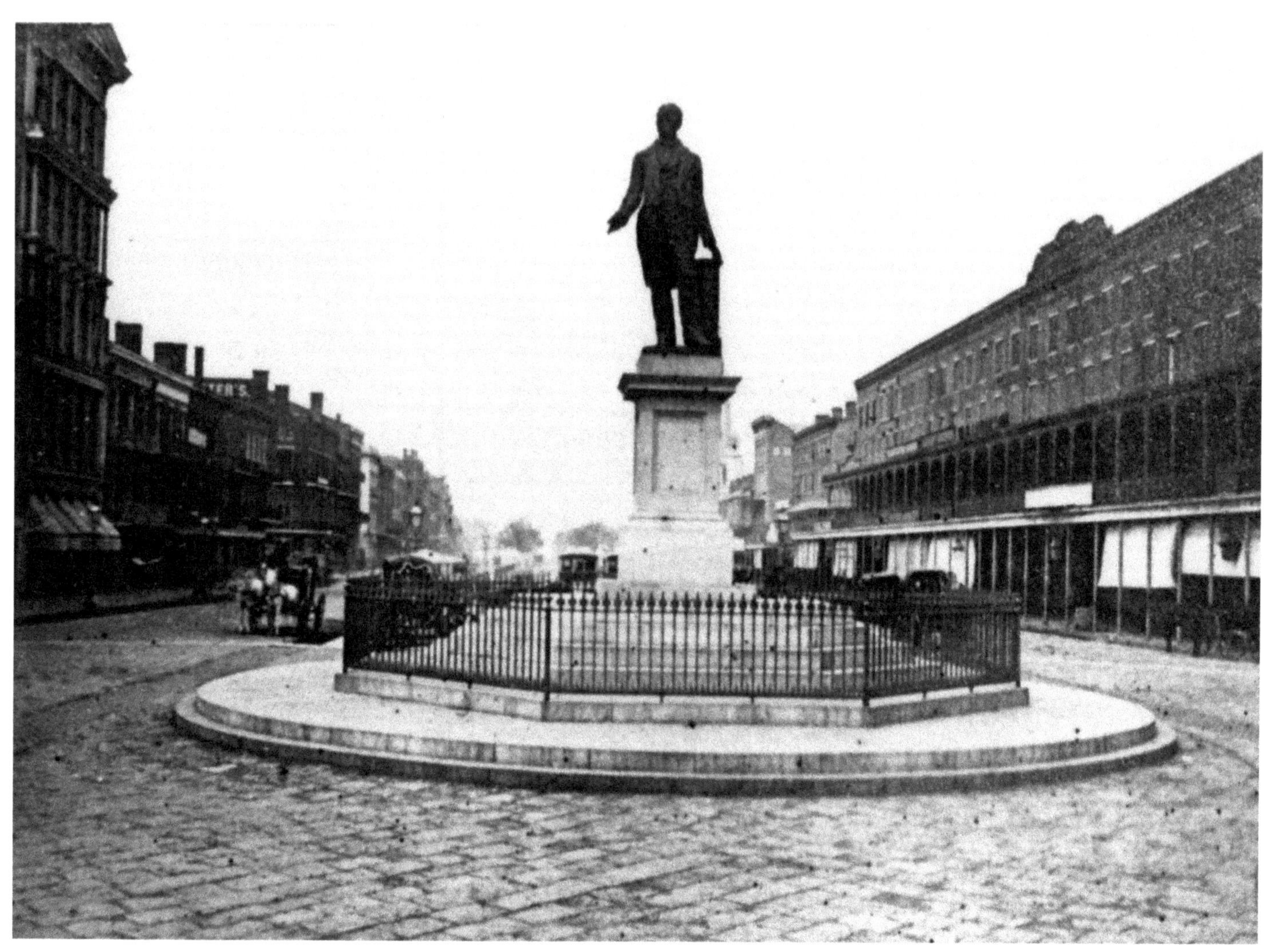

A statue of statesman Henry Clay stands in the middle of New Orleans' Canal Street in this photograph from around 1865. It was created by Joel T. Hart and dedicated in 1860. Clay, "the Great Compromiser," was revered in the South for his efforts to strike a balance in Congress between the slaveholding and free states. A street in uptown New Orleans is named for him. The statue was later moved to Lafayette Square.

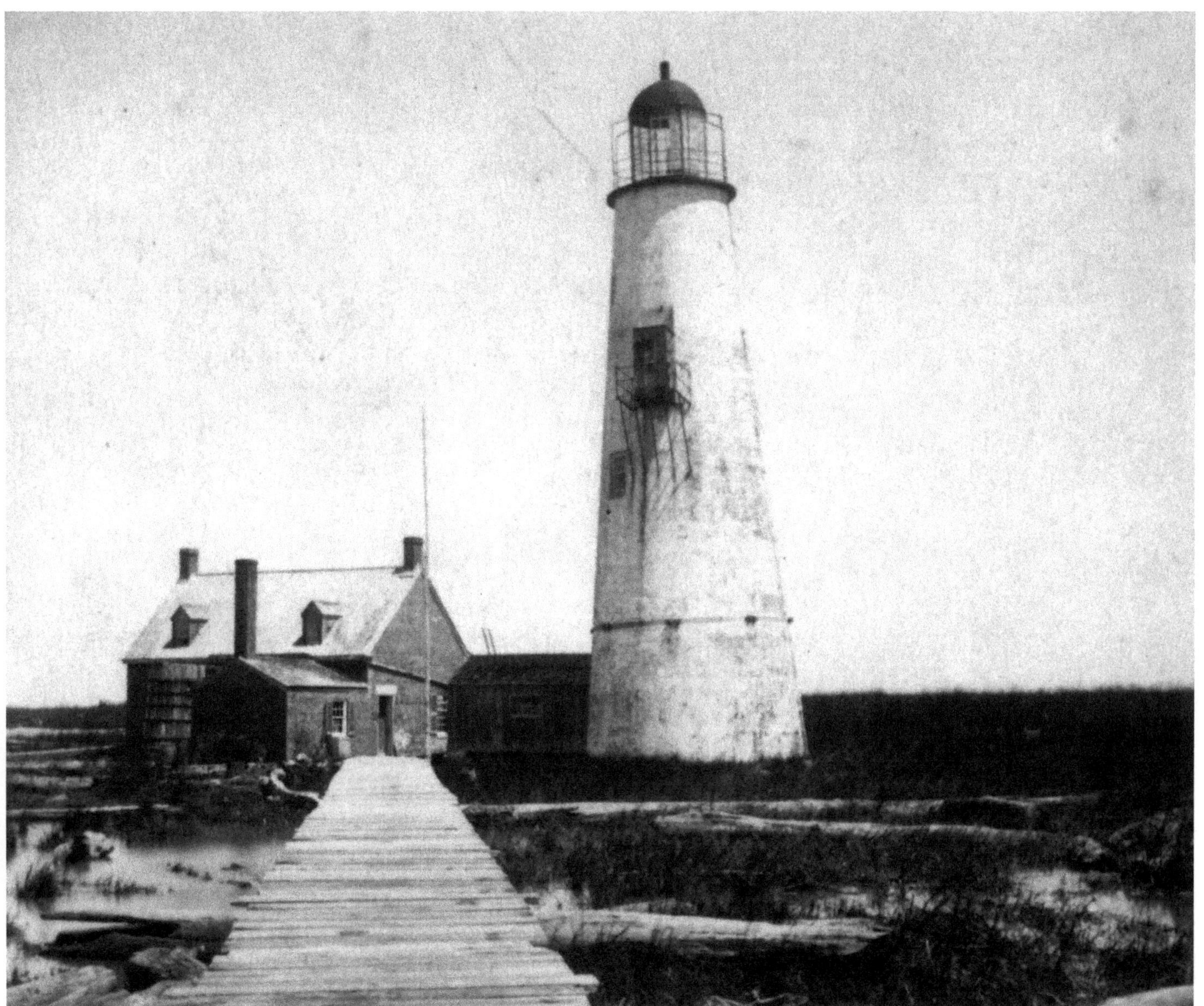

This 1867 image shows the lighthouse at Southwest Pass, the farthest south of several mouths of the Mississippi River. Also seen are the lighthouse keeper's house and the wooden boardwalk leading up to it. The second such brick structure to be built in that location, it was ill-adapted for its swampy base and soon began leaning dangerously like its predecessor. It was replaced in 1871 with a house of lighter skeletal design, which still stands although it is no longer functional.

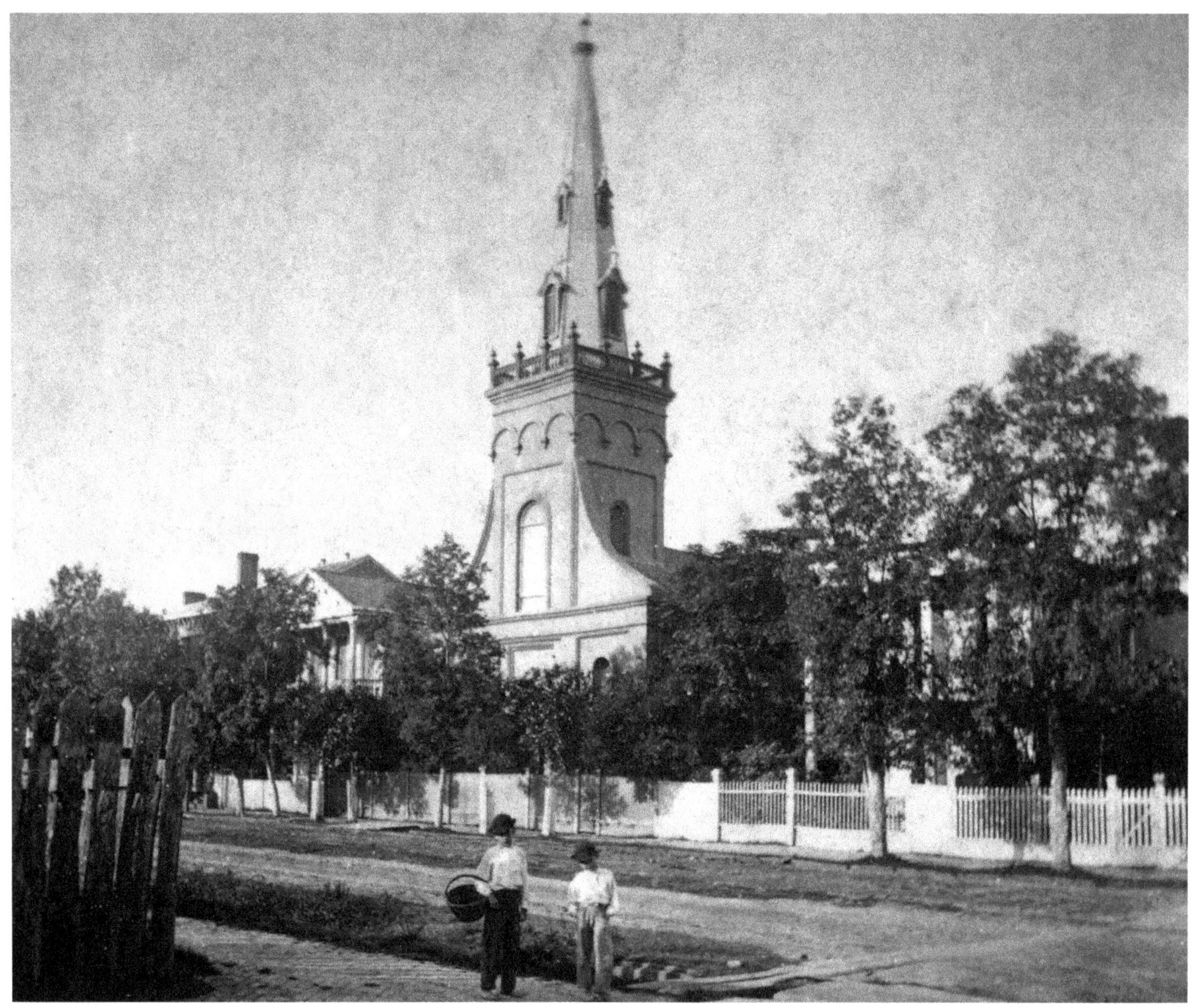

Notre Dame de Bon Secours (Our Lady of Good Succor) Catholic Church on Jackson Avenue in 1872. Early Catholic churches in New Orleans were built to accommodate congregations representing various nationalities, so that they could be ministered to in the language commonly spoken—in this case French. Notre Dame was designed by architect dePouilly in a modified Romanesque style. When this church was damaged by a hurricane in 1918, it was not repaired and was demolished in 1925.

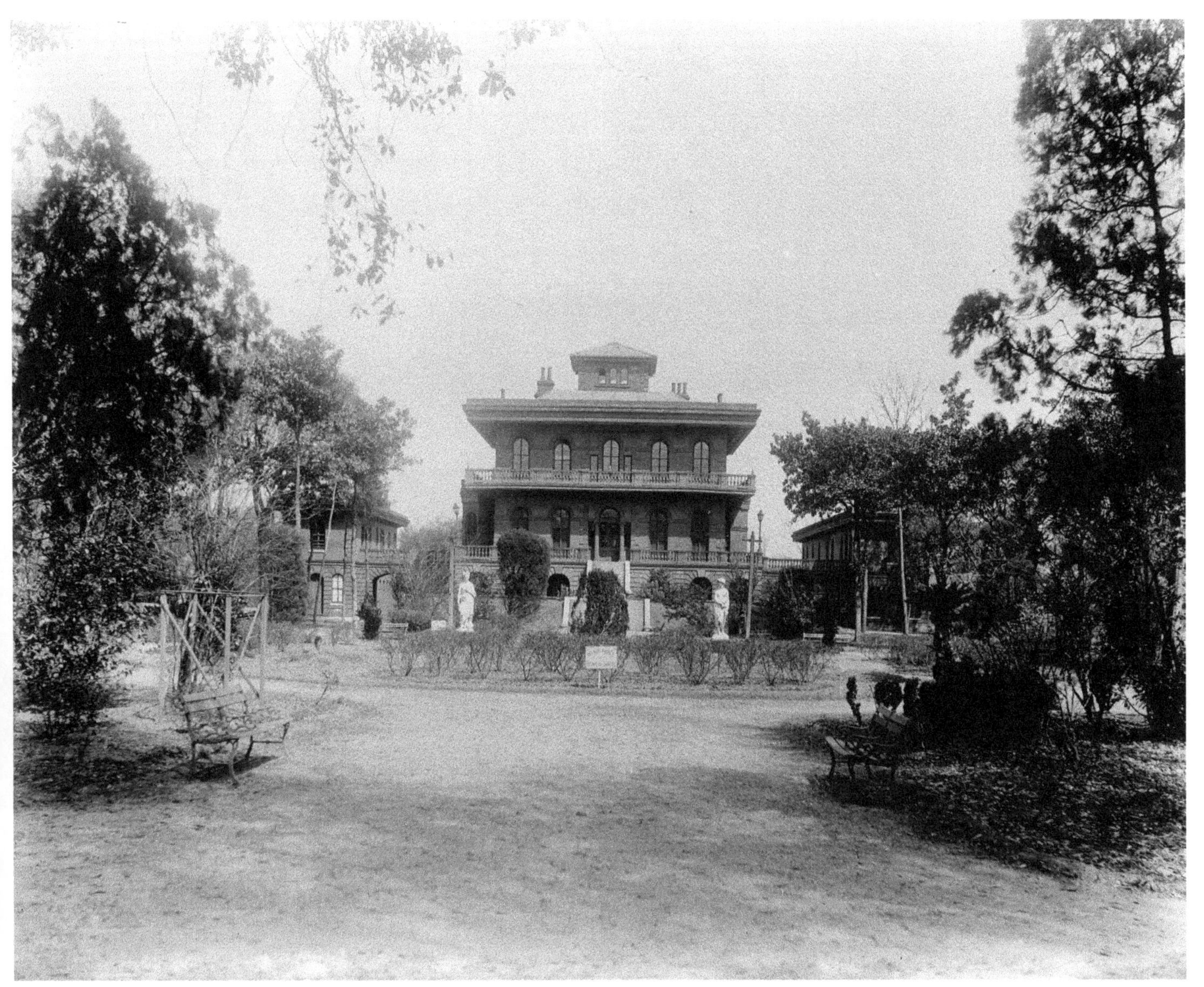

The headquarters of the Louisiana Jockey Club of New Orleans is seen in this photograph from the late nineteenth century. Designed by James Gallier, Jr., and built in 1865 for the prominent Luling family near Bayou St. John, it was sold to the Jockey Club in 1871 when the club took over management of the Fair Grounds Race Course nearby. It served as the club's headquarters for the next 20 years and still stands today, but is not open to the public.

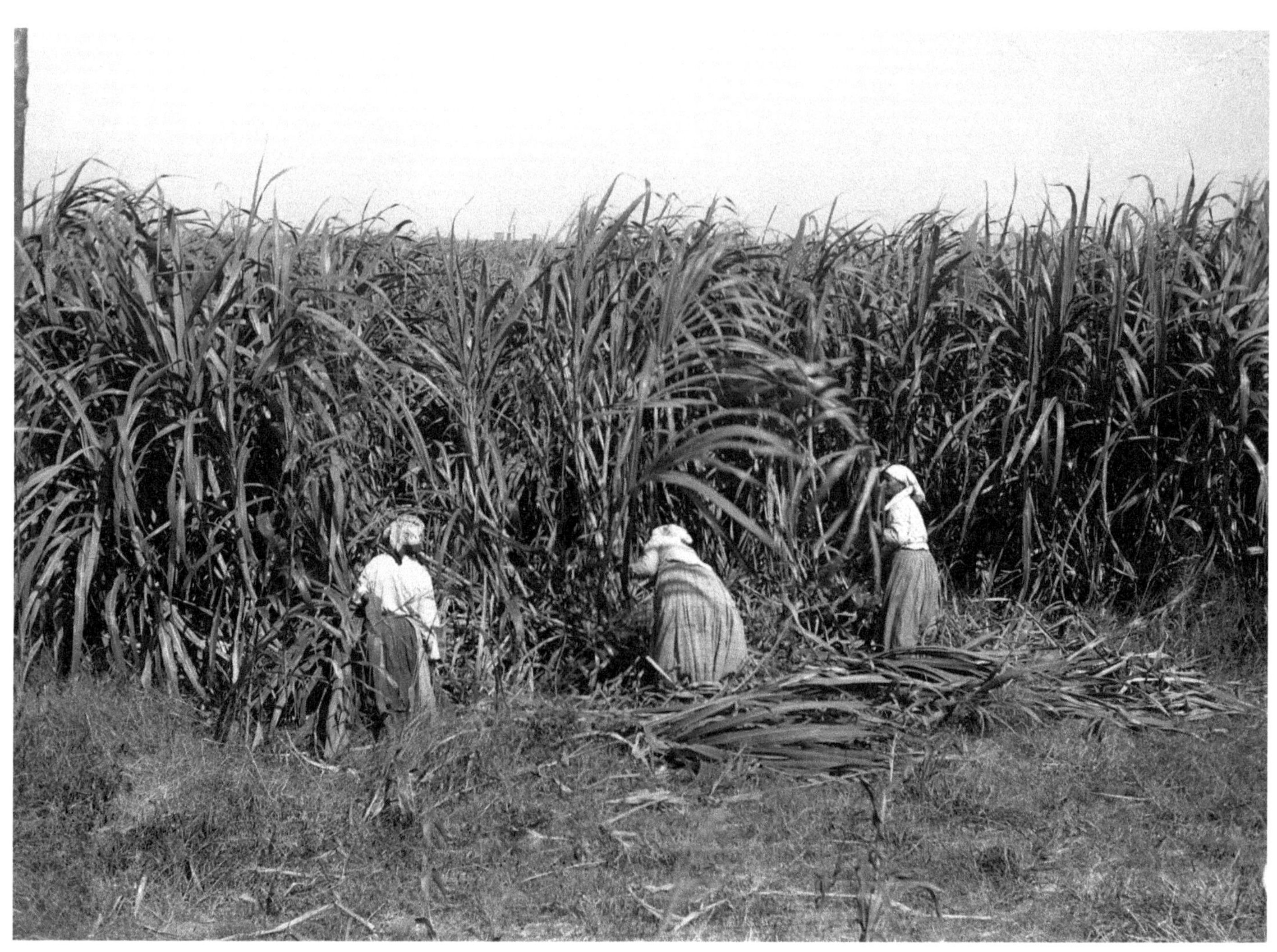

Three women harvest sugarcane by hand in southern Louisiana in this photograph from the 1880s. Sugarcane has been a leading agricultural product for south Louisiana for nearly 300 years, since its introduction by the Spaniards in the 1700s. Etienne de Bore, the first mayor of New Orleans, revolutionized the industry by being the first to produce granulated sugar. Today most sugarcane is harvested by machinery.

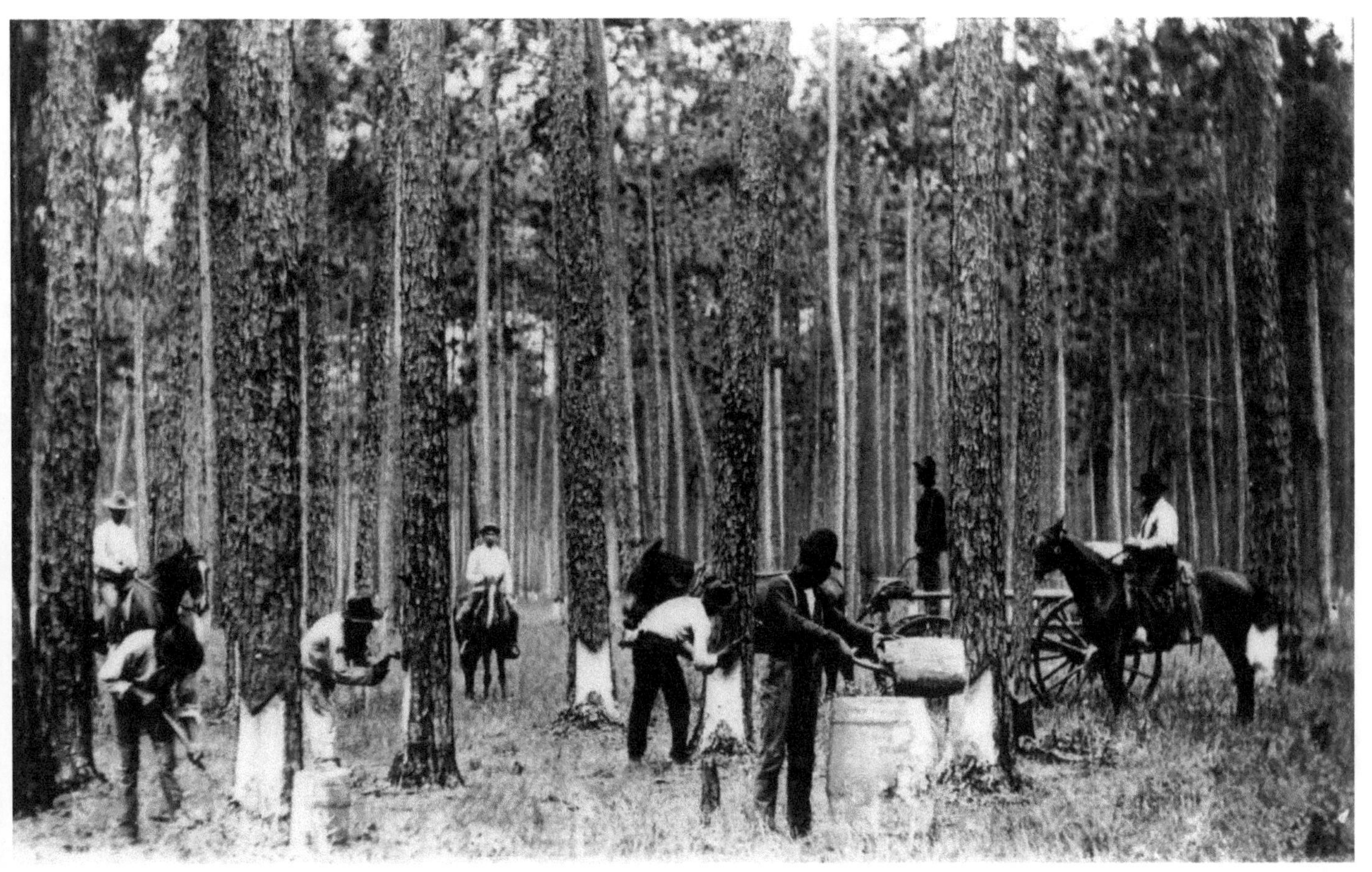

Workmen gather pine tar for the manufacture of turpentine in a forest outside Covington as three foremen on horseback supervise. In the late nineteenth century, the extensive pine forests north of Lake Pontchartrain were an abundant source of pine tar, used in making various products, including lacquers, turpentine, and the pine resin itself, which served as a lubricant for stringed musical instruments.

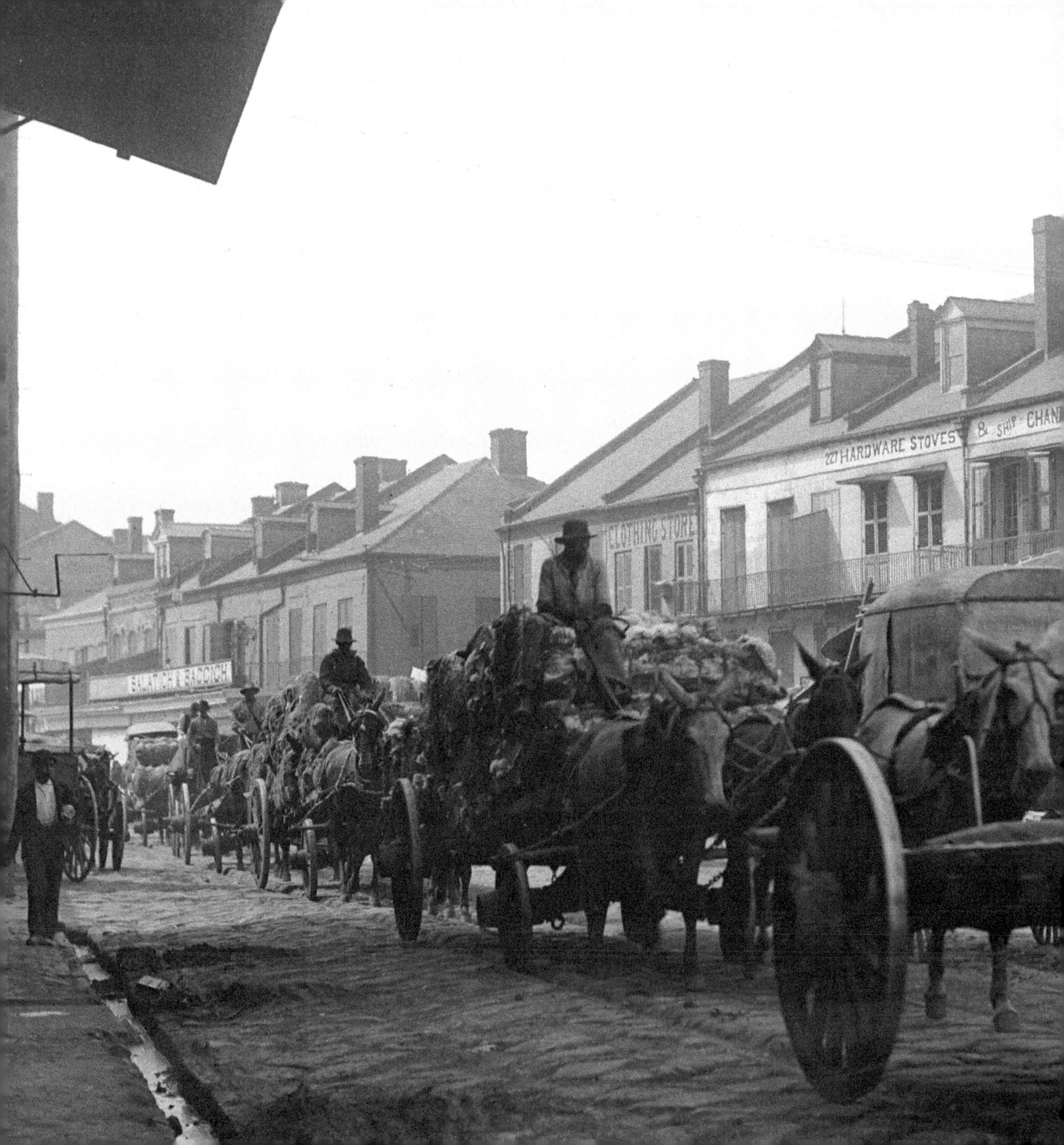

227 HARDWARE STOVES
& SHIP
CLOTHING STORE

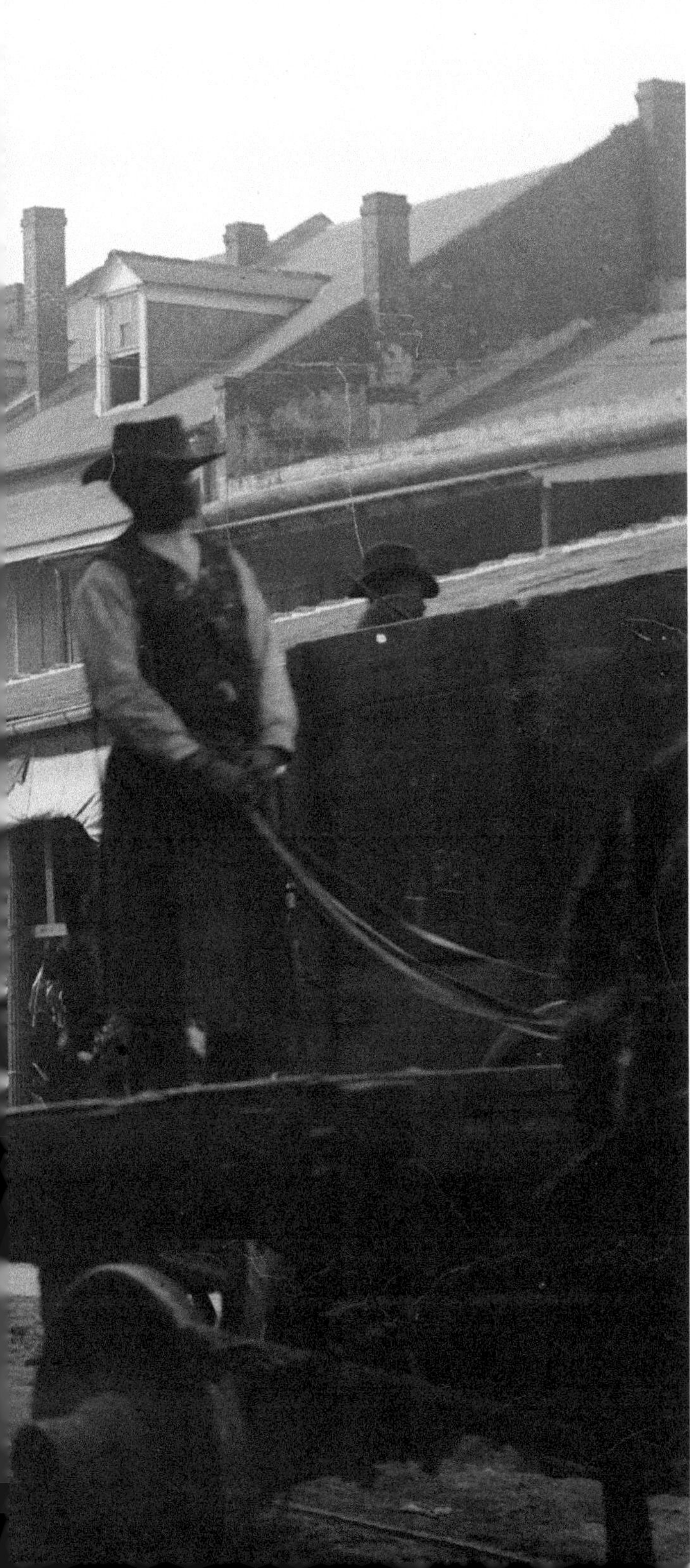

Horse-drawn wagons deliver produce and other goods to the French Market in this image from the late nineteenth century. Begun in 1791 during the Spanish colonial era and still doing business on the same site, the French Market is the oldest city market in the United States. Long before the advent of prepackaged foods, people bought their produce fresh from the farm at public markets like the one in New Orleans.

The exterior of the A. Albert & Son Photographers and Stationer store in Alexandria is seen in this image recorded in 1886. By today's standards, early photography was very crude, requiring heavy glass plates and other encumbrances, but in its time it was a revolutionary method of permanently capturing visual images. Before personal cameras were introduced into the marketplace, professional photographers were always very much in demand.

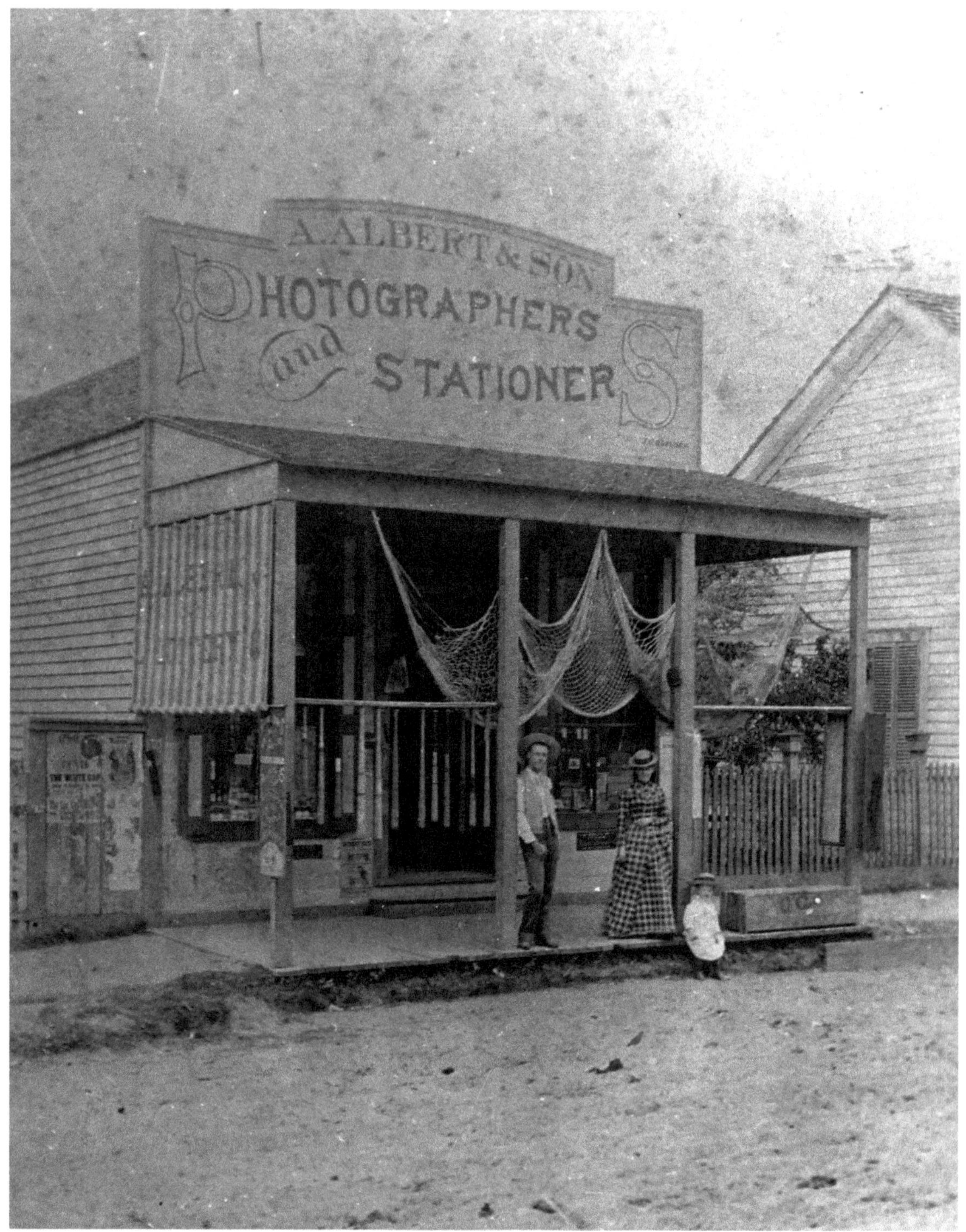

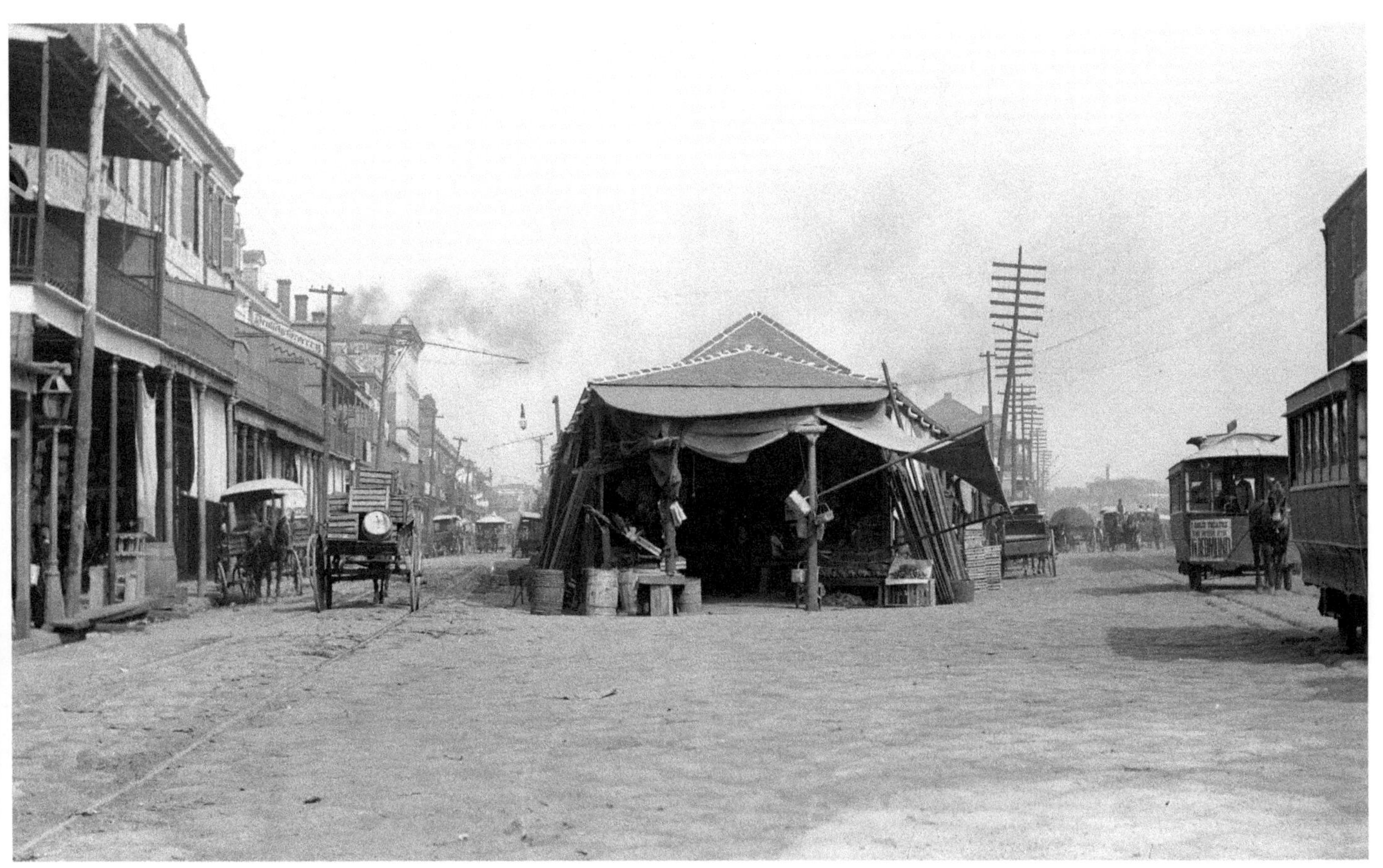

Horse-drawn streetcars roll up and down the streets on both sides of the old French Market in this image, sharing busy thoroughfares with horse-drawn carriages bringing produce to the market. This photograph was taken by legendary photographer William Henry Jackson (1843–1942), whose landscapes of the Rocky Mountain West were among the first images recorded from that part of the country. He is perhaps best known for his iconic 1873 photograph of Colorado's Mount of the Holy Cross.

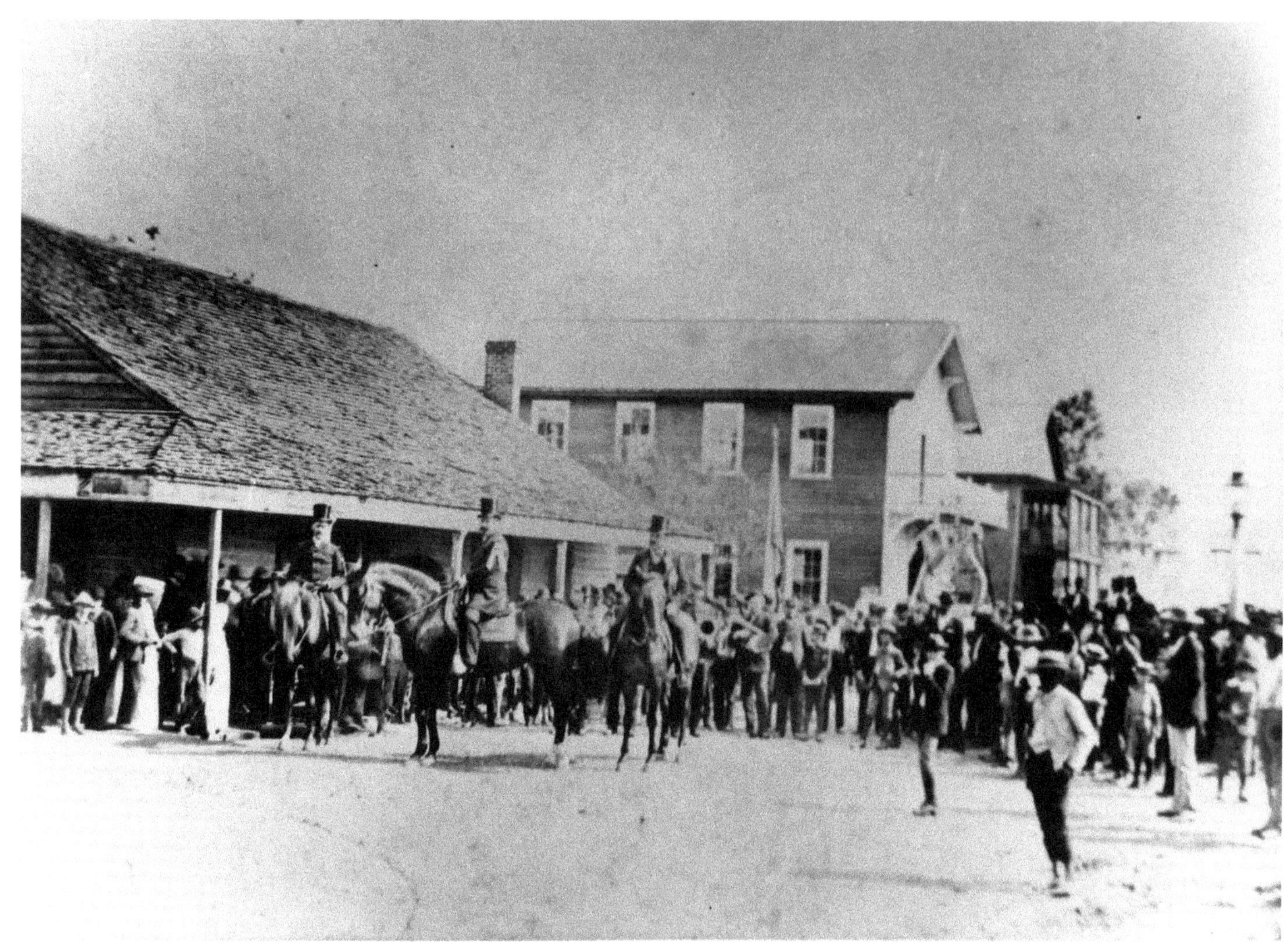

A firemen's parade is seen in Thibodaux in this image from around 1886. During a time when most structures were built of wood and most methods of illumination were flame-generated, fire was a constant threat to lives and property. Fire fighters were a very important component of every community and they often used parades on special occasions to publicly display their latest mobile firefighting apparatus.

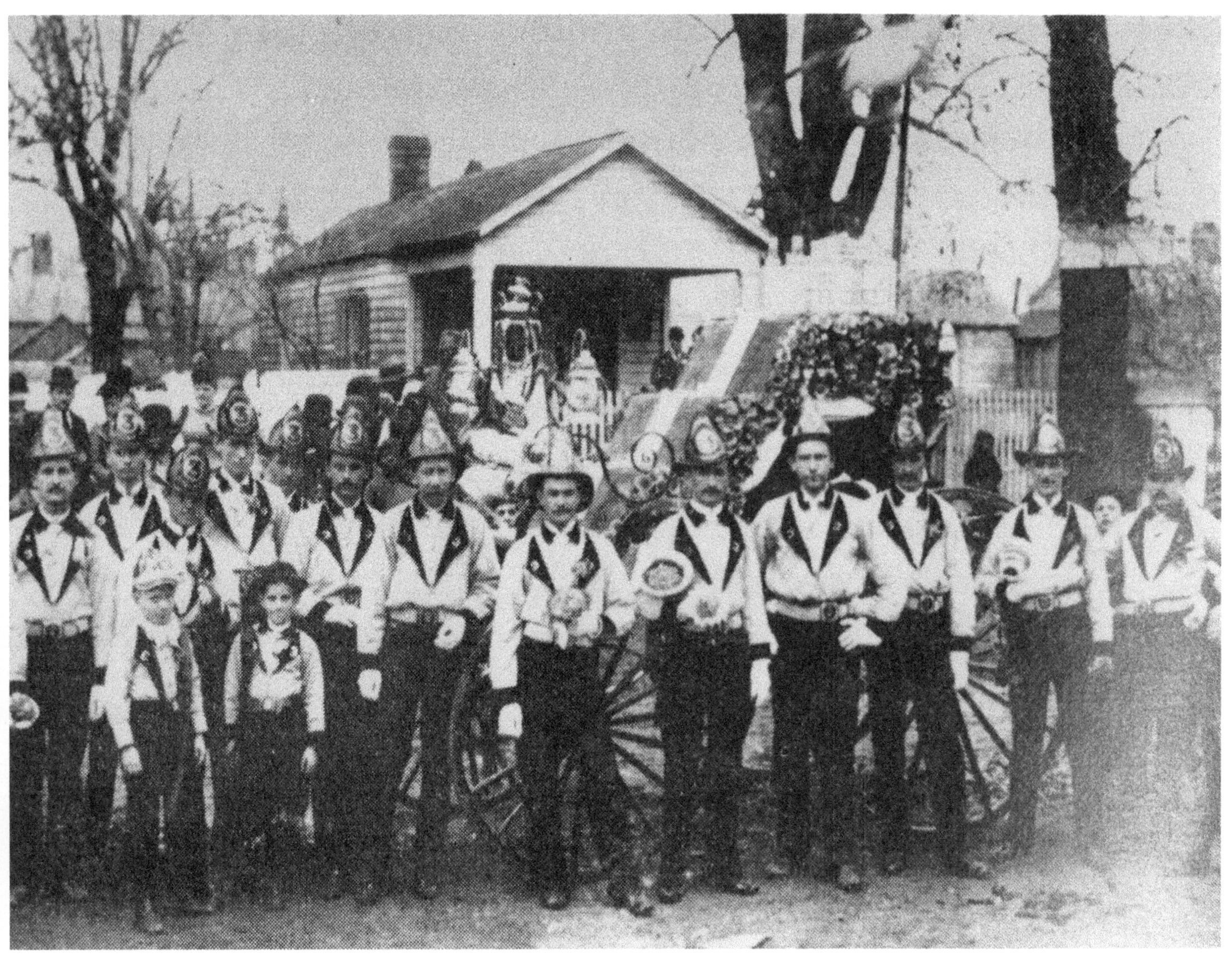

Members of the Number 3 Fire Company of Baton Rouge pose for this 1887 group shot outside their fire station. In large cities, fire districts were established and assigned numbers to cut the size of the area a fire company would have to cover, which improved response time. If the fire posed enough of a threat, companies from other districts were often called in to assist the company in whose district the fire was occurring. This multi-alarm system came to define the intensity of a fire.

A horse-drawn wagon bearing the casket of former Confederate States of America president Jefferson Davis rolls along a downtown street in New Orleans in December 1889. Born in 1808, Davis served as Secretary of War under President Franklin Pierce and in the U.S. Senate before becoming the only president of the secessionist states. He died in New Orleans on December 6, 1889, and was initially buried in Metairie Cemetery, then was moved to Richmond, Virginia, in 1893.

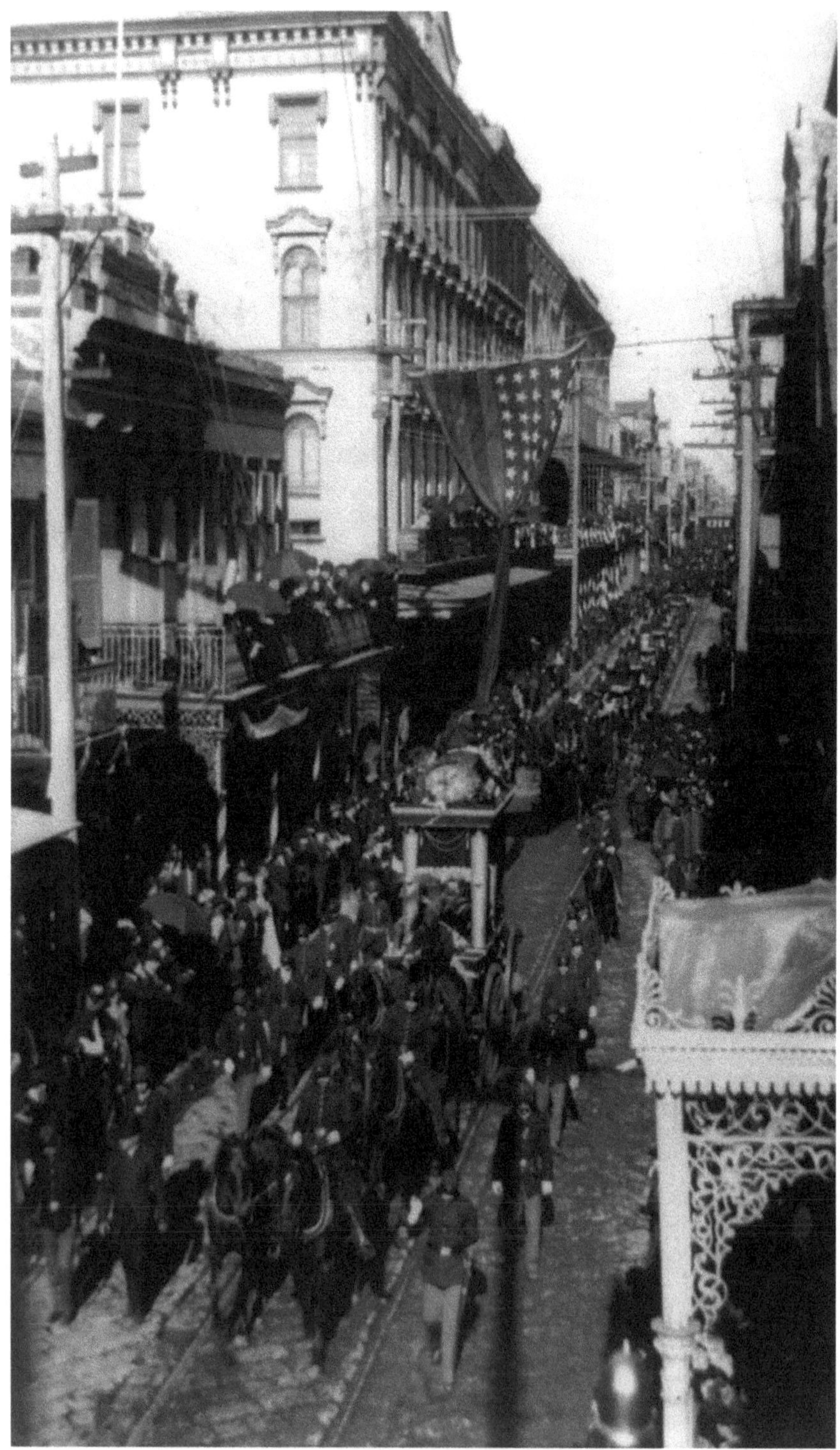

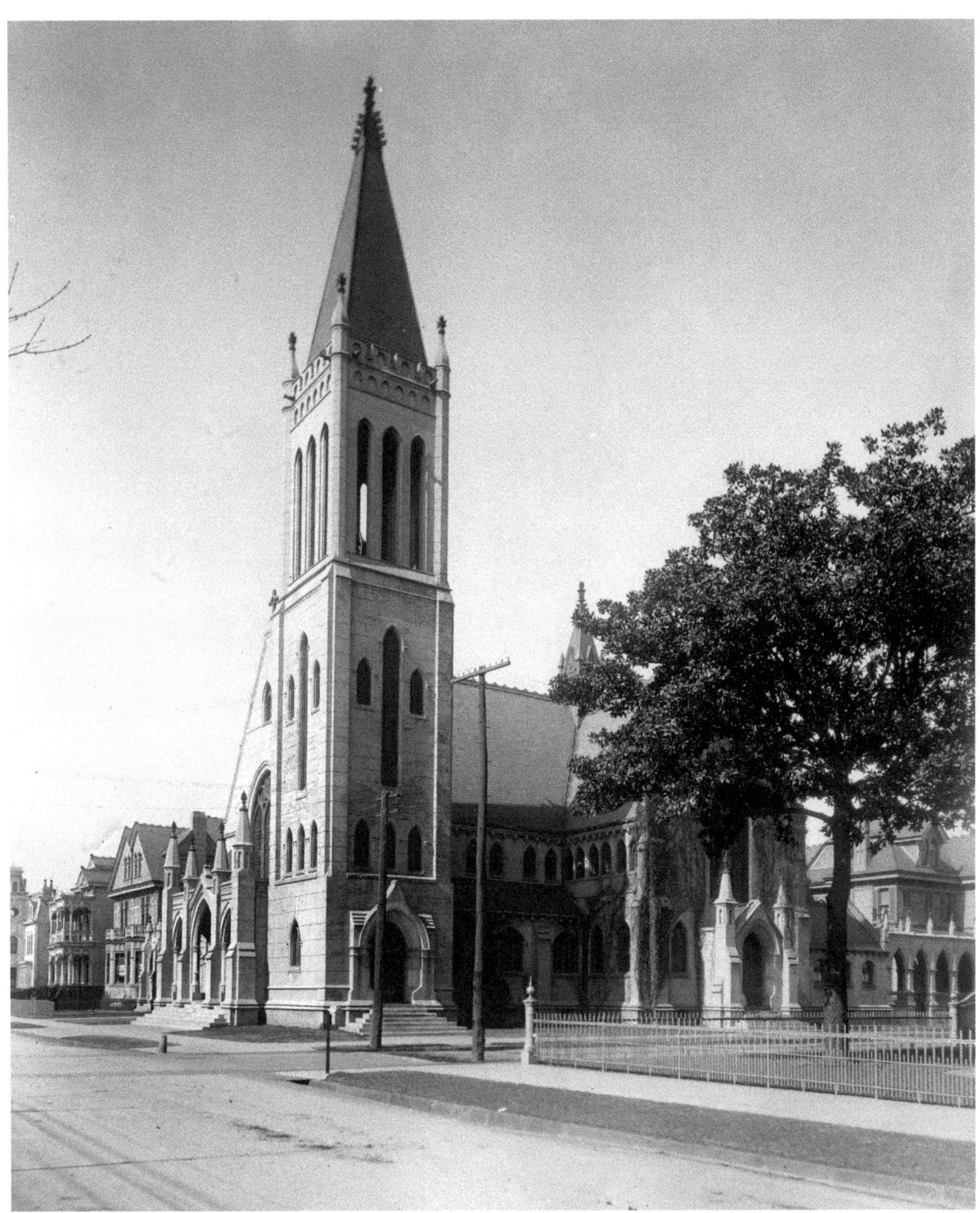

Christ Church, the Cathedral of the Episcopal Diocese of Louisiana, was the fourth church bearing that name in New Orleans since the founding of the diocese in 1805. It was designed by architect Lawrence B. Valk of New York and consecrated in the late 1880s. Absent its pointed steeple, the church still stands today at the corner of St. Charles Avenue and Sixth Street in the city's Garden District.

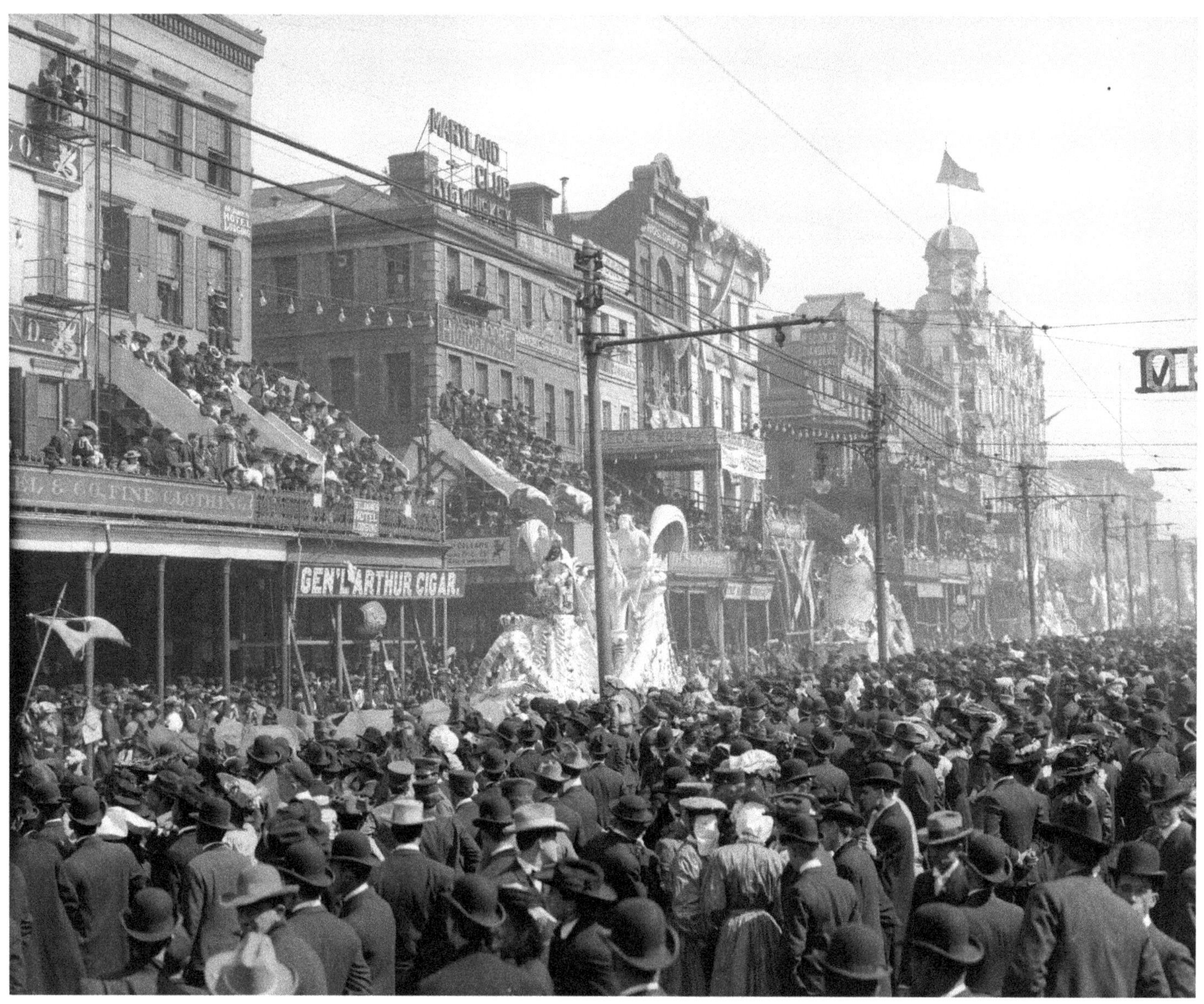

Crowds jam the wide breadth of Canal Street in New Orleans to watch the Rex parade on Mardi Gras Day around the turn of the century. Mardi Gras, meaning "Fat Tuesday" in French, is always the day before Ash Wednesday, which begins the Lenten fasting season that precedes Easter, 45 days later. Rex, a parading organization founded in 1872, features the "King of Carnival" on a special thronelike float on Fat Tuesday.

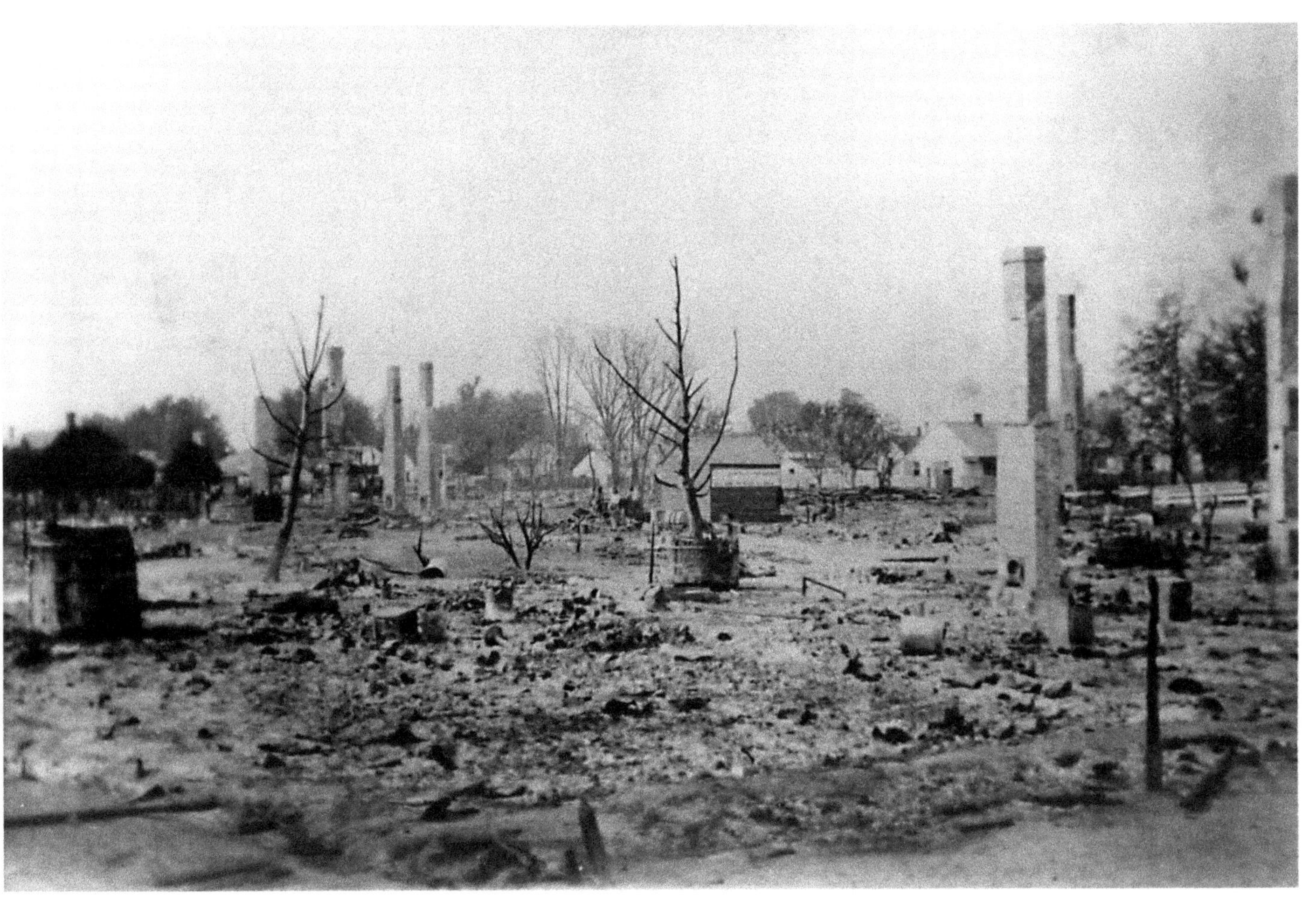

The ruins of Napoleonville are seen after a disastrous fire. Named after the French emperor who sold Louisiana to the United States and designated the seat of rural Assumption Parish, Napoleonville was hit by two conflagrations—on November 1, 1884, and again on December 2, 1894.

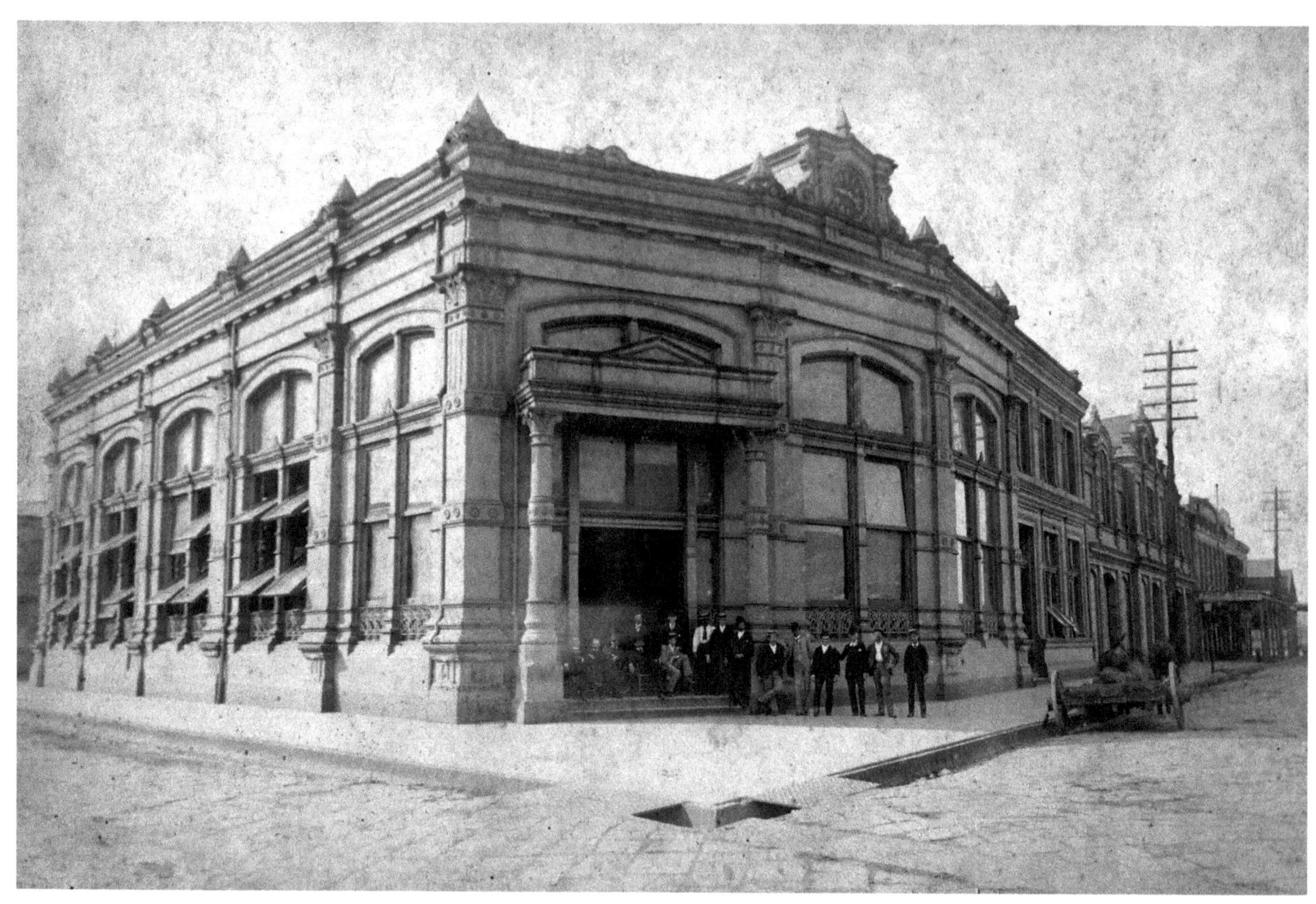

The Louisiana Sugar Exchange Building, which stood on the corner of Bienville and Front streets adjacent the New Orleans riverfront, is seen here in 1890. The Exchange was established to set prices and quality standards for its namesake product and was a key center for the commercial sugar trade in the late nineteenth and early twentieth centuries. The building was demolished in 1963.

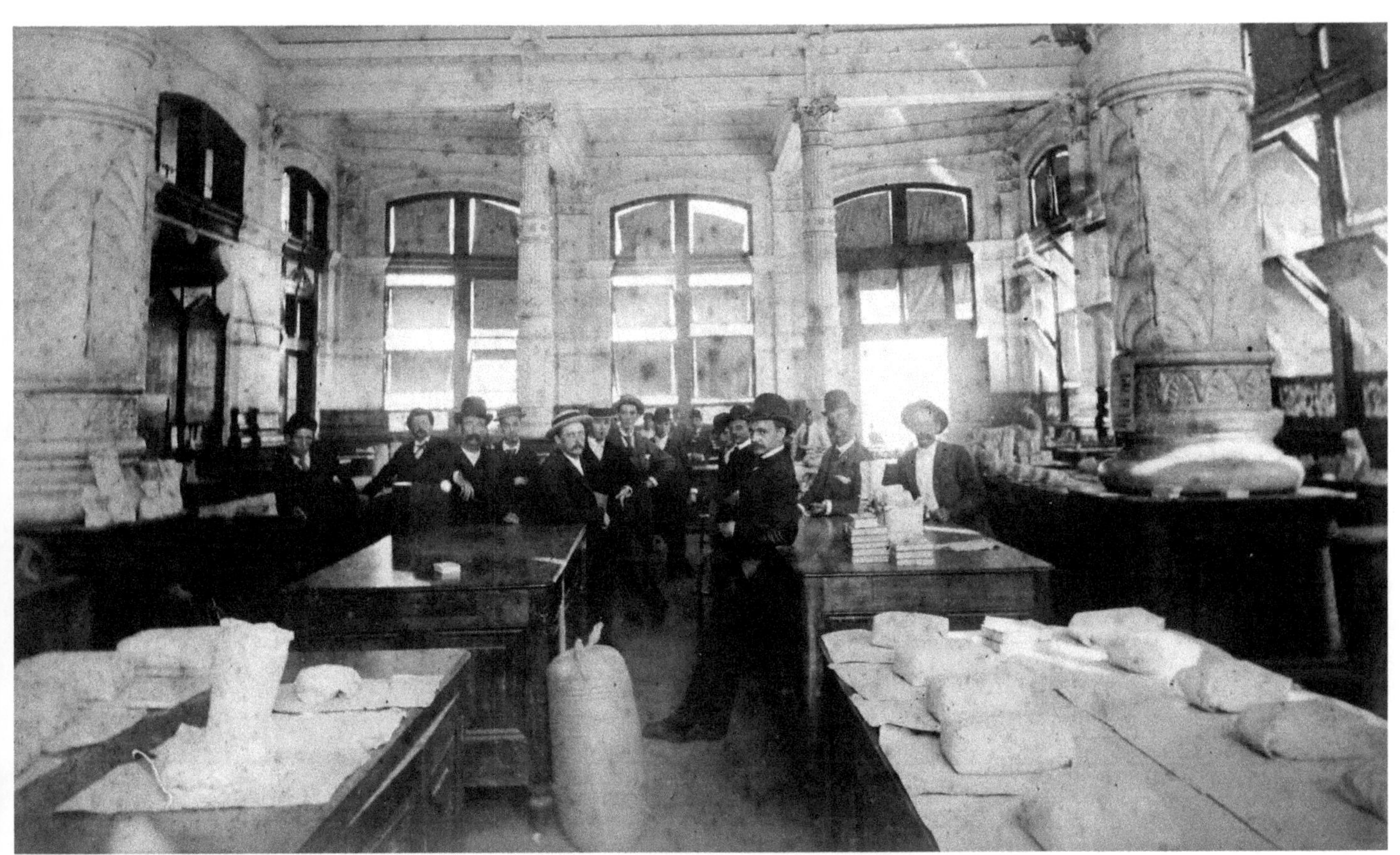

Traders gather on the floor of the Louisiana Sugar Exchange along with bags of sugar readied for market here in 1890. Sugar is still a leading crop and manufactured product of Louisiana, but the importance of the Exchange declined as government regulations stabilized market prices in the mid-1900s.

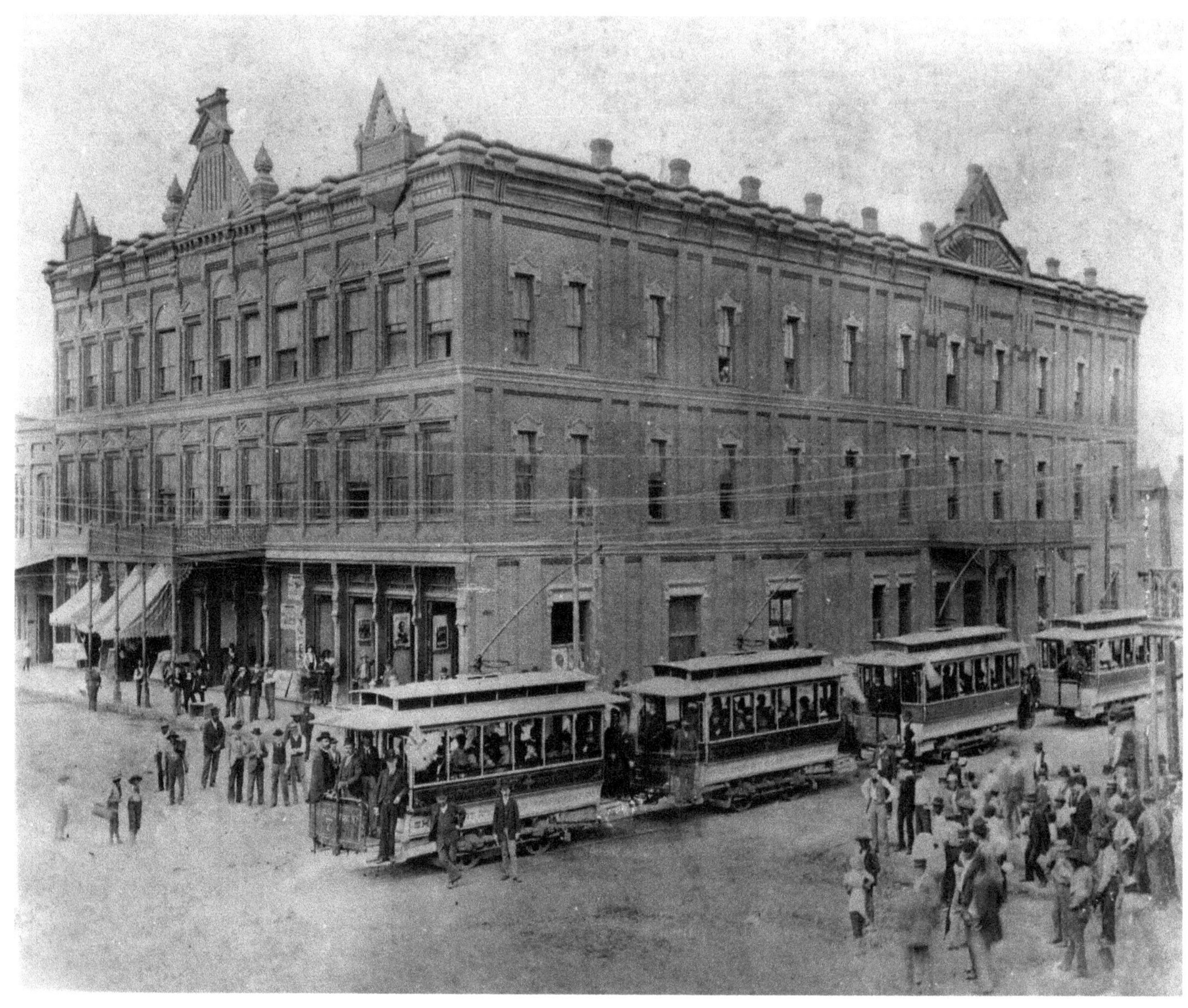

The first electric-powered streetcars in Shreveport make their grand appearance on October 4, 1890. Curious onlookers watch the parade of the new vehicles at the corner of Texas and Market streets in the city's downtown area.

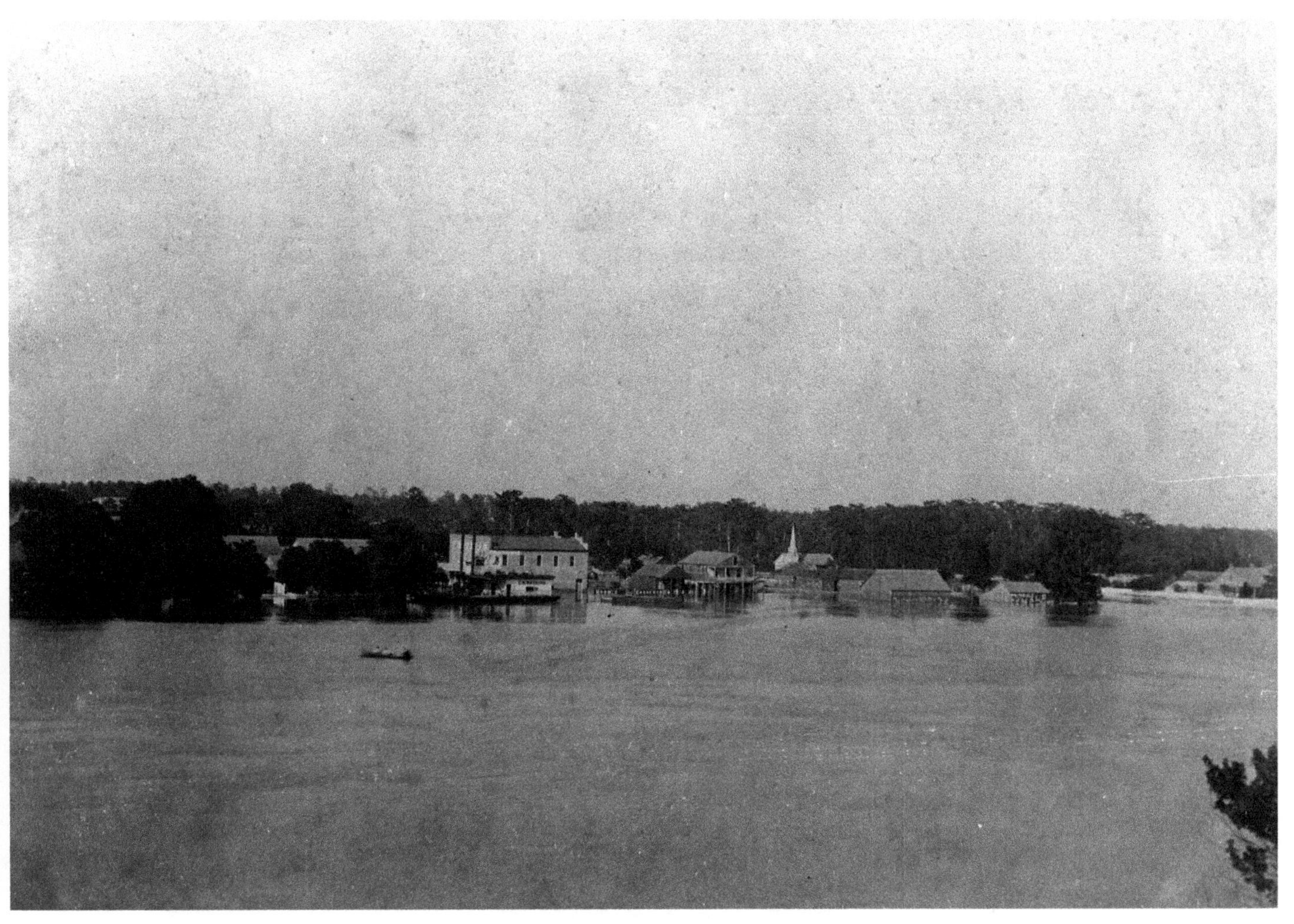

Swollen over its banks in 1892, the Red River floods the small city of Pineville directly across the river from Alexandria. The ferryboat *C. R. Watkins* is visible at left-center, and a Baptist Church steeple is visible in the background. The 1,000-mile-long Red River marks the geographical dividing line between the low-lying coastal plain of southern Louisiana and the higher elevations of the north.

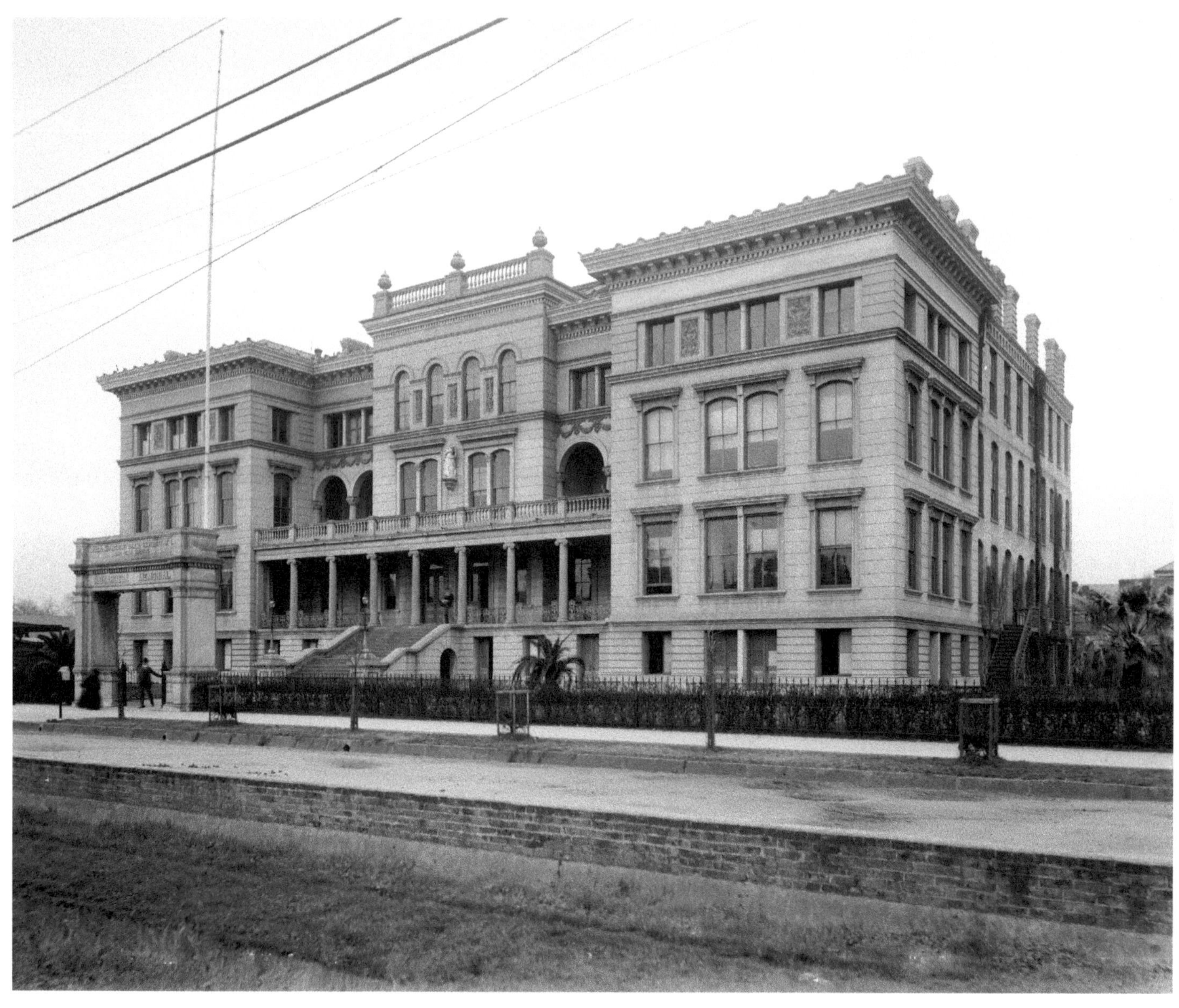

The front of Richardson Memorial Hospital on Canal Street in downtown New Orleans is shown here shortly after the hospital opened in 1893. Named for Dr. T. G. Richardson, former dean of Tulane University's Medical Department, it was used as a training hospital for future doctors and other medical personnel. It no longer stands.

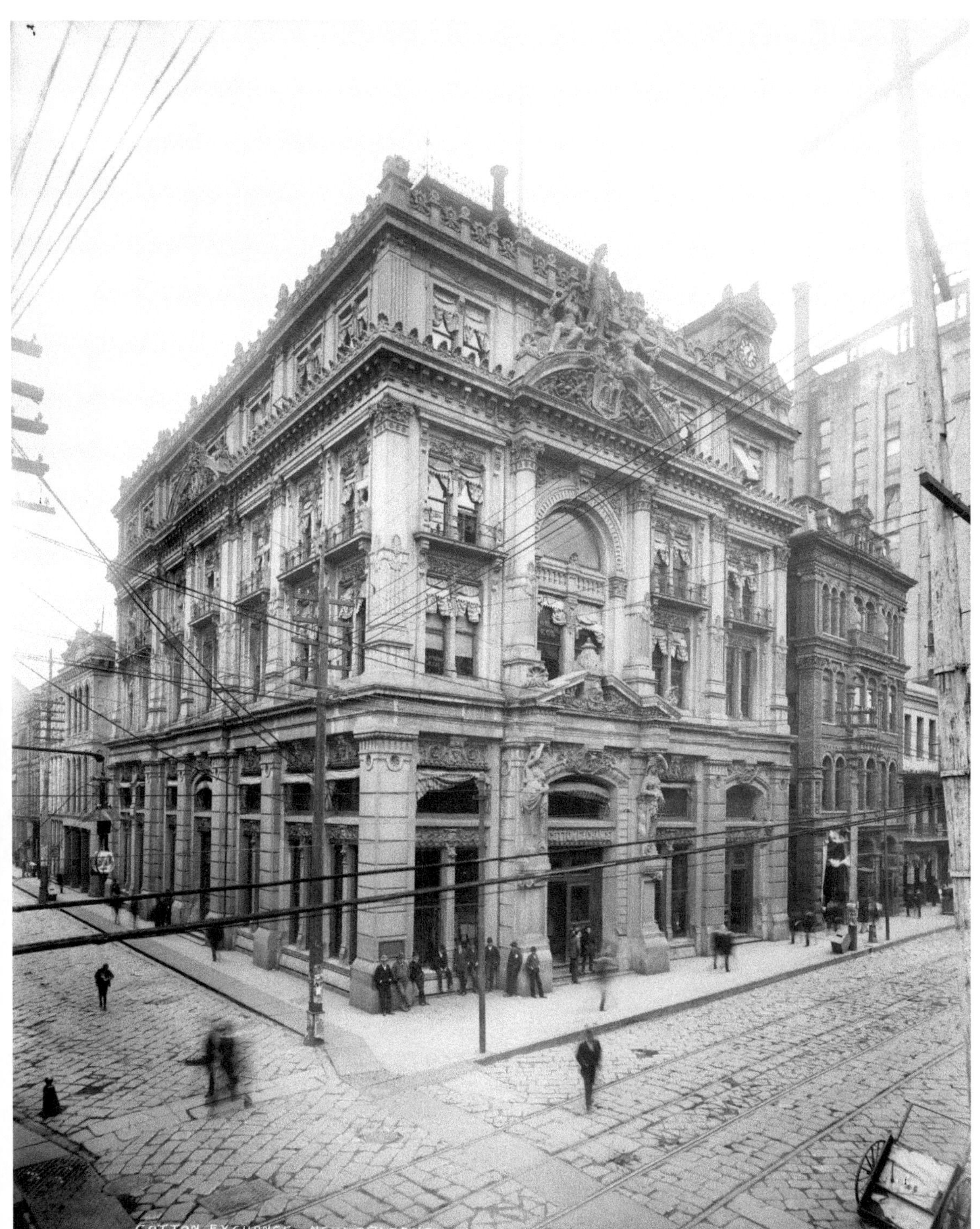

With one of the most ornately decorated exteriors of any building in downtown New Orleans, the Cotton Exchange was a hub of activity centering on this key agricultural crop in the late nineteenth century. Like the Sugar Exchange, it was established in 1871 as a central clearinghouse to set uniform cotton pricing and quality standards. This building was replaced with another structure in the early 1920s that still stands, today housing a hotel.

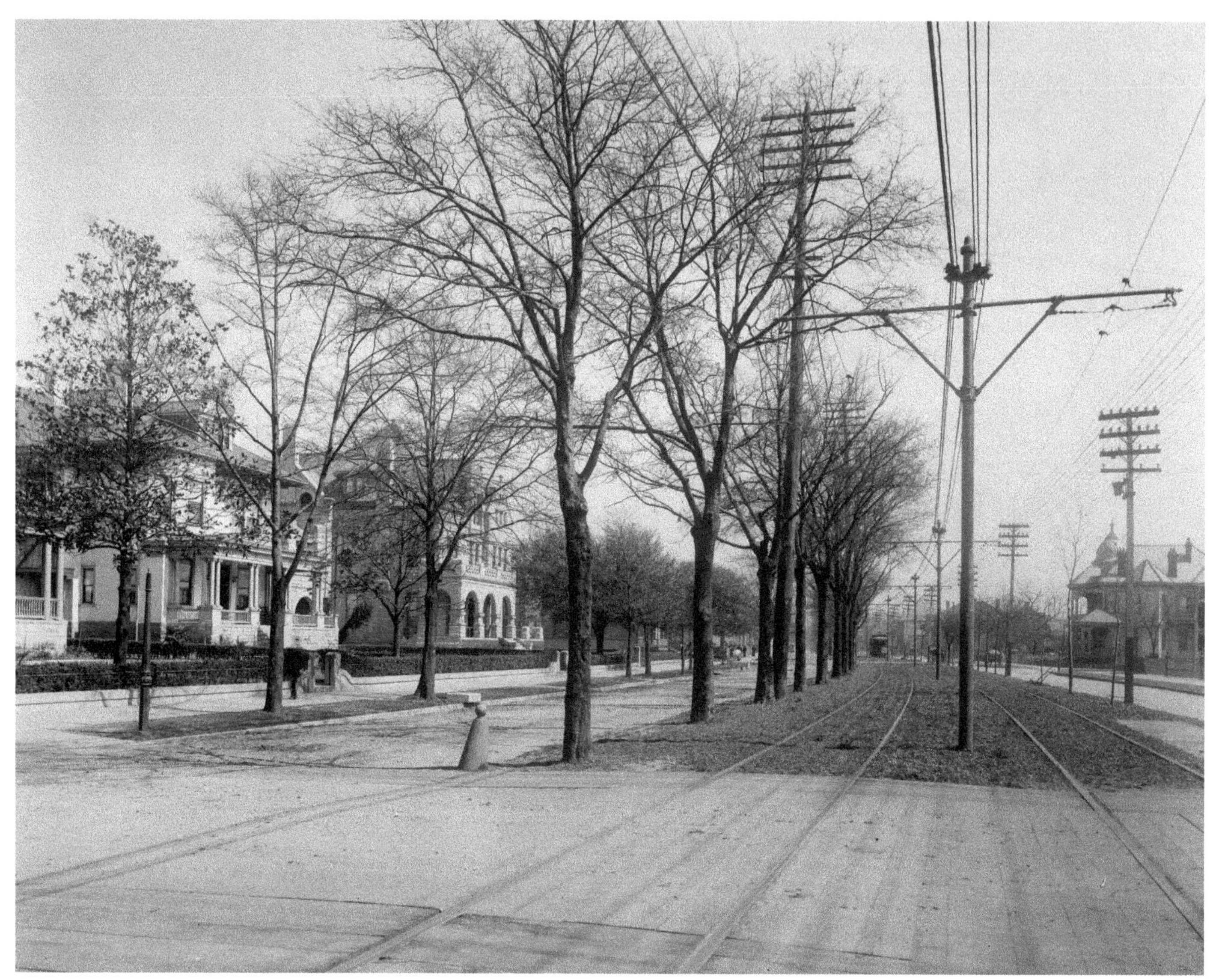

A distant streetcar plies the St. Charles Avenue streetcar line in this image from the 1890s. The streetcar seen here and others of its type were replaced by the distinctive olive-green Perley A. Thomas Series 900 cars, about 35 in all, built in 1923, and which are still running today. The St. Charles Line is the oldest continuously operating urban transport line in the United States, and is a popular New Orleans tourist attraction today.

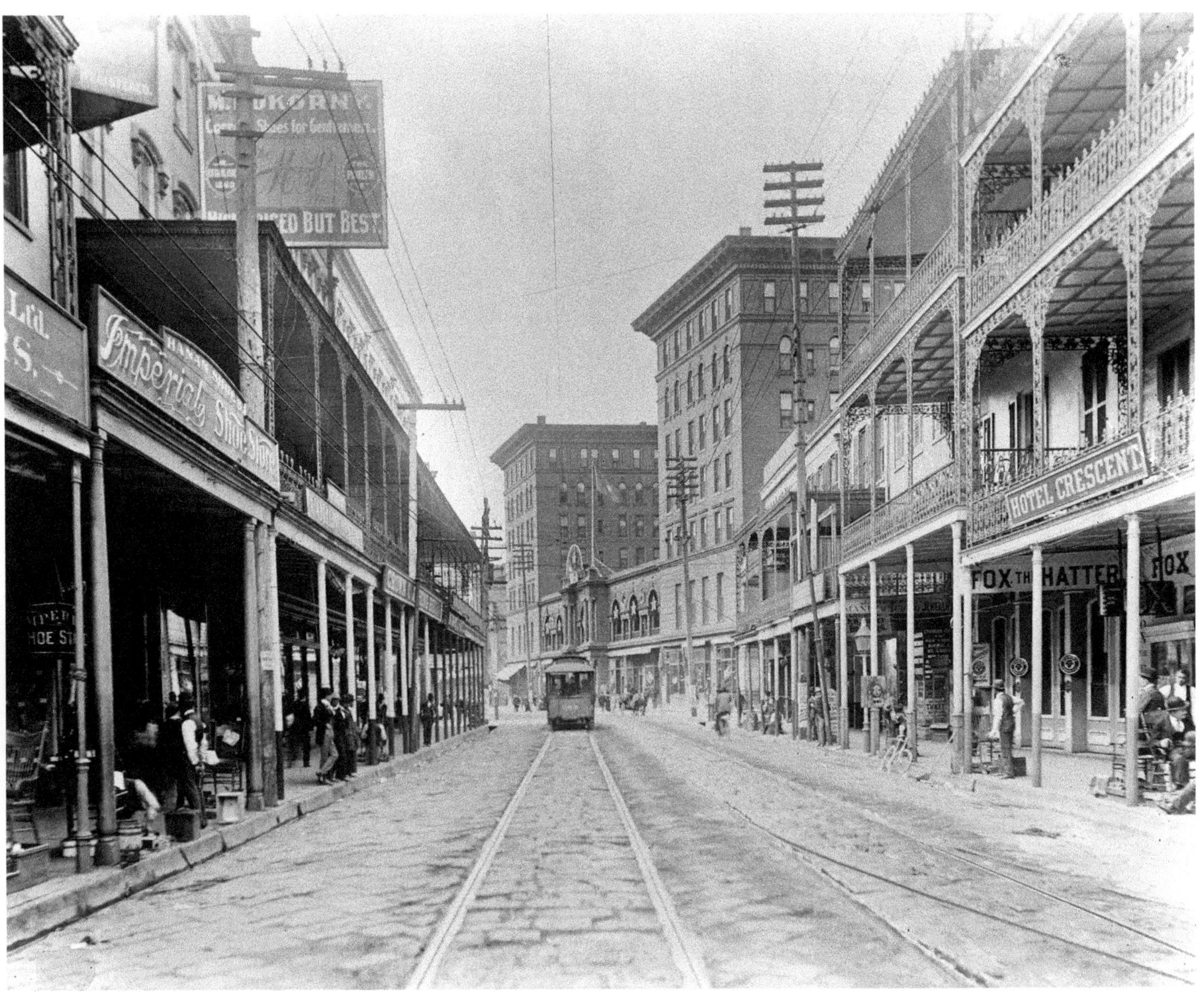

An electric streetcar rolls up St. Charles Street in downtown New Orleans late in the century. Until the entire length of St. Charles Avenue, from Canal Street to the Mississippi River, was given its present uniform name, its downtown section was designated St. Charles Street. Vintage streetcars still traverse the St. Charles Avenue Line, following the same route originally laid out in 1835.

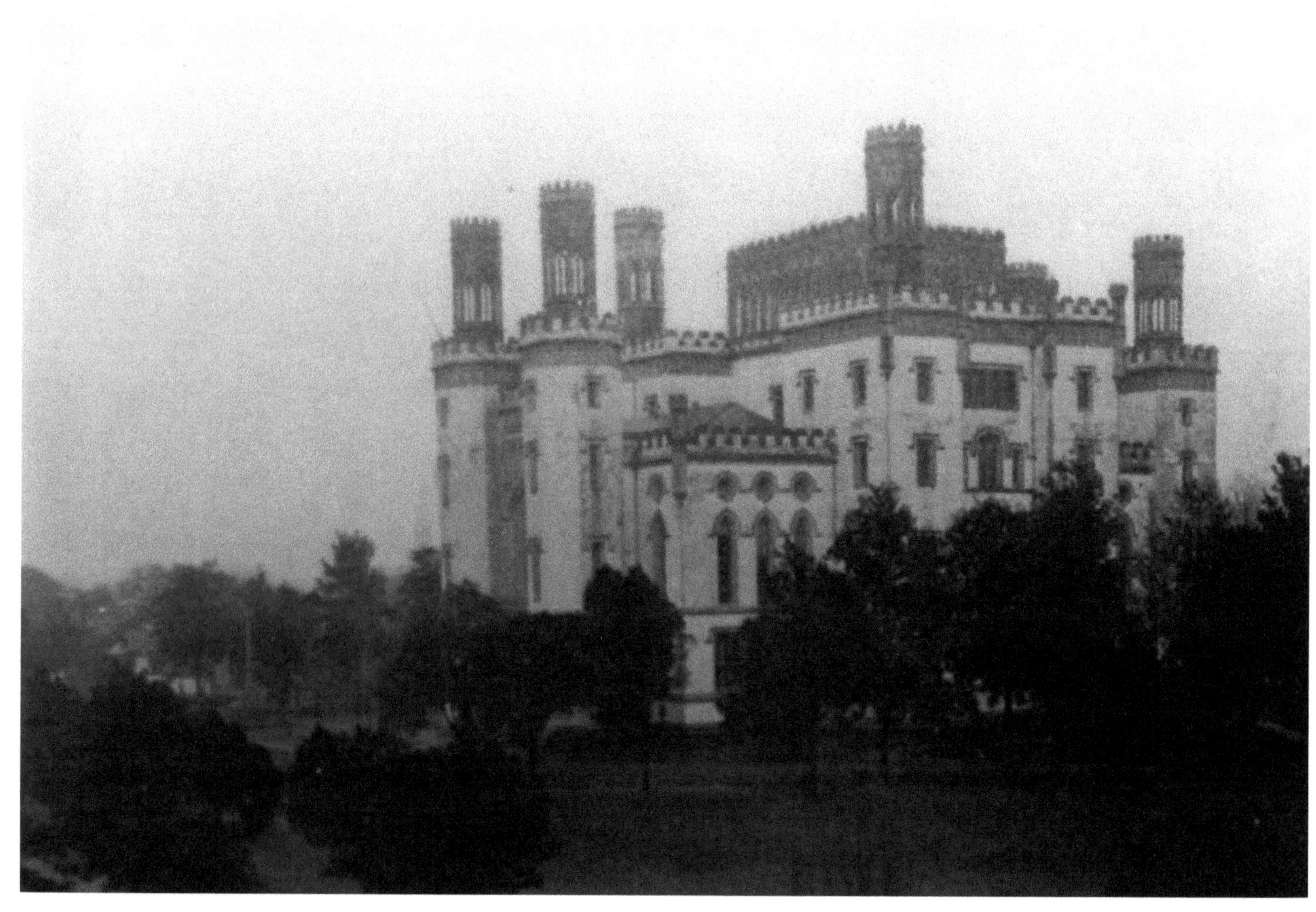

The Old State Capitol in Baton Rouge stands fortresslike in the mid-1890s. Designed by architect James Dakin and located on a bluff overlooking the Mississippi River, its Gothic Revival, European castlelike exterior prompted author Mark Twain to ridicule it as "pathetic." Abandoned in 1932 when the newer, larger Capitol opened nearby, it is now a National Historic Landmark and revered as an architectural masterpiece. It houses a museum devoted to Louisiana's political history.

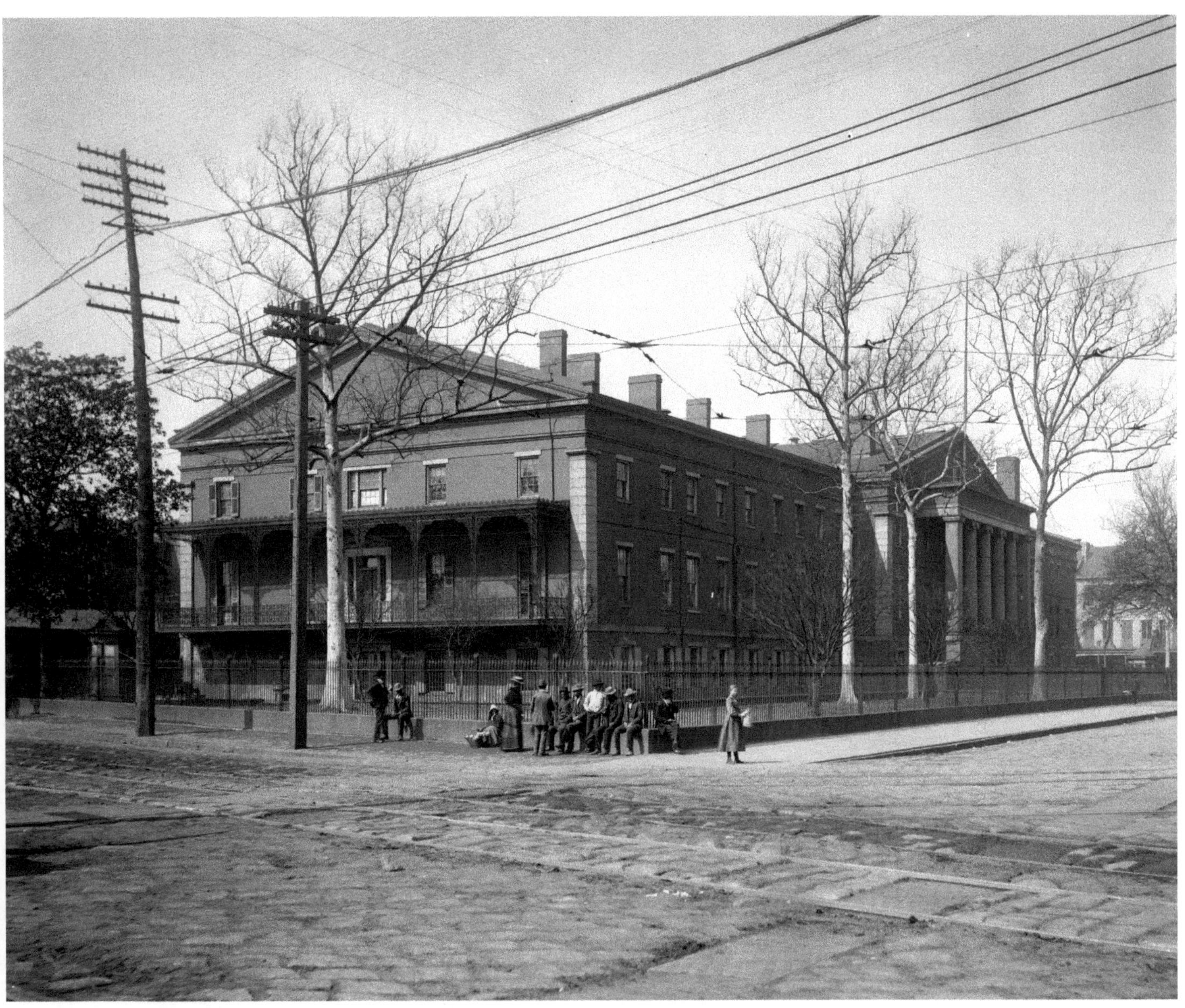

The Old United States Mint on Barracks Street on the edge of the French Quarter, New Orleans. Founded in 1839, the mint was still operating when this photograph was taken. It has the distinction of being the only mint to produce both United States coins and coins of the Confederate States of America. During its years of operation, the Mint produced more than 427 million gold and silver coins of nearly every denomination, with a total face value of over $307 million. The mint still stands today as a unit of the Louisiana State Museum, and portions of it are open to the public. Many of the types of coinage minted there can be seen inside the museum, along with original equipment used to manufacture the currency. The Old Mint also houses other artifacts, including an extensive jazz collection.

In 1897, workers at the Old U.S. Mint punch out metal blanks on which images will be stamped in the manufacture of coins to be circulated as official currency.

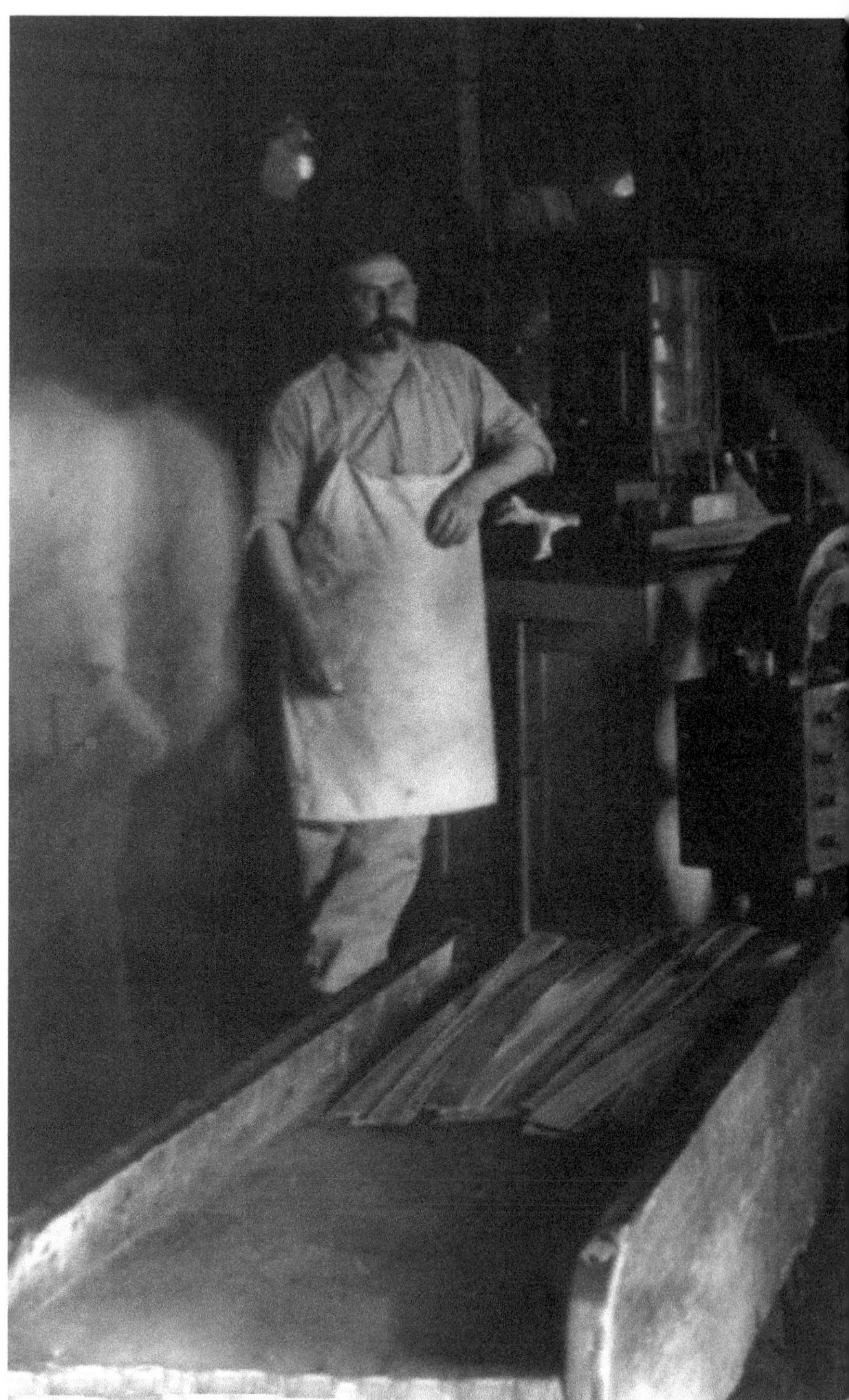

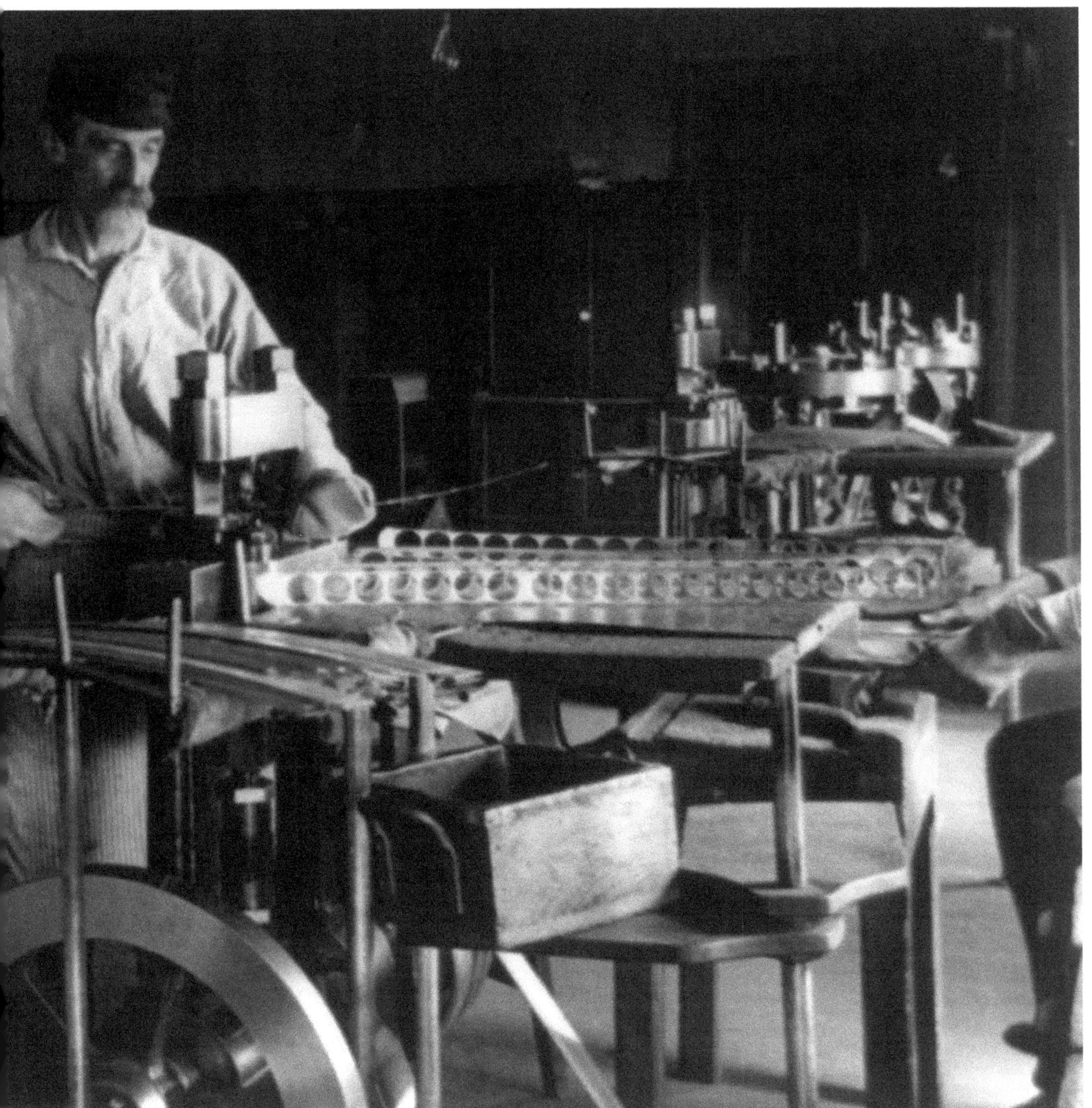

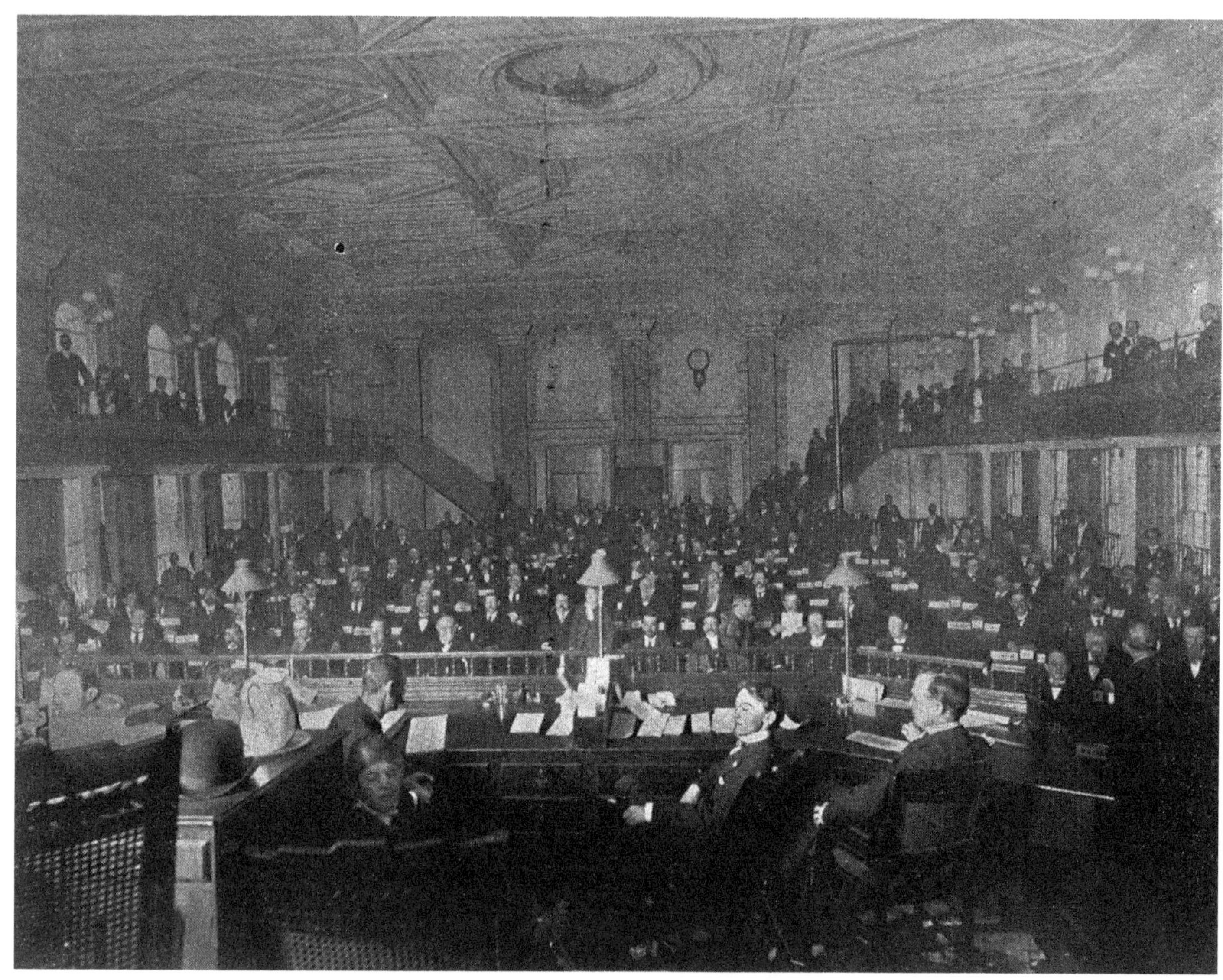

Delegates to Louisiana's 1898 State Constitutional Convention convene in the legislative chamber of the Old State Capitol in Baton Rouge. This Constitutional Convention enacted many of the Jim Crow laws enabled by the U.S. Supreme Court's "separate but equal" ruling in the 1896 *Plessey v. Ferguson* decision, based on a New Orleans test case. The last of the Jim Crow laws were repealed by the most recent constitutional convention held in 1974.

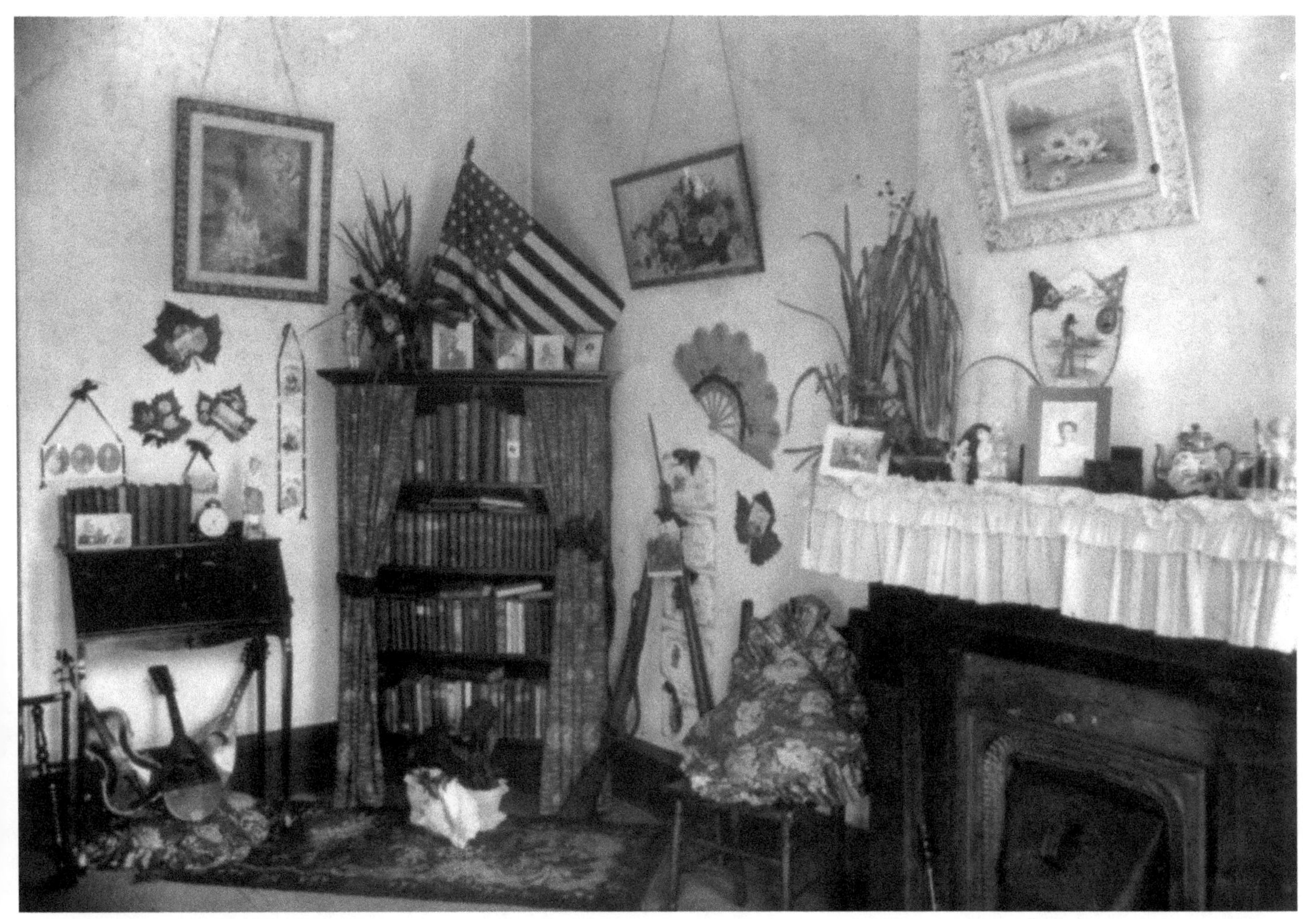

Books, musical instruments, and other objects useful in classroom instruction stand in the corner of the home of a teacher here in the late 1890s. Blacks and whites were taught at separate schools throughout the South in the years between the 1896 *Plessey v. Ferguson* decision and the *Brown v. Topeka Board of Education* case in 1954, which marked the end of the Jim Crow era.

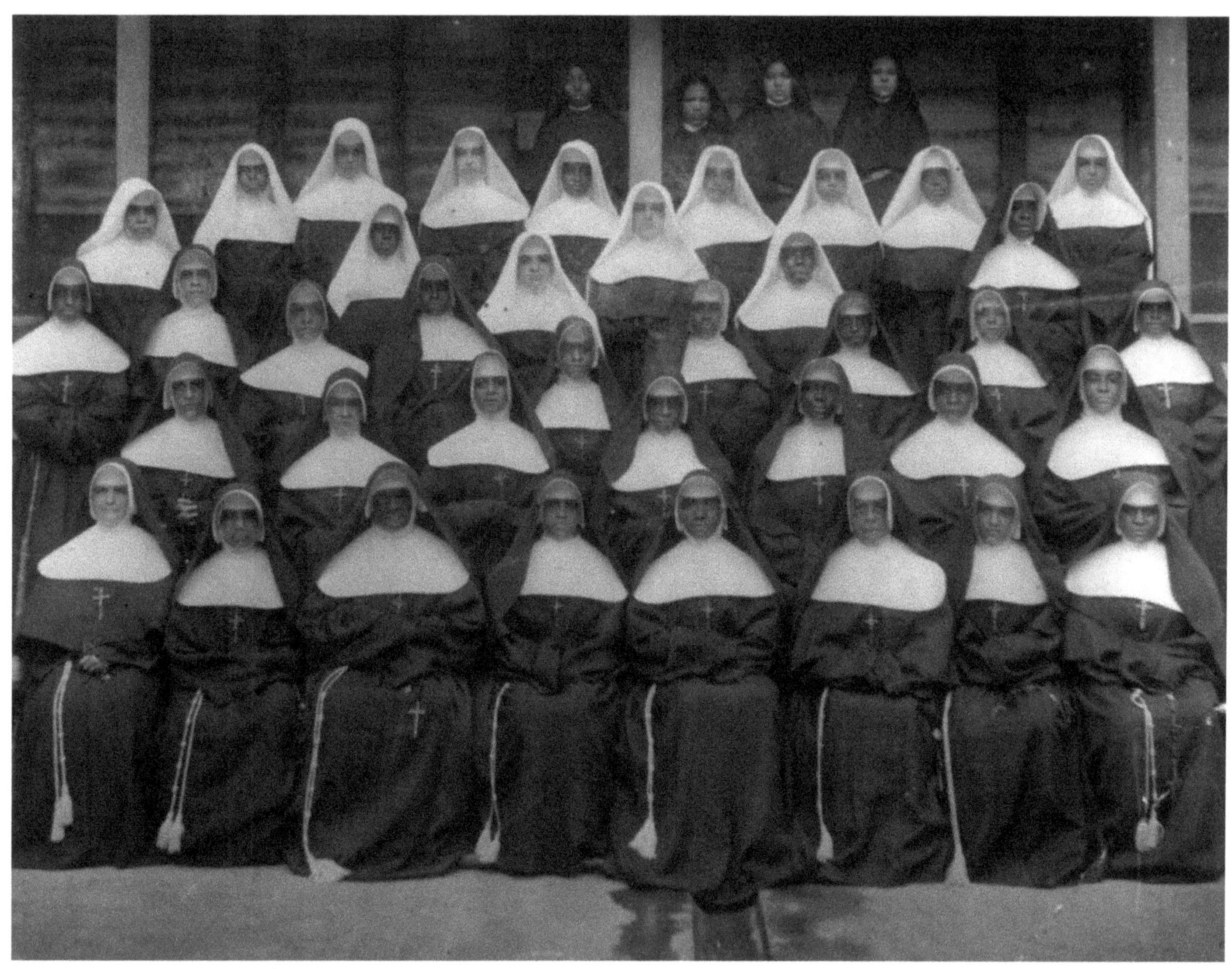

A group of nuns, Sisters of the Holy Family, gather for mass late in the 1890s. One of the few Roman Catholic orders made up of African-American women, the Sisters of the Holy Family was founded in 1837 by Sister Henriette DeLille, who is now being considered for sainthood by the Catholic Church. Today with 200 members, the order operates schools for poor children, nursing homes, and retirement centers.

A water tower is under construction in Thibodaux next to the Lafourche Parish Courthouse in the years surrounding the turn of the century. Thibodaux's most famous citizen was Edward Douglass White, who served on the U.S. Supreme Court from 1894 to 1921, the last 11 years of which were spent as Chief Justice. Thibodaux was also the site of a violent 1887 sugarcane workers strike that resulted in the deaths of 30 or more workers.

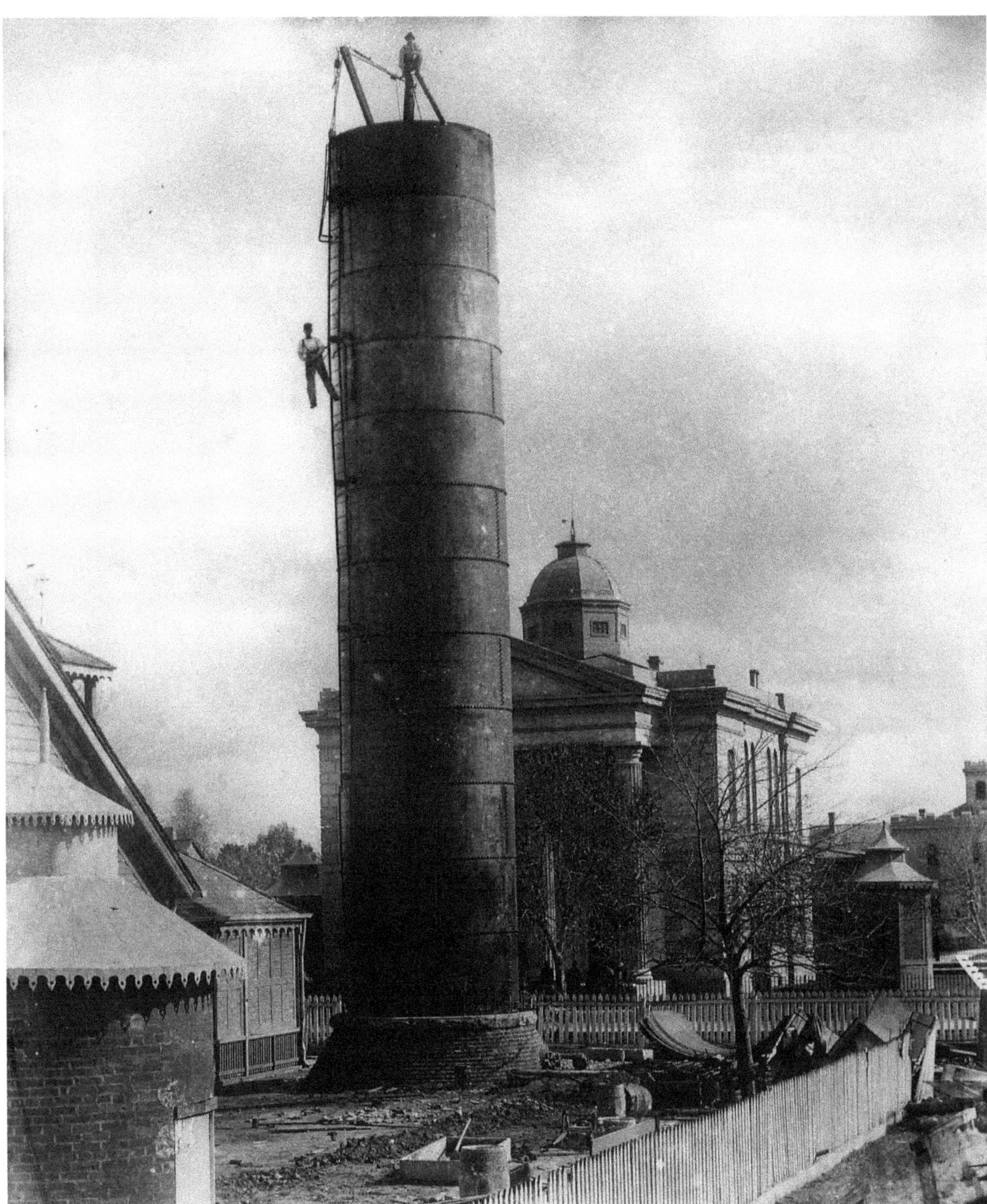

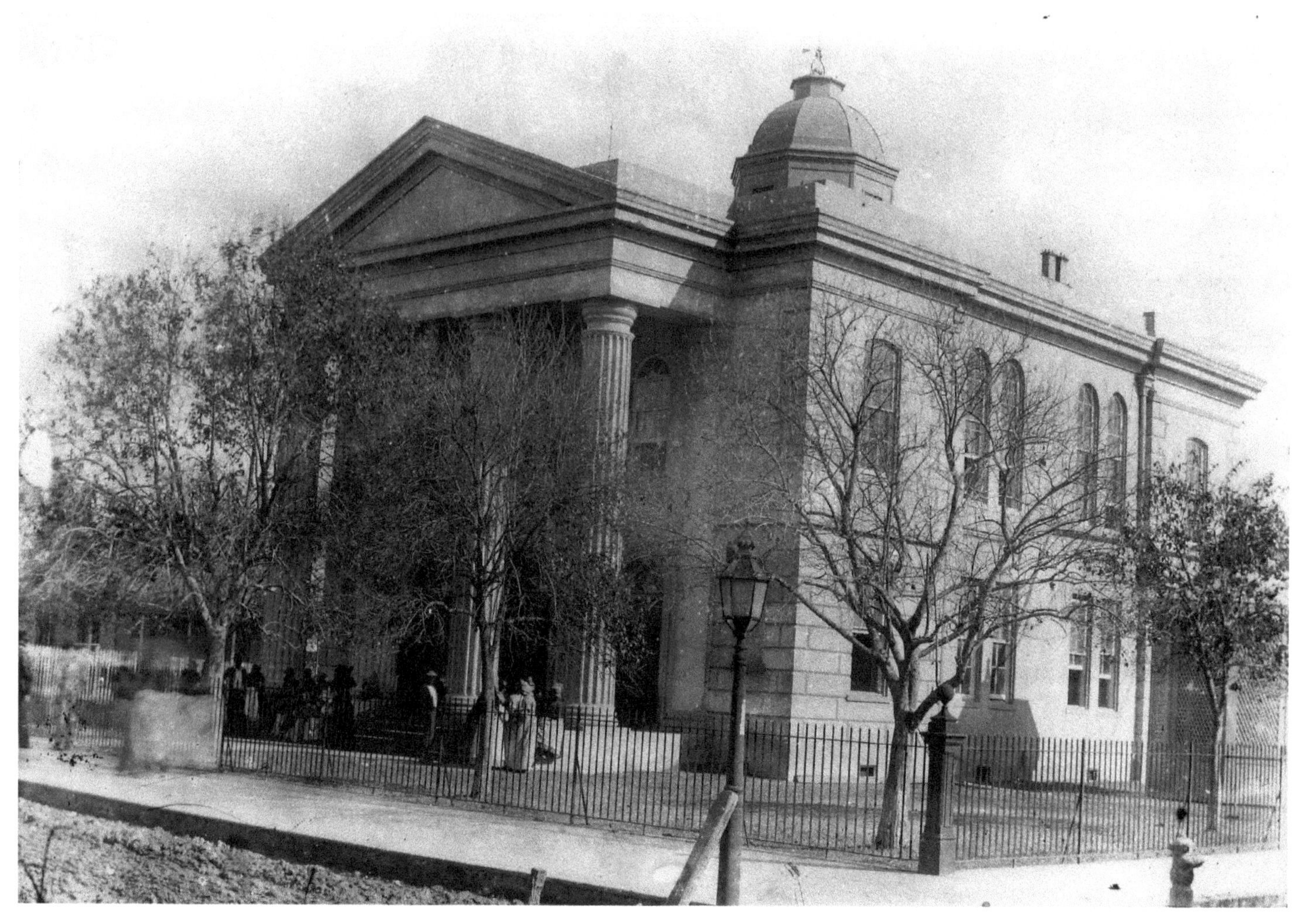

People mill around the front entrance of the Lafourche Parish Courthouse in Thibodaux in this image from the turn of the century. Settled in the 1700s by French Acadians exiled from Canada (nicknamed "Cajuns"), the mid-sized city was named for Henry Schuyler Thibodaux, who owned a nearby plantation and was acting governor of Louisiana in 1824. The courthouse, built in 1860 on land donated by Thibodaux, still stands today.

Booms and Calamities

(1900–1919)

The visit of President William McKinley to New Orleans in 1901 and the enthusiastic reception he received there were rightly perceived by many as an acknowledgment of the city's importance to the rest of the nation at the beginning of a new century. Despite the slow decline in steamboat commerce along the Mississippi River, product diversification would soon open up other markets for the city, especially international ones. Improvements in the design and capabilities of transoceanic maritime vessels and innovative methods of keeping shipping channels free of silt allowed the port to expand and increase its stature in the international marketplace.

In the northwestern corner of the state, oil discoveries transformed an entire region into a large-scale boomtown. Derricks pumping thousands of barrels a day mushroomed all over the rural countryside surrounding Shreveport, and pipelines hundreds of miles long pumped crude oil to refineries on the Texas Gulf Coast. Like most boomtowns in our nation's history, millionaires were made overnight and the prosperity spilled over into the surrounding communities, resulting in much-needed improvements to infrastructure.

Good economic fortune was not enjoyed statewide, however, and large pockets of poverty remained. During the early years of the twentieth century, Louisiana was visited by some of the leading photographers of the day, and the images they captured were not always flattering. Lewis Wickes Hine documented exploitative child labor conditions in the state's oyster canneries, and Walker Evans and Dorothea Lange documented rural poverty. These iconic images served their purpose, helping result in the passage of stricter child labor laws and, in later years, federal relief programs.

Also during this time, serious flooding along the Mississippi in the 1910s resulted in the destruction of thousands of acres of crops and the displacement of tens of thousands of residents. These disasters would result in the strengthening of levees and the construction of spillways a decade later. This was also a time when Louisiana became a key location for military bases and combat training sites, creating a significant economic impact that has lasted to the present. By the end of World War I, the state was enjoying record prosperity and assimilation into the national mainstream. The boom would soon turn to bust, however, and Louisiana would have to pick up and start over again.

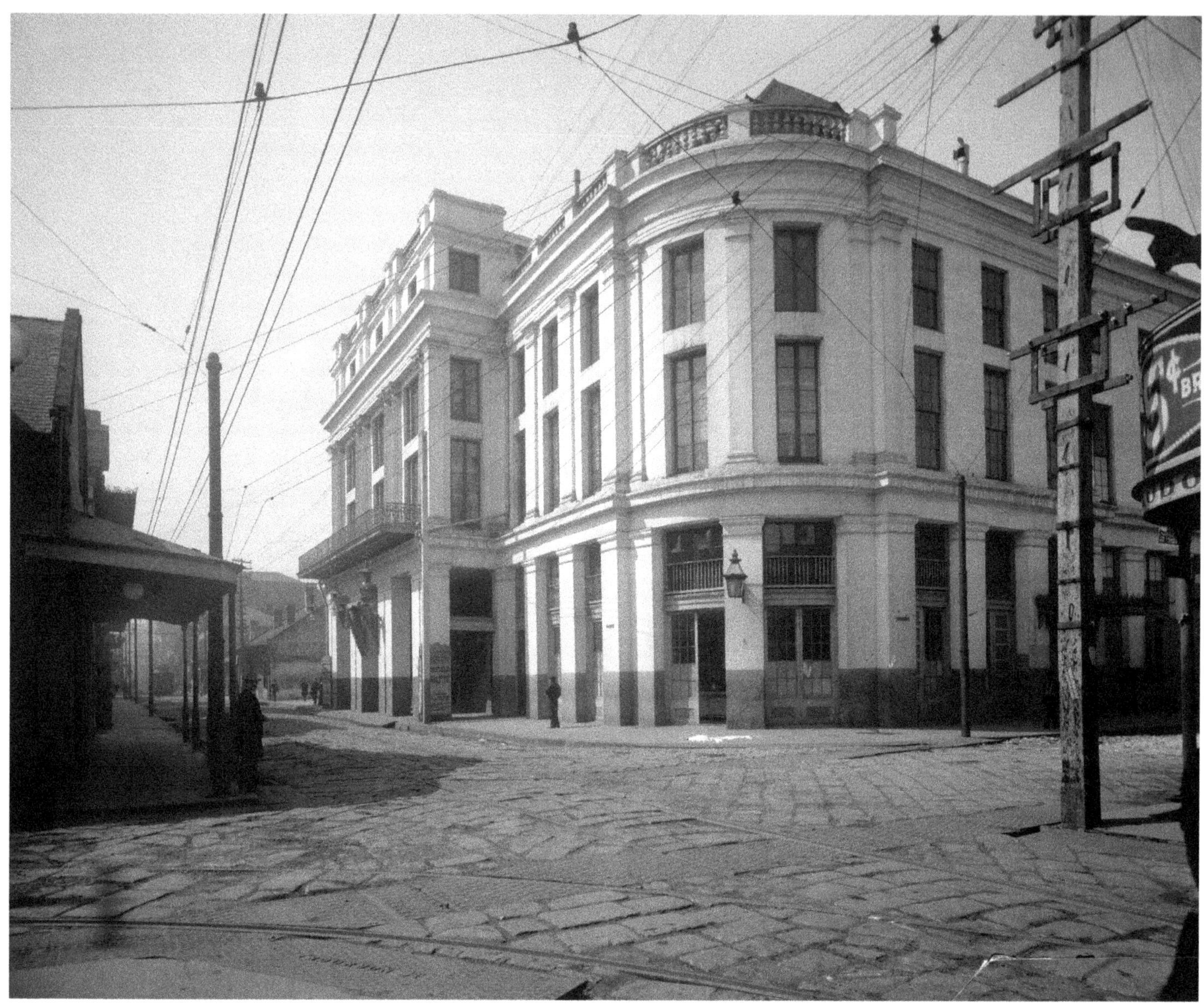

The historic old French Opera House stands at the corner of Bourbon and Toulouse streets in the French Quarter in this photograph from around 1900. Designed by famed architect James Gallier, Jr., it opened on December 4, 1859, and for the next 60 years was the center of social activity in New Orleans. The house staged operas, Carnival balls, debuts, benefits, receptions, and concerts. On December 4, 1919, it burned to the ground and was not rebuilt.

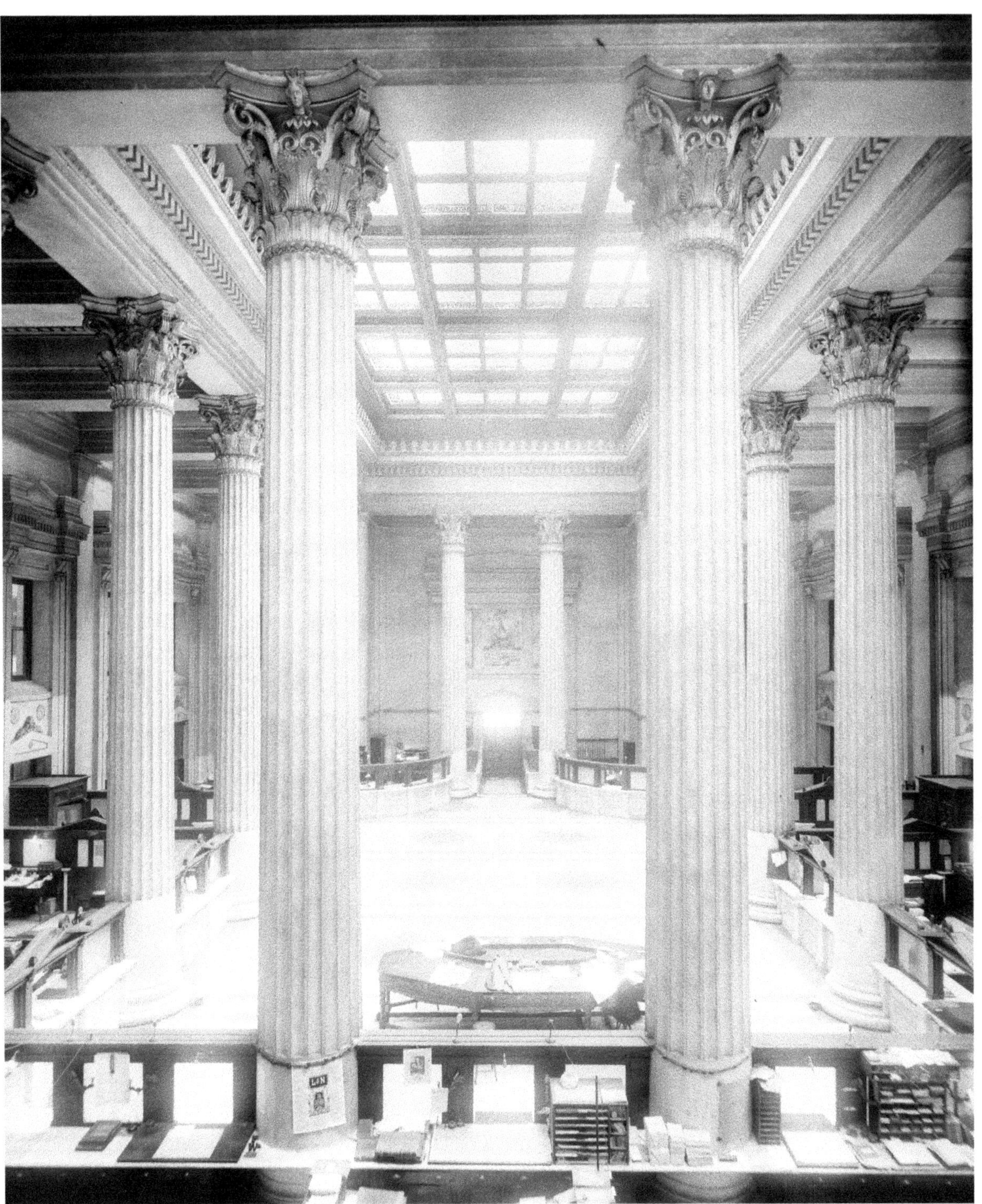

The elaborate Corinthian columns inside the old U.S. Customs House are featured in this image from around 1900. Located on Canal Street in New Orleans a few blocks from the river, the Customs House was built between 1848 and 1881 and housed the local customs office and other federal offices. Designated a National Historic Landmark in 1974, it reopened in 2008 as the Audubon Insectarium, the largest free-standing American museum dedicated to insects.

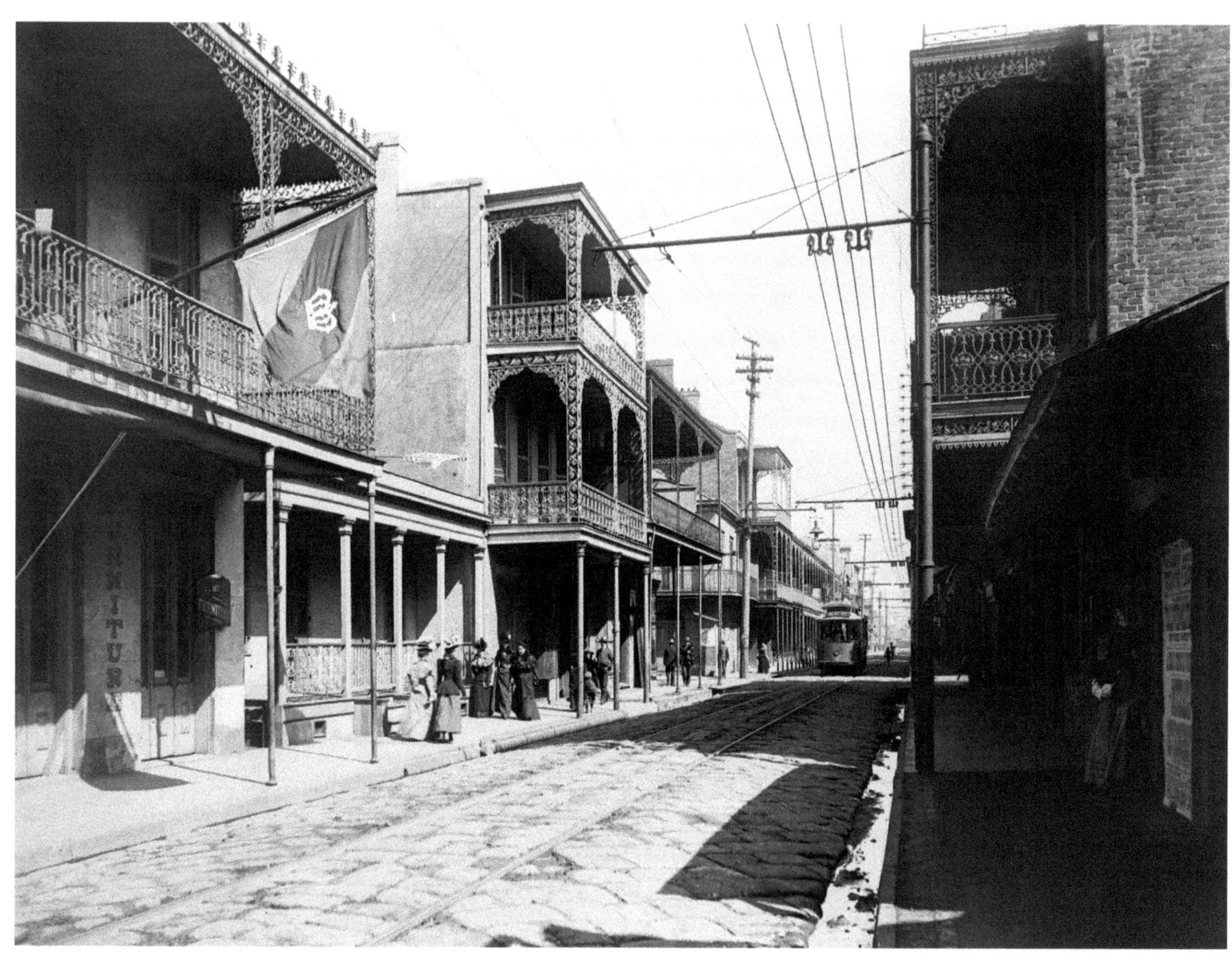

A scene along Royal Street in the French Quarter of New Orleans in the early 1900s. The iron lace balconies visible in the image, many of which can still be seen today, reflect styles of the Spanish colonial period that lasted from 1763 to 1803. The overhead wires no longer exist and the French Quarter is now served by underground electric cables. Royal Street today features many art galleries and antique shops and is a favorite destination for tourists.

The old City Hall on St. Charles Avenue in New Orleans is shown here as it looked around 1900. Also known as Gallier Hall after its architect, James Gallier, Sr., it was built in the 1840s in the Greek Revival style and served as New Orleans' City Hall until the mid-1950s. It still stands today and is used for formal city functions. Many of New Orleans' most famous people have laid in state here, prior to burial.

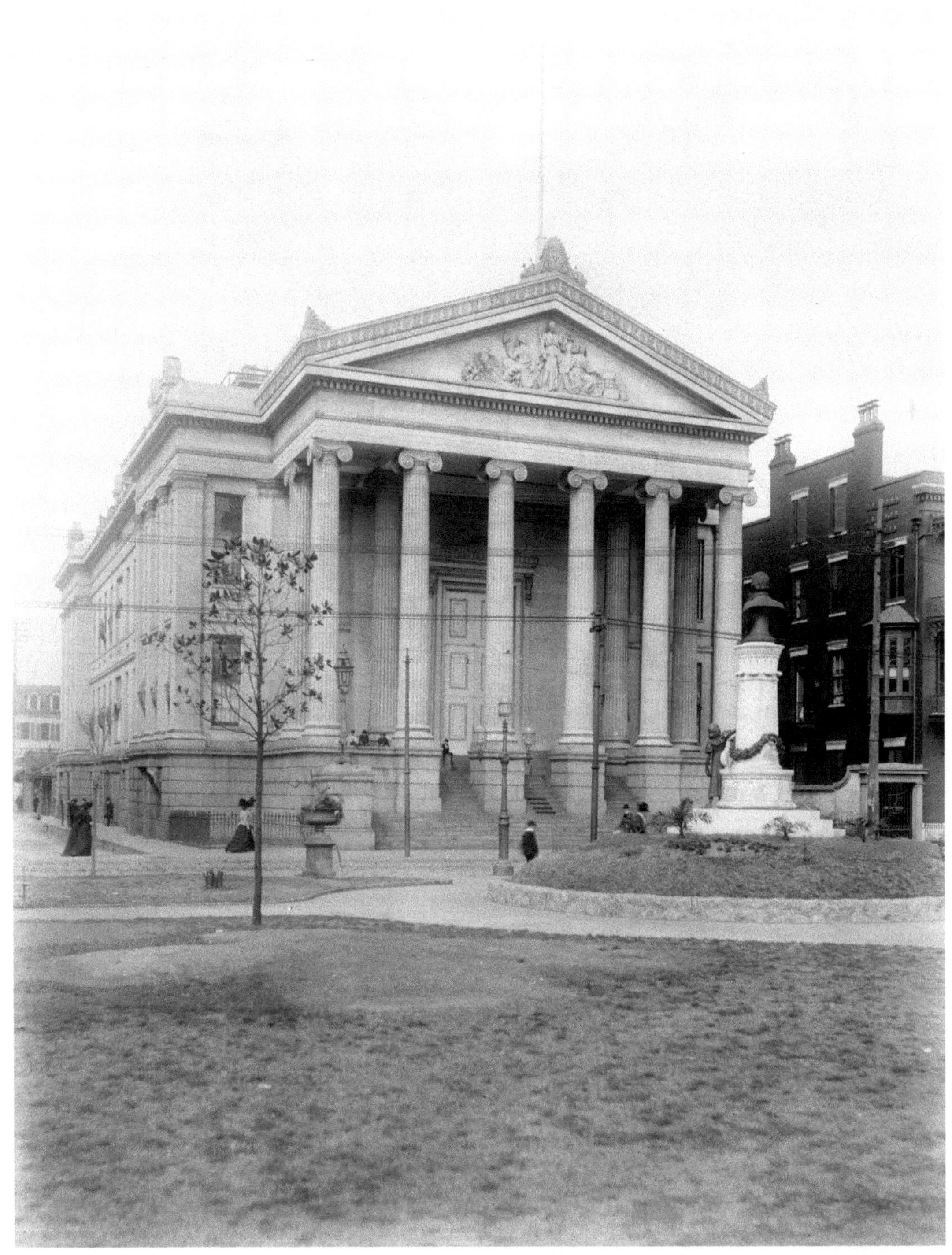

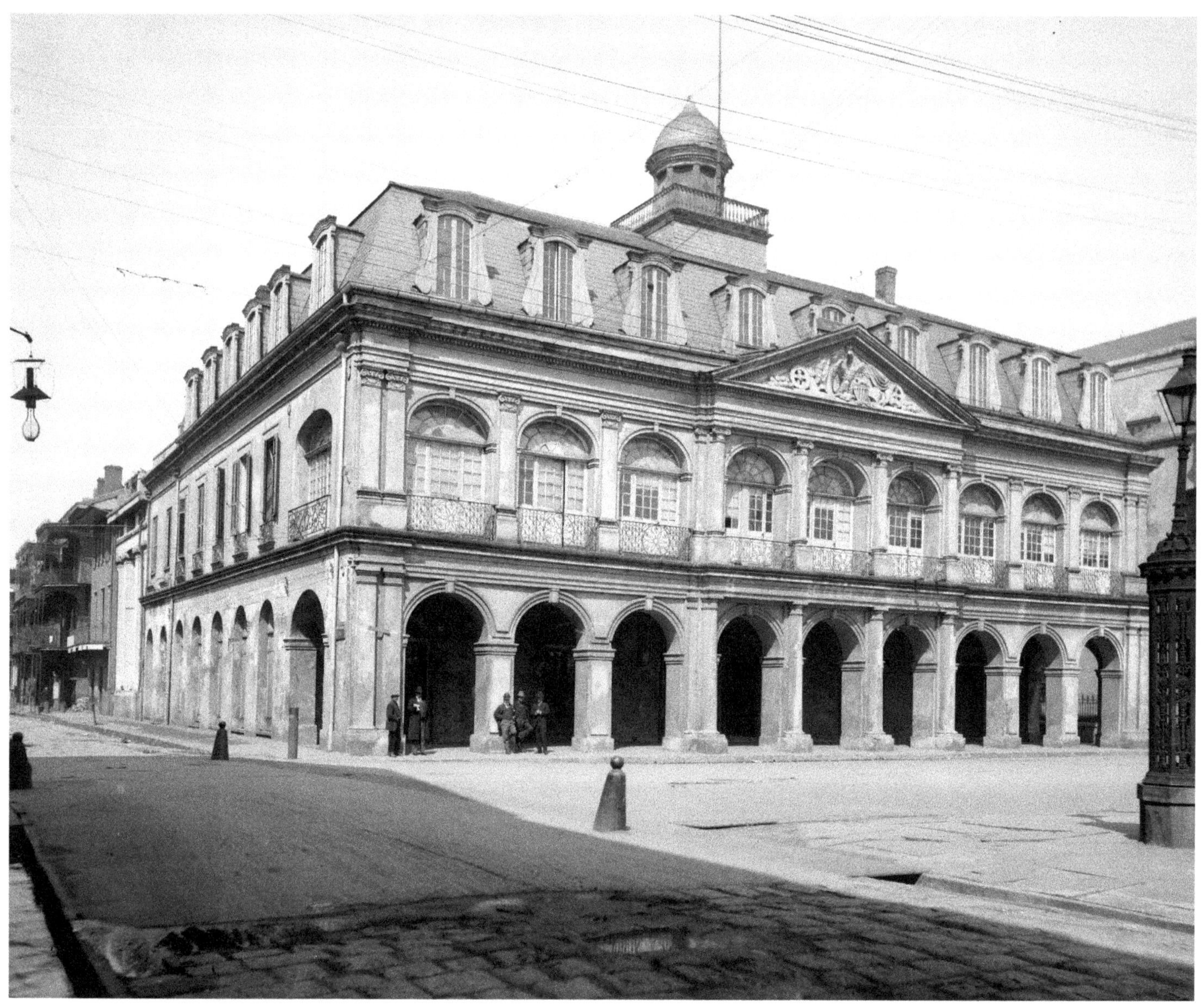

Seen here fronting on Jackson Square around 1900, the Cabildo dates to the mid-1790s and was the seat of the Spanish colonial government in New Orleans prior to the Louisiana Purchase, which was signed in one of the Cabildo's rooms in 1803. Serving today as a unit of the Louisiana State Museum, the Cabildo was the scene of a fire in 1988 that destroyed its upper floors and cupola. They were rebuilt to exact standards of the old building.

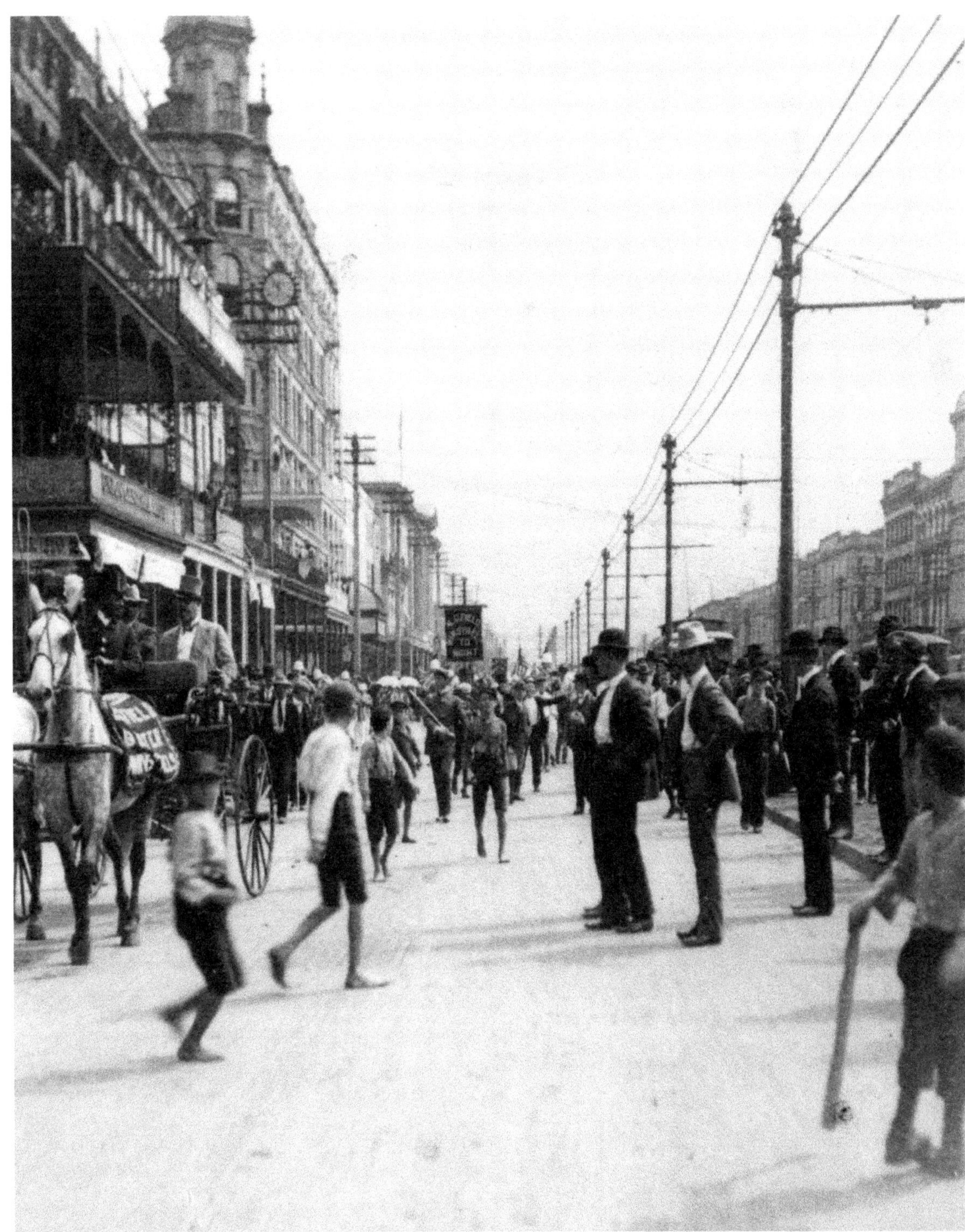

A busy Canal Street in downtown New Orleans in the early 1900s. Named for a canal that was never built, the street is one of the widest thoroughfares in any city in the United States. In the 1800s, Canal Street was the "neutral ground" or demographic dividing line between what were considered the French and American sectors of the city. Neutral ground is now defined as a median between lanes of any street in New Orleans.

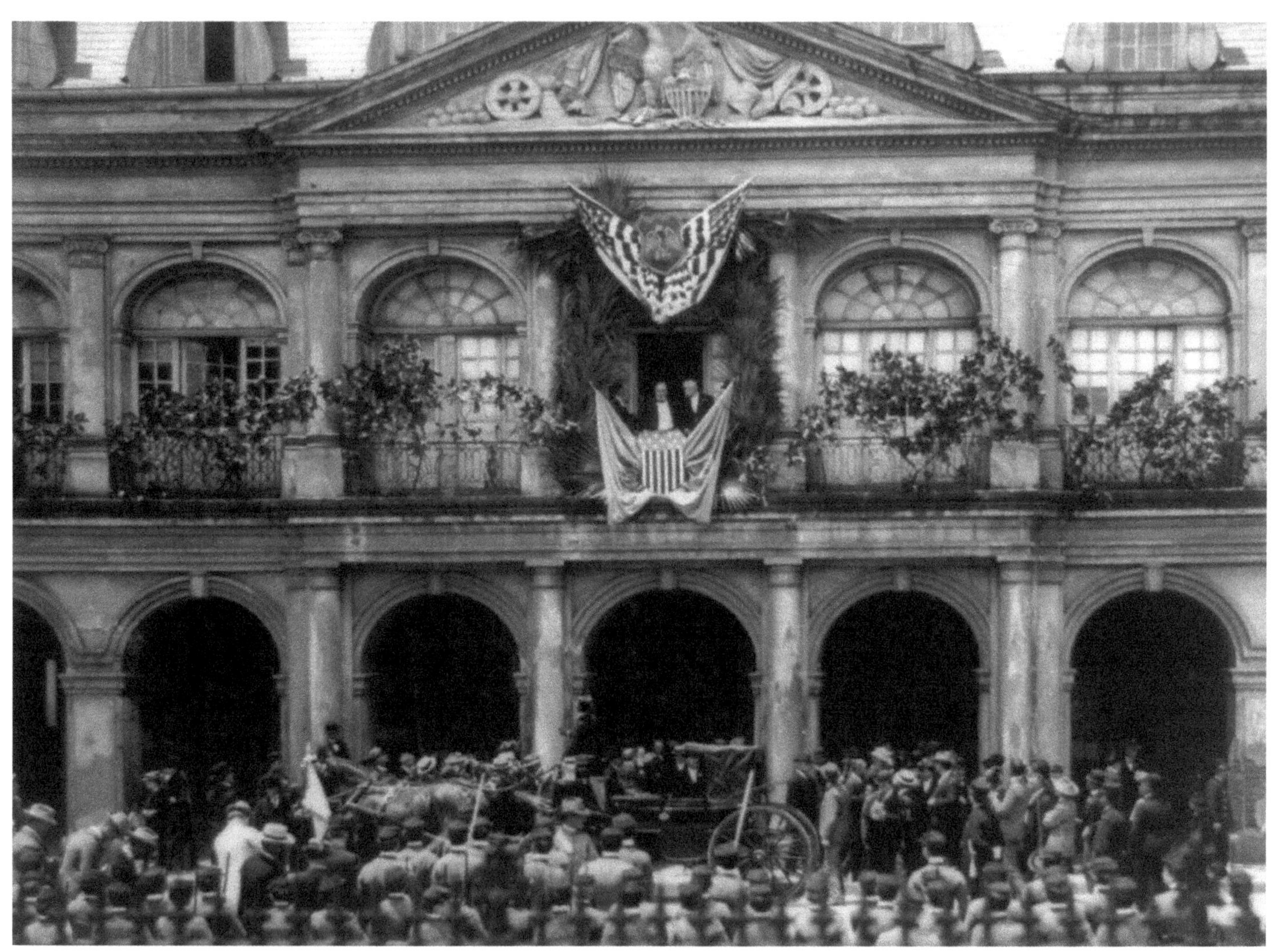

President William McKinley makes one of his final speeches from the balcony of the Cabildo during a visit to New Orleans in May 1901. An audience is seated in Jackson Square in front of the building to hear the speech. McKinley told the crowd, "My visit has been delightful," and he vowed to return soon, but on September 6 he was shot by a crazed anarchist while attending the Pan-American Exposition in Buffalo, New York, and died eight days later.

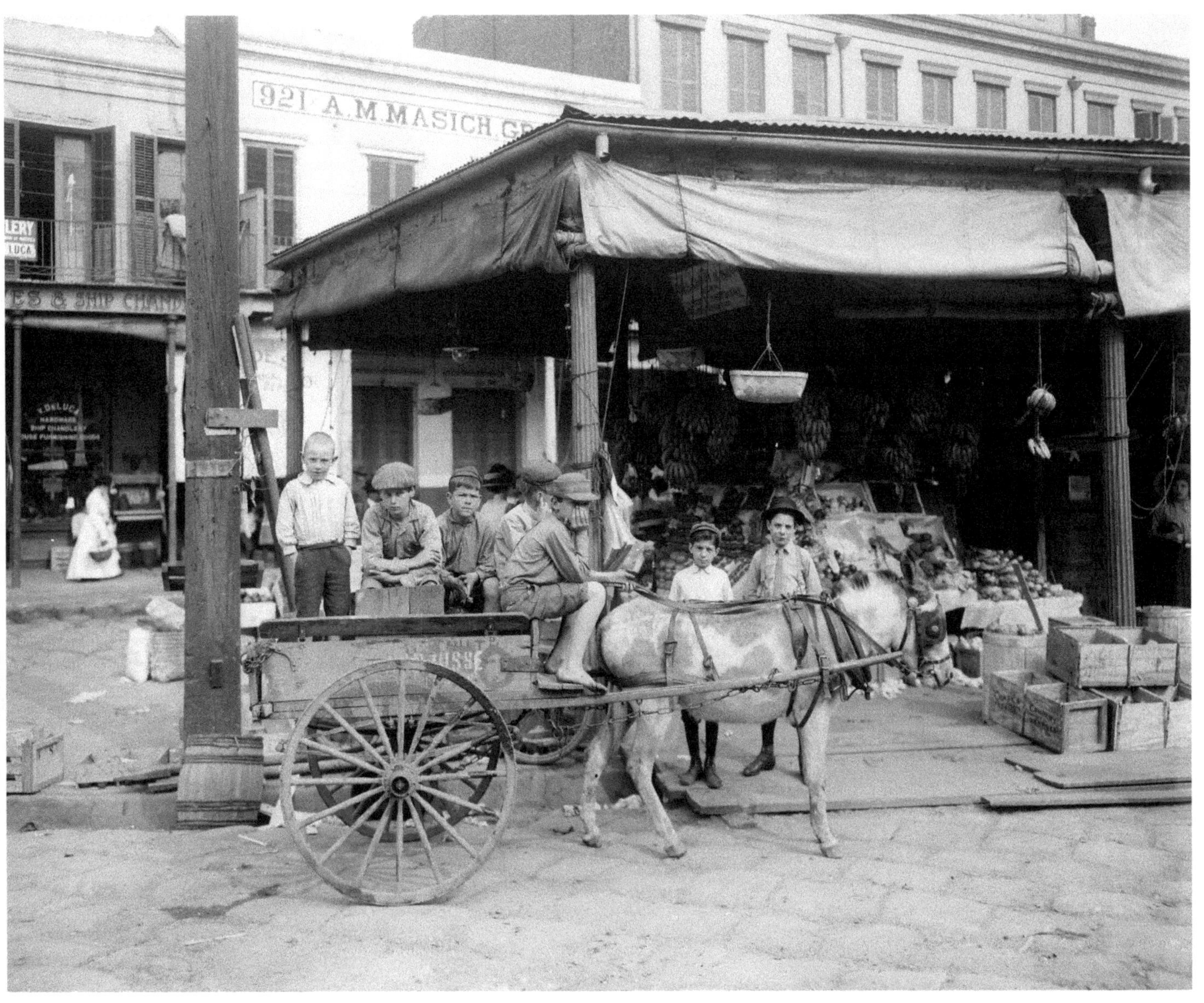

A group of young boys pose on and around a mule-drawn cart near the French Market in this early century image. Empty wooden produce crates and produce displays, including bananas and other fruit, are visible in the background.

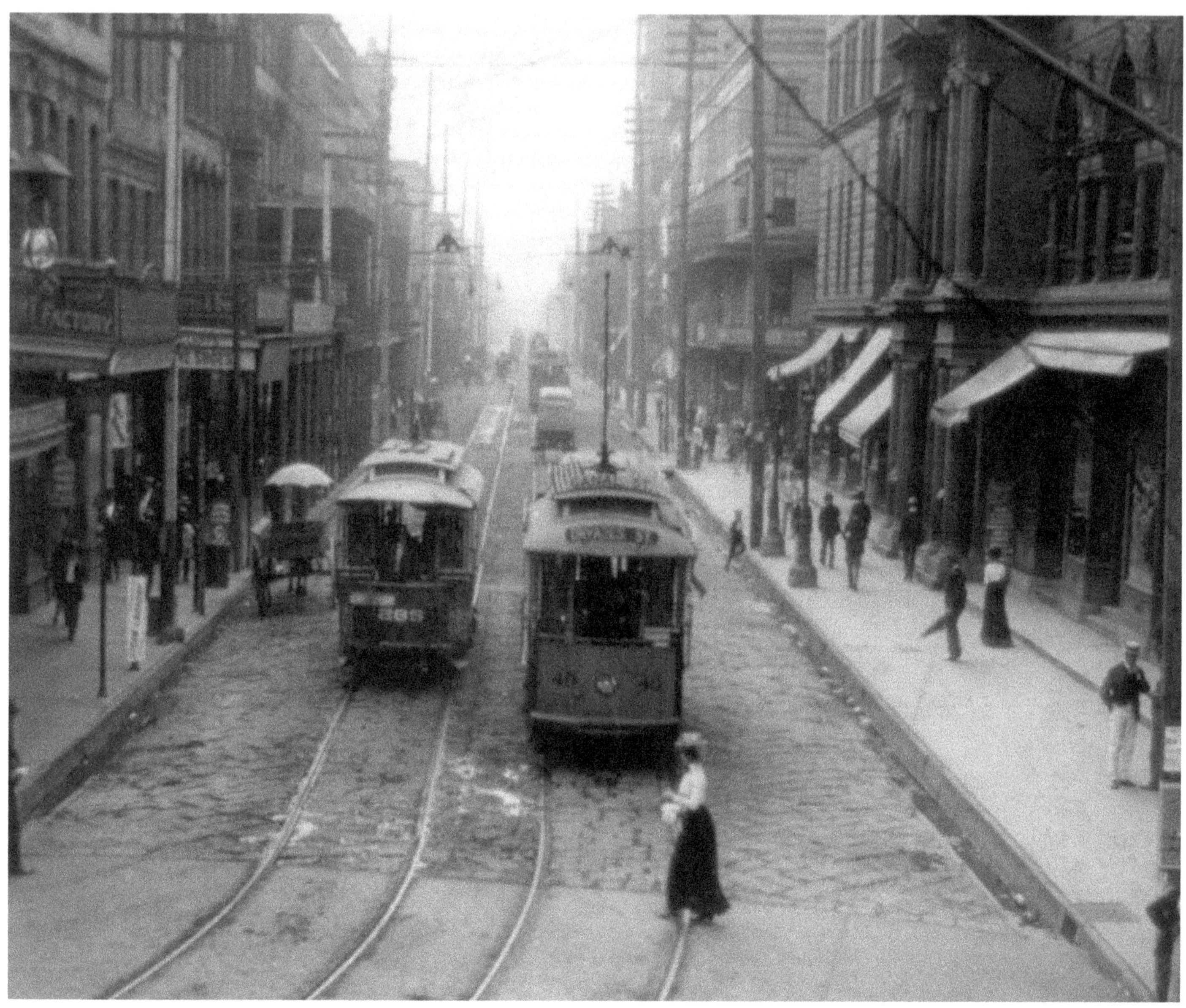

Streetcars roll side by side along St. Charles Street in downtown New Orleans in this view from around 1901. The streetcars seen in the picture were replaced in the early 1920s by the Perley Thomas Series 900 models, which still roll along the length of St. Charles Avenue today. The car at right is headed for Dryades Street, which at the time was the hub of retail commerce for the city's African-American population. Only one set of tracks remains on this section of St. Charles for streetcars heading uptown.

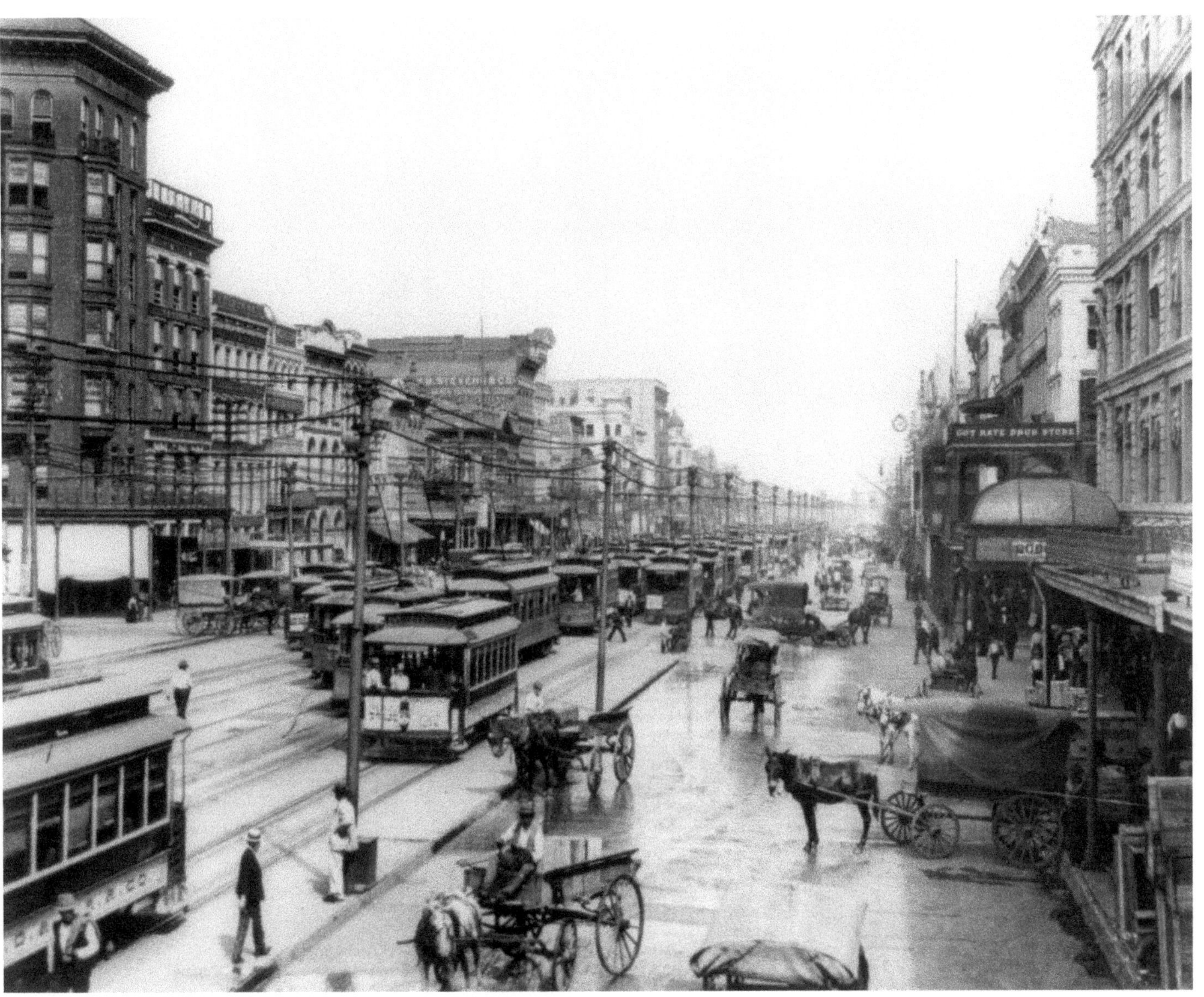

A fleet of electric-powered streetcars crowd the "neutral ground" of Canal Street, while horse-drawn carriages occupy both sides of the street itself. Many of the buildings seen here around 1902 still stand today. Streetcars were taken off Canal Street in 1964 and replaced with buses, but newer-model red streetcars were reintroduced in the early 2000s and have been very popular with tourists and locals alike.

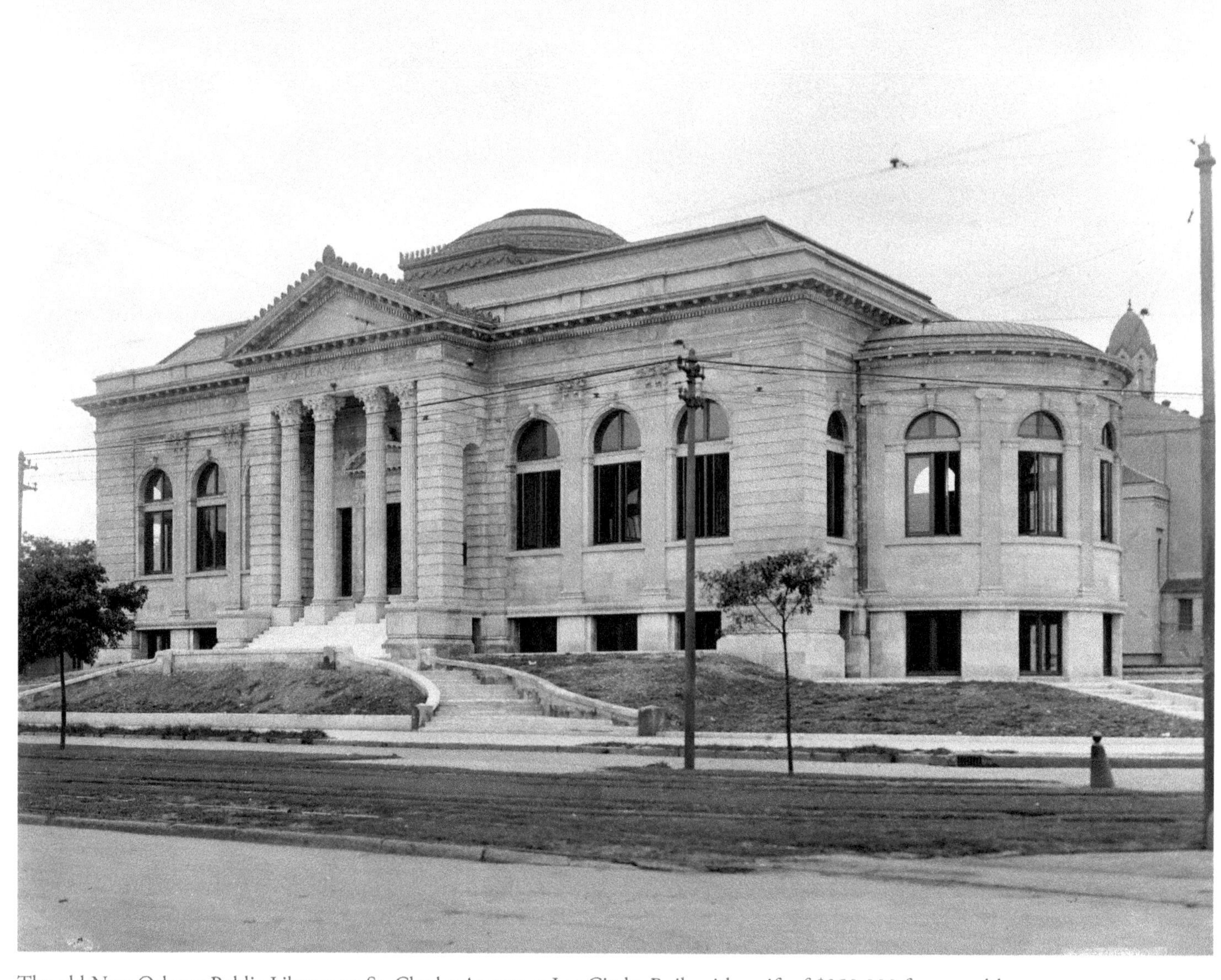

The old New Orleans Public Library on St. Charles Avenue at Lee Circle. Built with a gift of $250,000 from wealthy industrialist-philanthropist Andrew Carnegie in 1908, the library was a distinctive architectural landmark whose loss was lamented when it was razed in the 1960s and replaced with a modern glass-and-steel structure that would, for a time, house the K&B drugstore chain headquarters.

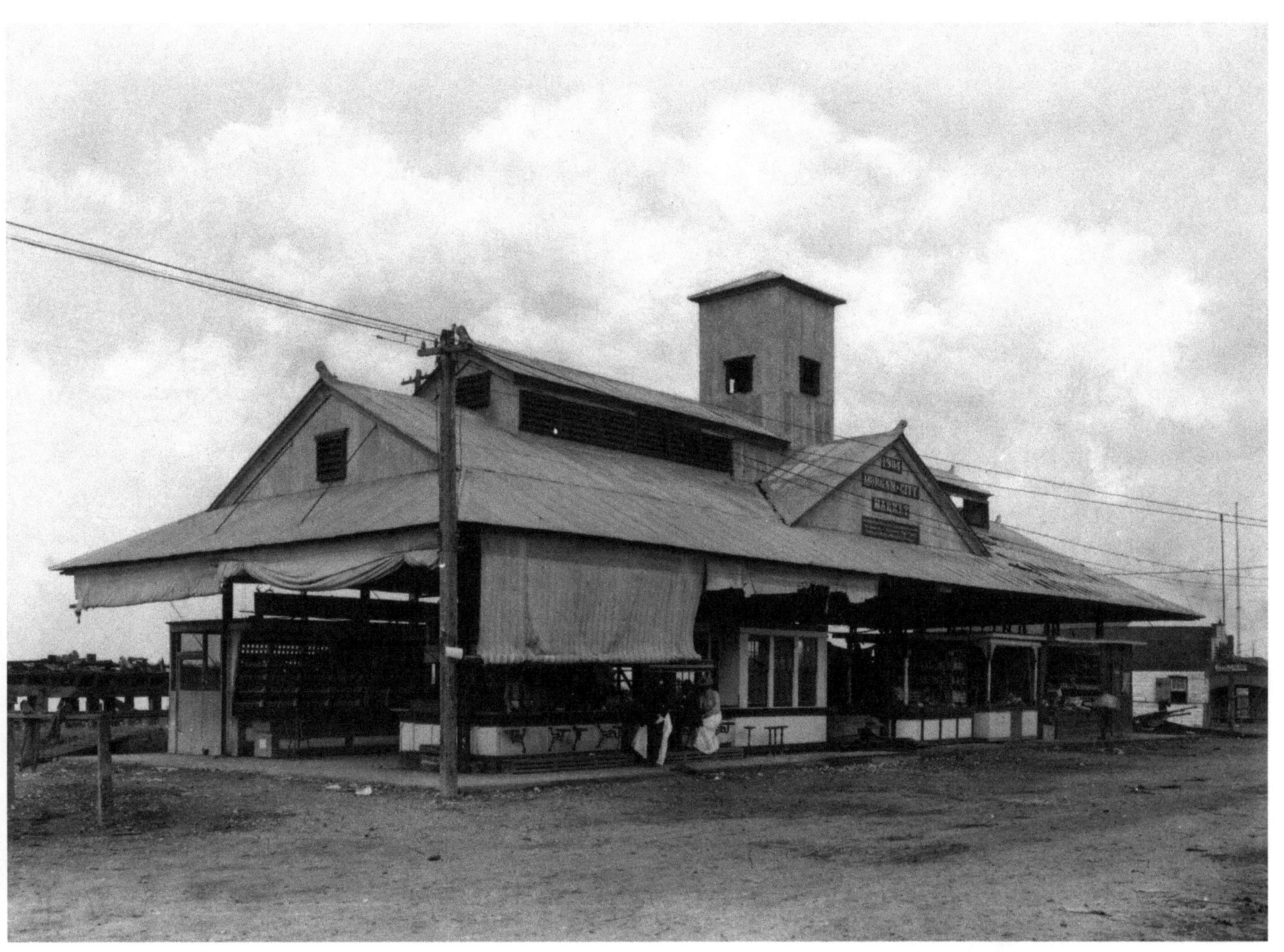

An outdoor market in Morgan City is open for business early in the new century. Morgan City, on the Atchafalaya River in St. Mary Parish, is about 70 miles west of New Orleans and has long been the center of a thriving fishing and seafood industry. Today it is also a hub of the oil-drilling industry and a busy "jumping-off" point for workers shuttling to and from the offshore rigs in the Gulf of Mexico.

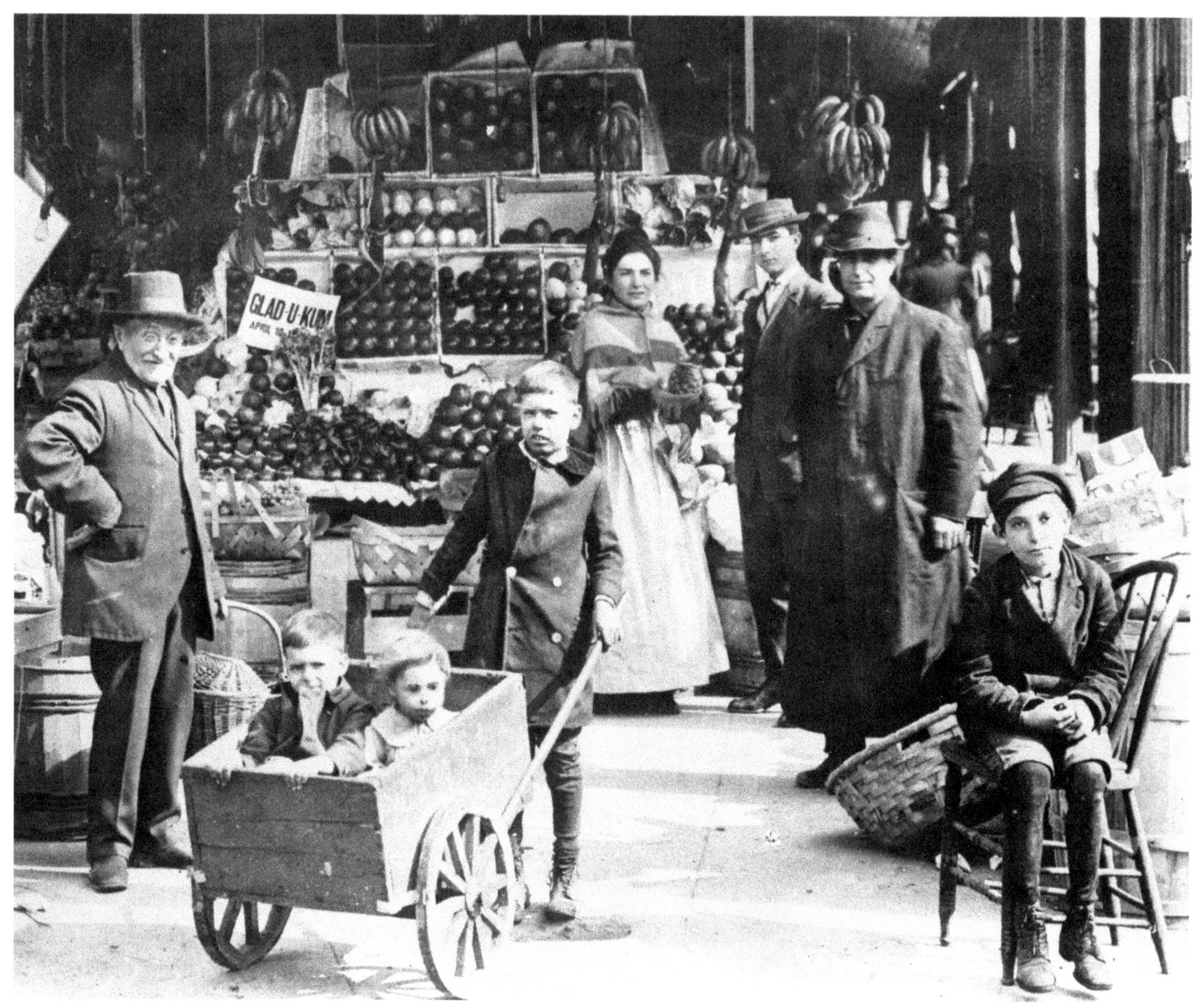

Members of what appears to be a family pose in front of a fruit stand in New Orleans, possibly the French Market, sometime in the new century. Produce vending was very often a family-run business in New Orleans, particularly among recent immigrants to the city.

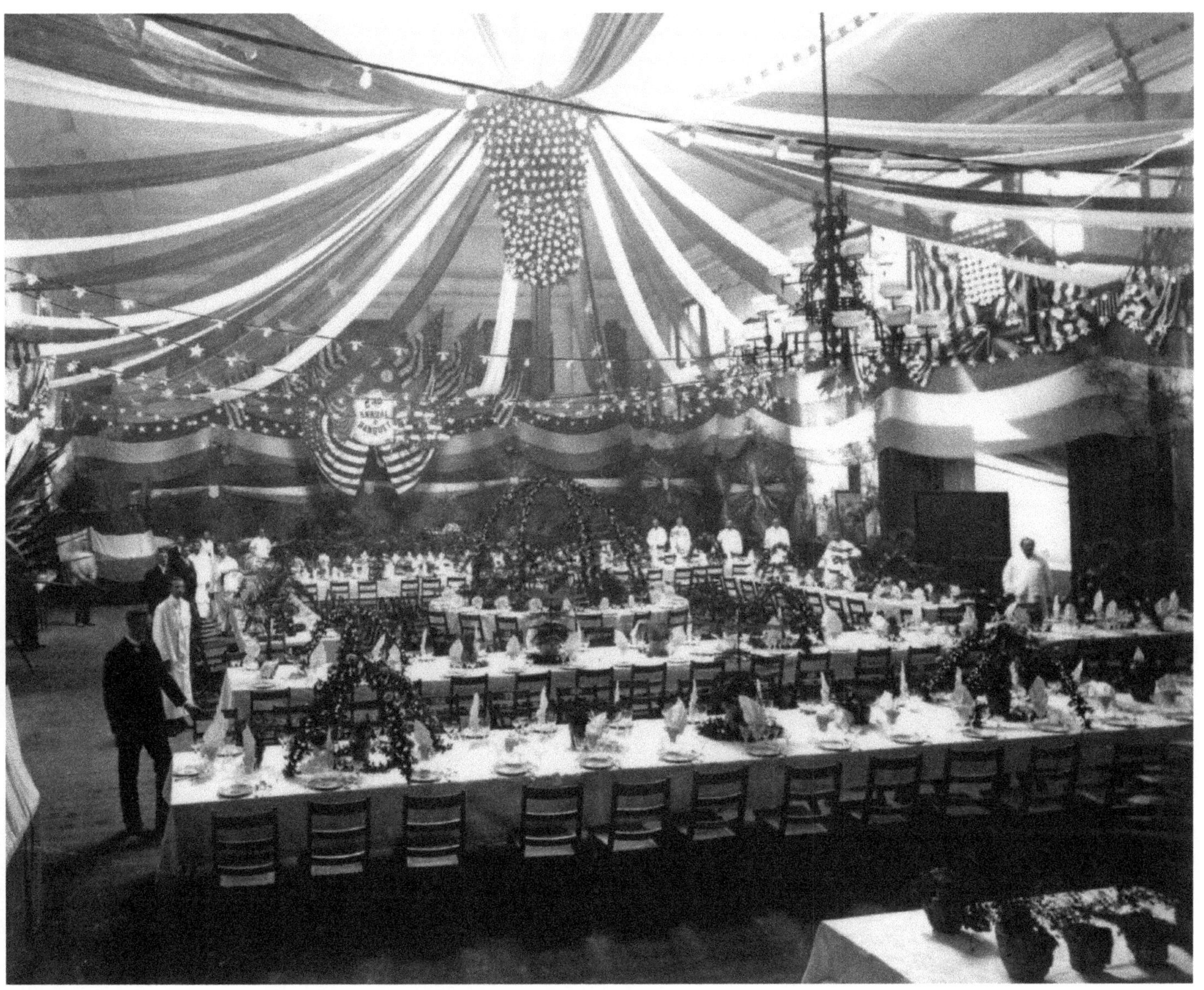

President Theodore Roosevelt was on hand to address the Second Annual Banquet of the New Orleans Board of Trade during his visit in 1904. Roosevelt, who had succeeded the assassinated President McKinley three years earlier, was the second Chief Executive to visit New Orleans while in office. The city has been visited by every sitting president since.

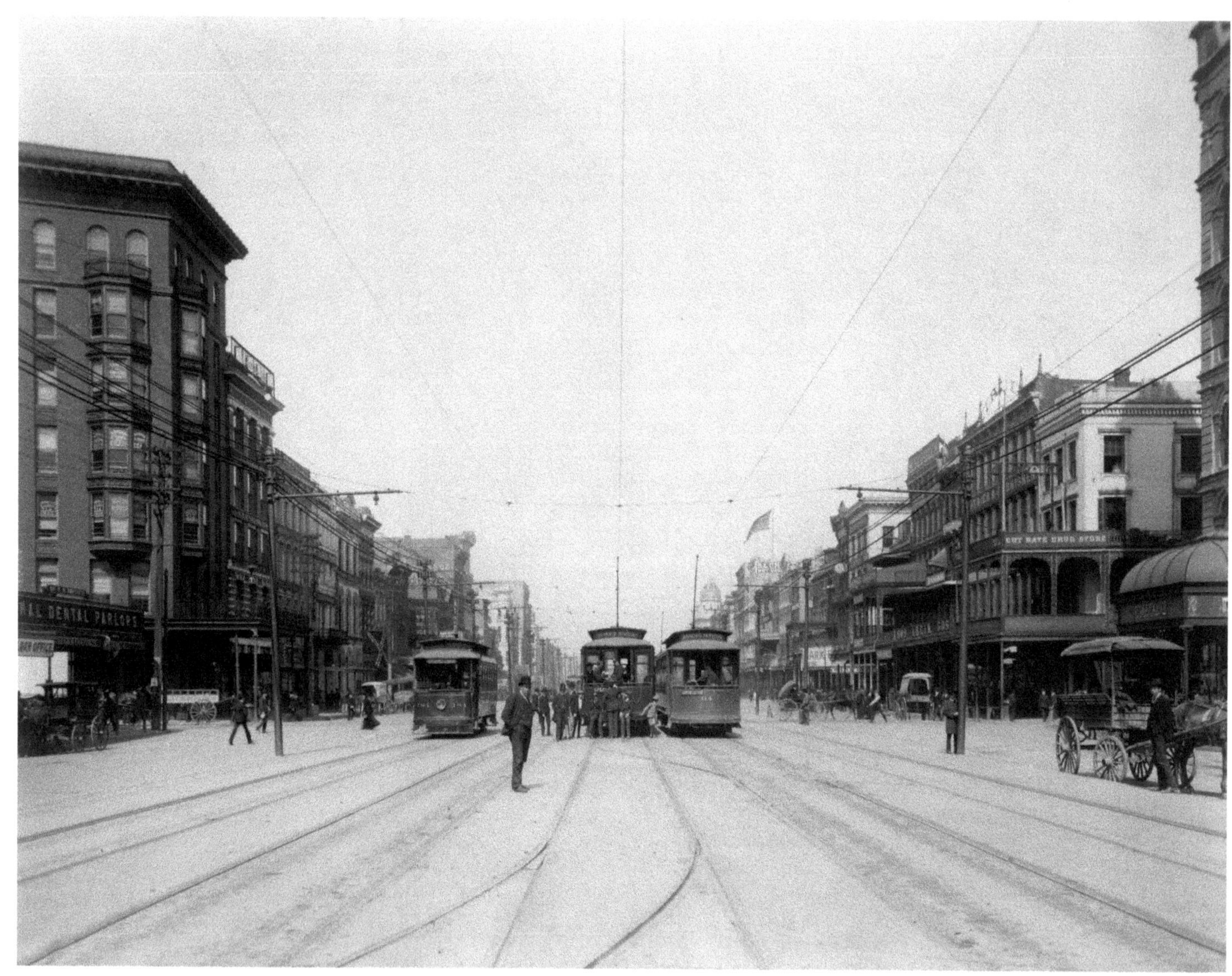

Streetcars line up three abreast on the "neutral ground" of Canal Street in 1907. The busy hub of downtown New Orleans, Canal Street, for many years, featured upscale department store chains and was a fashionable shopping mecca, as well as an entertainment district lined with movie theaters. Many of the former department stores have since been converted into major chain hotels and condominiums, and plans are in the works to restore the old theaters.

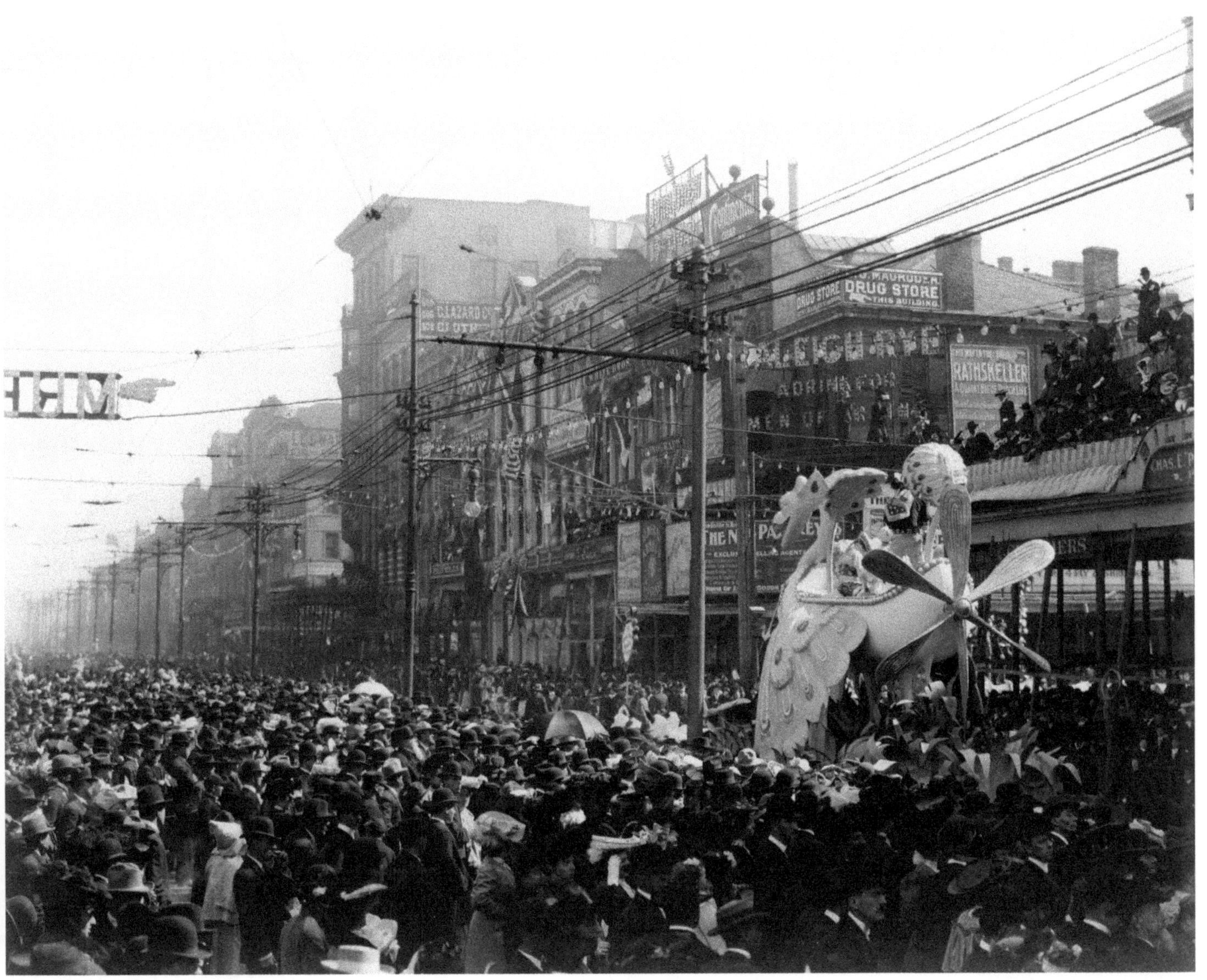

The Rex parade moves along a very crowded Canal Street on Mardi Gras Day 1906. Every year a prominent member of the city's business community would be chosen to "reign" as Rex for the day, nicknamed "the Lord of Misrule." By tradition, the King of Carnival is toasted by the mayor outside Gallier Hall on St. Charles Avenue, which, for 100 years, served as the New Orleans City Hall.

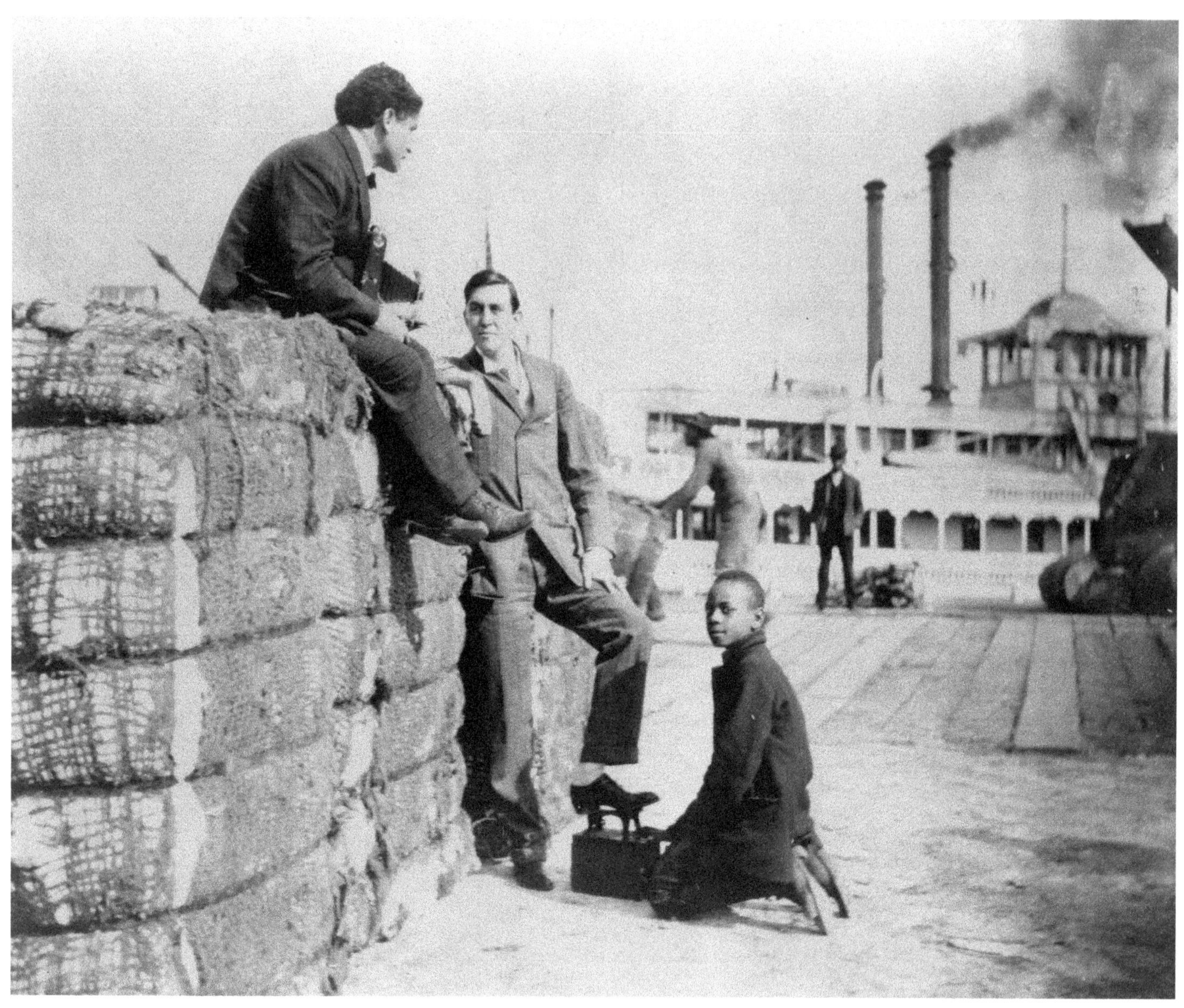

The famous magician and escape artist Harry Houdini sits on a cotton bale on the New Orleans riverfront in 1907 talking to a man who is having his shoes shined. A riverboat is visible in the background. Houdini, whose real name was Erich Weiss, was born in Hungary in 1874. He traveled widely throughout the United States promoting his death-defying stunts, including escaping while being submerged upside-down in water and chained.

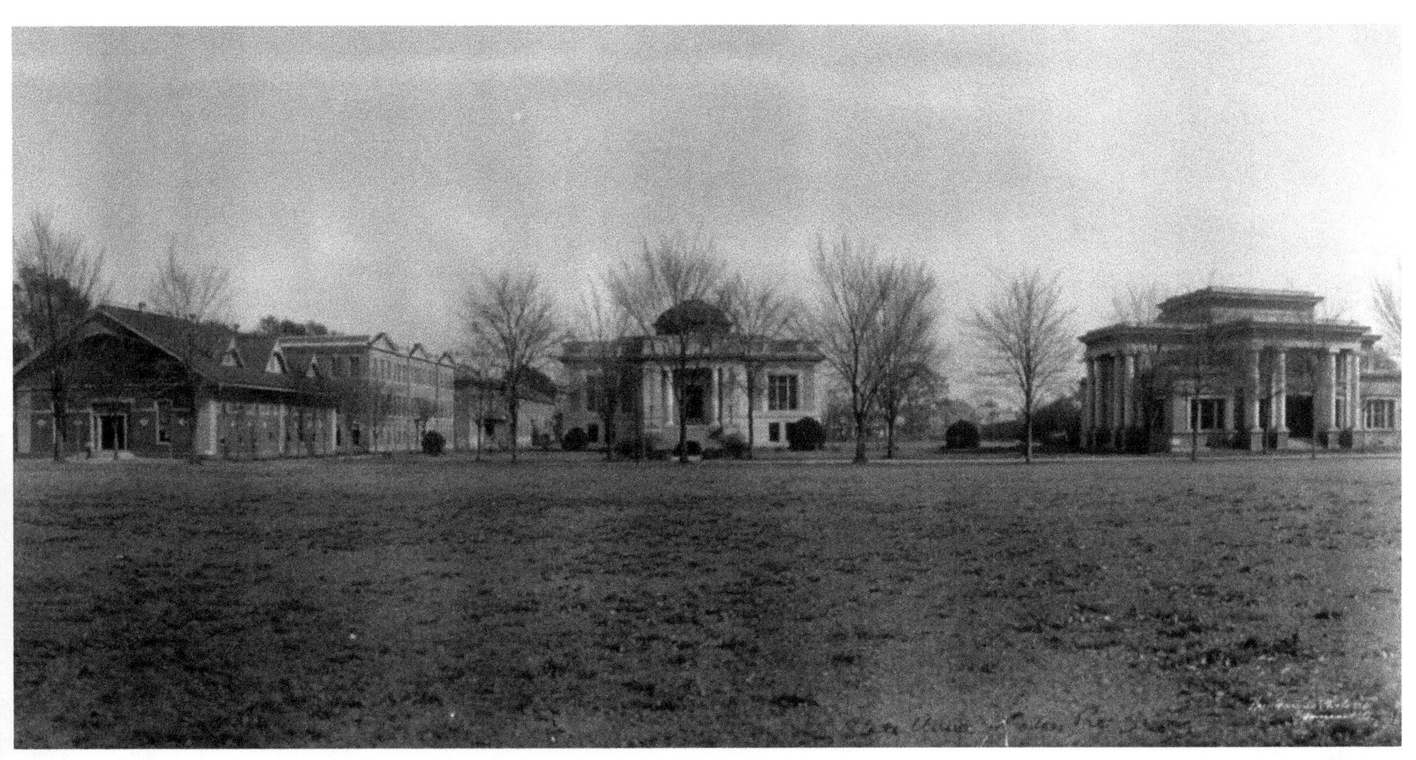

The campus of Louisiana State University in Baton Rouge as it appeared in 1909. The flagship college of the Louisiana State University System, the LSU campus in Baton Rouge was founded in 1860. Its first superintendent was General William T. Sherman, later a Civil War hero for the Union. Today's LSU campus occupies about 650 acres and encompasses 250 buildings. LSU Tigers football, which began in 1893, won national championships in the 1958, 2003, and 2007 seasons.

Following spread: This rooftop panorama of downtown New Orleans offers a look at the city as it appeared in 1909.

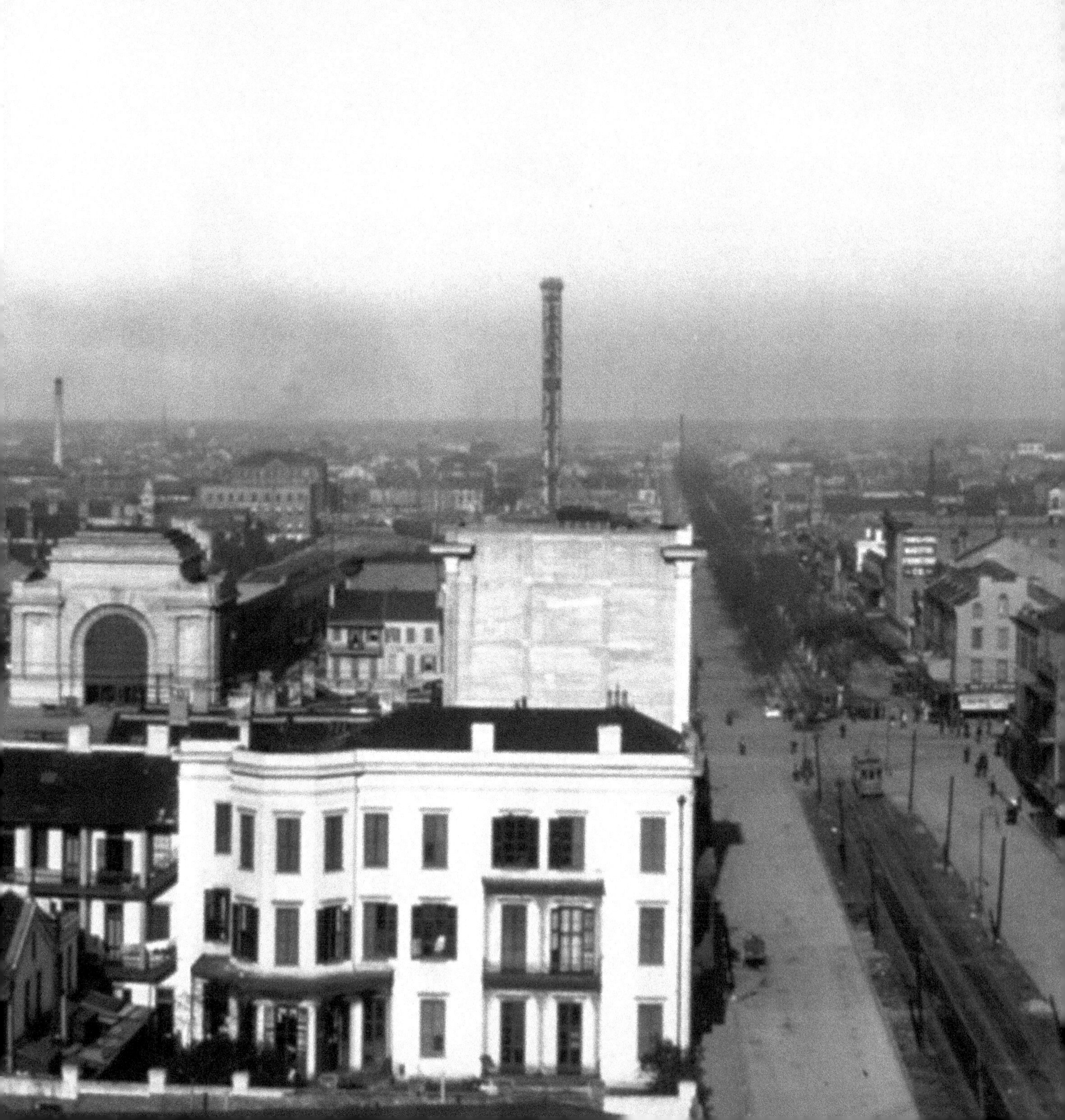

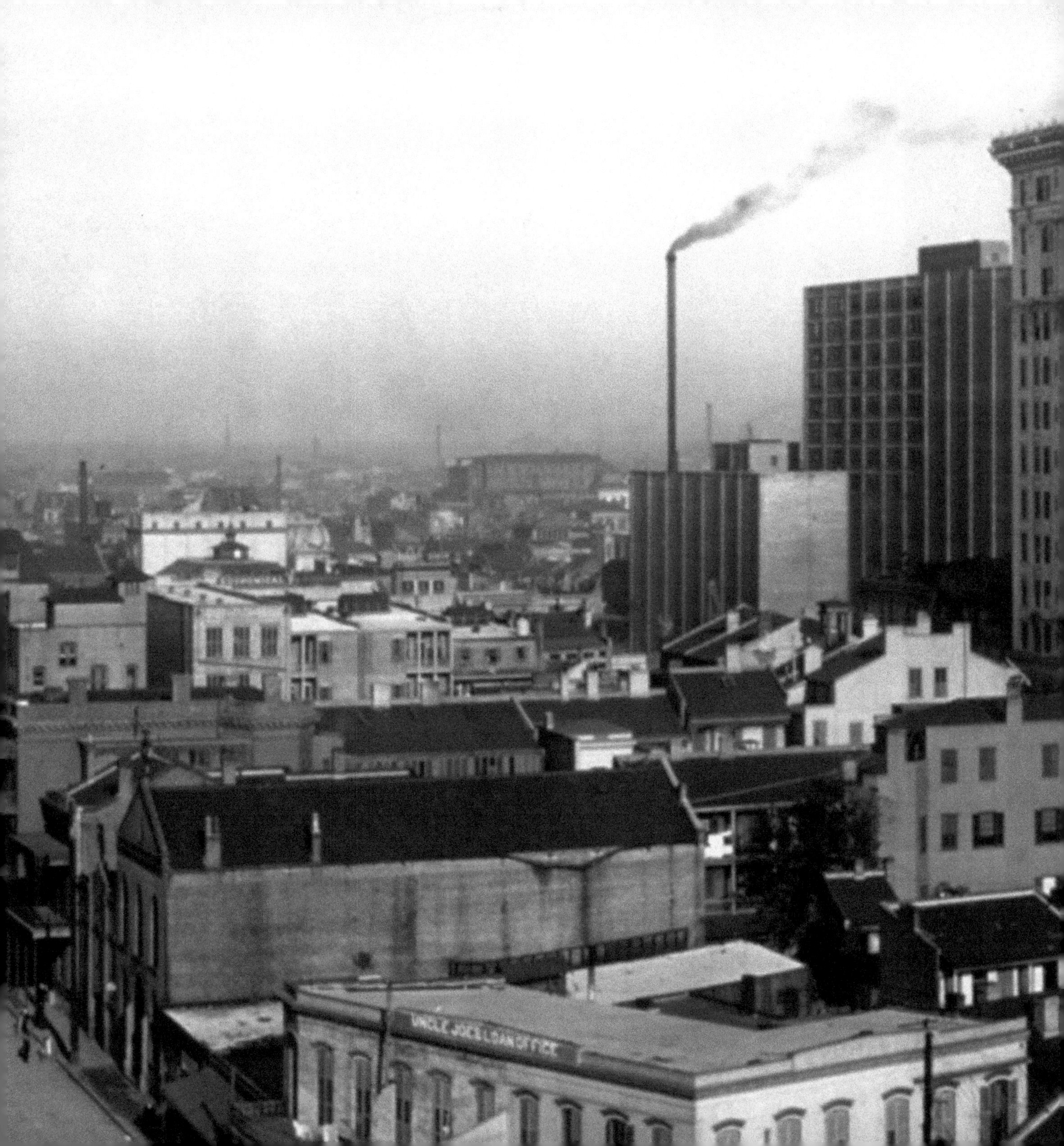
UNCLE JOE'S LOAN OFFICE

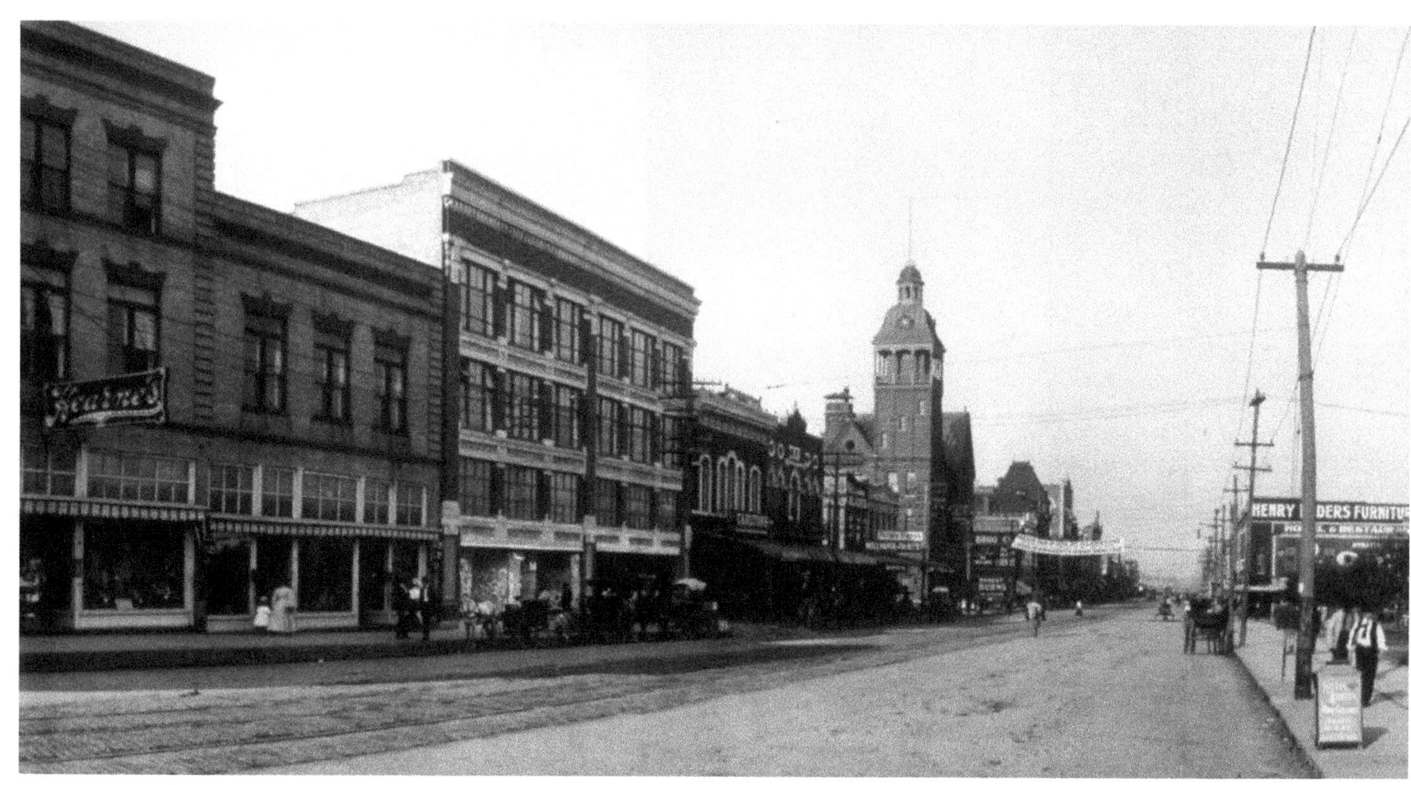

Downtown Shreveport as it appeared around 1910. Located on the Red River in the northwest corner of Louisiana, Shreveport was named for Captain Henry Shreve, who designed the first flat-bottomed, shallow-draft steamboats to run on the Mississippi River and its tributaries. He also designed the first snag-removal boats and oversaw the operation that broke up an 1830s logjam on the Red River.

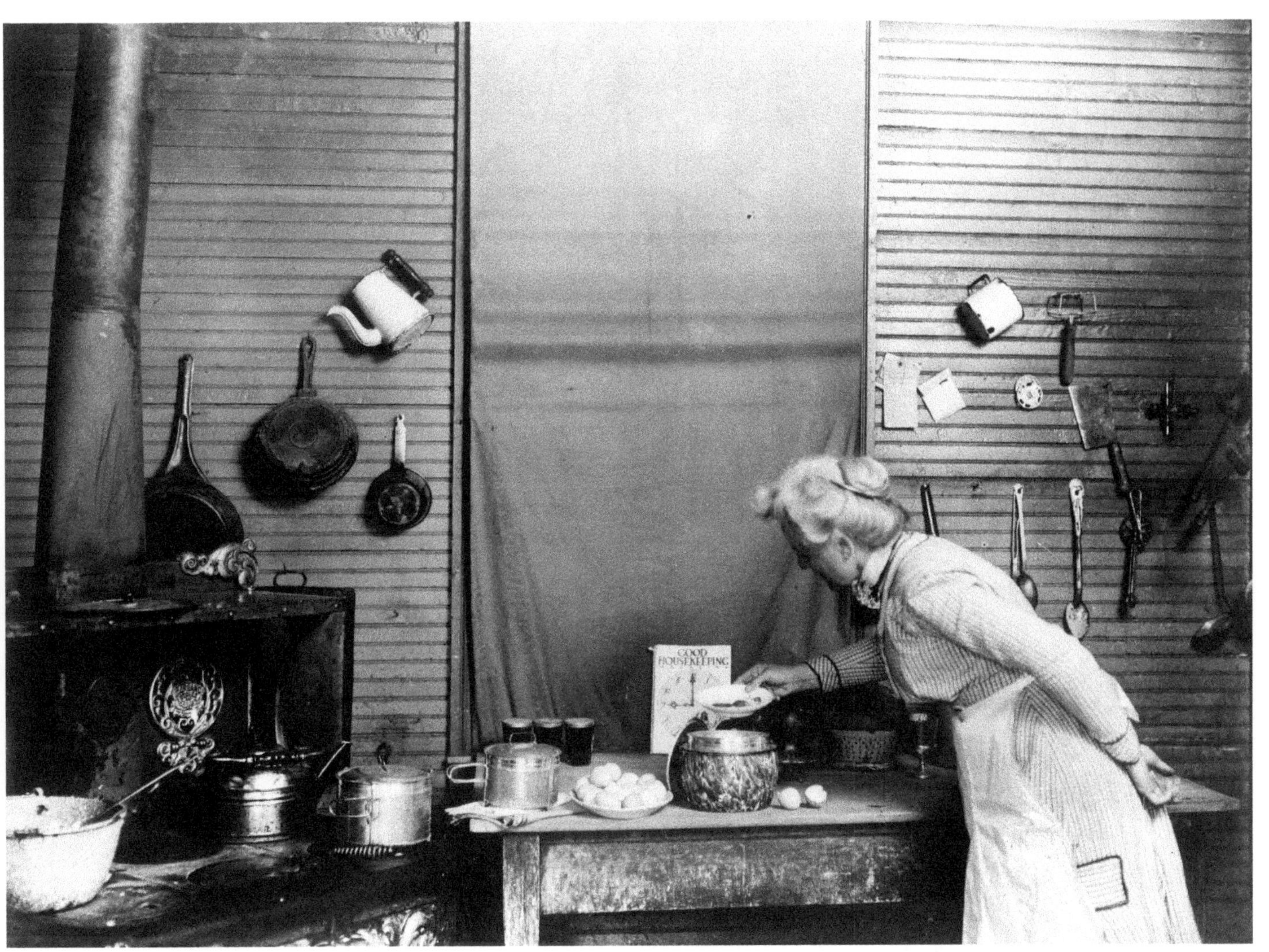

A woman separates an egg in a kitchen in Crowley around 1910. The image was part of a series titled "Modern Cooking" by J. G. Ewing, a noted photographer of the day.

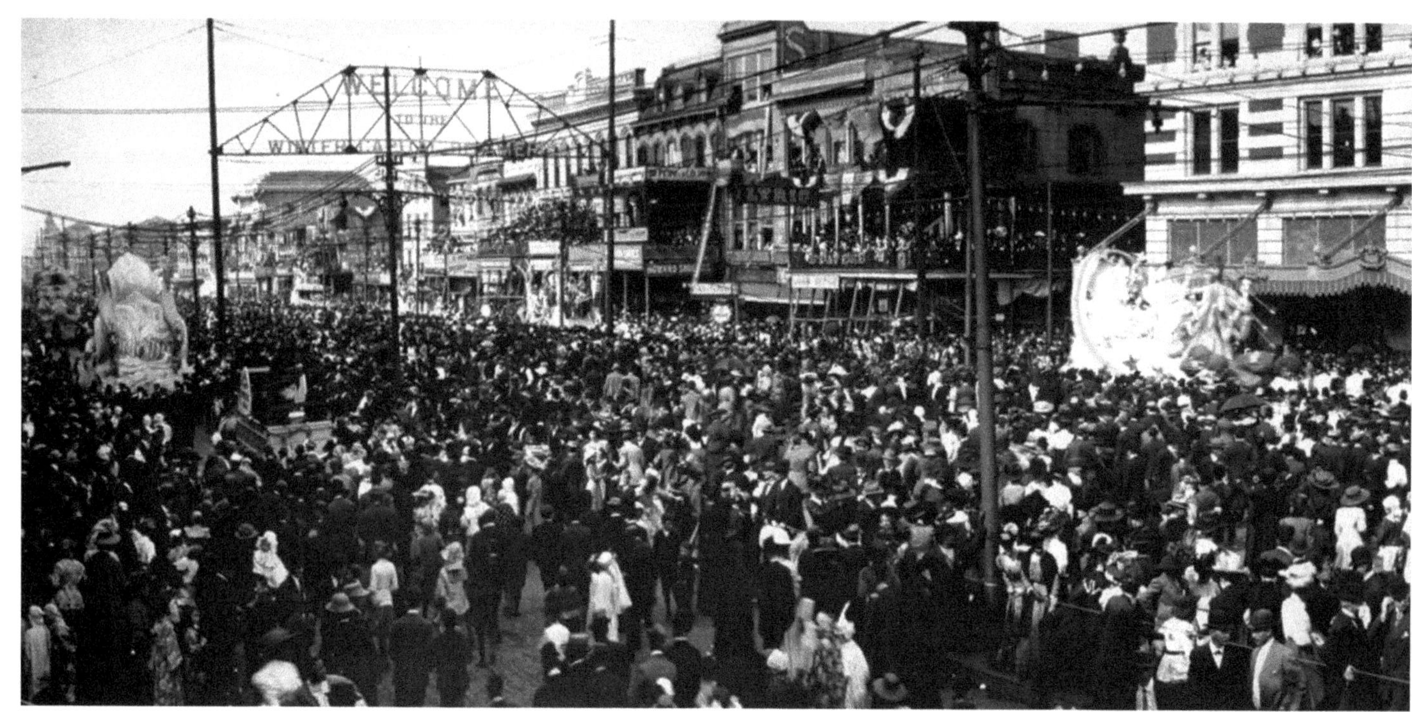

Floats from the Rex parade roll along both sides of Canal Street through crowds gathered to celebrate Mardi Gras around 1910. Mardi Gras has been held almost continuously in New Orleans since 1857, the only exceptions being during the Civil War, the two world wars, and a police strike in 1979.

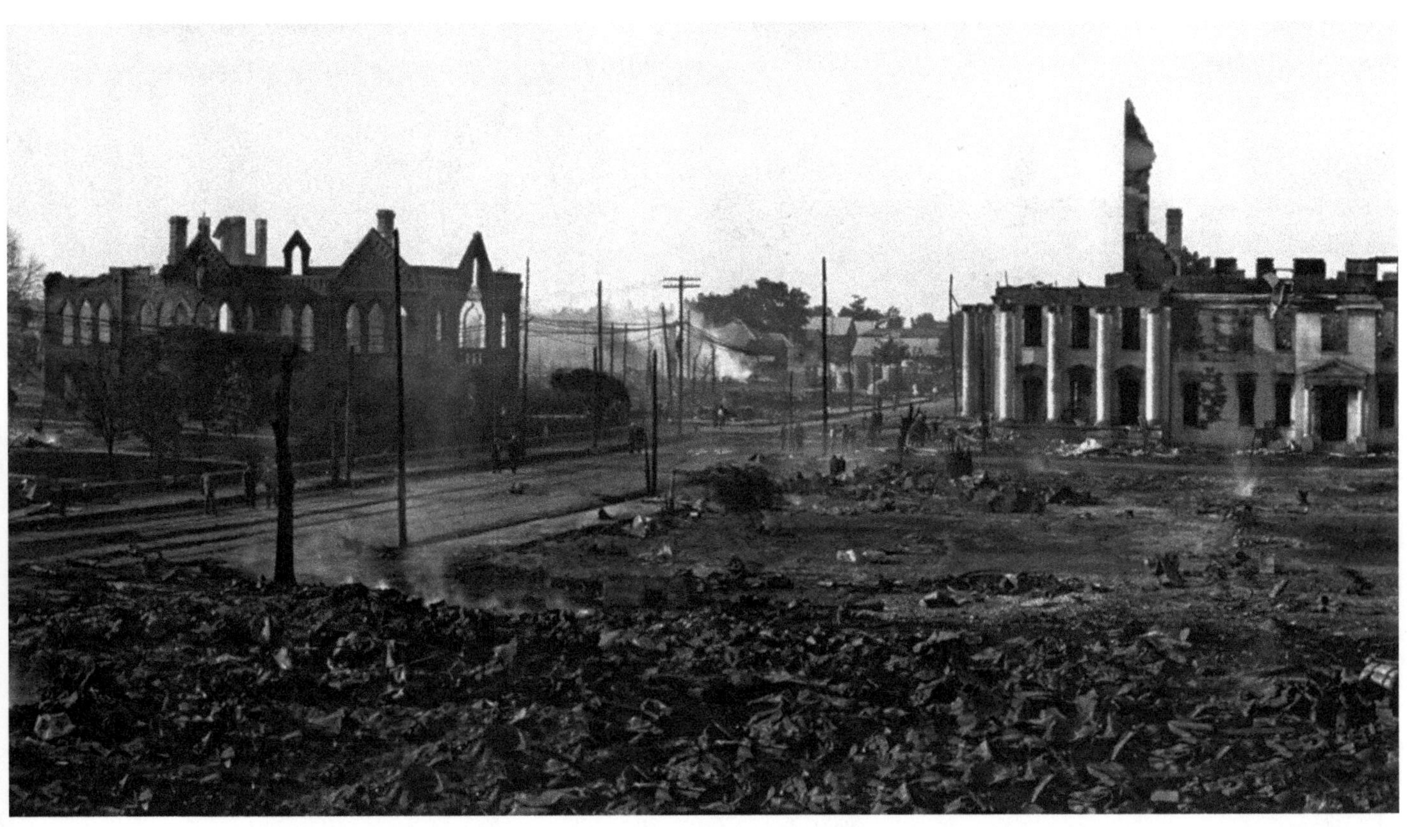

A devastating fire that struck Lake Charles on April 23, 1910, flattened a seven-block area of the city and left the old Catholic Church and neighboring structures gutted shells. Also destroyed in the blaze was the newly constructed Calcasieu Parish Courthouse, the Lake Charles City Hall, and a fire station. Nearly half of the city's population of 15,000 was made homeless, and damage was estimated around $4 million.

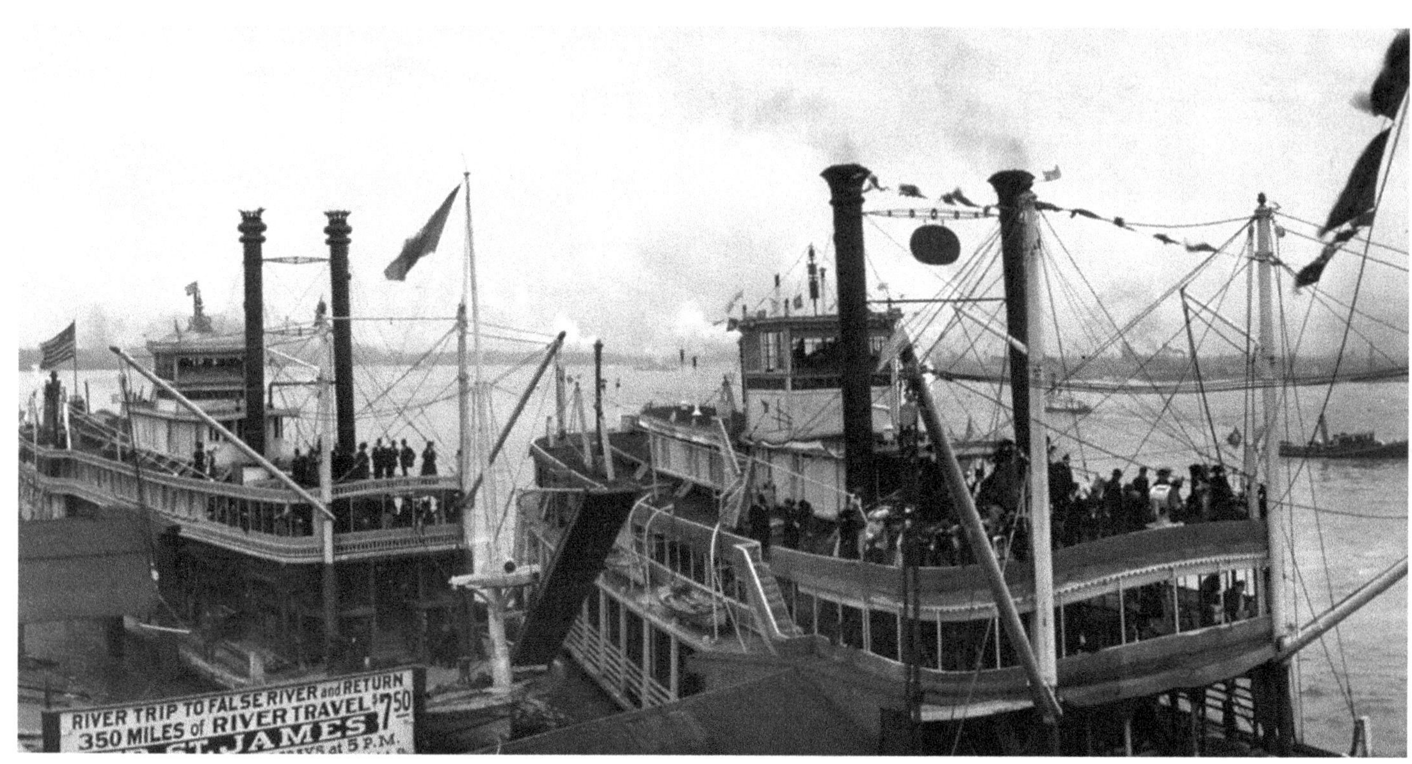

The packet steamboat *St. James* takes on passengers in New Orleans for a 350-mile round trip to False River, above Baton Rouge, around 1910. By the early 1900s, steamboats plying the Mississippi and other western rivers began to lose their importance as railroads and other methods of ground transportation prevailed. Sightseeing excursions became a way of replacing revenues lost on cargo and passenger transport.

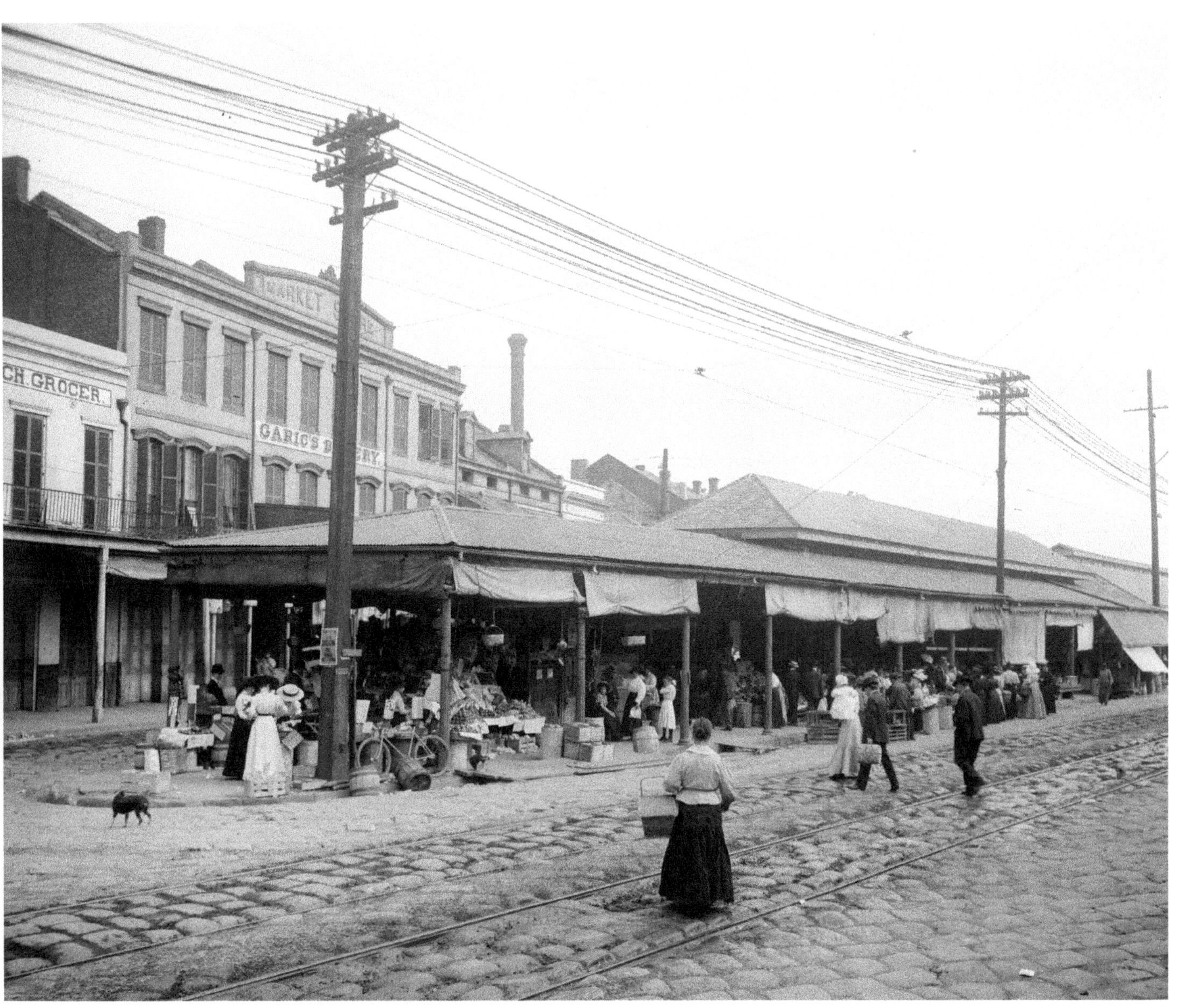

This shot was taken of the old French Market in New Orleans around 1910. Before the advent of supermarkets later in the twentieth century, people bought their produce directly from outdoor markets, usually early in the morning while the goods were still fresh. The French Market was extensively renovated in 2008 and is still very popular today, especially with restaurant chefs.

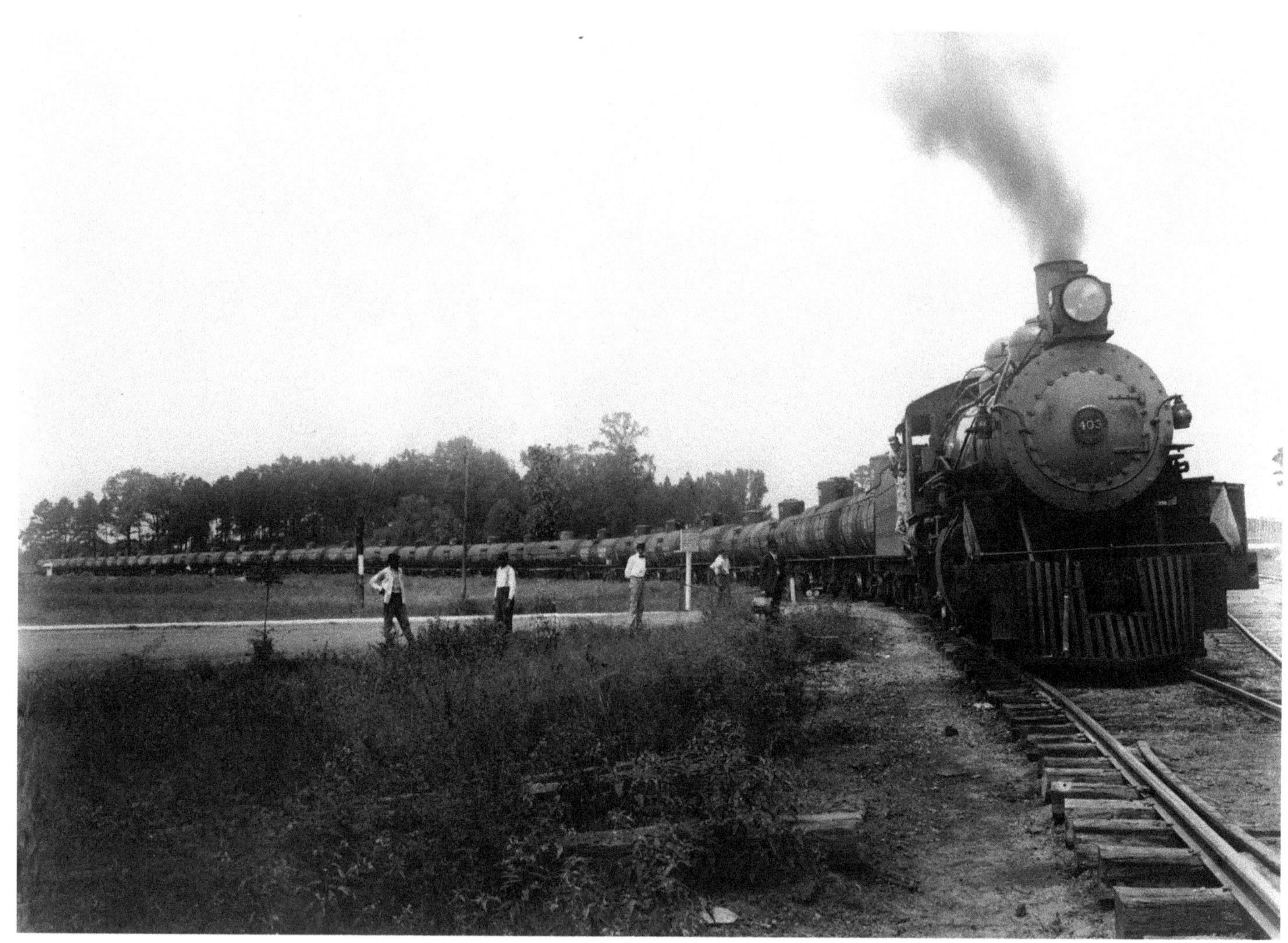

A steam train on the Louisiana & Arkansas Railway rolls along the tracks near Minden in northern Louisiana. Incorporated in 1898, the L&A ran from Hope, Arkansas, to Shreveport and New Orleans with branches serving Vidalia, Louisiana, and Dallas, Texas. Originally a freight line, it began passenger service in 1928 and ended it 40 years later. The L&A was bought out by the Kansas City Southern Lines and the name was discontinued in the 1960s.

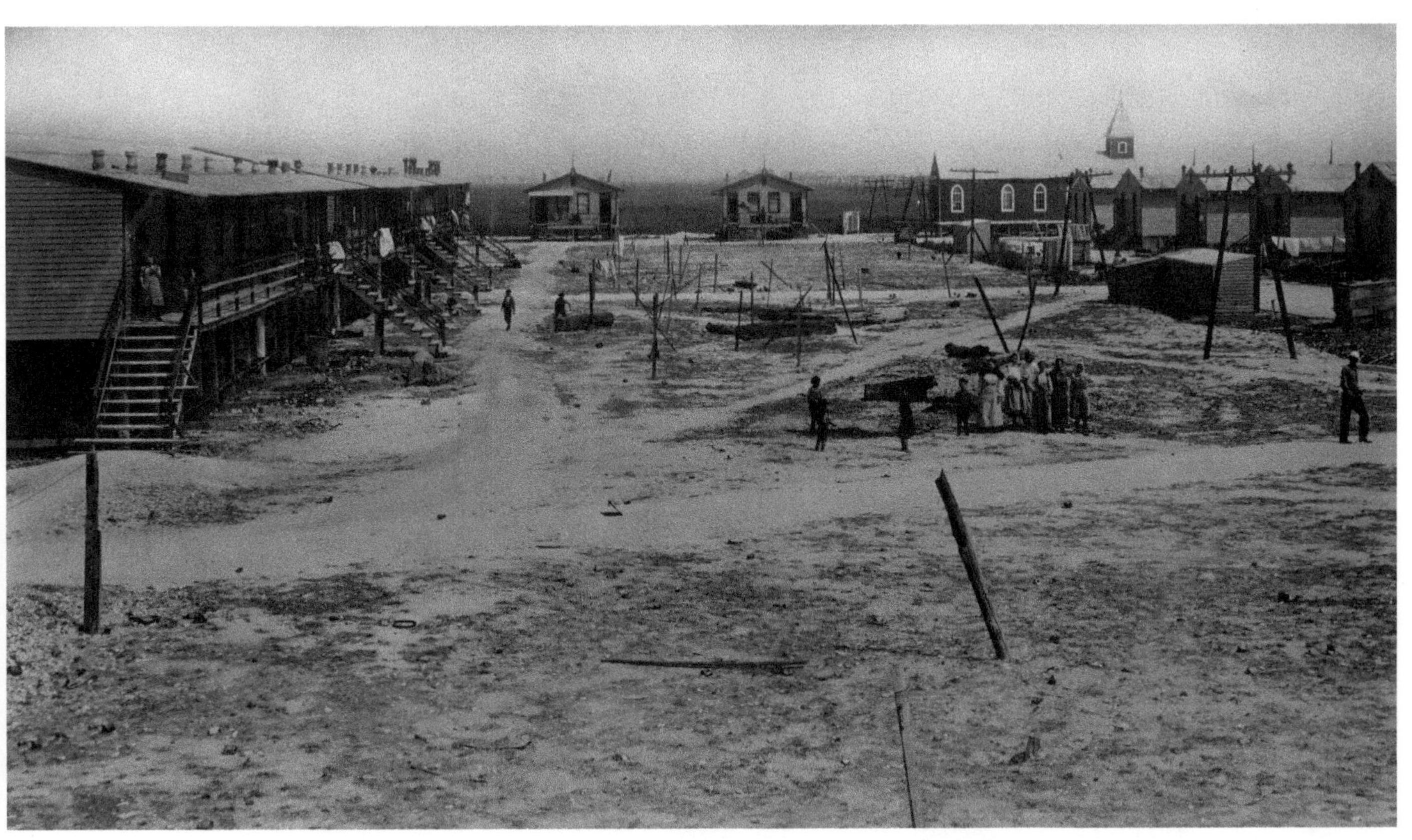

This photograph and the two that follow were taken by Lewis Wickes Hine (1874–1940) for the National Child Labor Committee in March 1911. Hine traveled around the country photographing conditions under which young children were working. This image shows the settlement of Dunbar, Louisiana, where oyster canning was the main industry. Children as young as four worked in the shucking and canning sheds there for long hours and low pay.

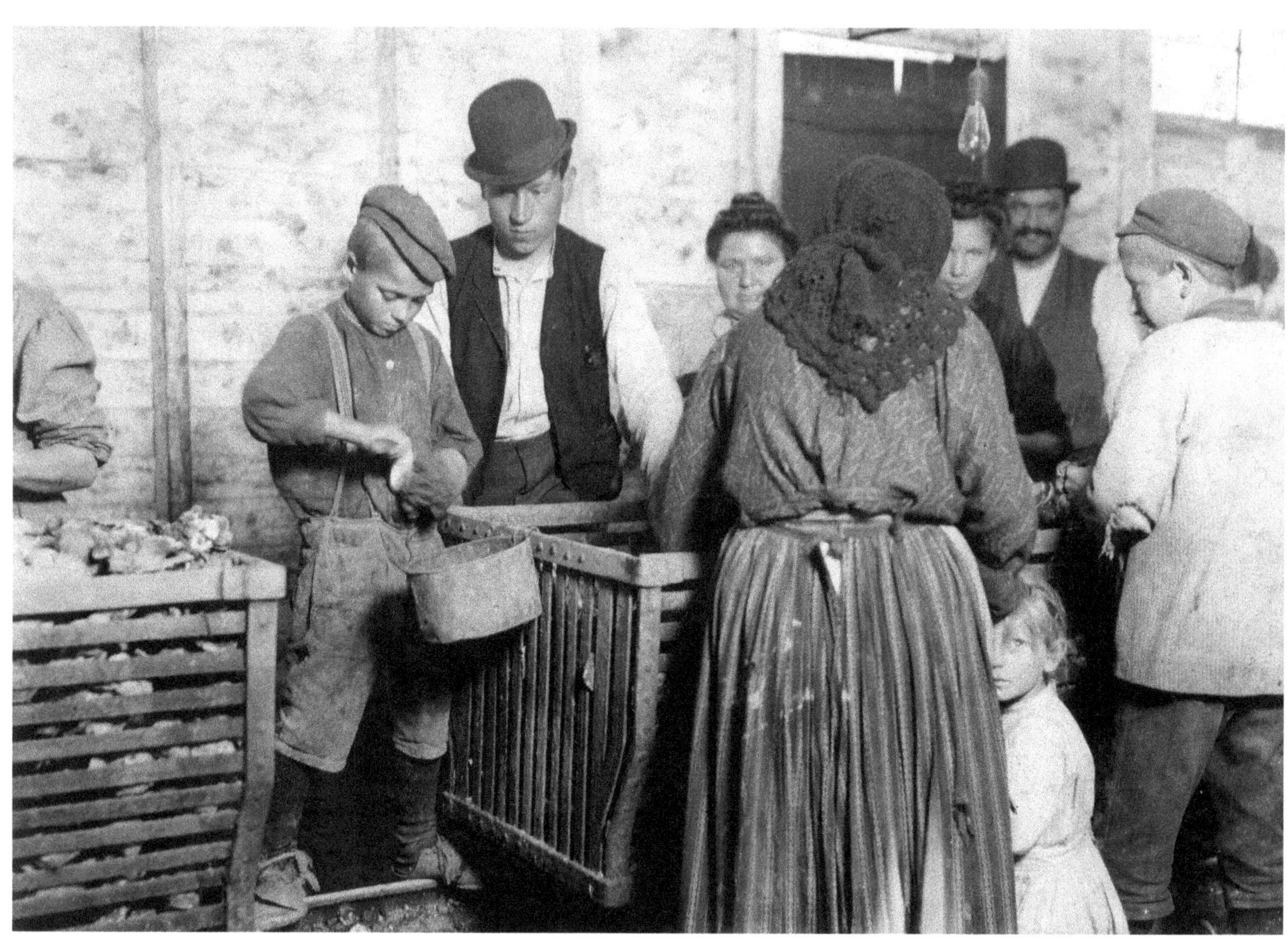

A nine-year-old boy named Johnnie shucks oysters under the watchful eye of the shucking boss, also known as a padrone. Workers, young and old and of all races and nationalities (many of whom were recent immigrants) worked in the shucking and canning sheds of Dunbar, often from 3:00 A.M. to 5:00 P.M. with only half an hour off for lunch. Many of Dunbar's temporary residents were imported from Baltimore, Maryland.

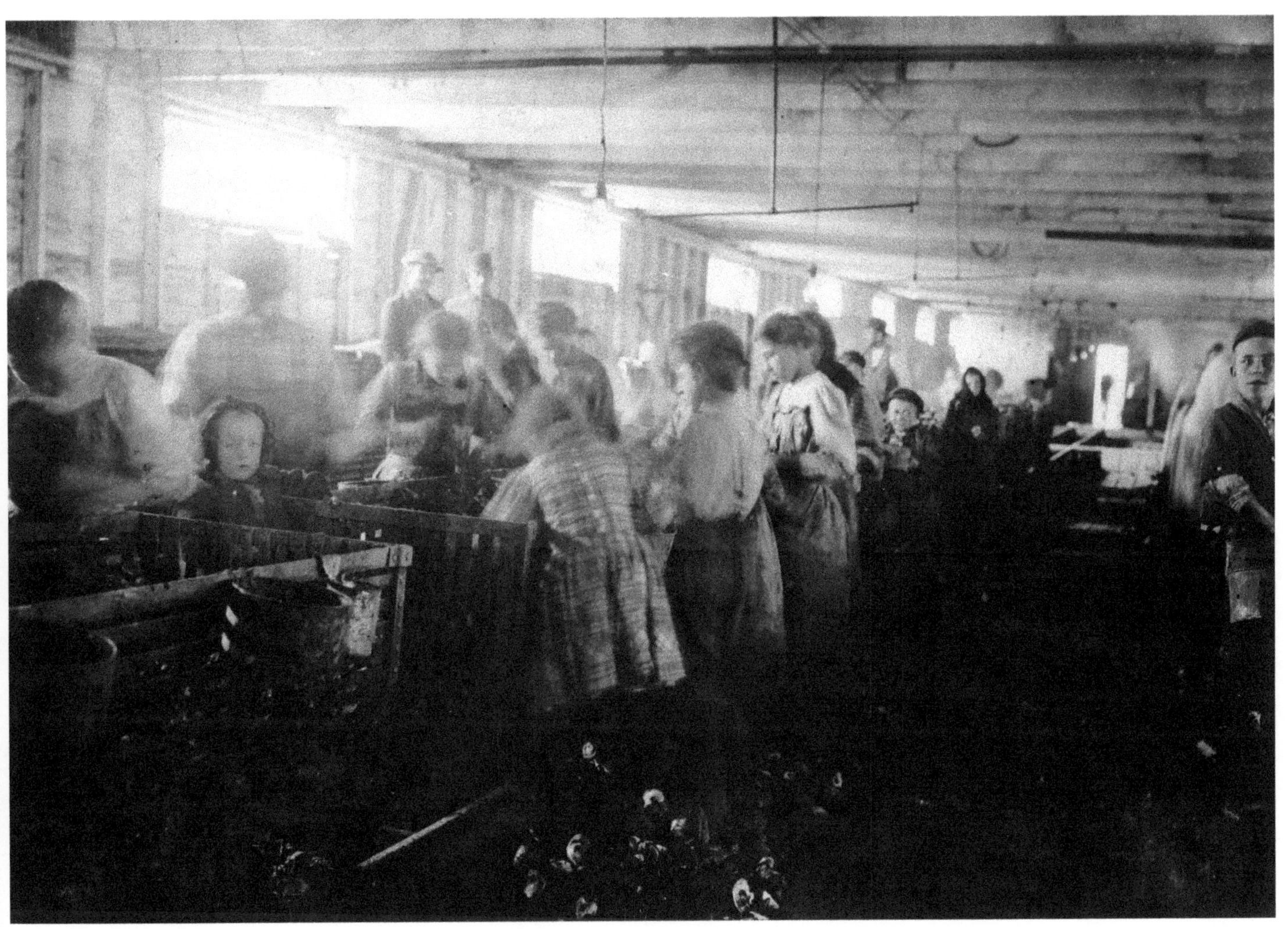

Oyster shuckers, most of them children, are seen working in one of the canning sheds in Dunbar. Trained as a sociologist, Hine used his cameras to document the often deplorable conditions of American laborers and recent immigrants. The photos he took of child labor conditions in the early 1900s shocked the nation and helped enact laws establishing minimum age requirements for workers. The Dunbar settlement which, at its peak, housed about 300 workers, no longer exists.

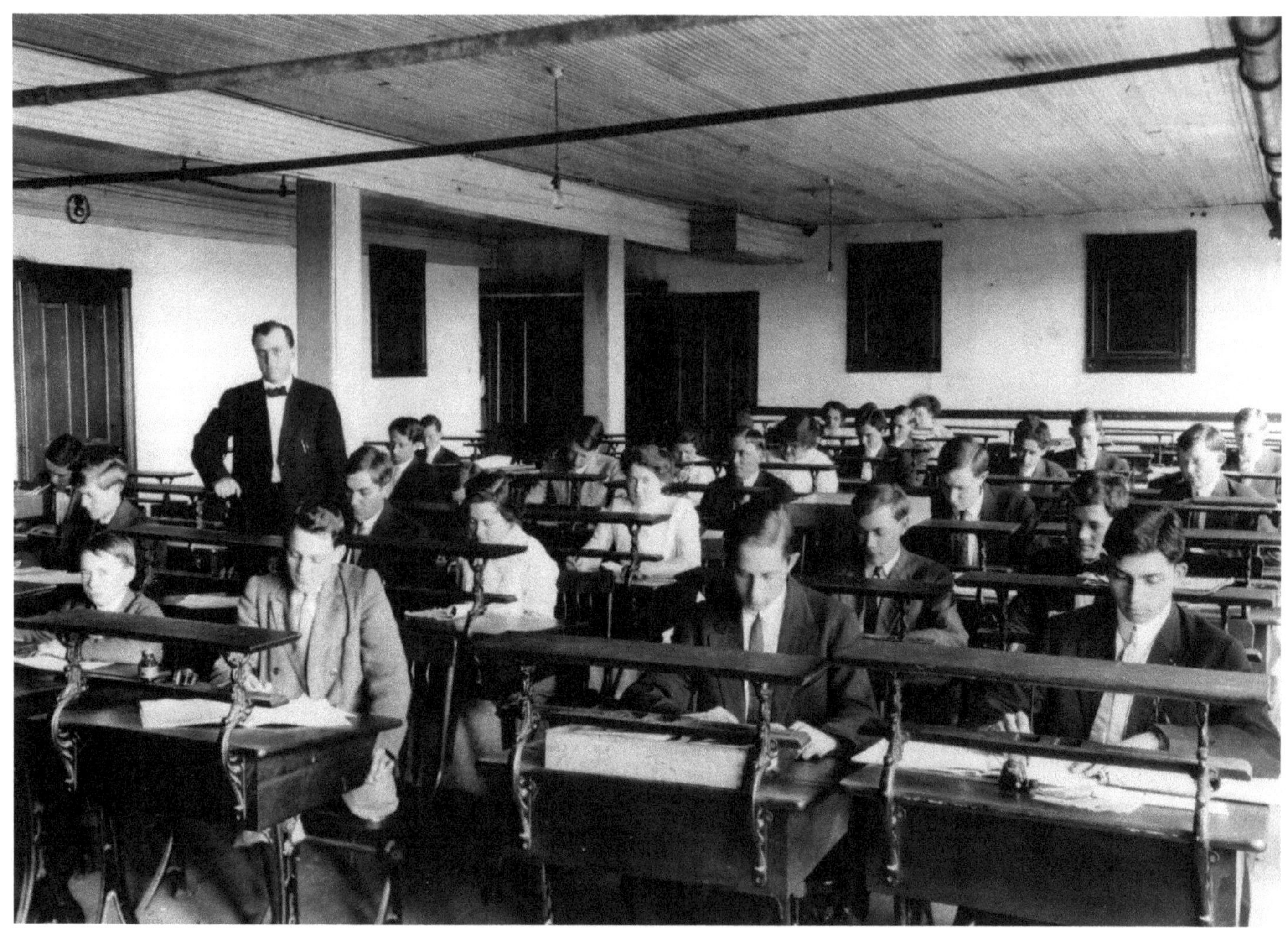

Students are seated in a bookkeeping class at Louisiana Industrial Institute and College in Ruston in the early 1900s. Founded in 1894, it became Louisiana Polytechnic Institute in 1921, and finally Louisiana Tech University in 1970. Today it is best known for its engineering programs and its athletics, especially men's football and women's basketball. At last count, Louisiana Tech was attended by students from 46 states and 68 countries with a total enrollment of nearly 11,000.

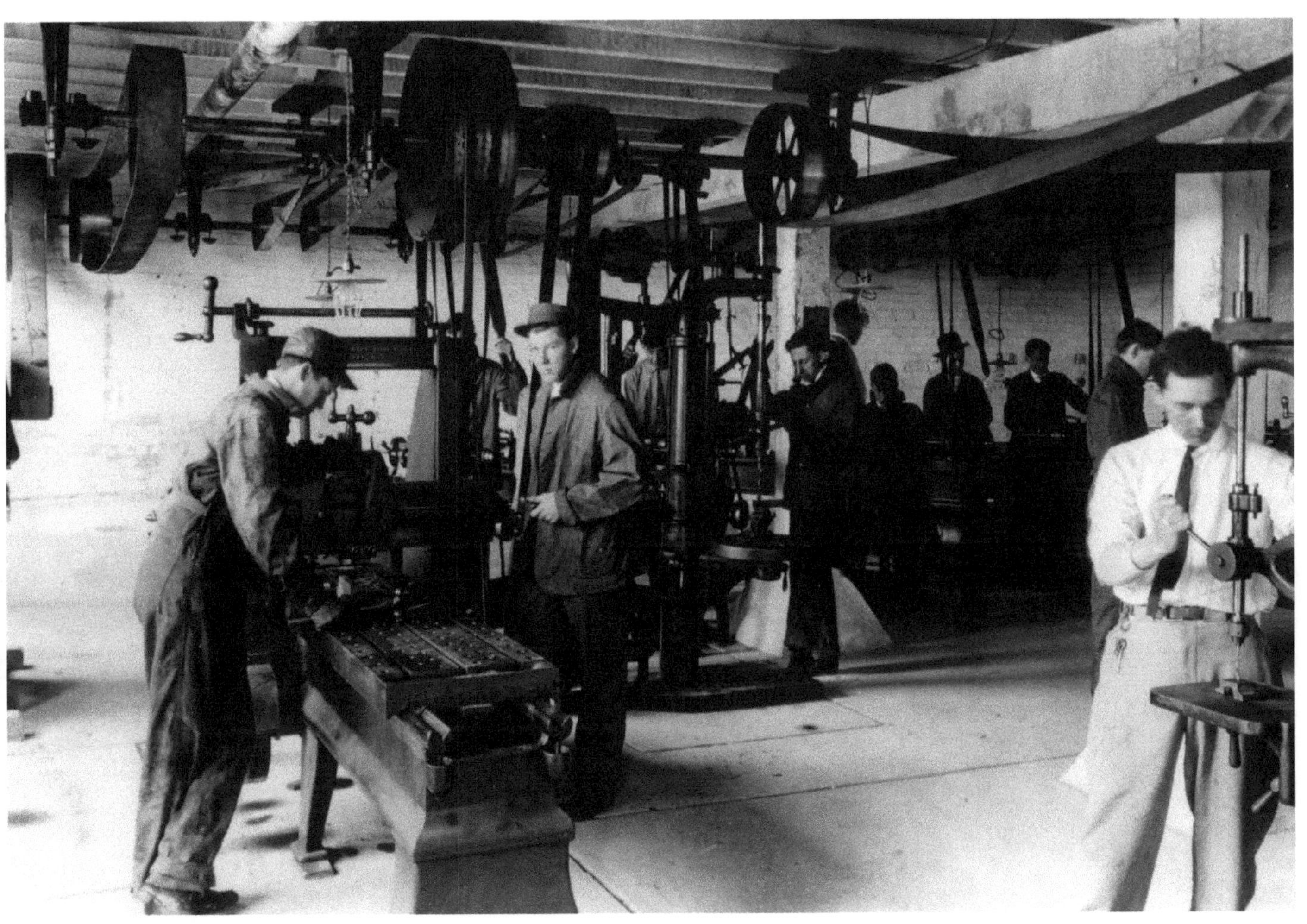

Students work in the campus machine shop at Louisiana Industrial Institute and College in Ruston, acquiring hands-on industrial training in the early 1900s. Technical colleges like this one grew in importance and popularity in the late 1800s and early 1900s as the Industrial Age increasingly demanded these kinds of mechanical skills.

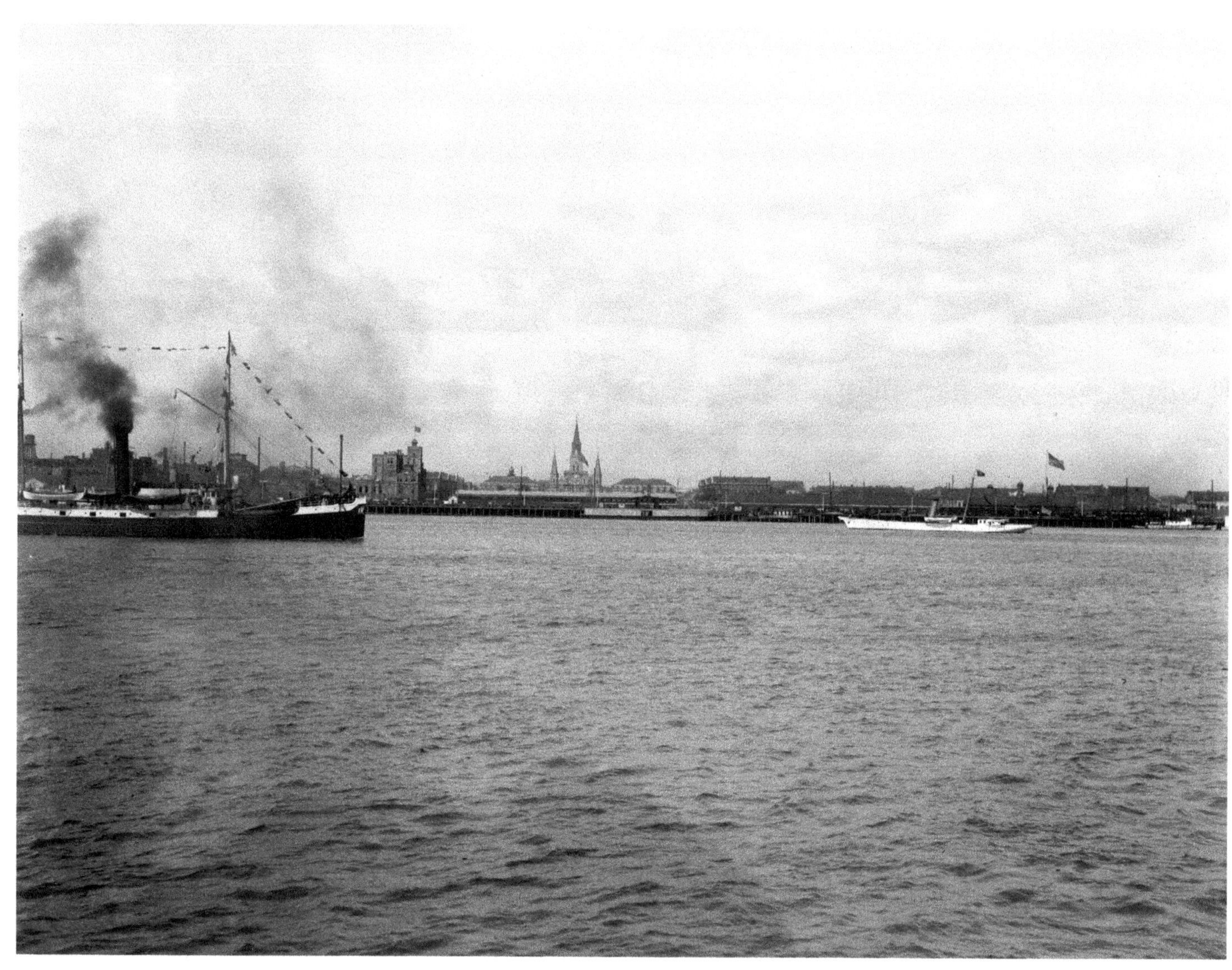

A cargo ship steams along the Mississippi River past the French Quarter in this image from the 1910s. The view is remarkably little changed today. The buildings in the distance at center—the Jackson Brewery, the Cabildo, St. Louis Cathedral, the Presbytere, and most of the riverfront wharves—are still standing. The cathedral as shown is missing its cupola, which was blown off by a hurricane in 1913 and finally replaced in 2008.

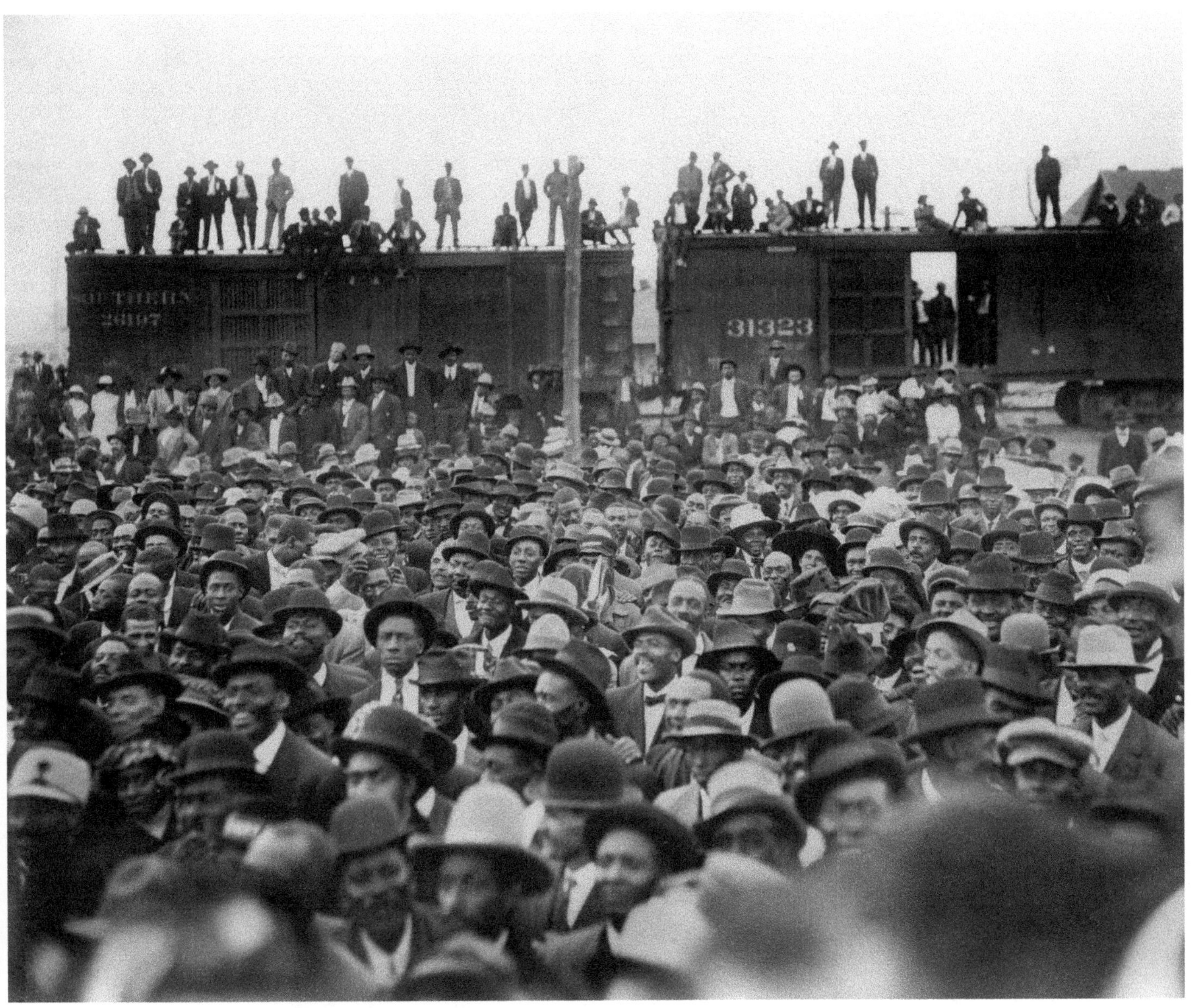

A large crowd of African-Americans gathers in New Orleans in 1912 to hear famed educator and social reformer Booker T. Washington give a speech. Many spectators stand on railroad boxcars in the background. During the Jim Crow segregationist era of the early 1900s, Washington (1856–1915) was the voice of moderation in seeking to help African-Americans improve their social status and working skills. He helped found the Tuskegee Institute in Alabama for that purpose in the 1880s.

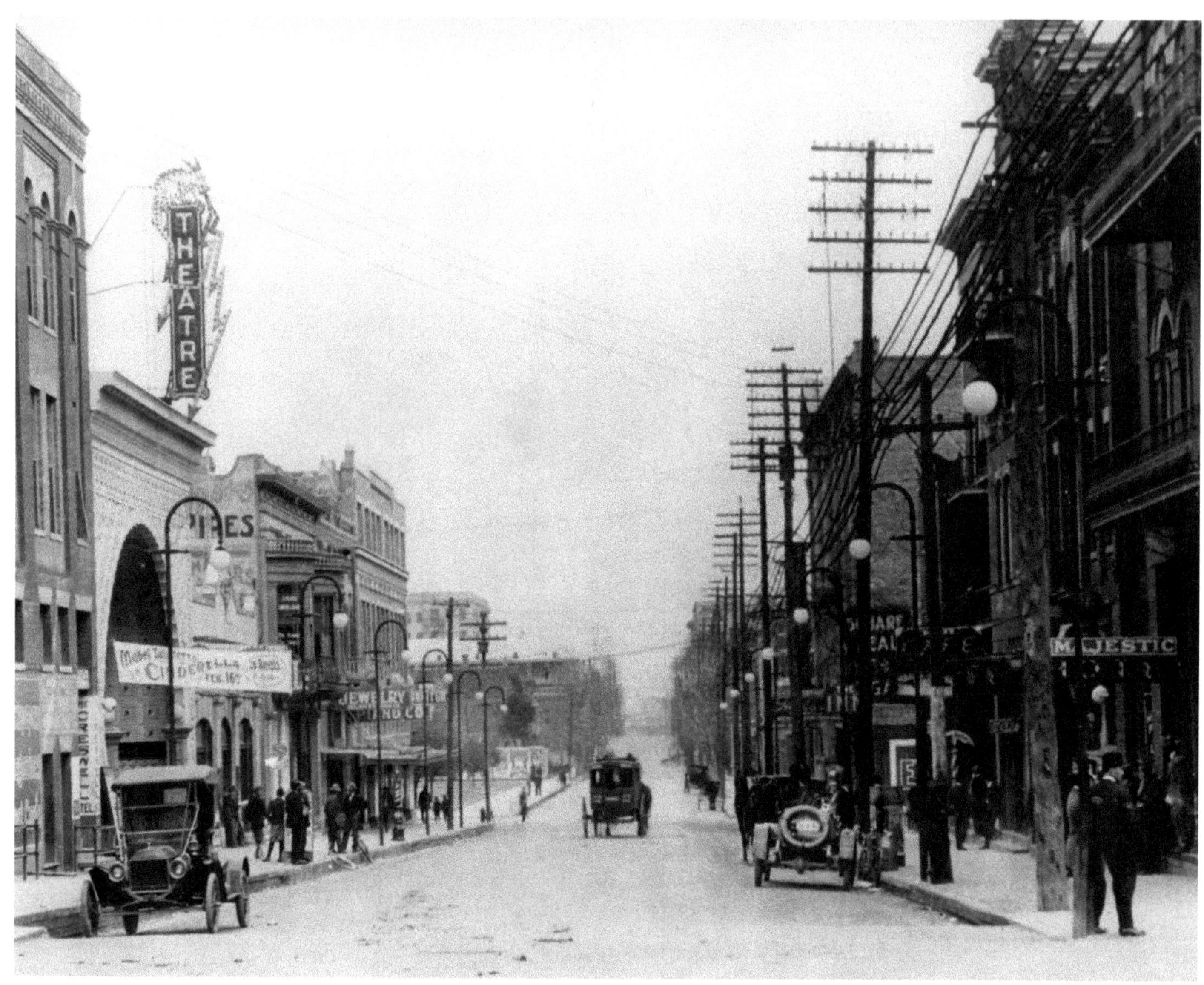

Cinderella starring Mabel Taliaferro is showing at a main street theater in Shreveport around 1913. The most famous theater in Shreveport was the Municipal Memorial Auditorium, where the *Louisiana Hayride* show would be staged between 1948 and 1960. Simultaneously broadcast over 25 radio stations, the *Hayride* helped spotlight up-and-coming country-western and rock stars like Hank Williams, Elvis Presley, Johnny Cash, Webb Pierce, Jim Reeves, Governor Jimmie Davis ("You Are My Sunshine"), and many others.

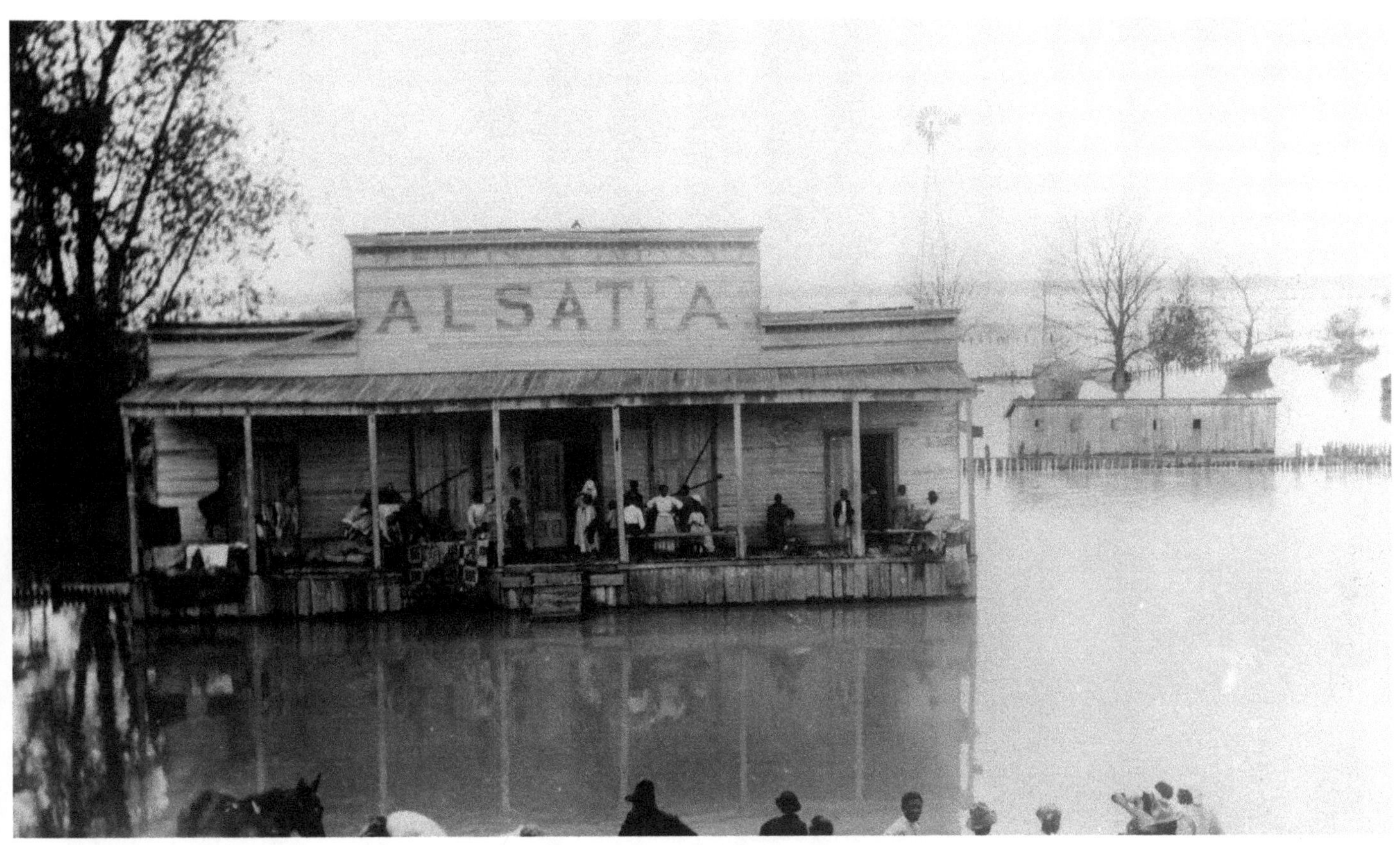

Floodwaters from the swollen Mississippi River inundate the streets of Alsatia in East Carroll Parish in 1912. The building is probably a combination general store and post office, which was common in small towns at that time. The population of the eastern portion of this rural agricultural parish in the extreme northeast corner of Louisiana was displaced by the flood and had to be evacuated. This photograph and especially the two that follow capture the misery faced by residents of rural areas along the Mississippi who were vulnerable to flooding prior to construction of levees.

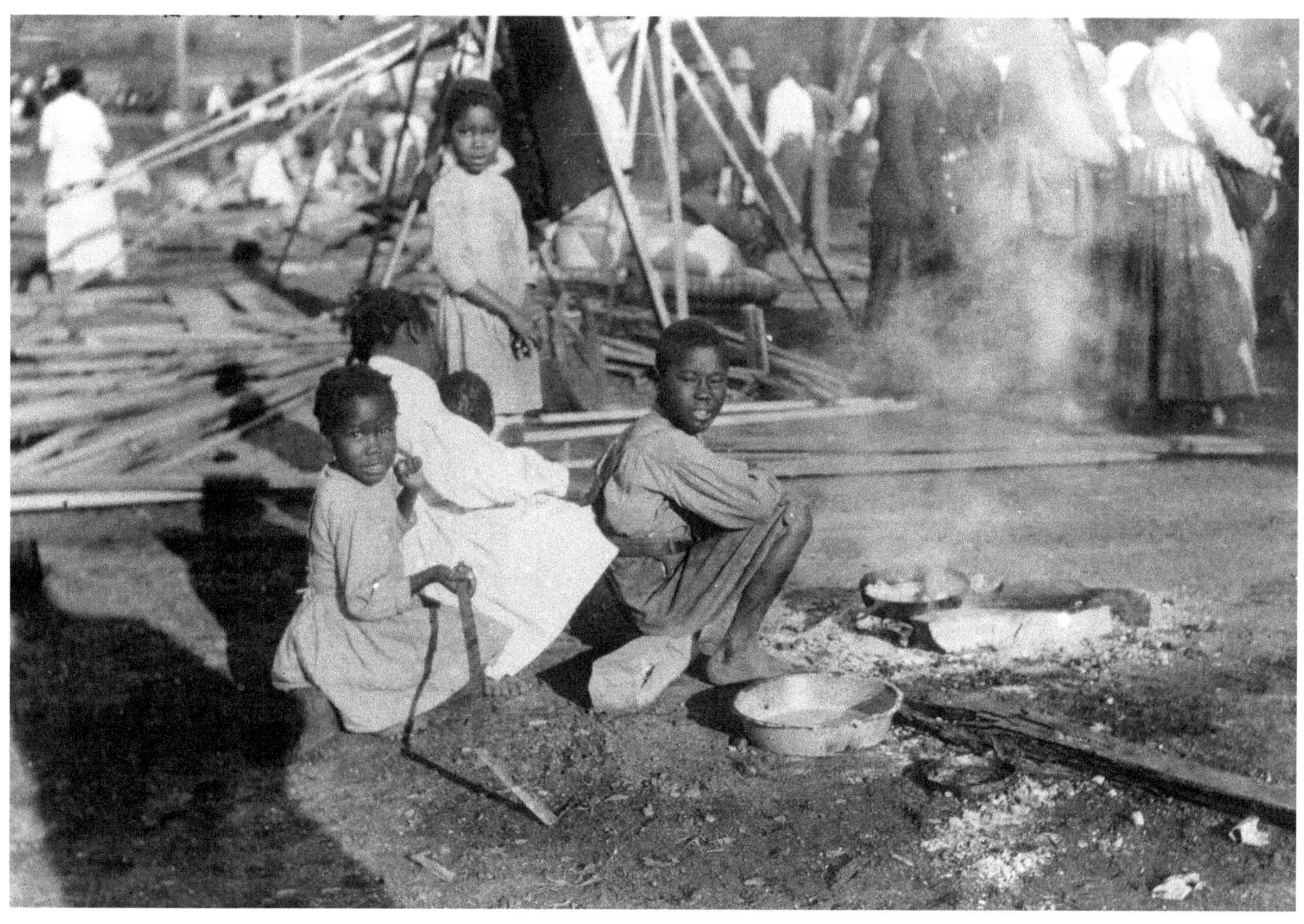

Children and their parents cook government-issued rations in a makeshift camp following the flooding that occurred in East Carroll Parish in April 1912. According to historical records, more than 1,000 square miles of active farmland went under water, in some cases as deep as six feet.

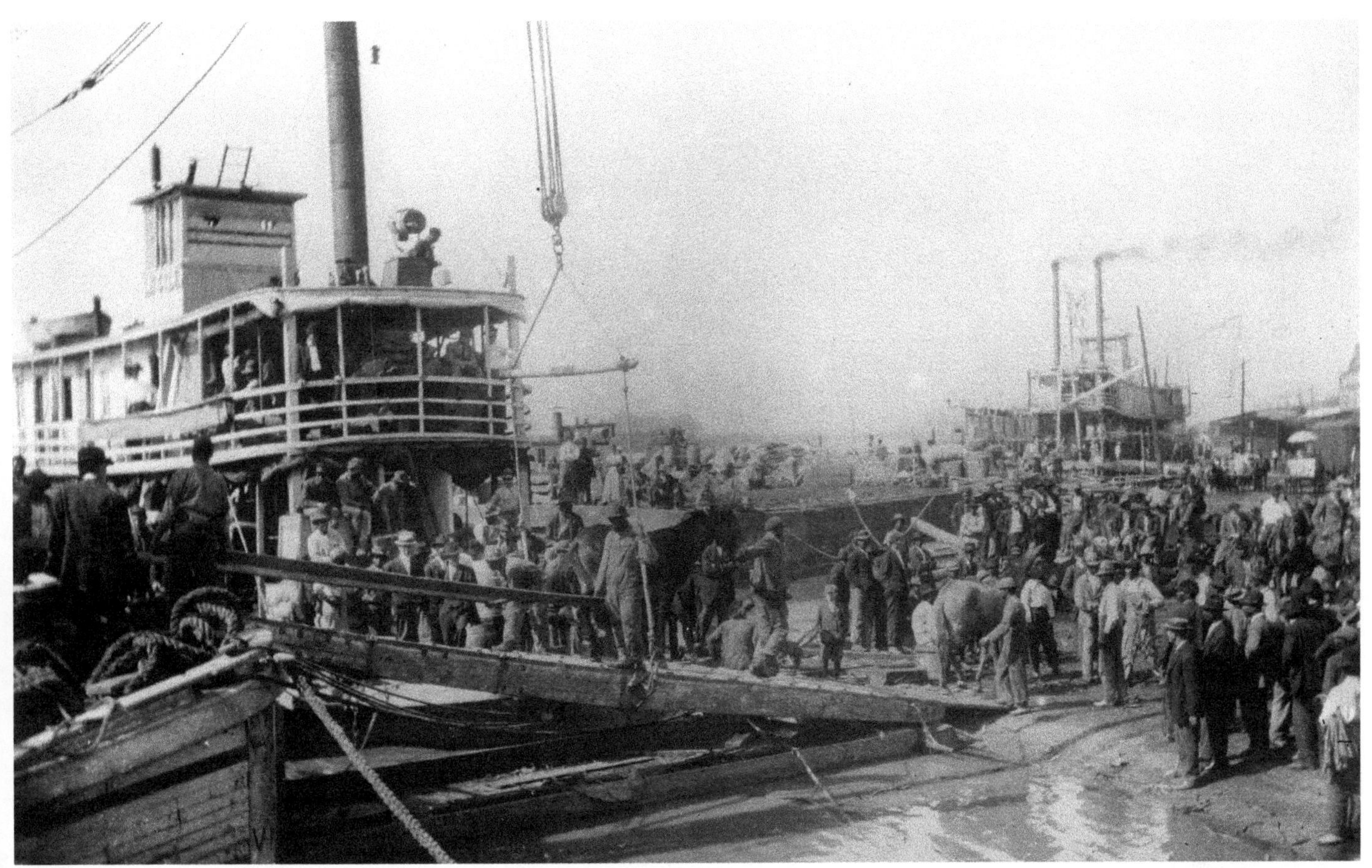

Evacuees from the April 1912 flood in East Carroll Parish board government-chartered steamboats along the Mississippi River. Most of the evacuees were transported about 40 miles downriver and temporarily housed in a cotton warehouse in Vicksburg, Mississippi, until the floodwaters subsided. This flood and two others that followed in 1913 and 1927 led to improved levee construction along most of the length of the lower Mississippi by the Army Corps of Engineers.

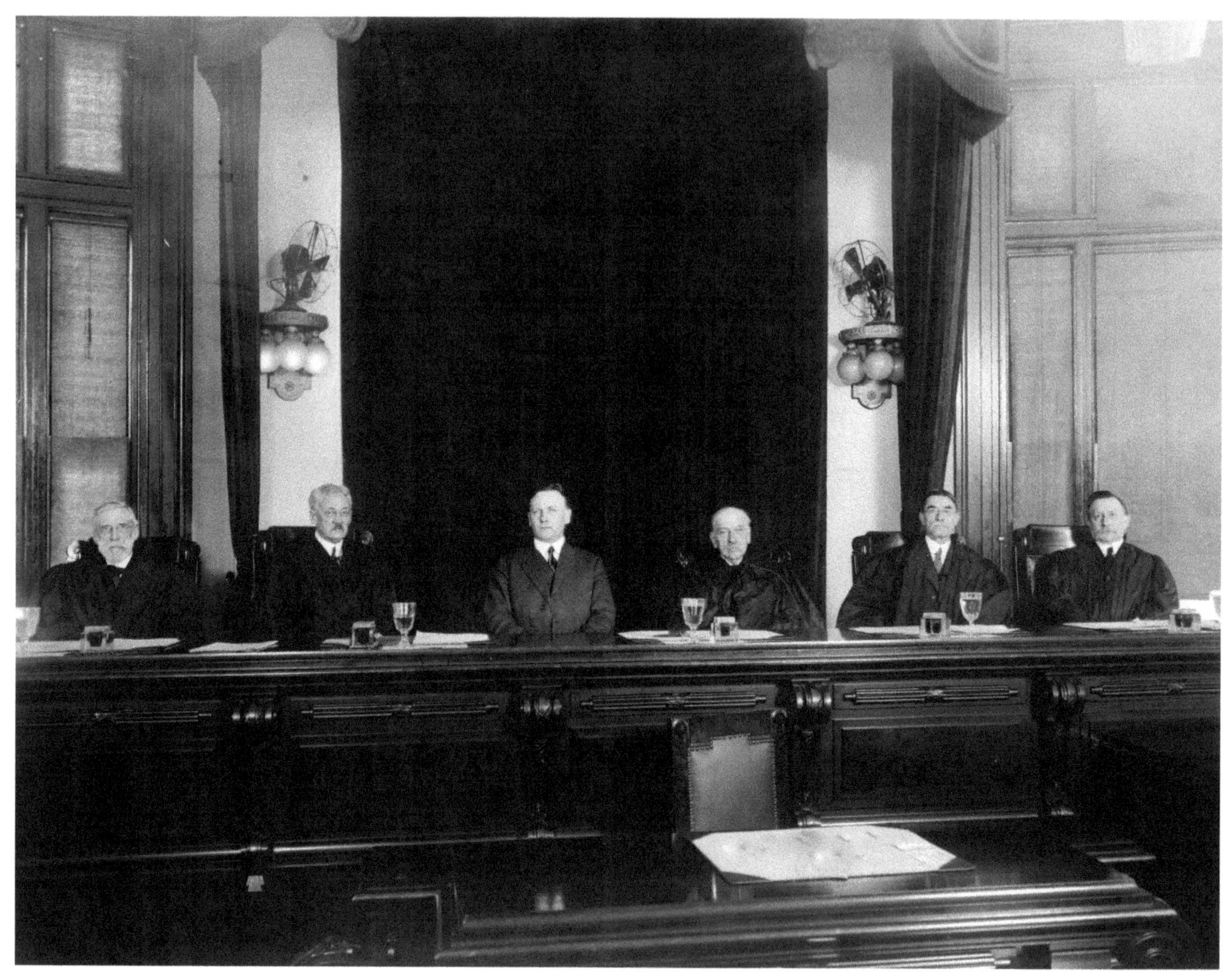

Governor Luther Hall (1869–1921) is seated at center in this 1913 group portrait of the governor and Louisiana Supreme Court. Prior to serving as governor from 1912 to 1916, Hall was a state senator, a state district judge, and a state appellate judge. For the three years prior to his death he was the state's assistant attorney general. Other justices serving at that time and seen here include Frank A. Monroe, Oliver O. Provosty, Alfred D. Land, and Walter B. Sommerville.

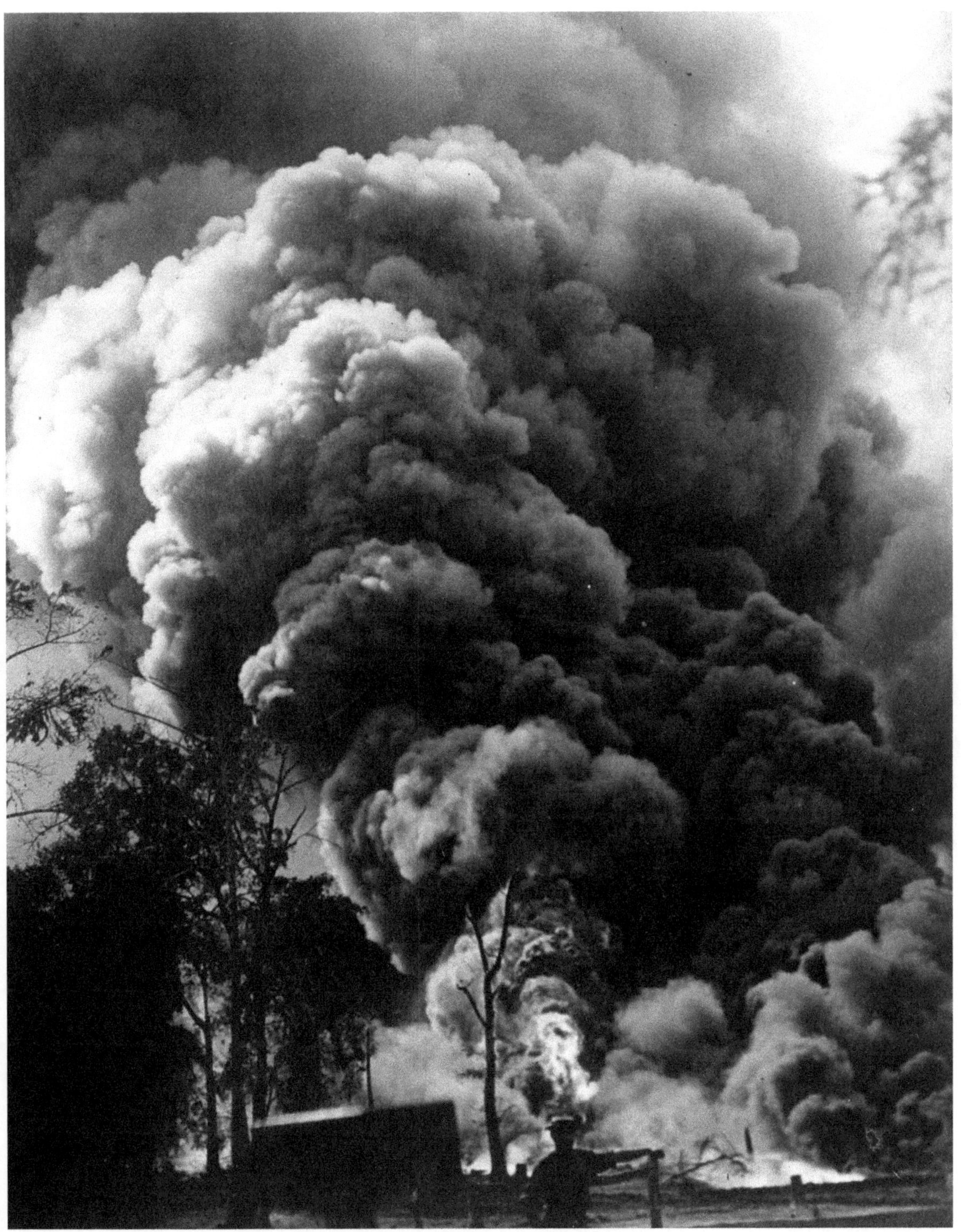

A disastrous fire destroys a Star Oil Company well in Mooringsport, northwest of Shreveport, on August 7, 1913. According to information accompanying the original photograph, it was the largest single well fire in the history of the United States up to that time, with an estimated 30,000 barrels of oil lost each day. Once a major oil town in upper Caddo Parish, Mooringsport is now a popular resort town. It is located on Caddo Lake, which straddles the Louisiana-Texas border.

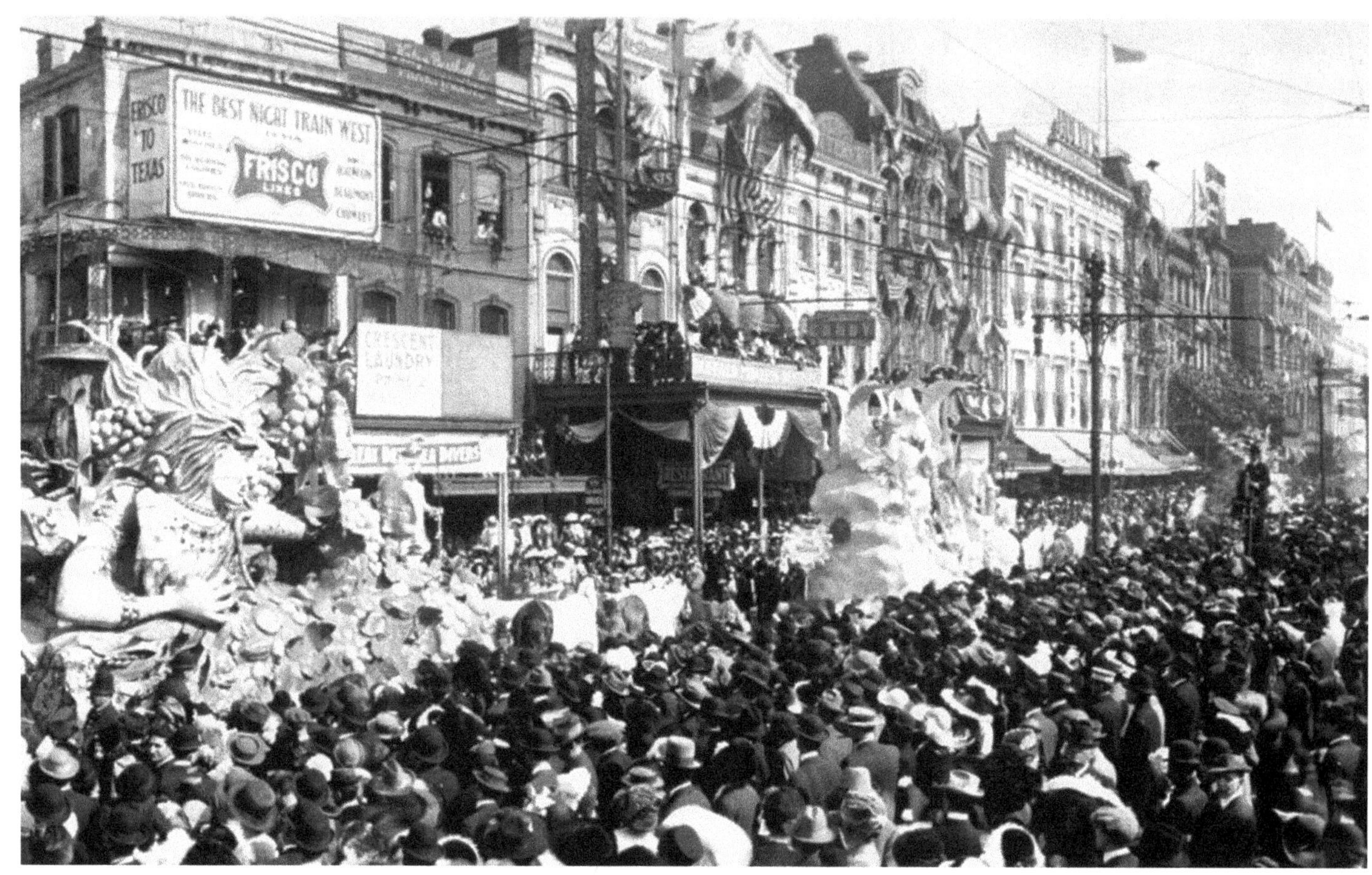

Floats in the Rex parade roll along Canal Street at its intersection with St. Charles Street (later Avenue) on Fat Tuesday, 1913. Carnival parades then, as now, started in uptown New Orleans and rolled along St. Charles to Canal where they disbanded. Fat Tuesday (Mardi Gras Day) is an official holiday in New Orleans and its surrounding area, with most businesses and government agencies closed. It falls on a different date each year, which depends on the date of Easter Sunday.

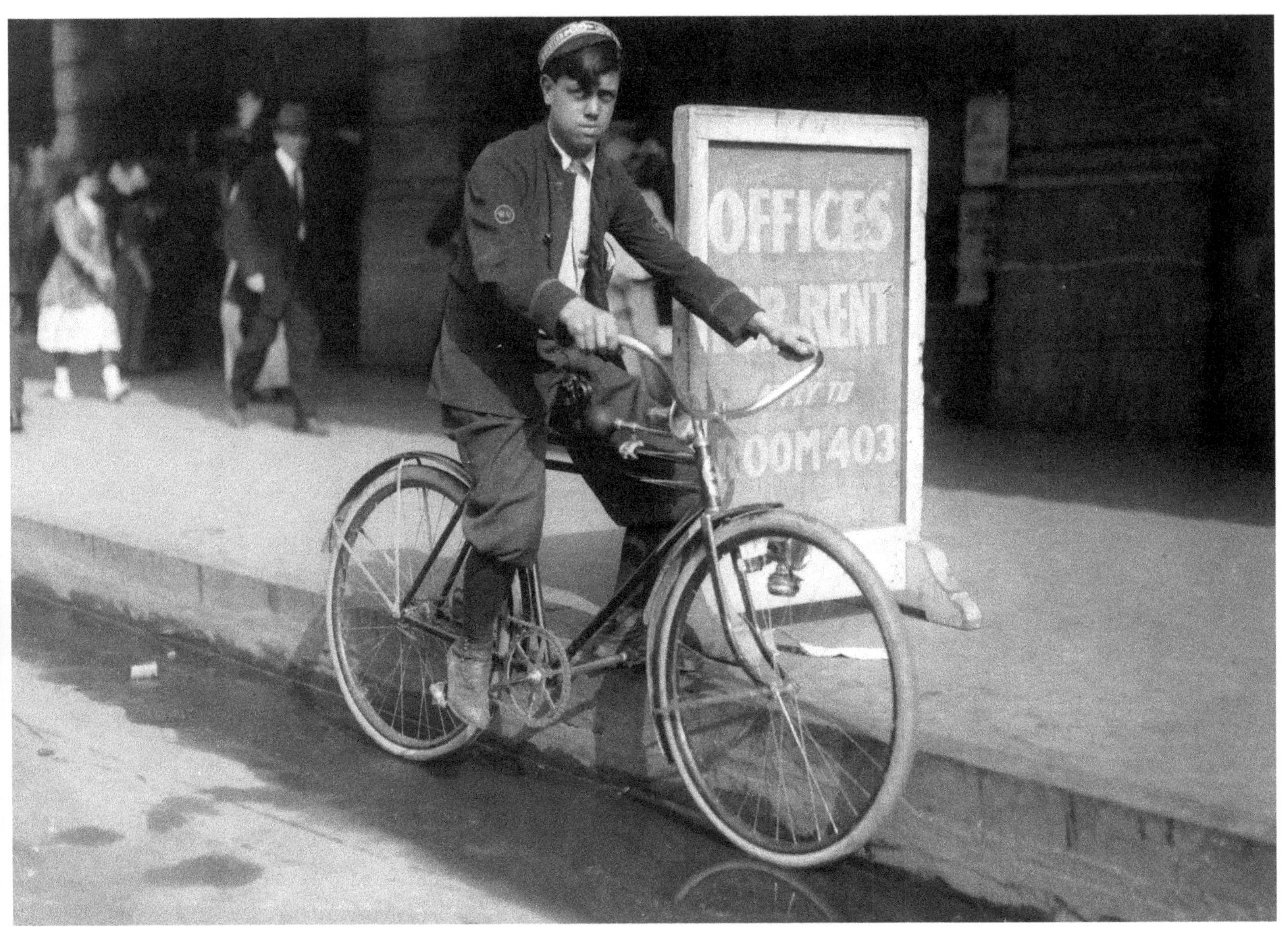

A messenger boy delivers a telegram through the streets of New Orleans in November 1913. Lewis Hine was still traveling the country, pictorially documenting instances of child labor. He wrote, "The telegraph companies are trying to obey the law and few violations occur." This messenger boy appears to be old enough to handle the job and seems to confirm Hine's assessment.

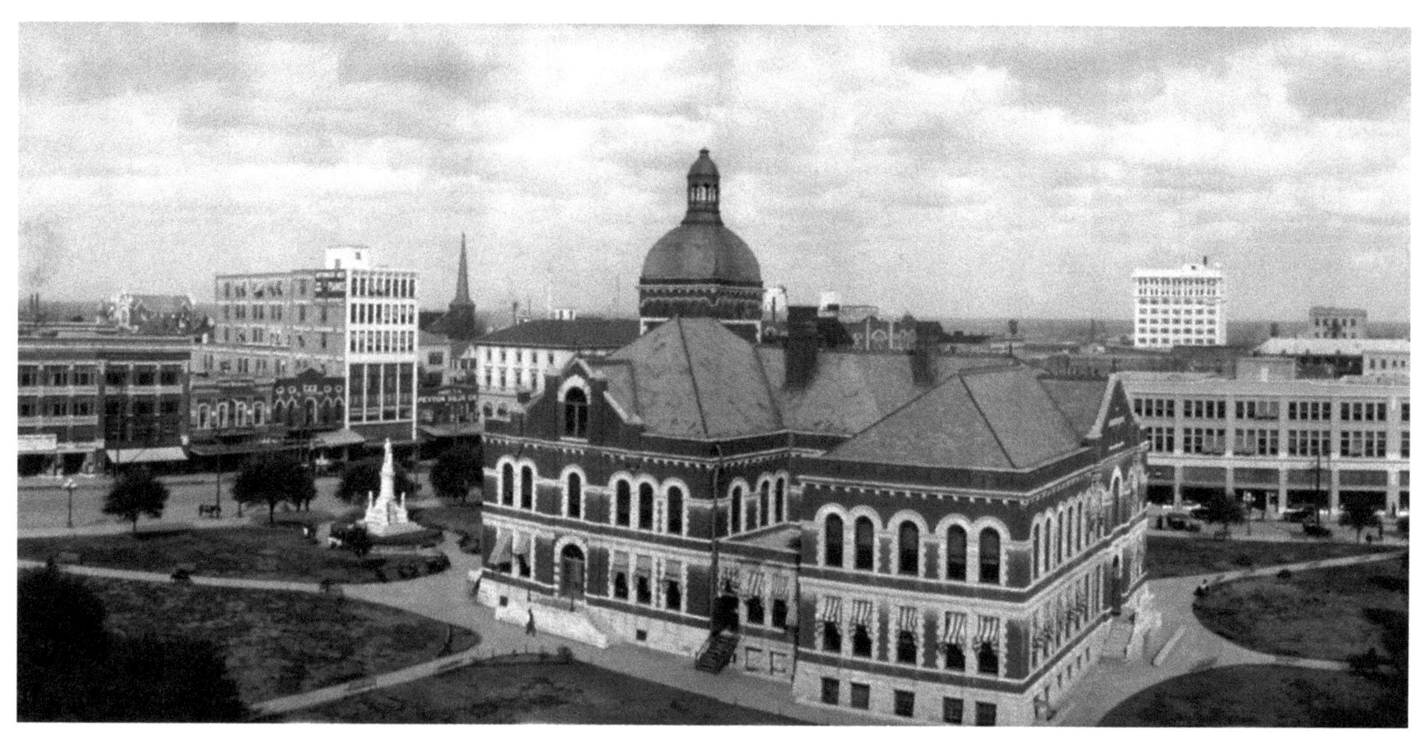

The old Caddo Parish Court House in Shreveport as it appeared around 1916. Built in 1855, the red-brick building with its distinctive dome topped by a cupola briefly served as the Louisiana State Capitol after the fall of Baton Rouge during the Civil War. It remained in use until it was replaced with a white-marble structure resembling a wedding cake in 1928.

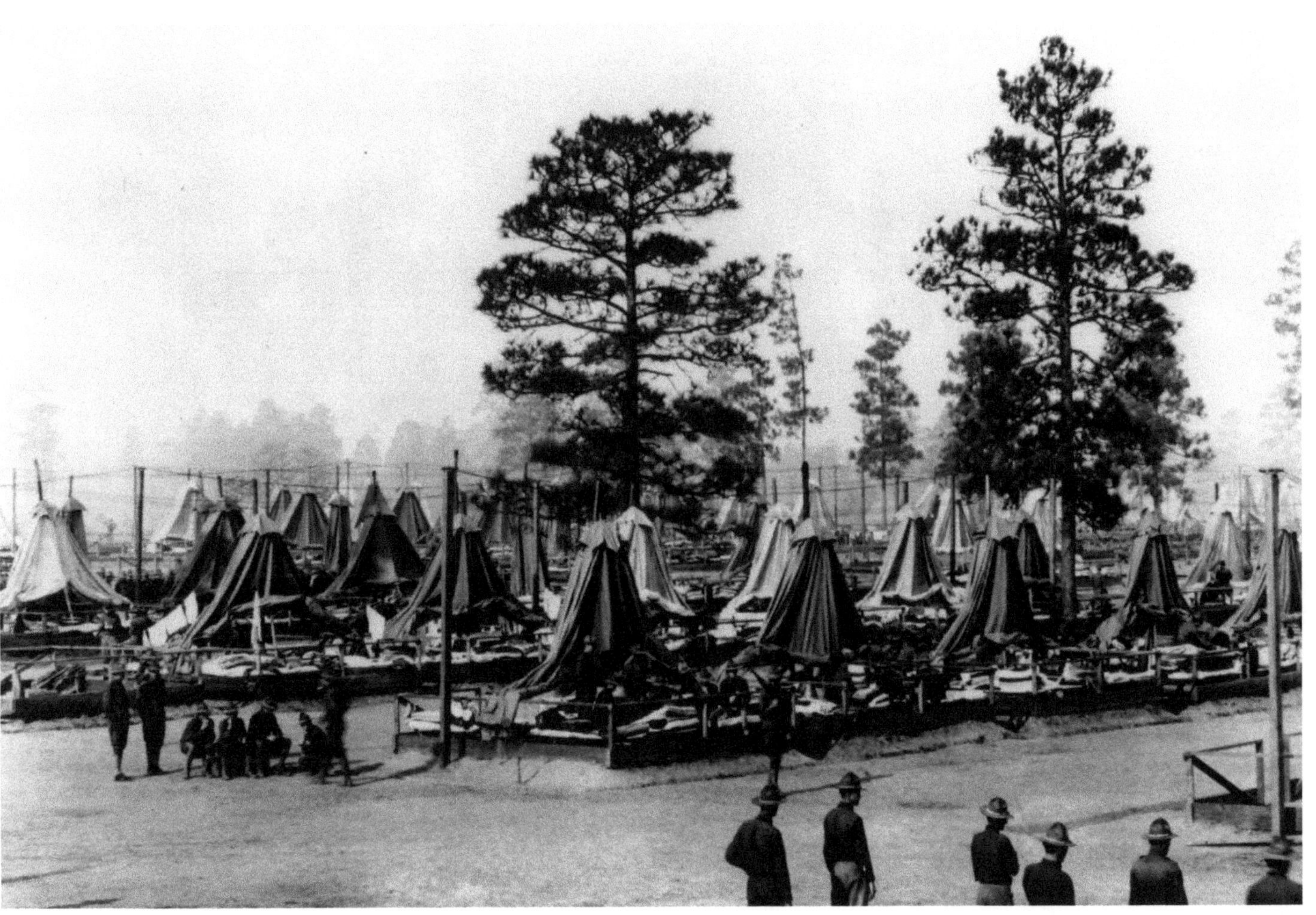

Soldiers relax at Camp Beauregard in 1918. The camp was located in Pineville, across the Red River from Alexandria, and was abandoned after the war in 1919 but returned to the government in 1940 for use as a World War II training area. Named for the New Orleans–born general whose battalion fired the first shots of the Civil War at Fort Sumter, the camp's hot, muggy weather made it a logical training location for American troops destined for service in similar climates. Today it is headquarters for the 225th Engineer Brigade, the largest engineer group in the army, and is also a National Guard training site.

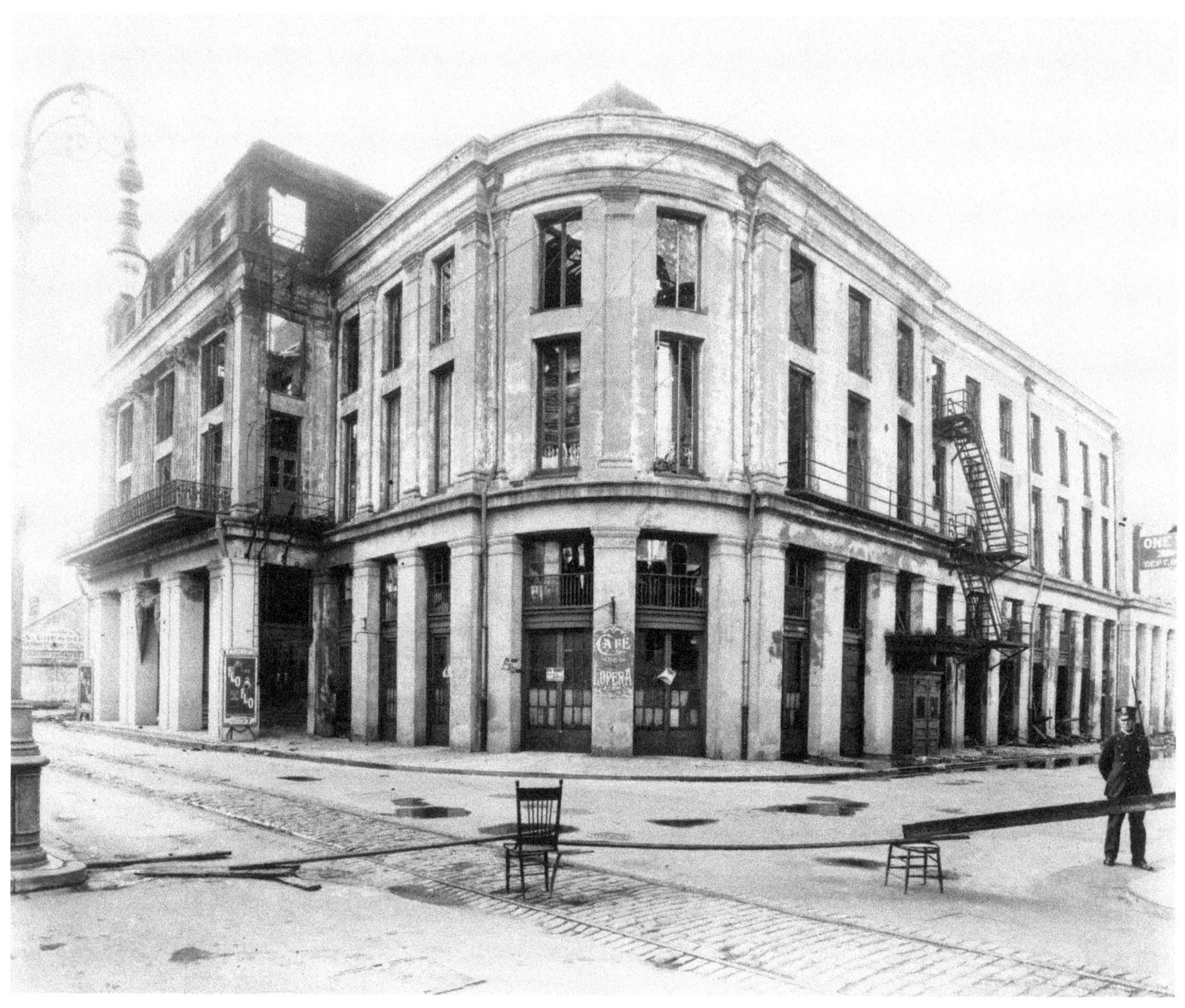

A lone policeman stands watch over the ruins of the old French Opera House in New Orleans after an early morning kitchen fire devastated the historic structure beyond repair on December 4, 1919. It had opened in 1859 with a production of Rossini's *William Tell,* and the following season acclaimed soprano Adelina Patti made her international debut at the house. During its heyday in the late 1800s and early 1900s, it hosted the American premieres of many of the greatest operas of Europe's master composers.

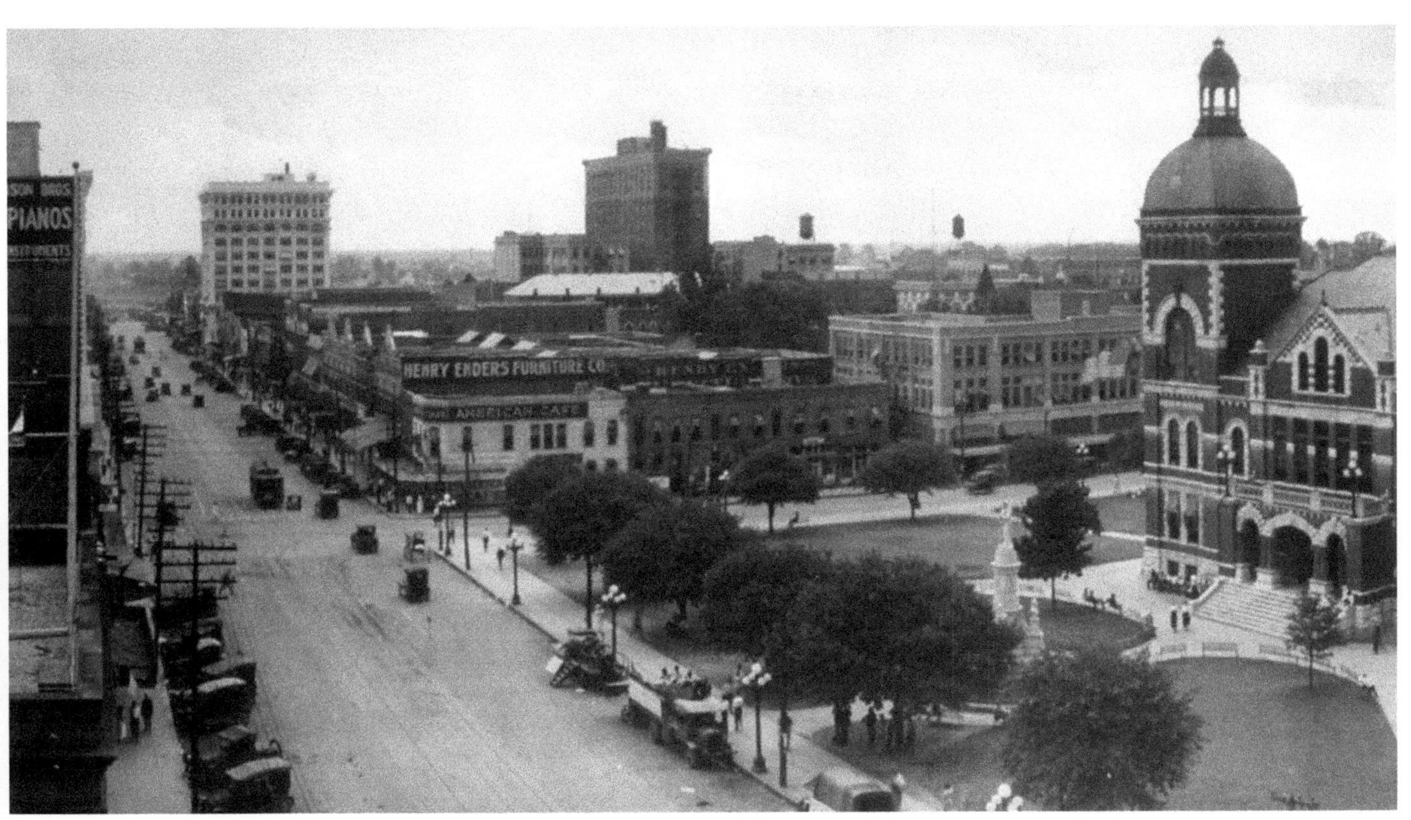

Electric streetcars and early model automobiles crowd out the few remaining horse-drawn wagons along this main thoroughfare in Shreveport in 1919. The old Caddo Parish Court House with its Confederate Soldiers monument in front is visible at right. A transportation hub on the Red River from its founding in 1836, Shreveport is the third-largest city in Louisiana today with a population of slightly more than 200,000.

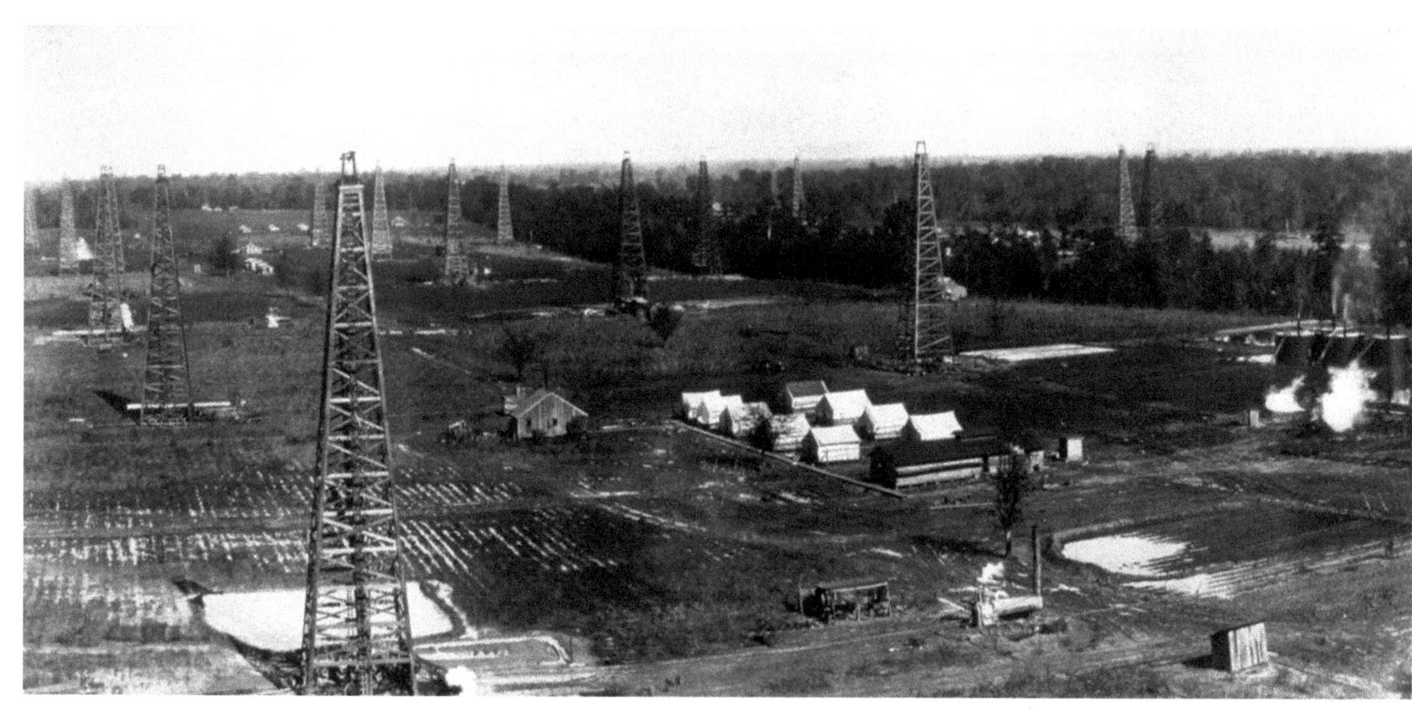

Row after row of oil derricks in 1919 point to the drilling operations at Bull Bayou in DeSoto Parish. A *New York Times* article on October 22, 1919, announced that the Sinclair Consolidated Oil Corporation had acquired the property, unveiling plans to build a 250-mile pipeline from there to the refineries in Houston. The pipeline would have the capacity to transport about 20,000 gallons of crude oil a day.

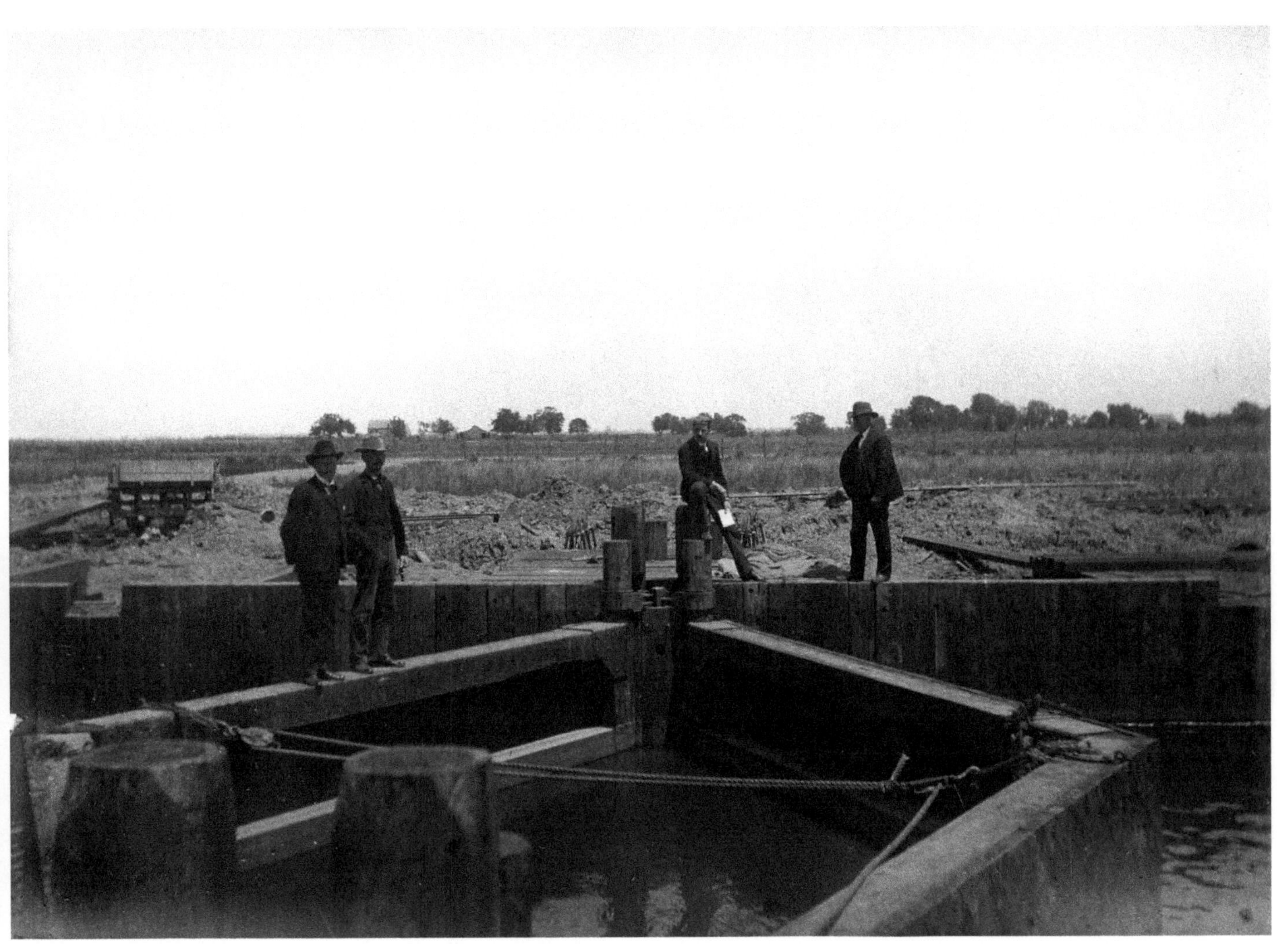

A group of men stand beside a navigation lock near Mermenteau in Acadia Parish. Located on the Mermenteau River and Bayou de Cannes, Mermenteau is now the site of a shallow-draft port facility roughly midway between the larger municipalities of Jennings and Crowley. Hydraulic engineering was in the process of replacing manual labor in the operation of canal locks around the time this image was recorded.

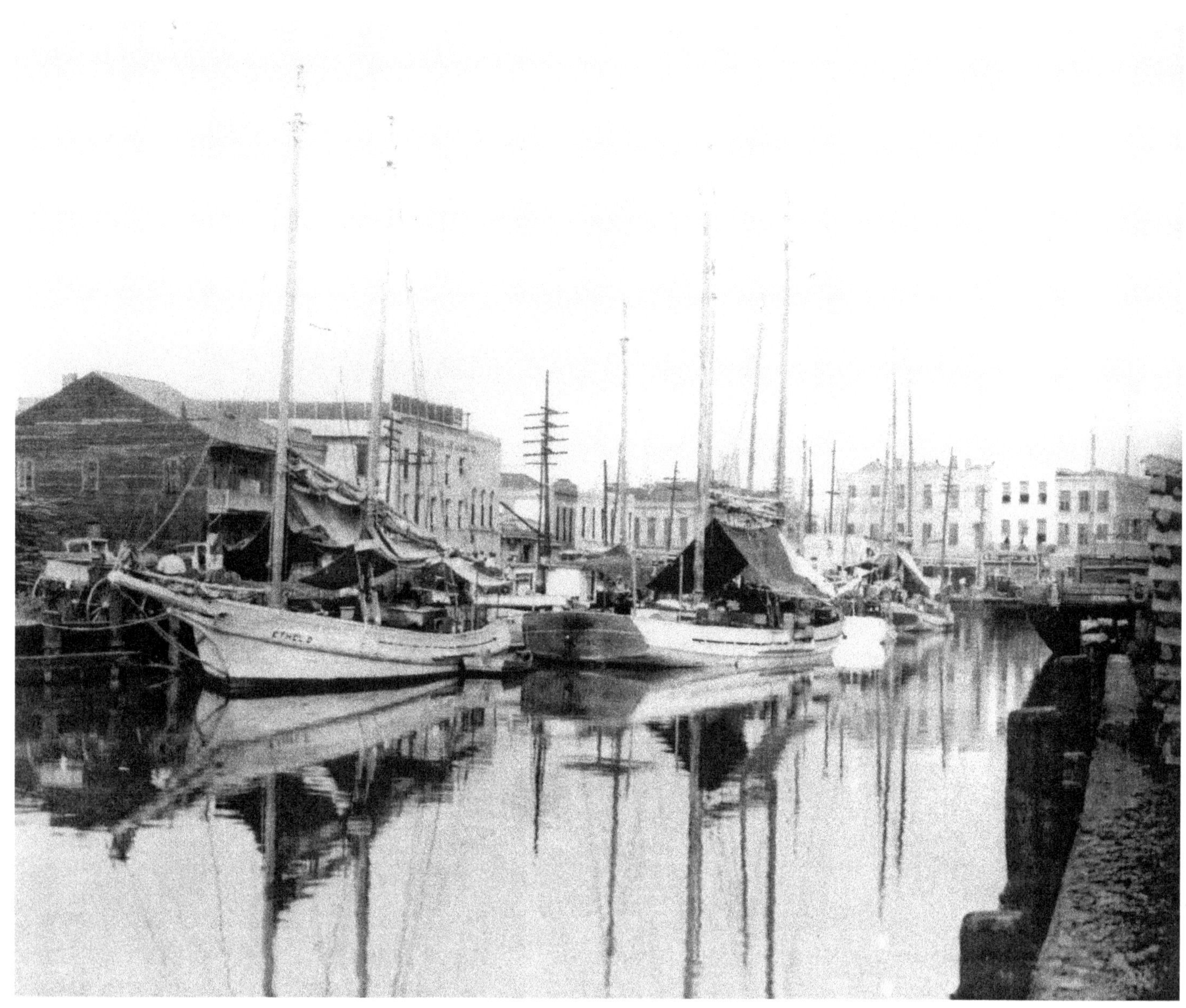

Boats crowd the banks of the New Basin Canal in New Orleans in 1919. Dug by manual laborers in the 1830s, the canal connected Lake Pontchartrain with downtown New Orleans several miles away, and was a main commercial artery for small boats. By the 1940s its usefulness had waned and it was filled in. All that remains today is its former entrance at the lake, now a yacht basin.

The Roaring Twenties and a Great Depression

(1920–1935)

The oil boom that had begun in north Louisiana early in the twentieth century continued into the 1920s. Hundreds of wells continued to pump out the black crude demanded by a prospering nation that was just beginning its love affair with the automobile. As motorized vehicles came into widespread affordability and private ownership, the demand for more and better roads increased concurrently. Large-scale road-building projects began to connect formerly isolated locales in Louisiana, bringing with them the blessings and complications of a new technology.

Denizens of the bayou country who had led pastoral, insular lives for centuries while preserving their French language and Old World customs were suddenly—and often traumatically—thrust into a modern world that threatened their cherished lifestyle. As oil wells in the north of the state dried up, new reserves were being tapped in the Gulf of Mexico. Formerly isolated fishing communities became hubs of activity as jumping-off points for workers going to and from the offshore rigs.

The Great Flood of 1927, which caused widespread havoc over a five-state region of the lower Mississippi, became the impetus for spurring the elevation and strengthening of levees along both sides of the river. The flood also spurred the creation of two spillways into which excess river flow could be diverted, sparing the chief population centers at Baton Rouge and New Orleans. Hurricanes aside, neither city has flooded as the result of swollen rivers since.

Like the rest of the nation, at the end of the twenties Louisiana fell into an economic tailspin. The Great Depression hit the Bayou State just as hard as everywhere else, if not harder. The harsh economic conditions under which many people lived only made them more keenly aware of their own poverty. Into this caldron of discontent strode Huey P. Long, one of American history's most colorful characters, both a self-professed champion of the downtrodden and a politician accused of dictatorial ambitions. Promising unprecedented reforms and delivering on many of his promises, "the Kingfish" rose to national prominence over a brief seven-year span before being cut down by a bullet in 1935. His death was just the beginning of a political era dominated by members of his family into the late twentieth century.

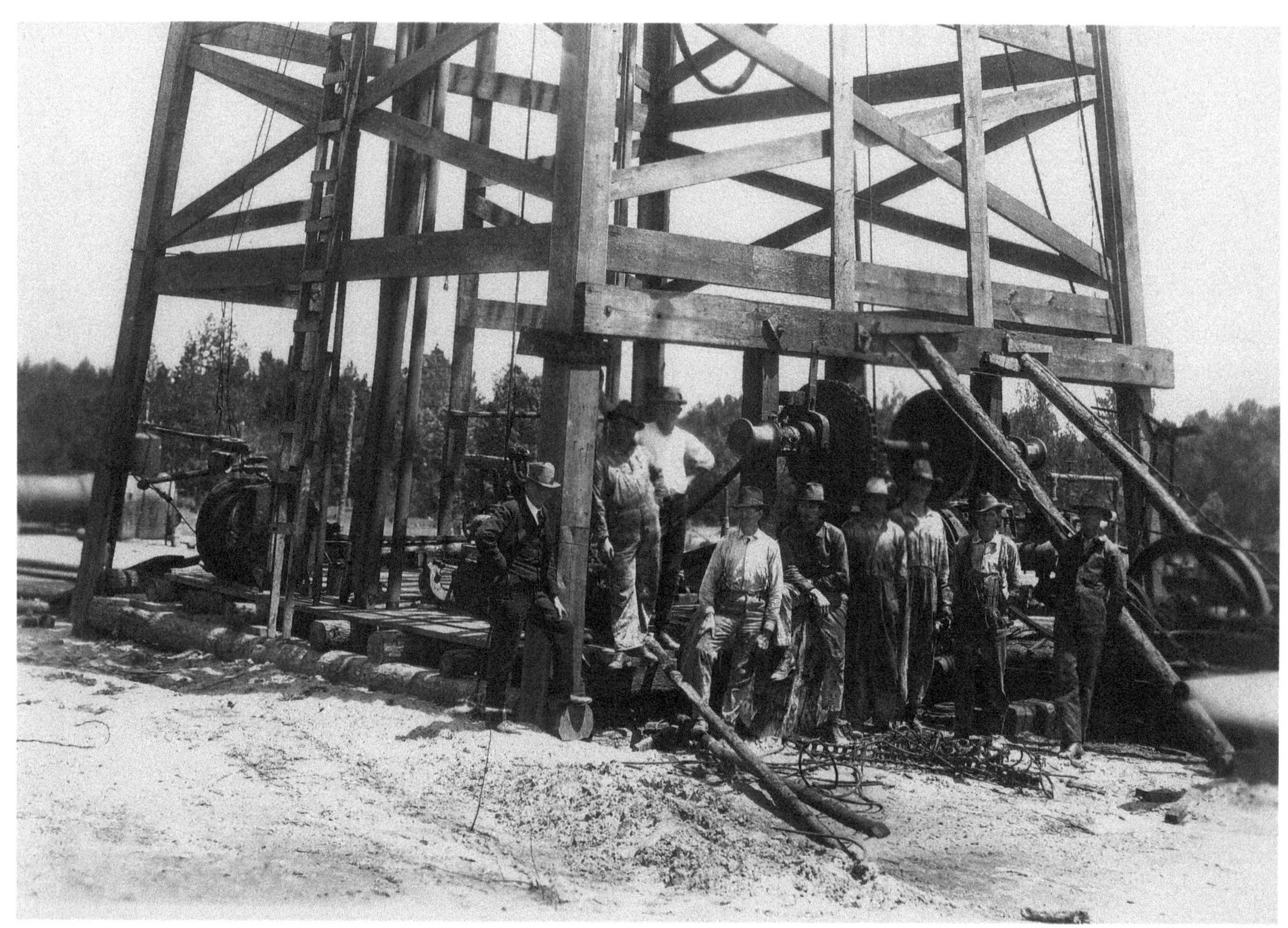

Oilfield workers pose at the foot of a drilling derrick in northern Louisiana around 1920. Drilling for oil became a big industry in the state's northwestern quadrant, centering on Shreveport, in the early 1900s. Wells in the north began to dry up by the 1920s but, not long afterward, oil was discovered in the Gulf of Mexico and the industry's focus shifted to the southern part of the state.

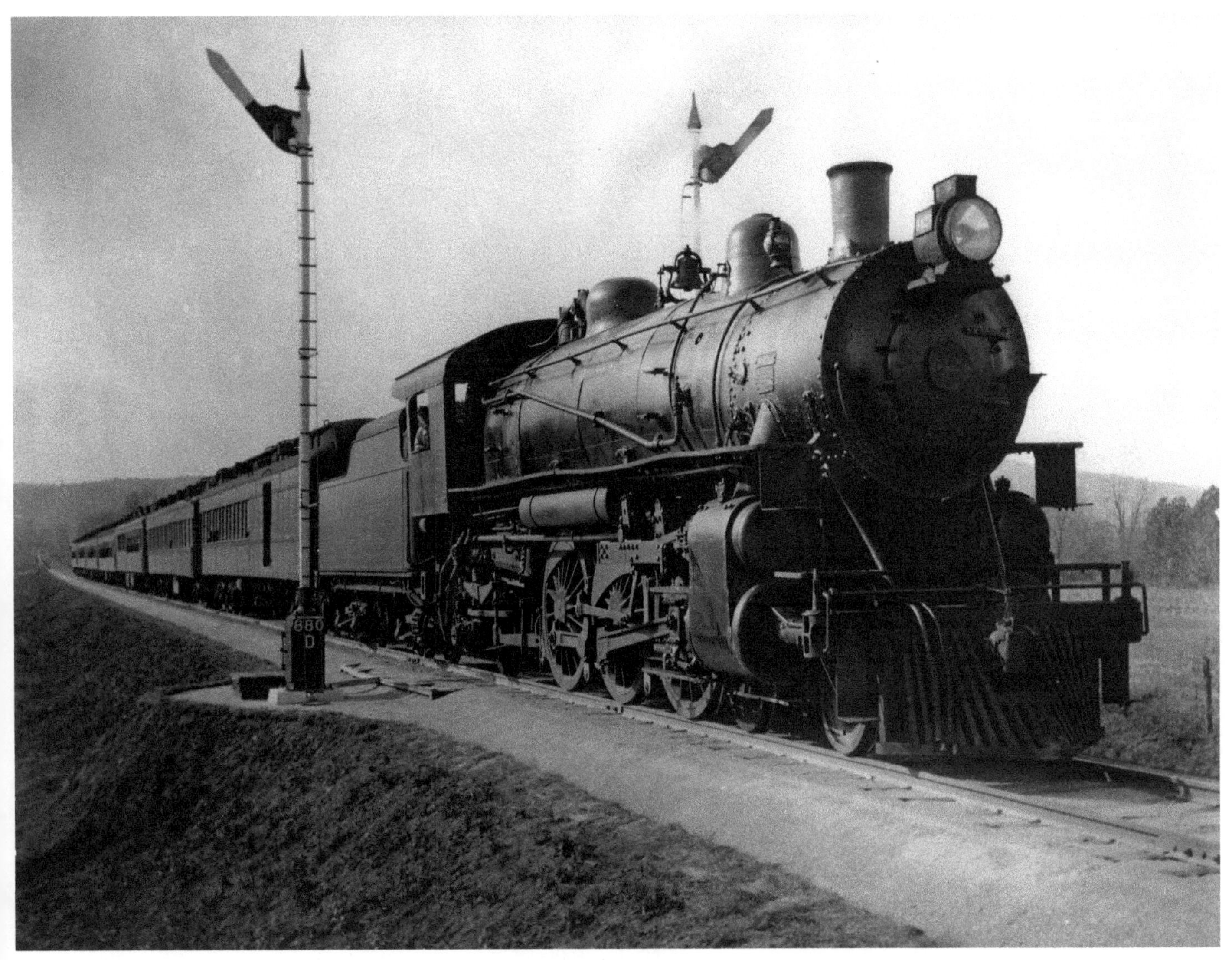

The Missouri Pacific Railroad's Sunshine Special passes twin semaphores while pulling a string of passenger coaches through northern Louisiana. Originally built in 1915 for service between St. Louis and large cities in Texas, the route of the Sunshine Special was extended into Shreveport in 1924 and New Orleans five years after that. It was taken out of service in 1955.

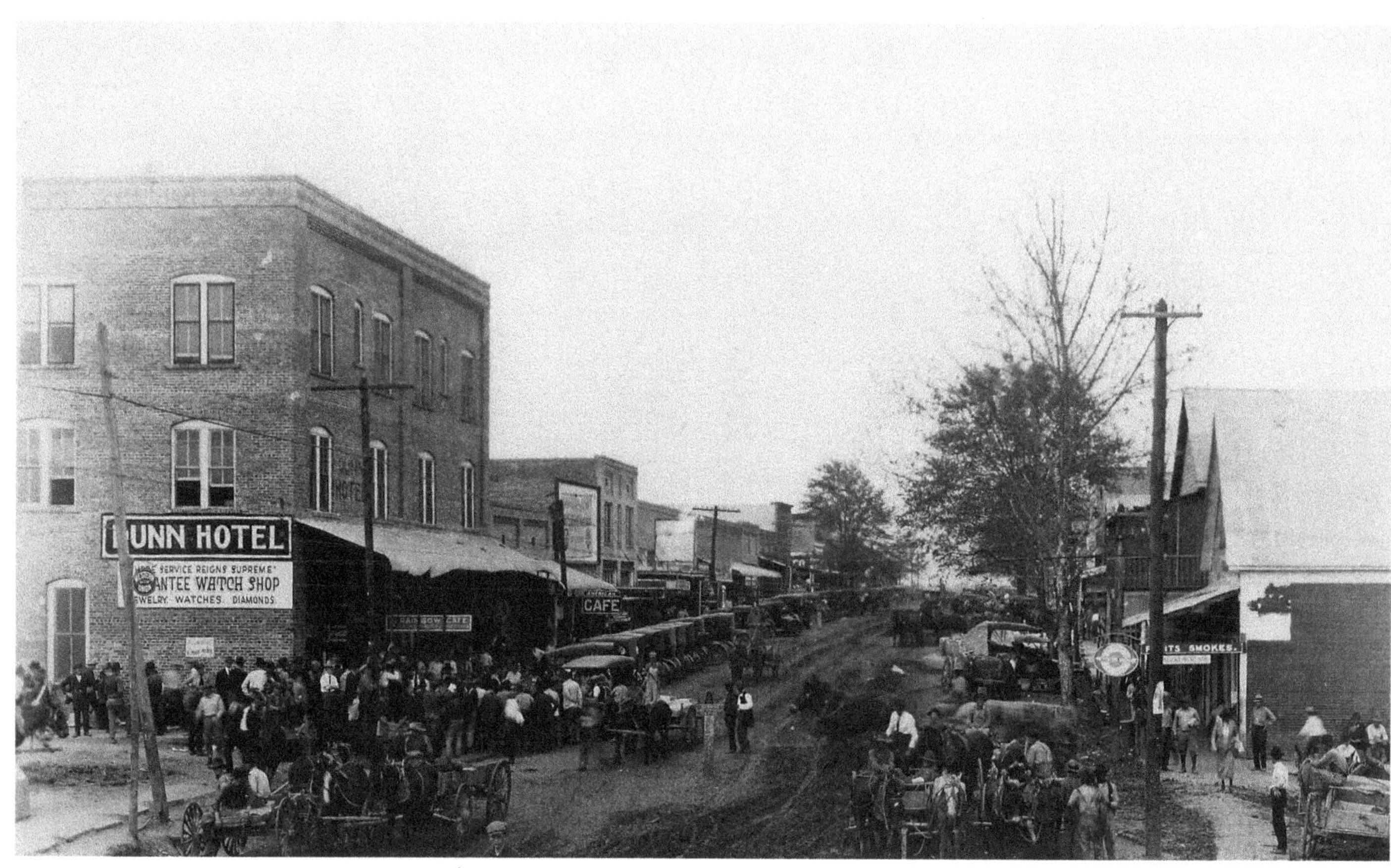

Haynesville's main street is full of activity in this photograph from around 1920. Horse-drawn carriages and automobiles share the street during the heyday of the oil boom in northern Louisiana. Haynesville, in Claiborne Parish just a few miles south of the Arkansas state line, was on the eastern edge of a vast subterranean oil reservoir that stretched into Texas. The boom was short-lived, as drilling drained much of the reserves within a ten-year span.

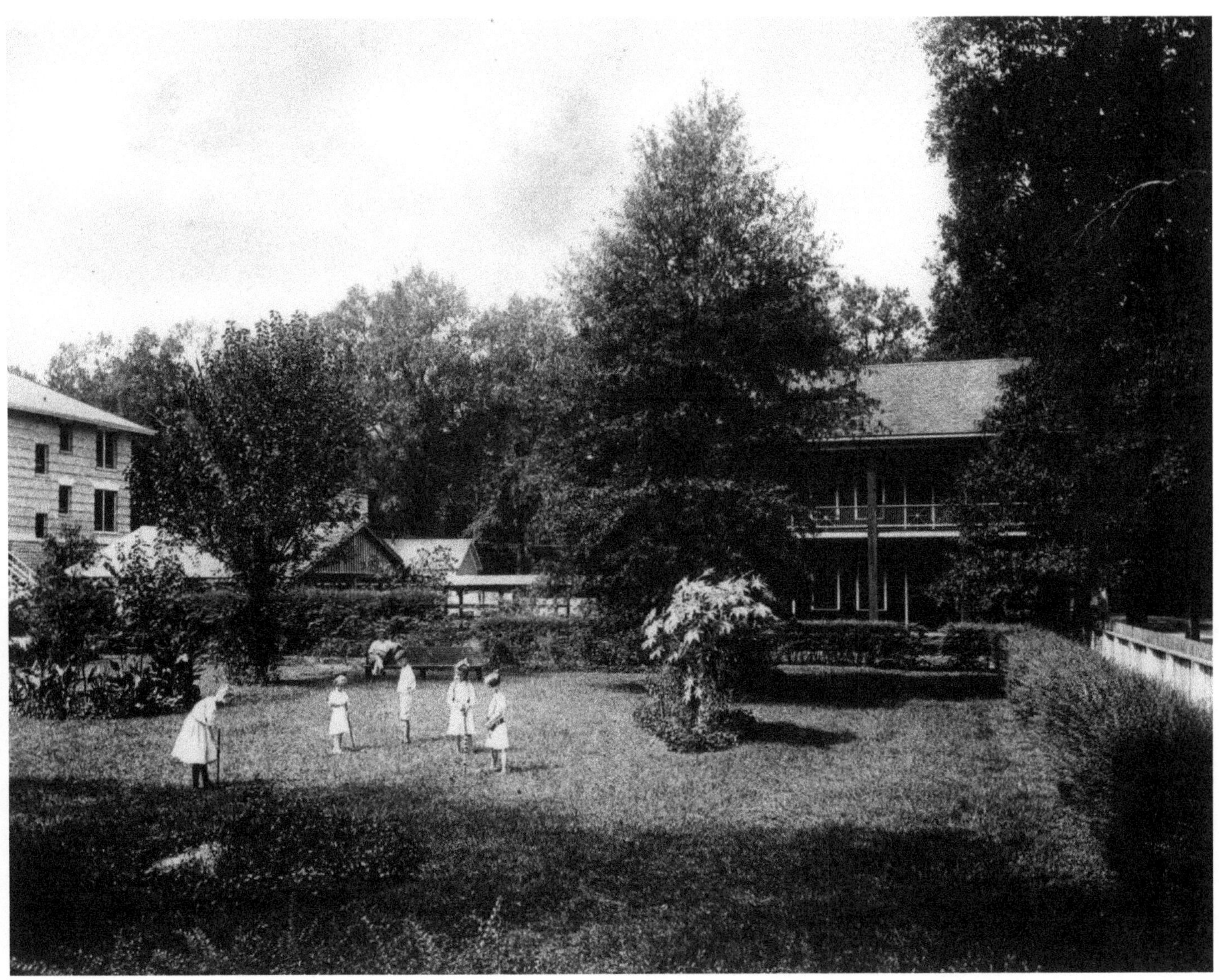

A group of five children play croquet on the lawn of the Playground of the Oaks Hotel in Hammond. Located about 50 miles northwest of New Orleans, Hammond was once a getaway destination for wealthy New Orleanians who had the means to leave the city during the hottest months of the year. Today it is the crossroads of two interstate highways and the hub of a fertile strawberry-growing region.

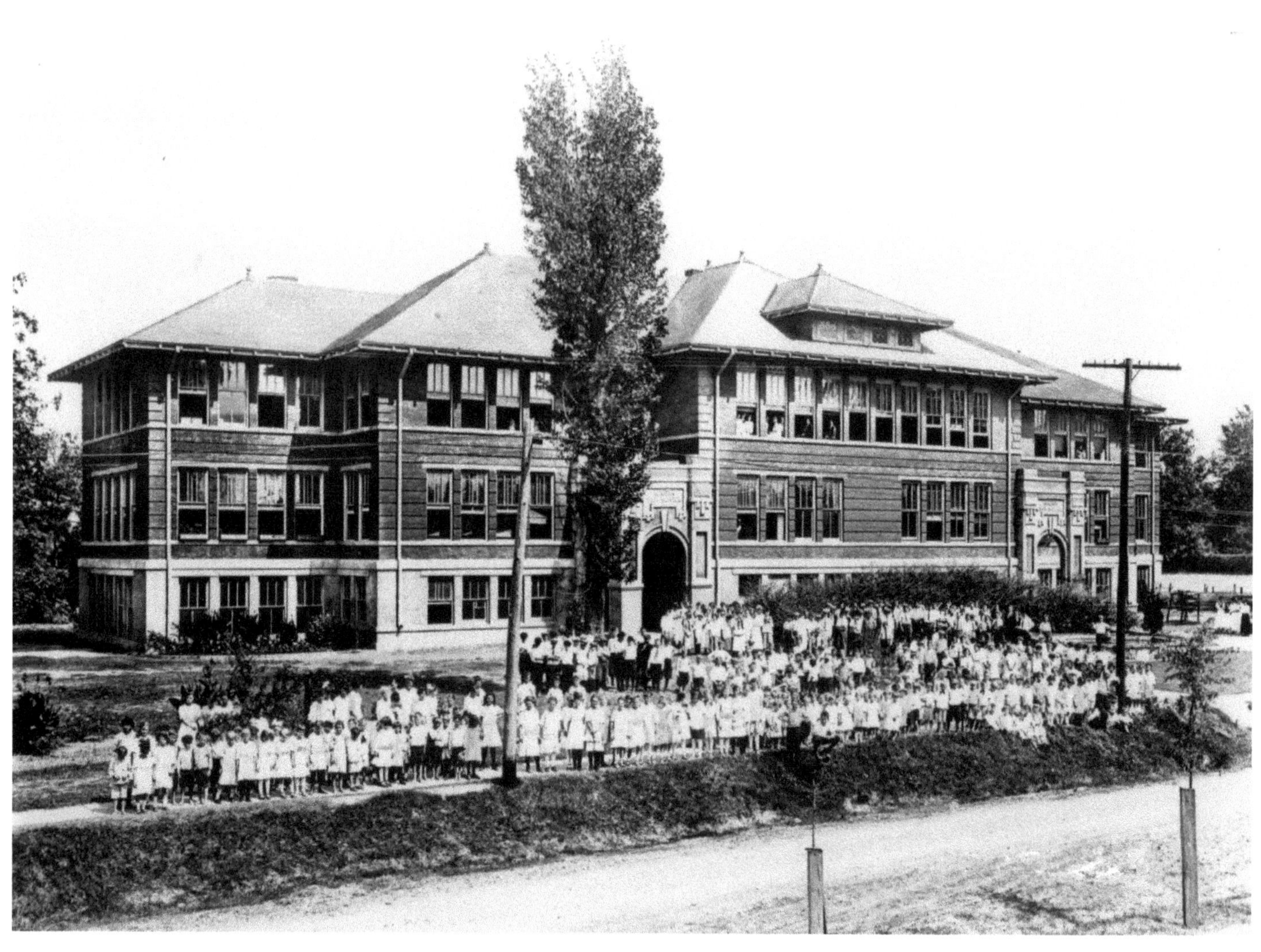

Students pose in front of Minden High School in Minden in this early-twentieth-century group portrait. The school is still in use today, following extensive renovations completed in 2007. The seat of Webster Parish, 28 miles east of Shreveport, Minden was founded in 1836 and named for a city in Germany. Famed country-western singer Hank Williams was married there on October 18, 1952, three months before his death. Minden is also the home of Northwest Louisiana Technical College.

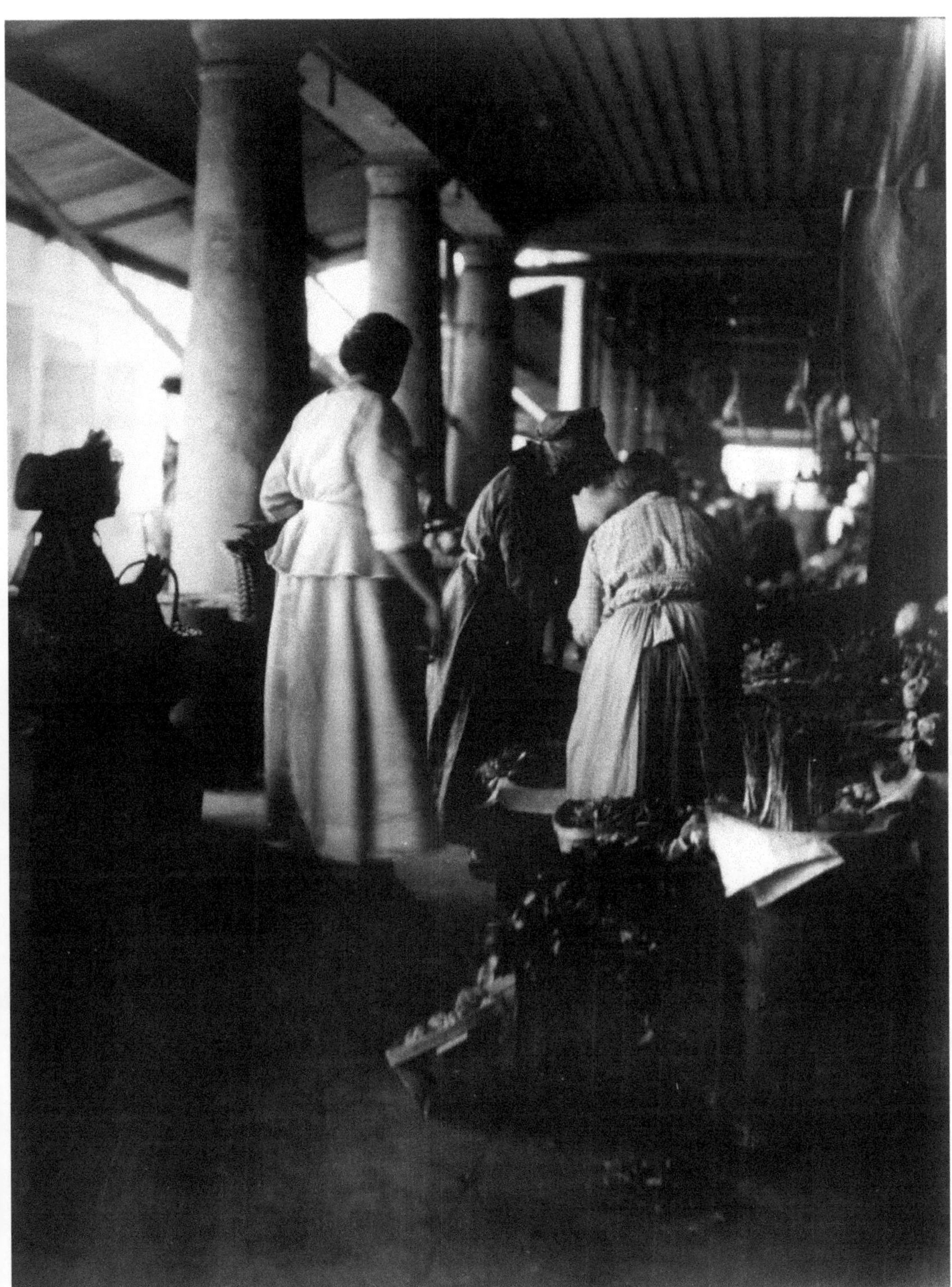

Women shop at an outdoor market, possibly the French Market, in New Orleans in this photograph from the early 1920s.

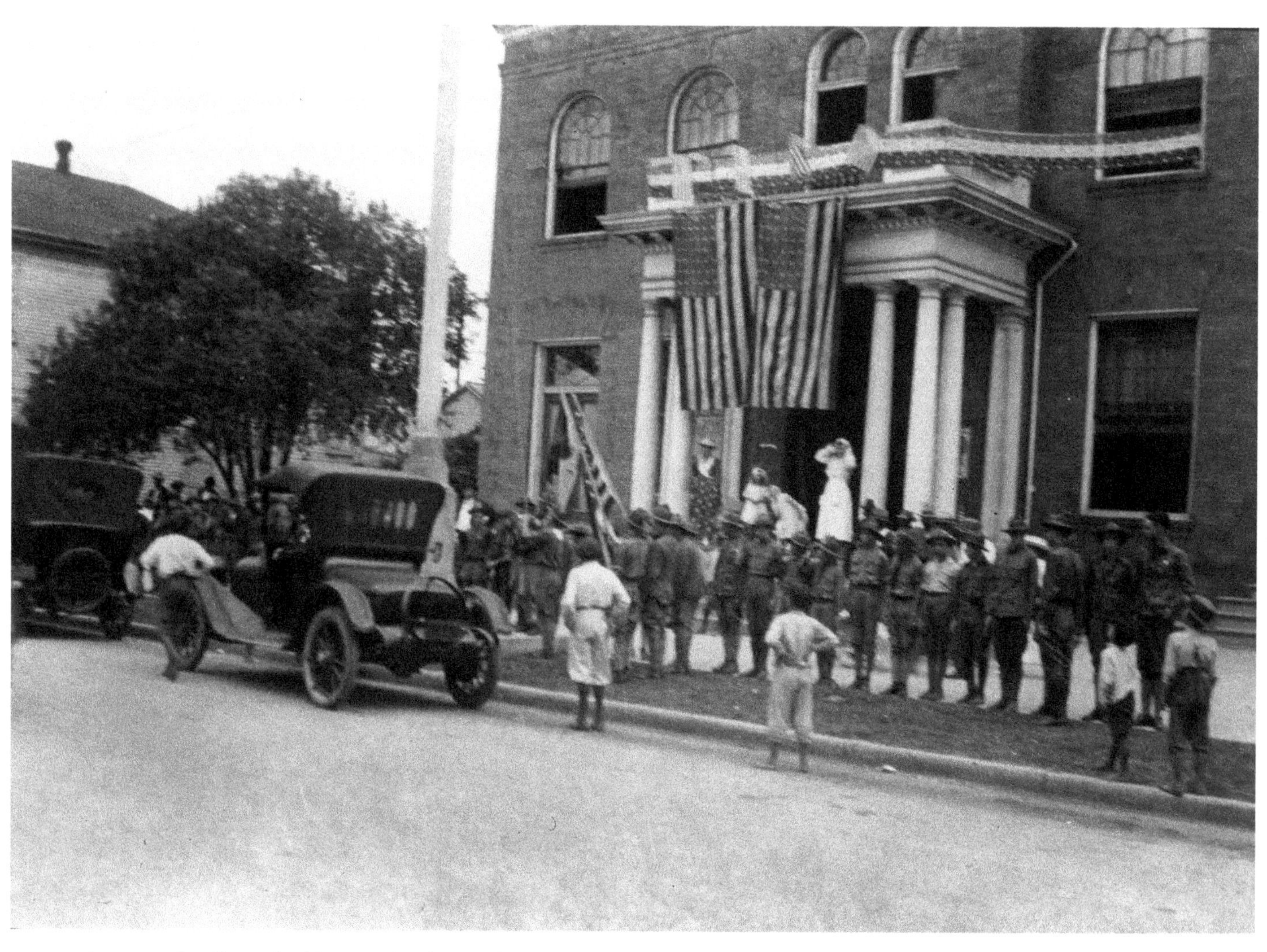

A group of uniformed soldiers are lined up and raising an American flag on a special occasion in front of the old City Hall in Baton Rouge around 1920. The offices of old City Hall, built in the late nineteenth century, would move into another building in 1935 and later into a much larger building that also houses the offices of East Baton Rouge Parish.

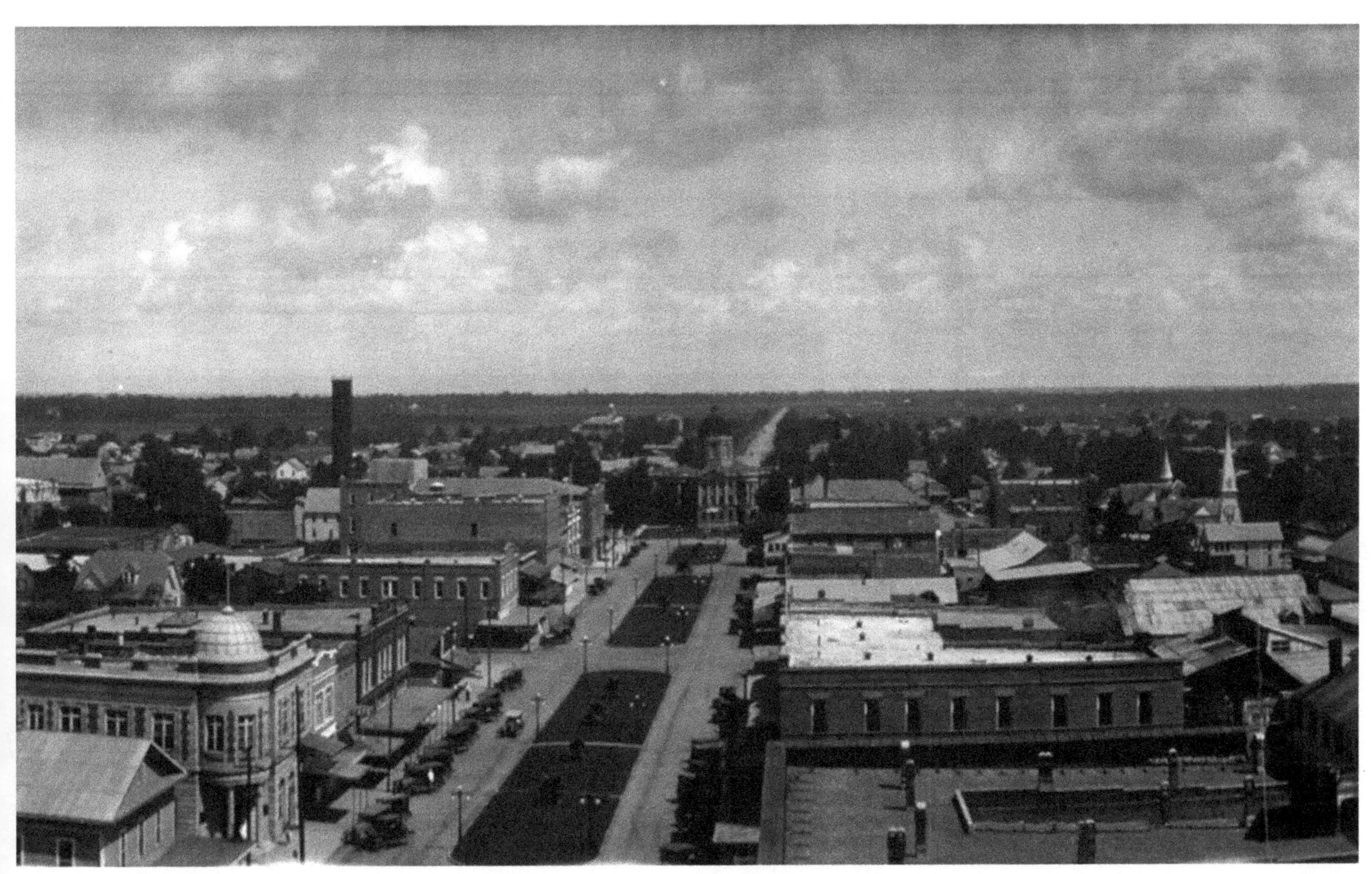

This rooftop view from 1921 shows Parkerson Avenue, the main street of Crowley, looking toward the old Acadia Parish Court House in service from 1903 to 1949. Crowley bills itself as the "Rice Capital of the World" and hosts an annual Rice Festival. In the early 1900s there were about a dozen rice mills in the Crowley area, several of which are still open, but the region has diversified into other crops and industries.

Following Spread: A streetcar rolls toward the busy intersection of Texas and Market streets in Shreveport's downtown business district in 1921.

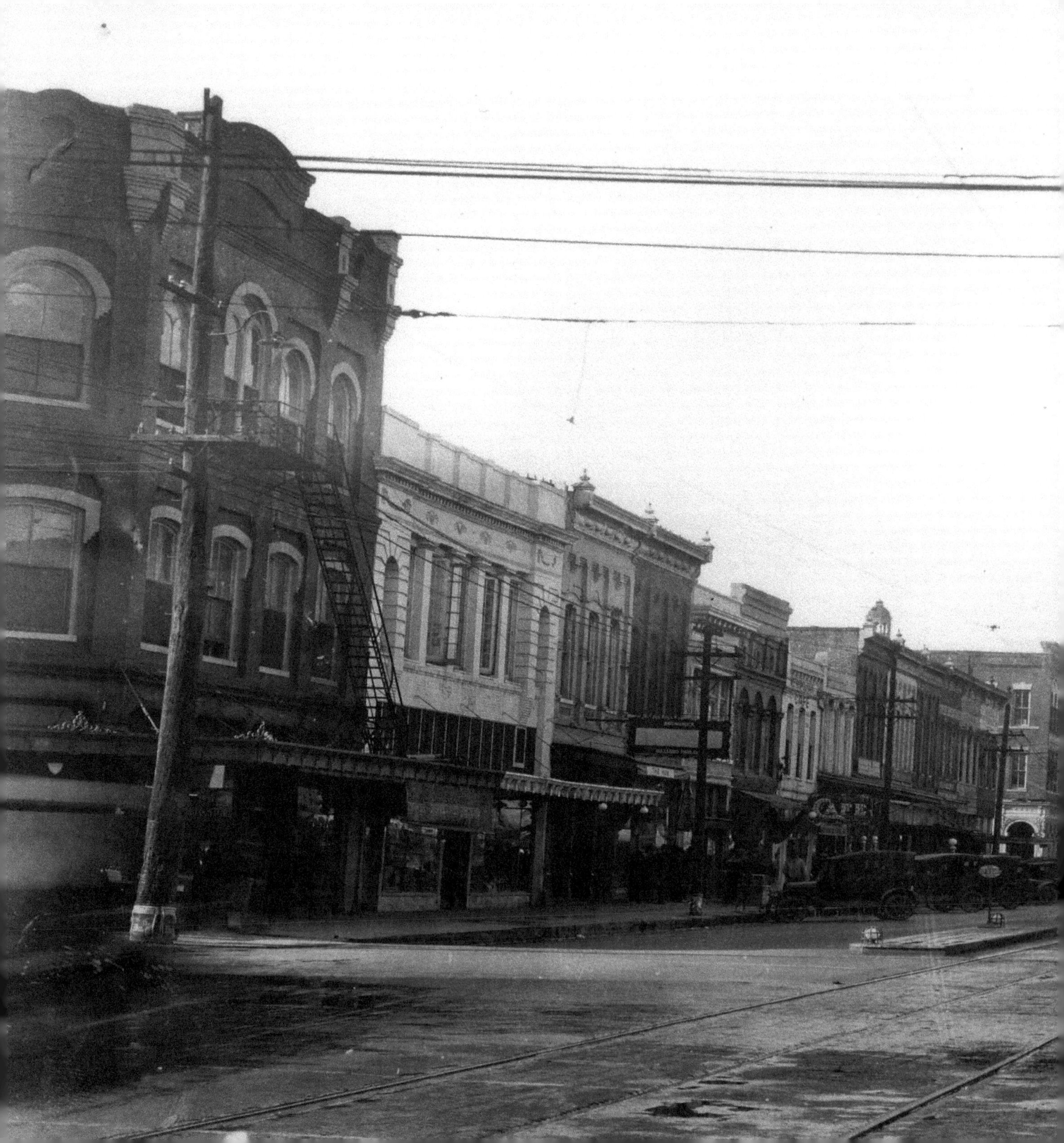
CAFE

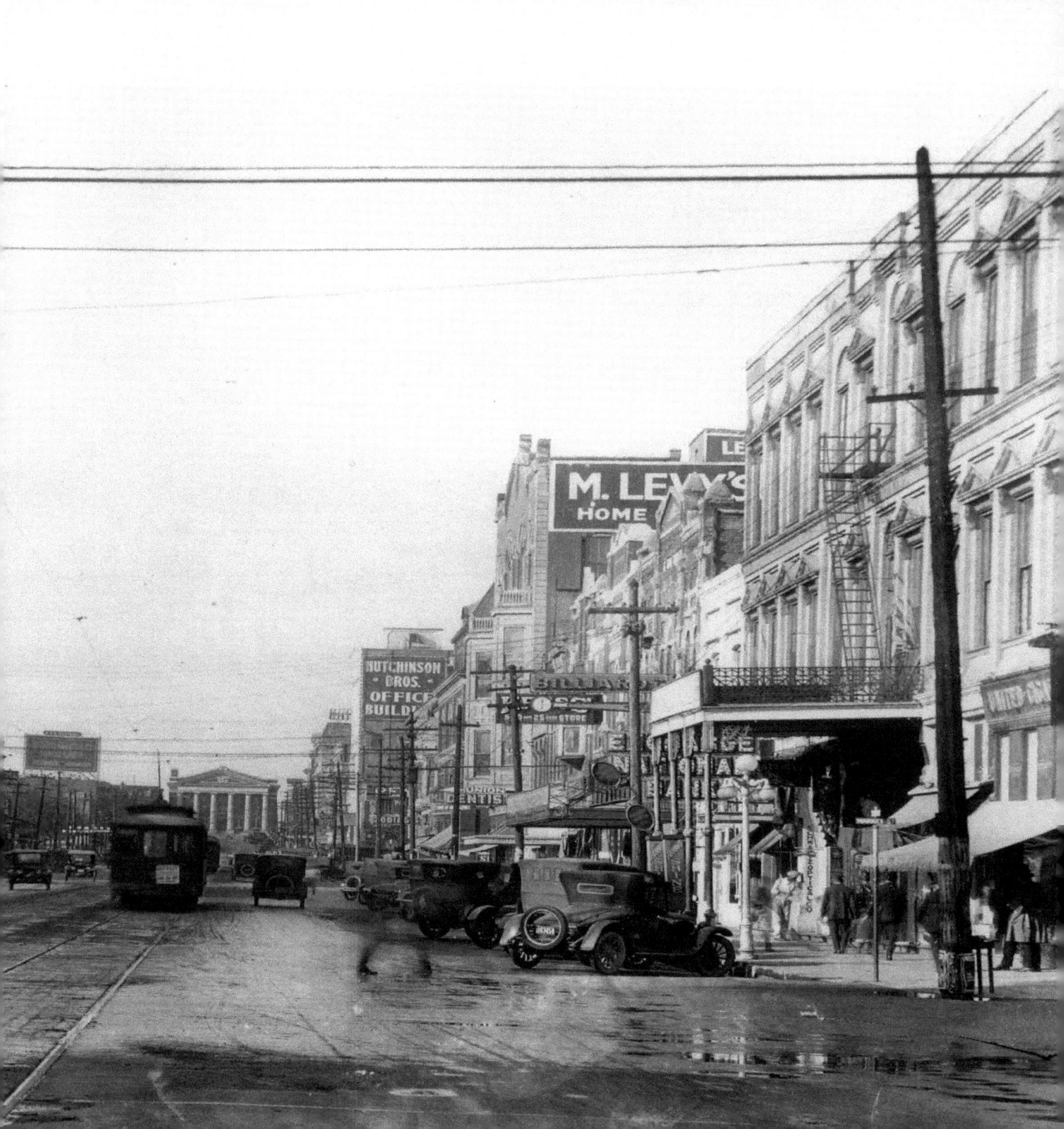
M. LEVY'S
HOME
HUTCHINSON
BROS.

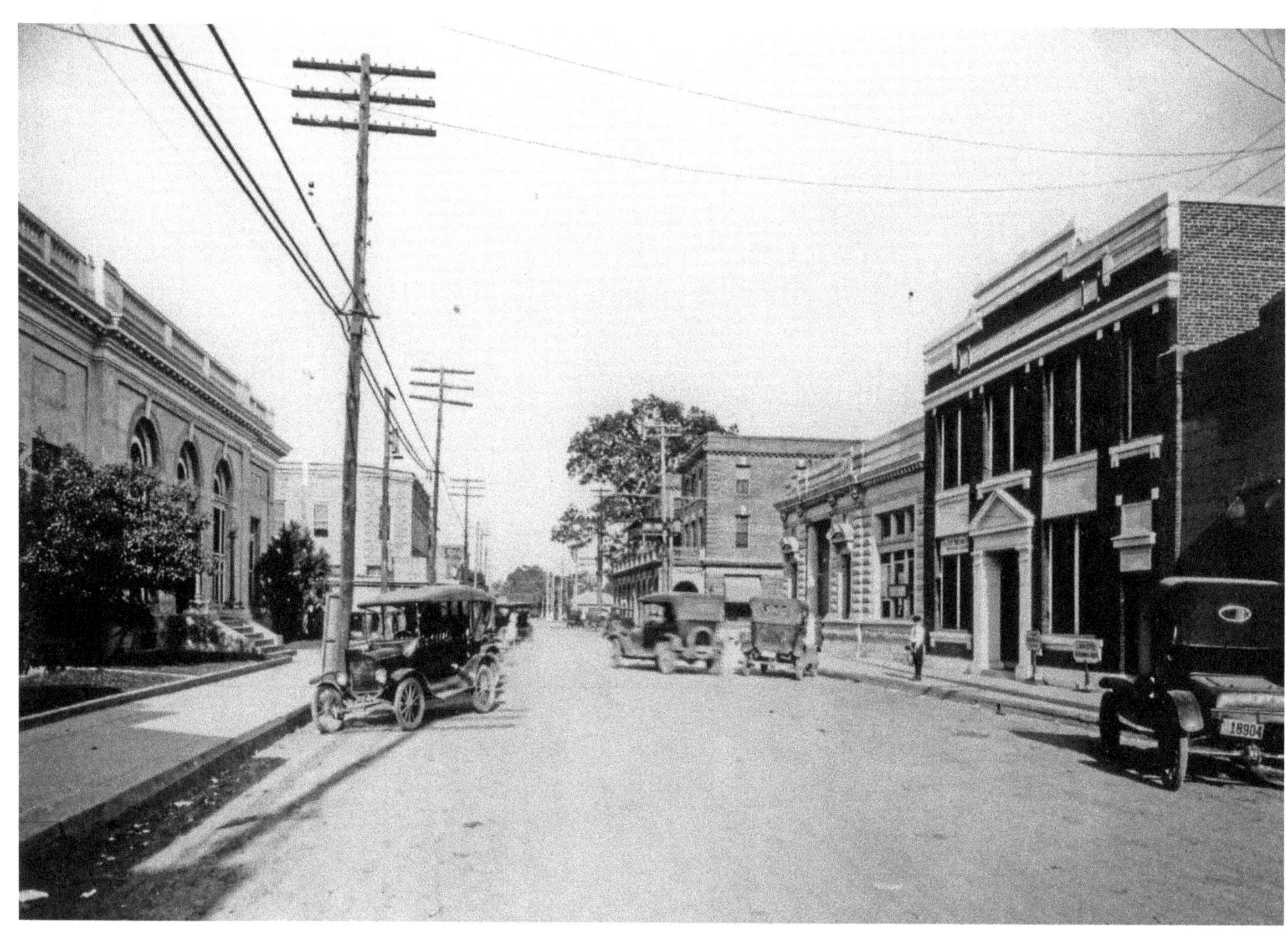

Scene in the business district of Lafayette in 1921. Named for the French Marquis de Lafayette, who came to the aid of the American colonists during the Revolution, Lafayette considers itself the unofficial "Capital of Acadiana," a grouping of southern Louisiana parishes with predominantly Cajun populations. Lafayette celebrates the Cajun cultural heritage with its annual Festival Acadiens et Creoles, featuring Cajun-Creole food, handicrafts, music, and dancing.

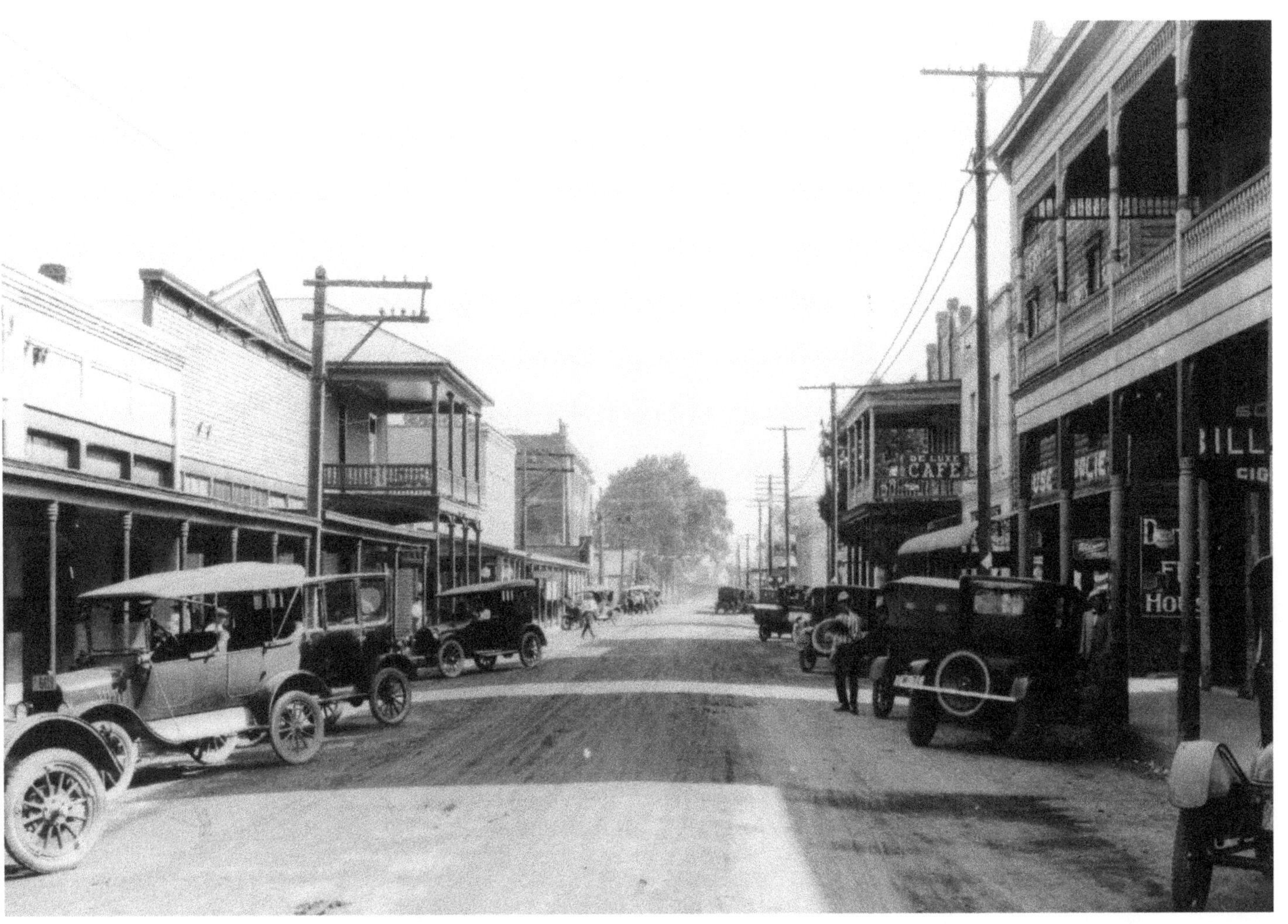

Lafayette lies in the center of a region settled by French Canadians, who were forced into exile by the victorious British after they assumed control of Canada following the French and Indian War in the mid to late 1700s. The term "Cajun" is a shortened form of *Acadian,* which describes the region of Canada bordering Nova Scotia and New Brunswick from which they were driven out.

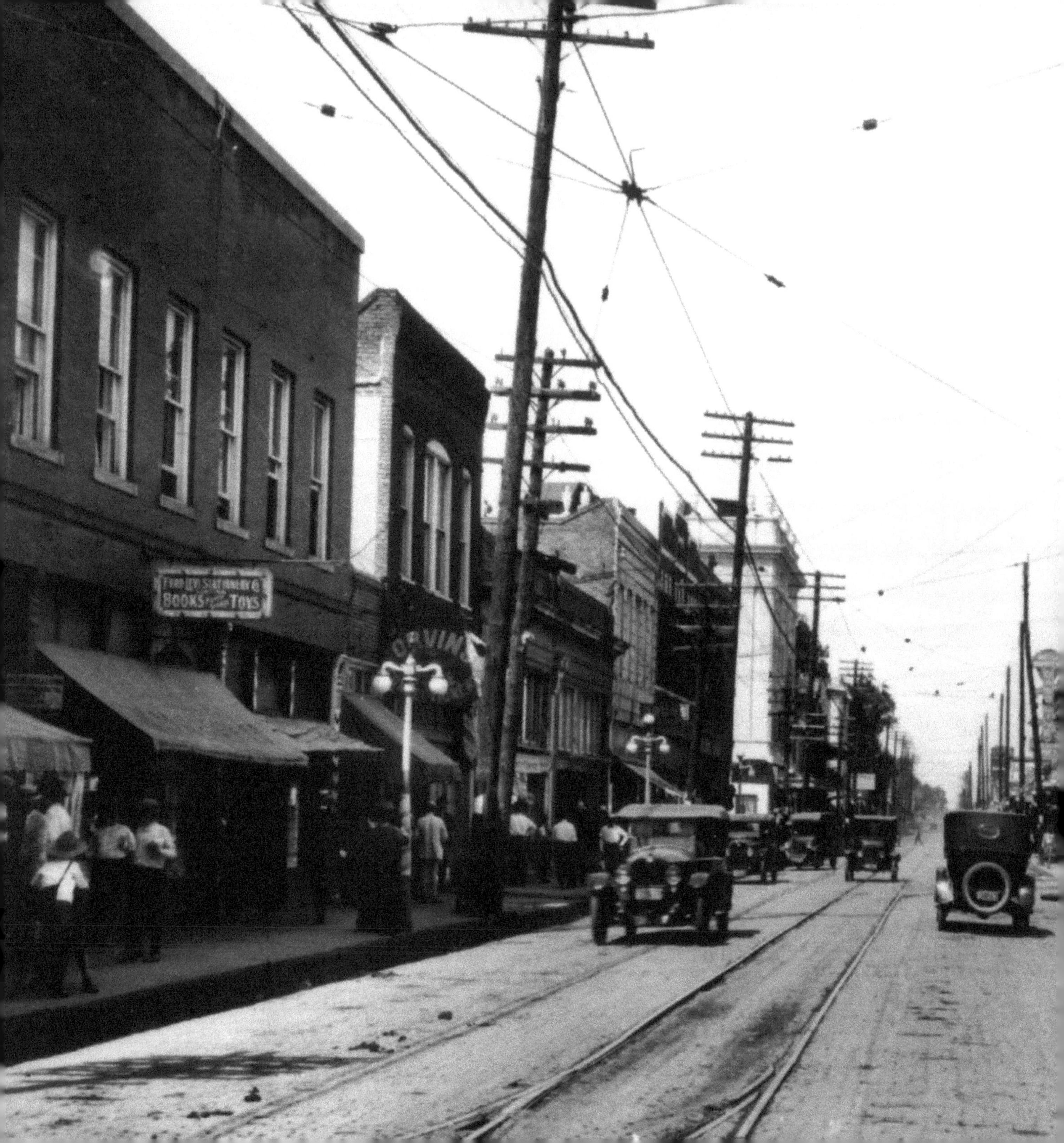
BOOKS TOYS

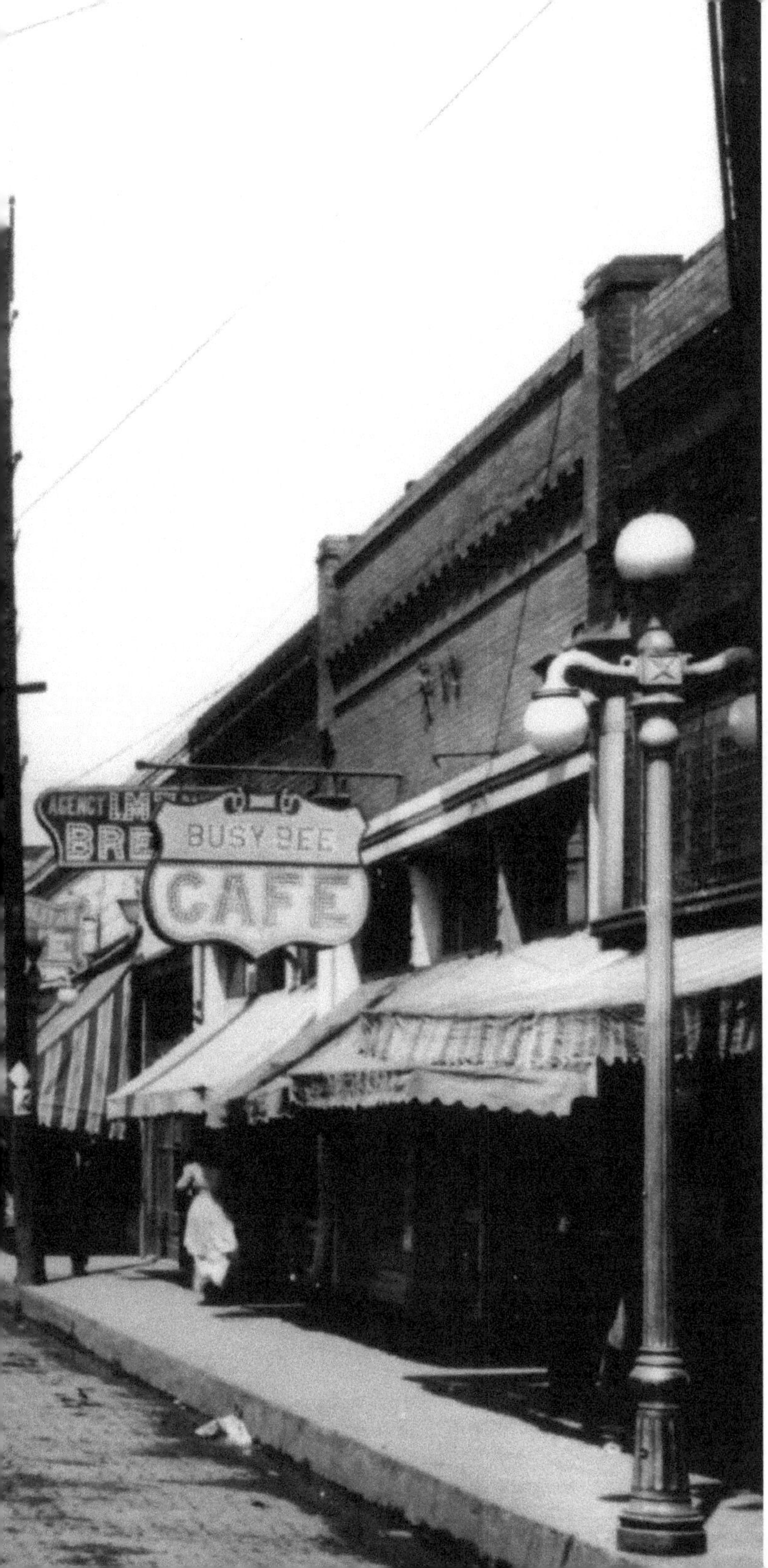

Scene in downtown Monroe in 1921. The main city and population center of northeastern Louisiana, it was named for James Monroe, President Thomas Jefferson's special envoy who helped negotiate the Louisiana Purchase from France in 1803. He later became the 5th President, serving from 1817 to 1825. The city of Monroe lies on the Ouachita River, across from its "twin city," West Monroe, and is the seat of Ouachita Parish.

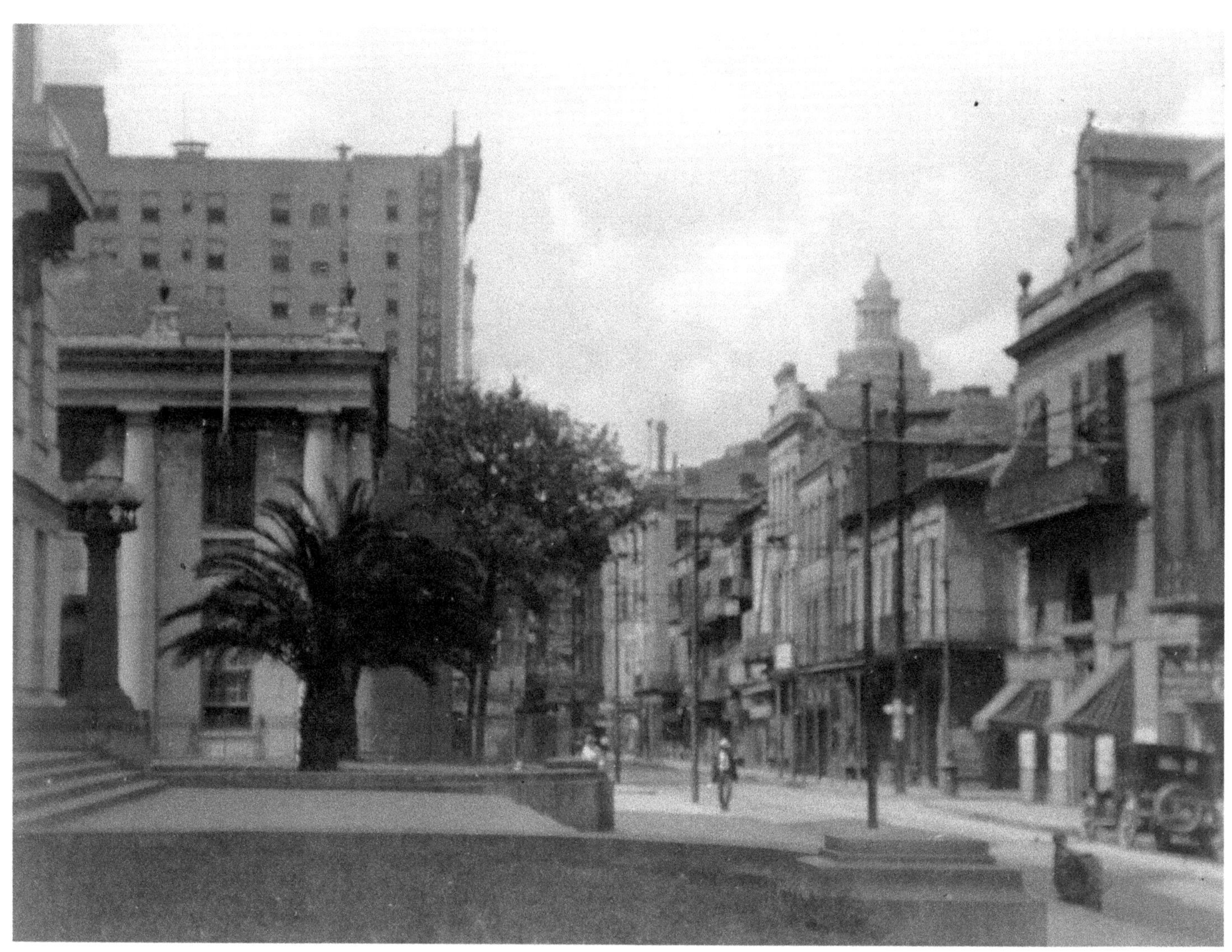

A section of Royal Street in the New Orleans French Quarter is seen from the front steps of the Louisiana Supreme Court Building in the early 1920s. The colonnaded tower in the background is the 20-story Hibernia Bank Building built in 1921 and, at the time, the tallest building in Louisiana. It still stands, renamed the Capital One Building after its new owners, and is a New Orleans landmark sporting colored lights at night for different holidays throughout the year.

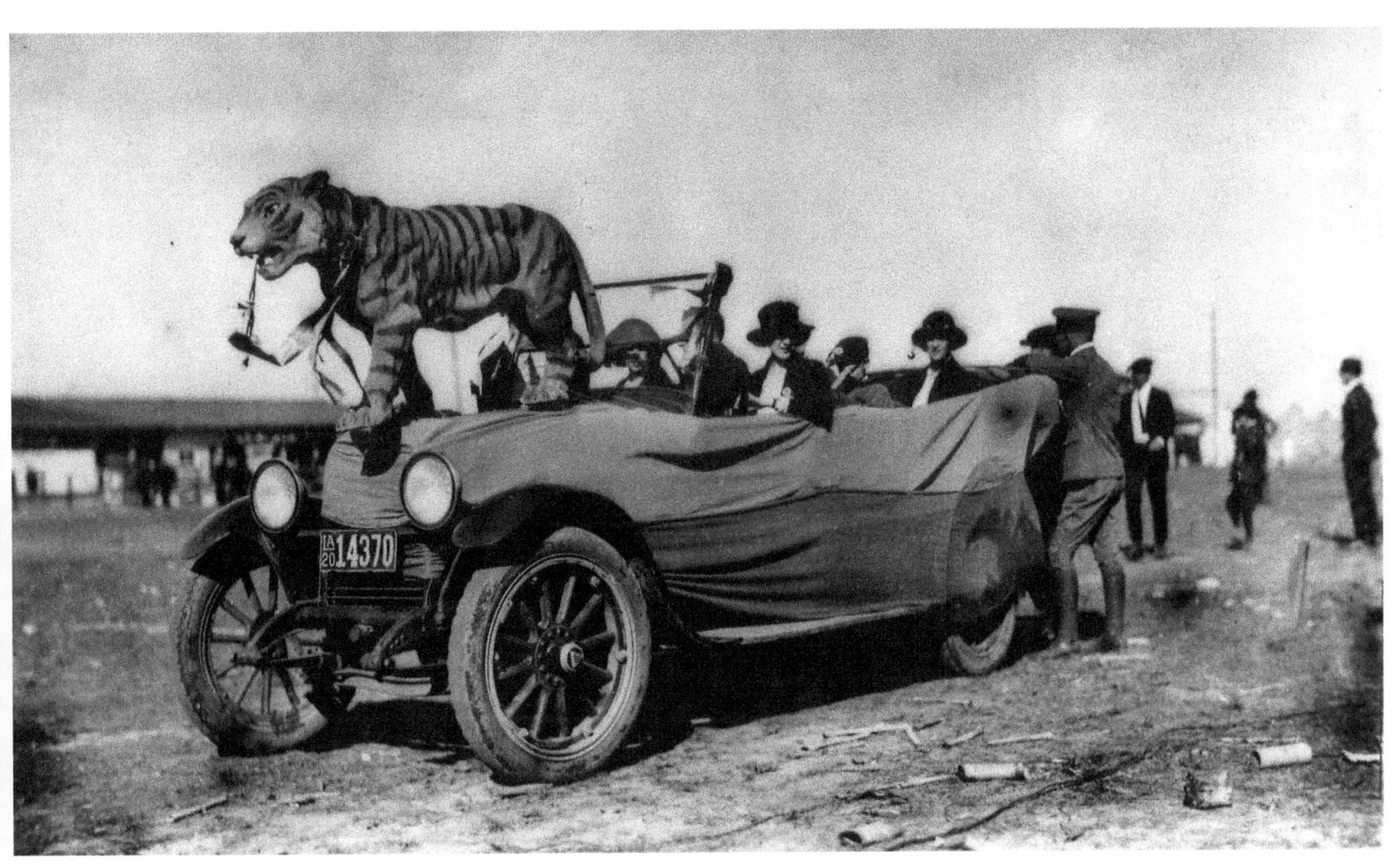

Enthusiastic Louisiana State University football fans pose inside an early convertible with a papier mache tiger mounted on the hood. "Mike the Tiger" has been the longtime mascot of the LSU Tigers, and these fans were in Shreveport for the 1921 gridiron match-up between LSU and the University of Arkansas Razorbacks. LSU won, 10–7. With a record of 33 wins, 19 losses, and 2 ties, the school currently holds the lead in an intercollegiate rivalry that dates back to 1901.

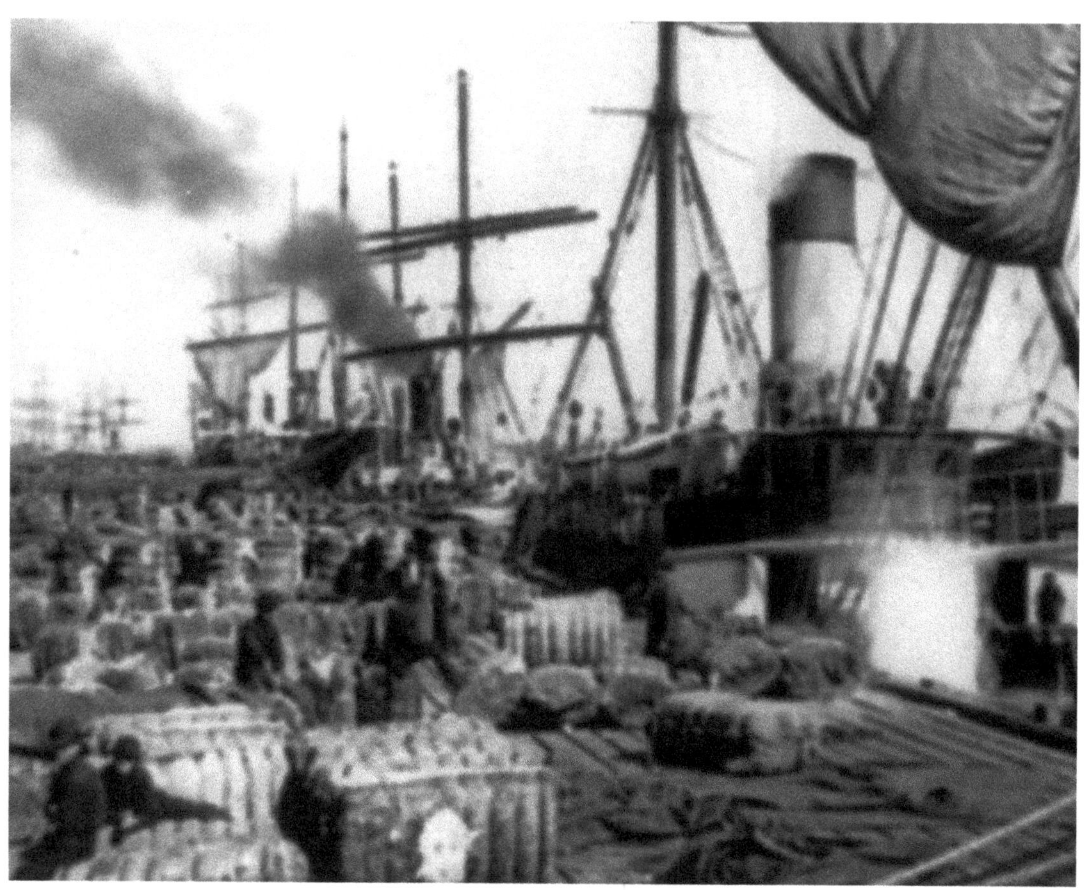

Bales of cotton sit on a busy wharf along the New Orleans riverfront, for loading onto nearby docked ships. Cotton continued to be an important Southern crop and export commodity well beyond the Civil War and into the twentieth century. It remains an agricultural staple of the region, but its importance has declined with the development of synthetic fabrics in the years following World War II.

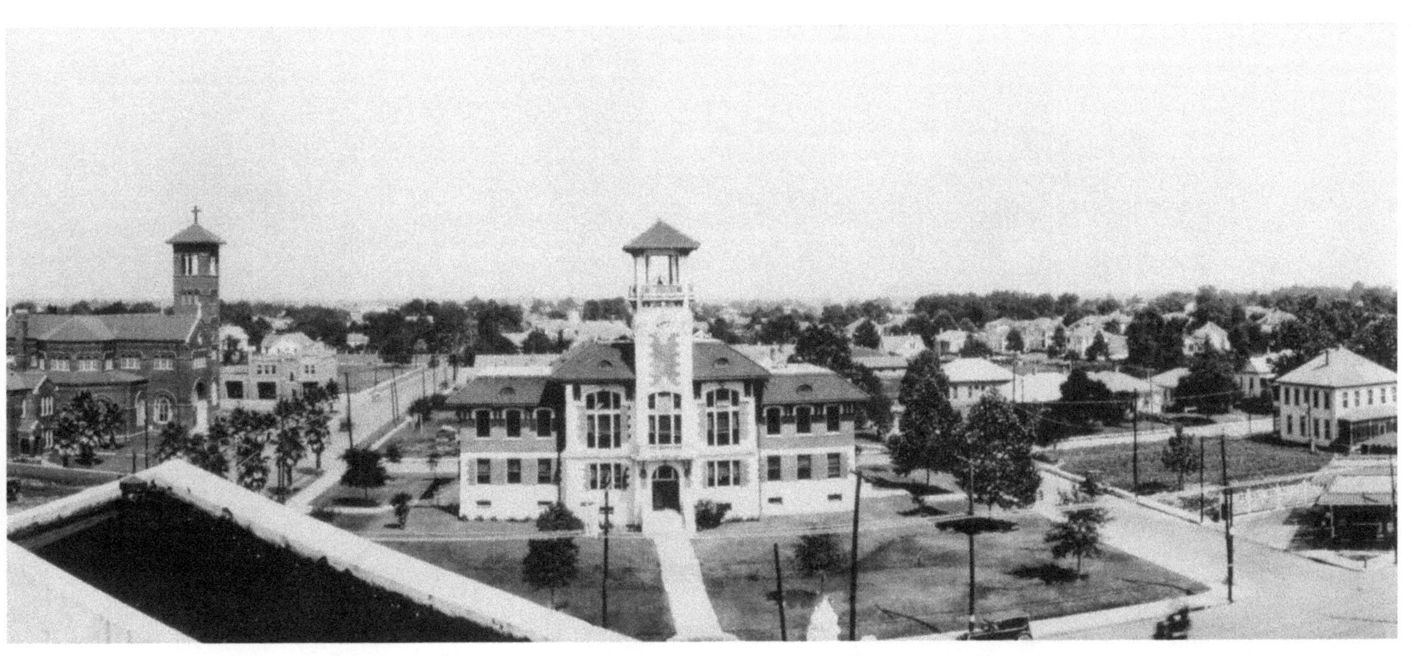

A 1923 rooftop panorama of Lake Charles. The chief population center of southwestern Louisiana, Lake Charles recovered from a disastrous fire in 1910 that destroyed more than seven downtown city blocks. Today it is the fifth-largest city in the state and a center for gaming, drawing residents from nearby Texas to its floating casinos along the Calcasieu River.

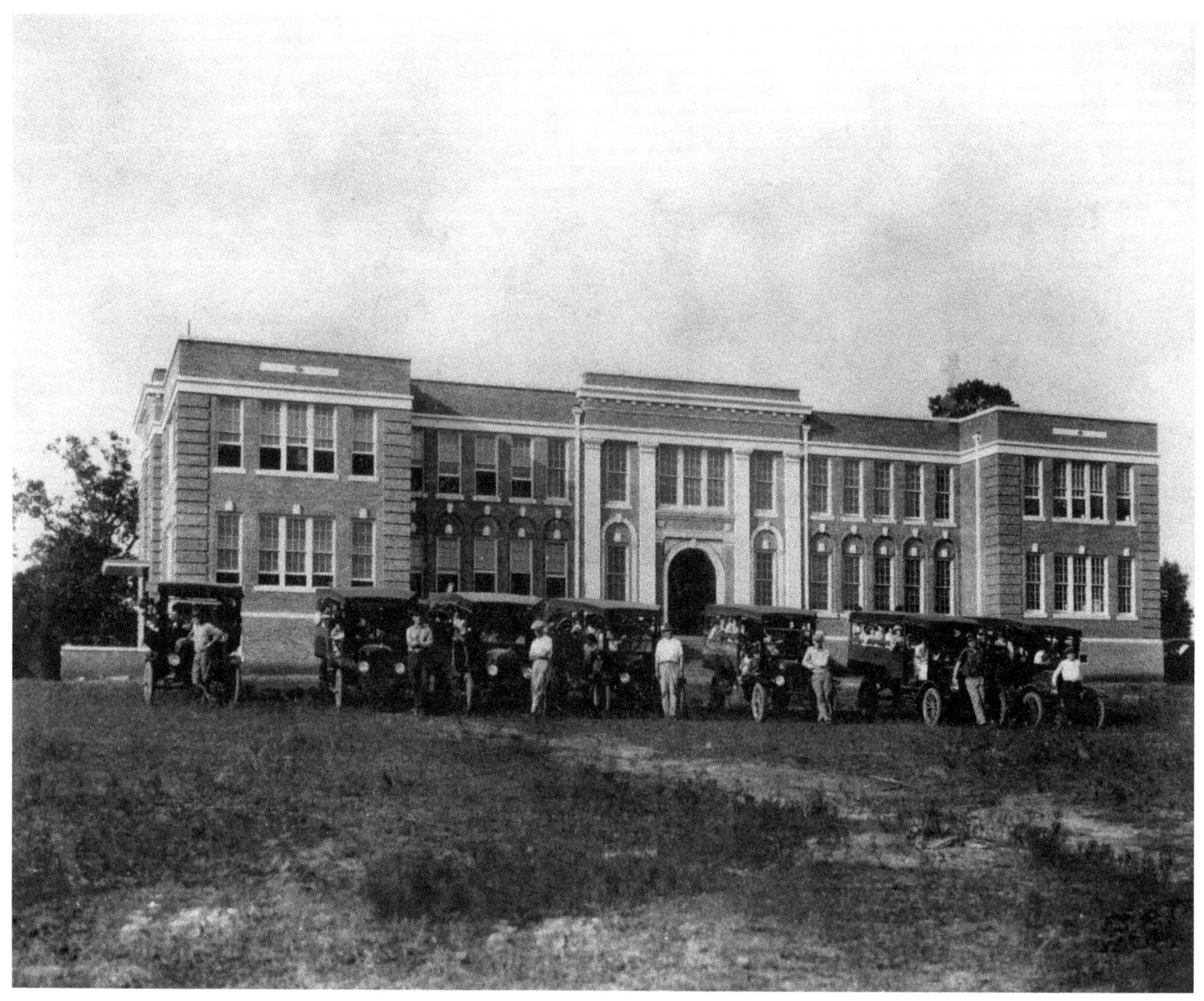

High school and transfer buses sit parked outside the old, no-longer-standing high school in Plain Dealing in 1923. Situated in the northern part of Bossier Parish with a population of just over 1,000, Plain Dealing was named for a local plantation with the same name. The hottest recorded temperature in the state's history, 114 degrees Fahrenheit, was measured in Plain Dealing on August 10, 1936.

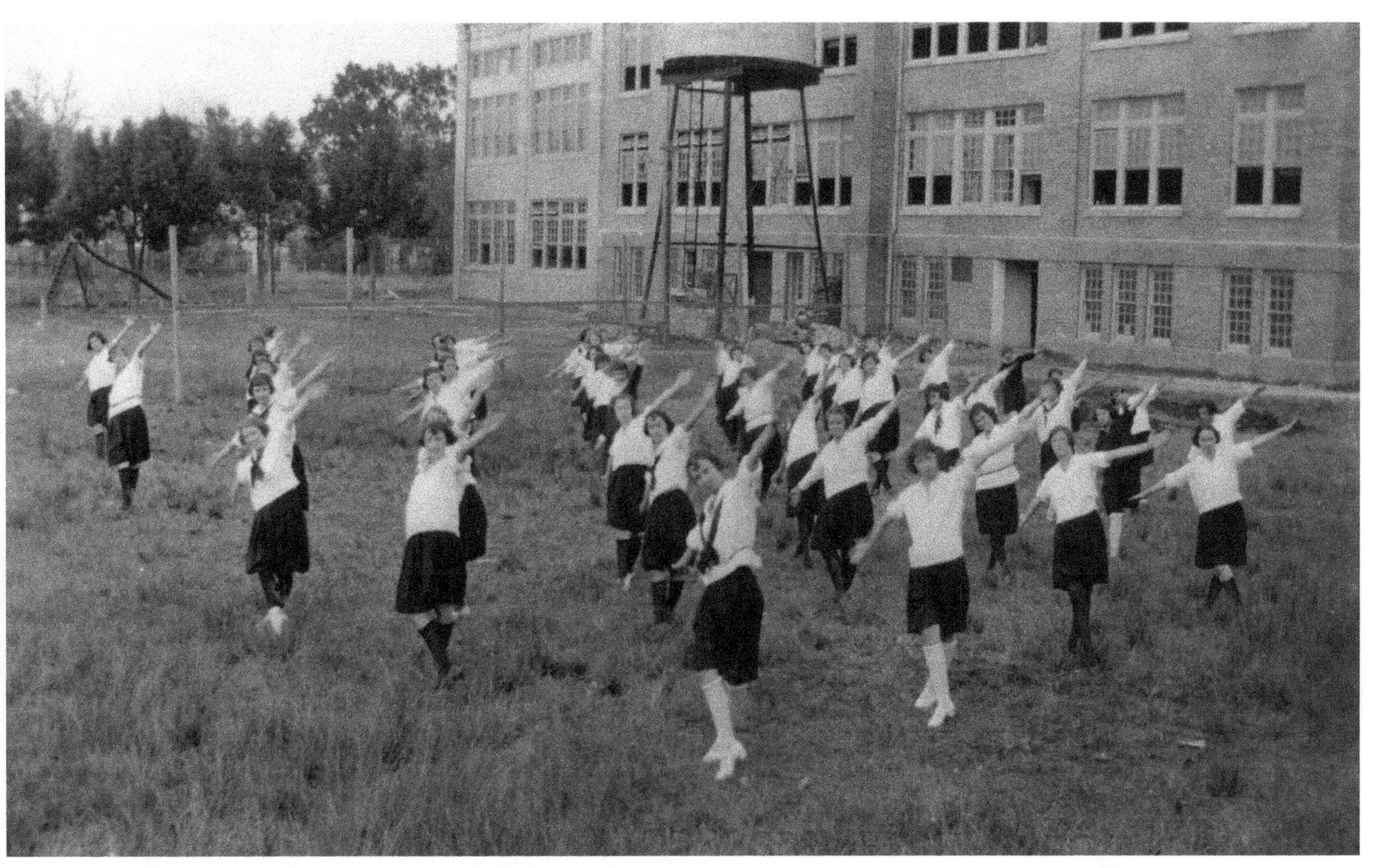

Students in their gym outfits are doing exercises or perhaps rehearsing a dance routine outside Patterson High School in Patterson in the early 1920s. Located in St. Mary Parish west of Morgan City with a population of more than 6,000, Patterson was settled in the early 1800s by Pennsylvanians of Dutch descent and originally known as Dutch Settlement. It was renamed for Captain John Patterson, a trader from Indiana who settled there in 1832.

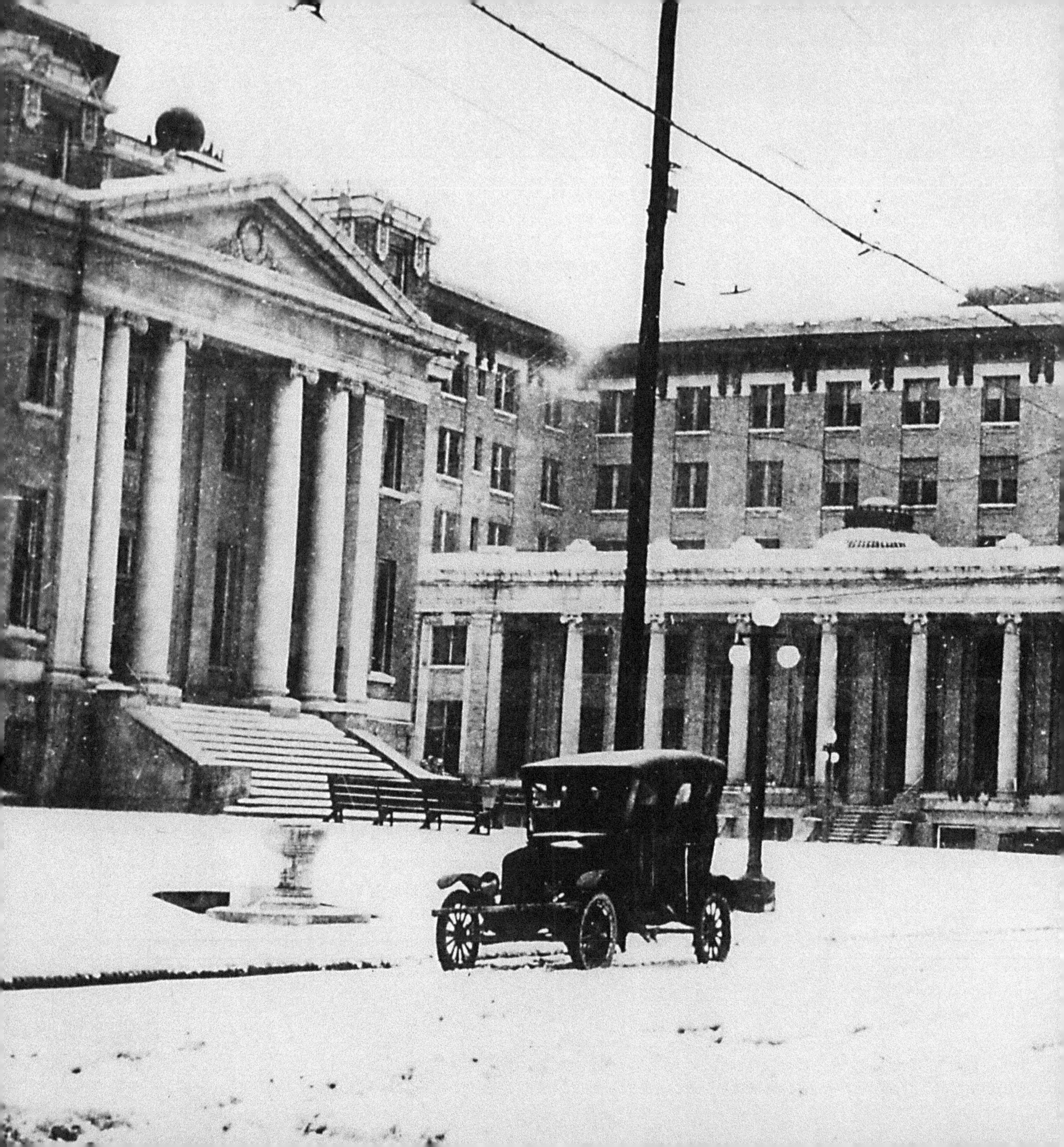

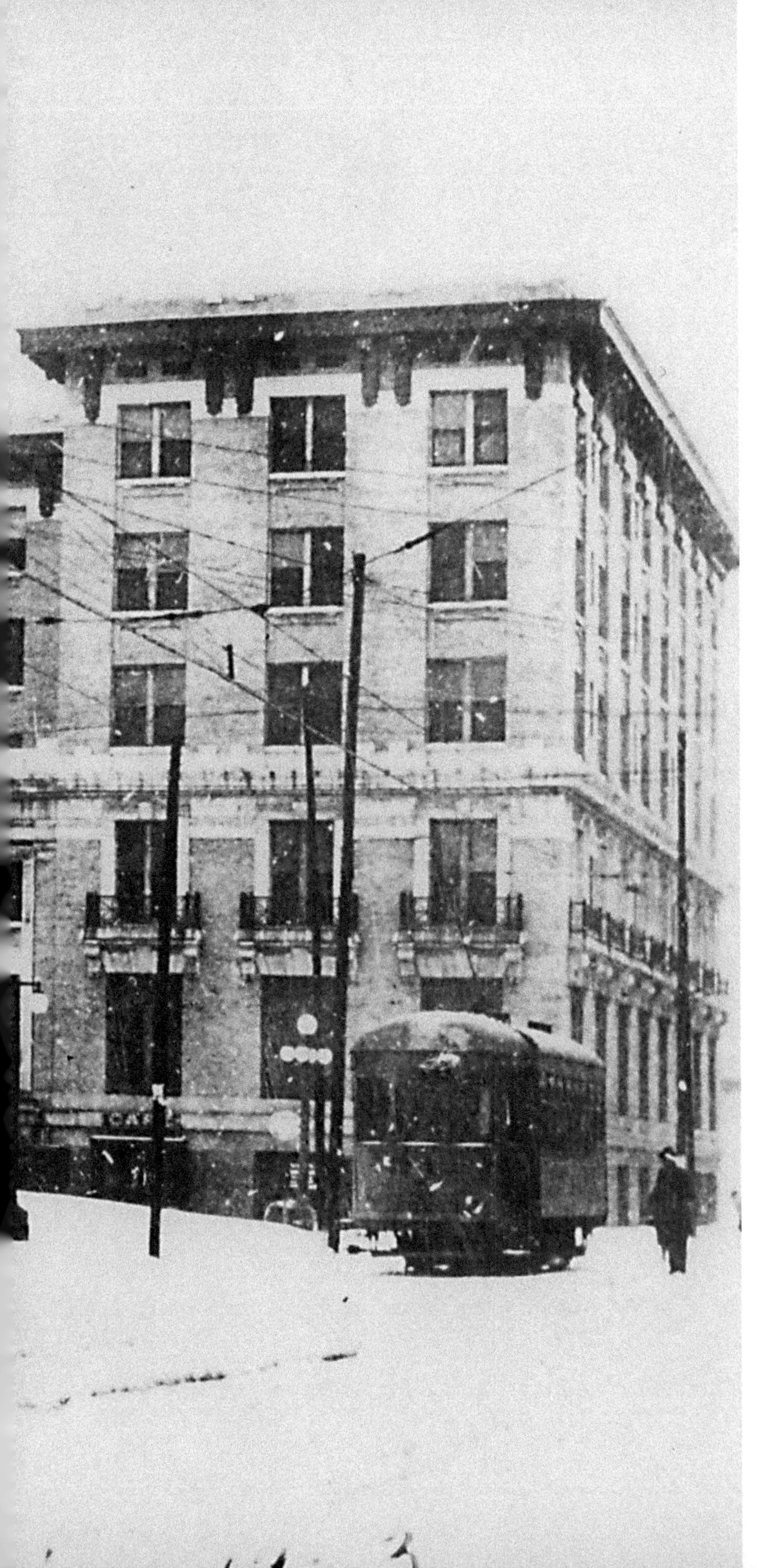

A lone automobile and a streetcar venture out onto Second Street during a rare snowfall that blanketed the streets of Alexandria to an estimated depth of four inches during the winter of 1923. The old City Hall is visible at left and the elegant Hotel Bentley, which was built in 1908 and still stands today, is at center. During nearby military maneuvers in the 1940s, generals Patton, Marshall, Eisenhower, and Bradley stayed at the Bentley.

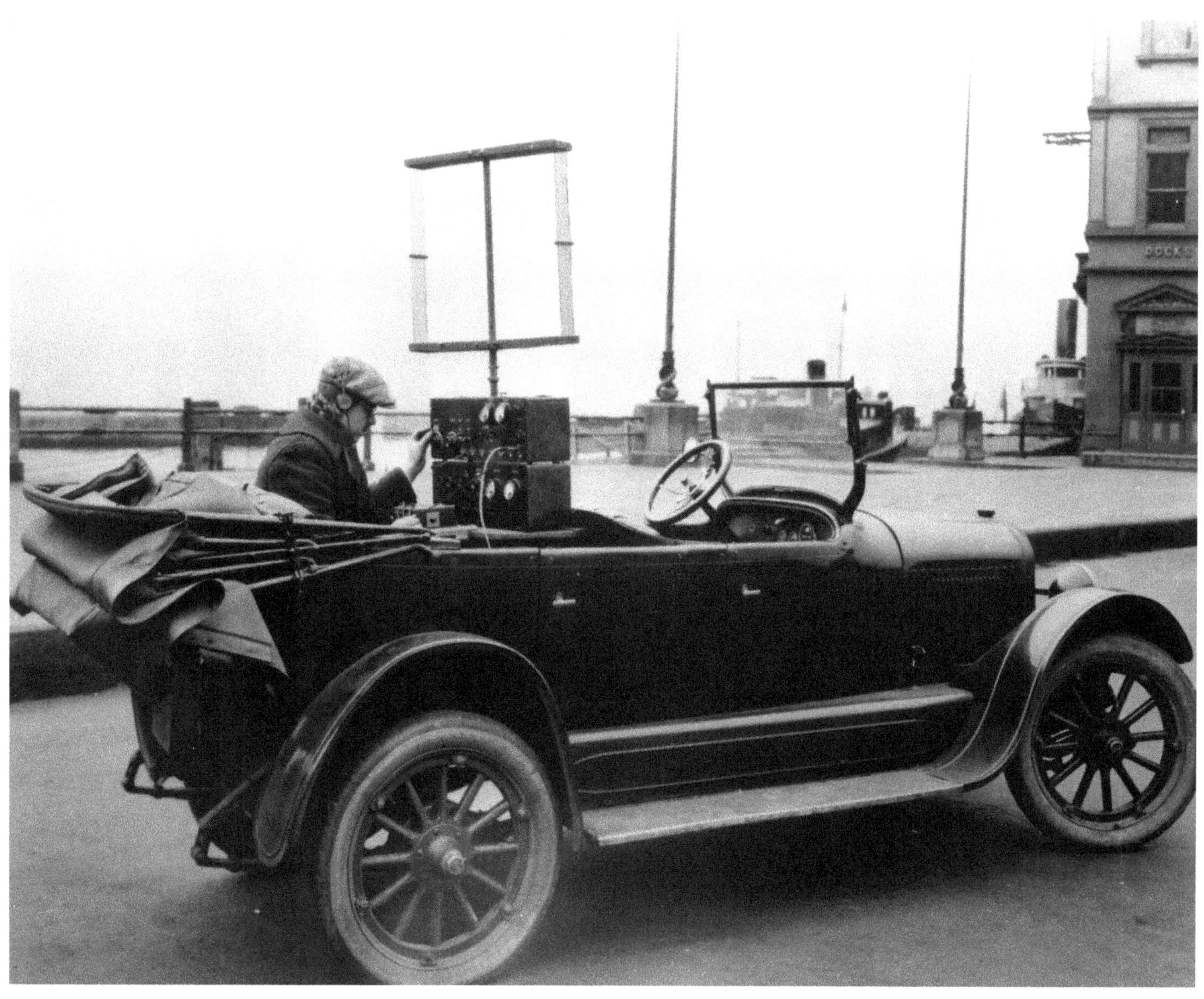

This man is operating a mobile radio telephone from the backseat of a convertible in 1924, probably near the Mississippi River. Mobile telephone service was in its infancy in the 1920s and only a few individuals and official agencies had access to it.

Early automobiles flank Third Street in Baton Rouge in 1925. Baton Rouge was founded in 1699, when French explorer Sieur d'Iberville, traveling up the Mississippi River, observed a reddish cypress pole draped with bloody animals and fish. The pole marked the boundary between the tribal hunting grounds of the Houma and Bayou Goula. The explorer called the pole "le bâton rouge," or red stick.

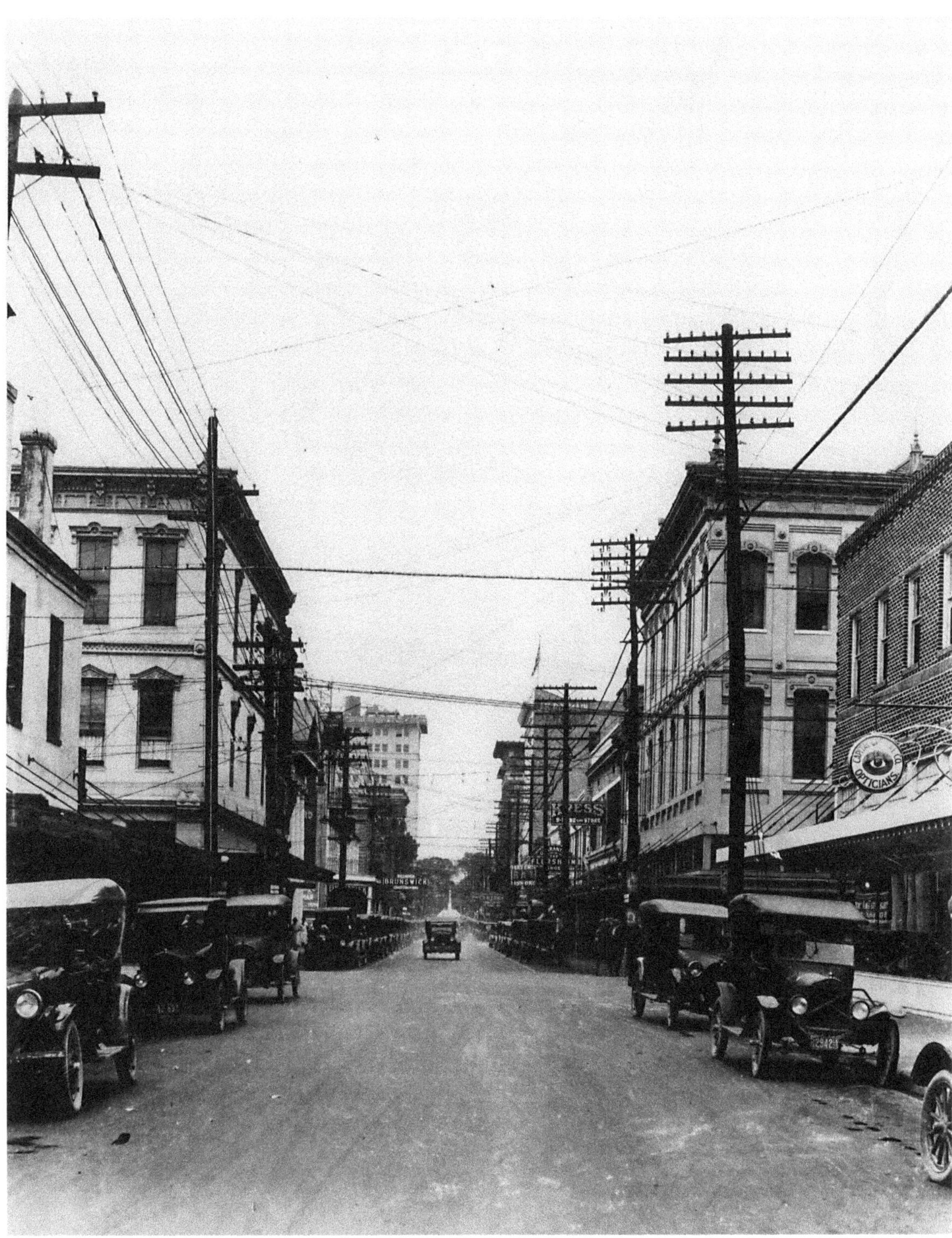

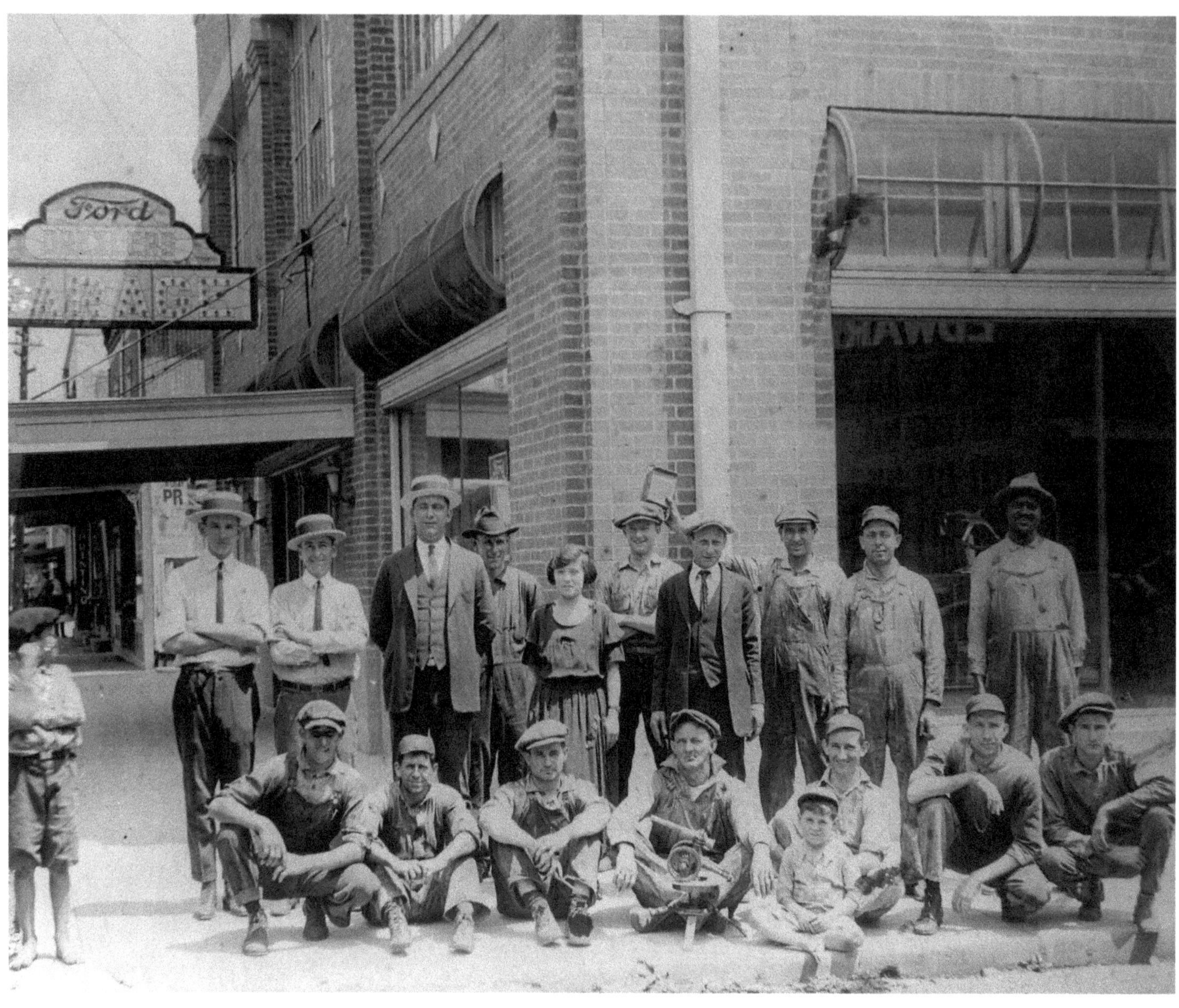

Employees of Drexler's Ford dealership in Thibodaux pose in front of their building. Thanks to Henry Ford and his encouragement of assembly line production in his Detroit automobile plants, cars started becoming affordable to the average American by the 1920s. Fords were among the most popular cars of that time, a distinction they still enjoy today.

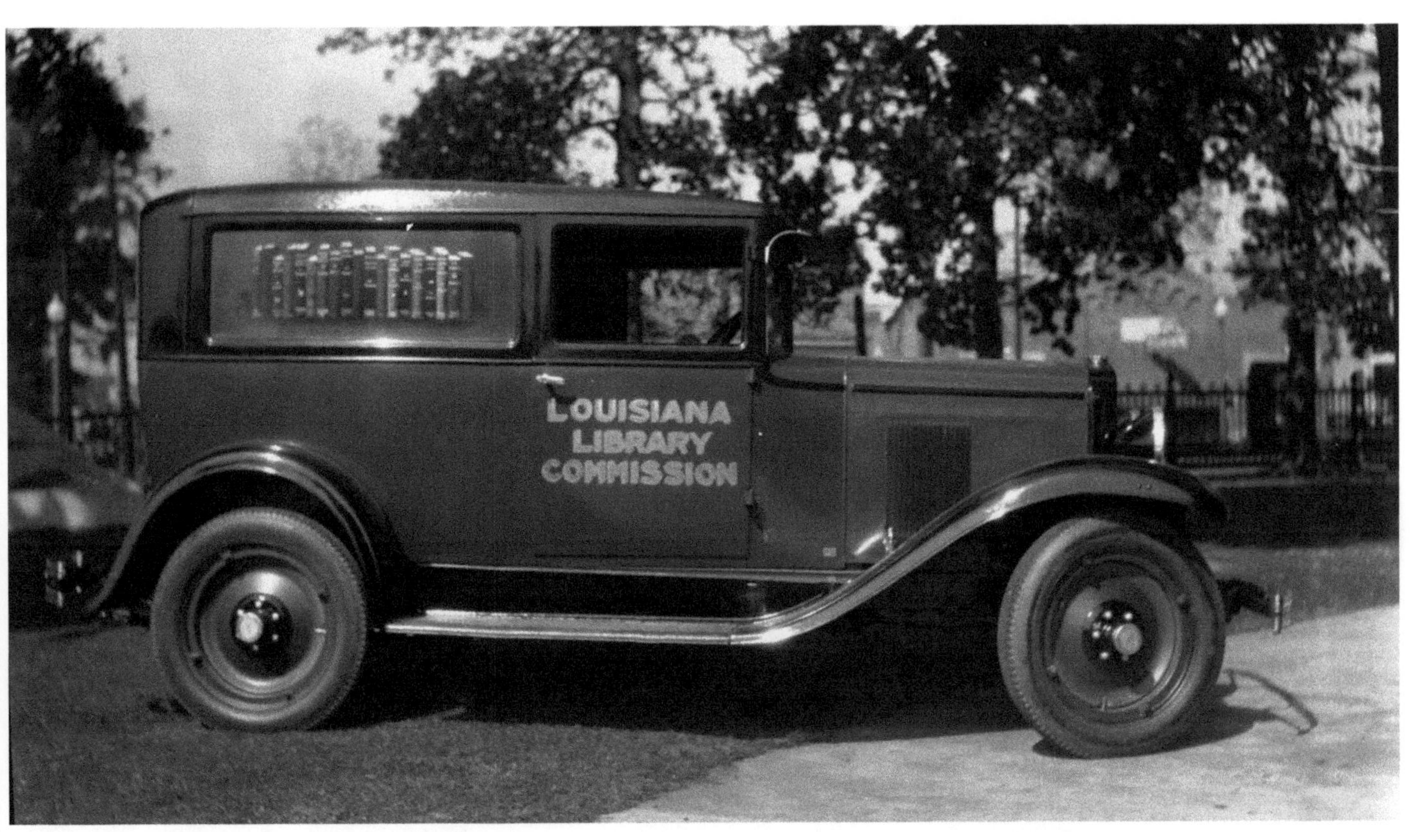

An early Louisiana Library Commission Bookmobile is parked in Concordia Parish around 1927. Many rural areas of the state did not have their own libraries nearby, so the bookmobile concept took root. Concordia Parish lies along the Mississippi River north of Baton Rouge and directly across from Natchez, Mississippi.

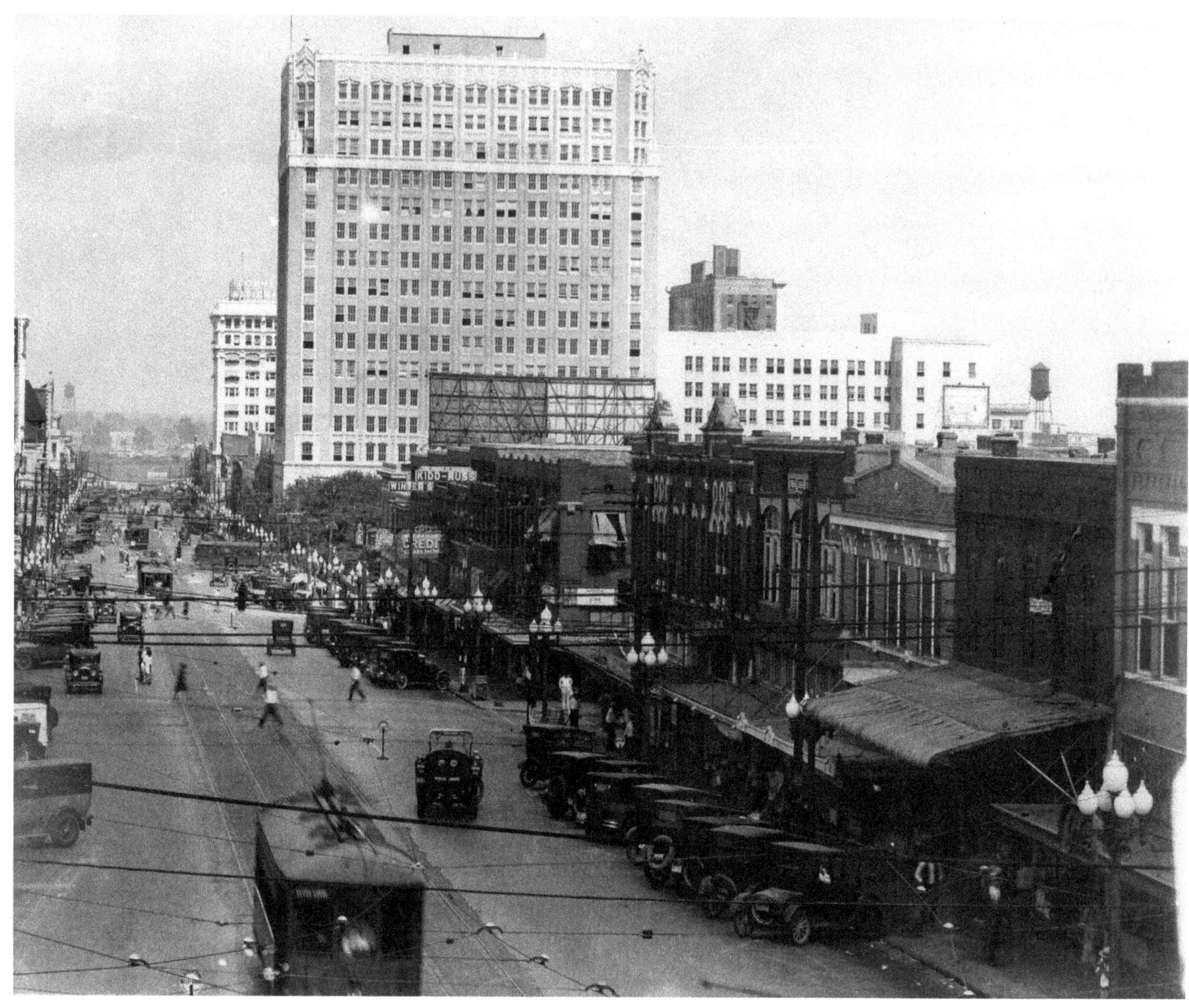

Facing east along busy Texas Street in Shreveport in the mid-1920s. Shreveport was founded in 1836 to serve the newly navigable Red River and the Texas Trail, a land route into the newly independent Republic of Texas.

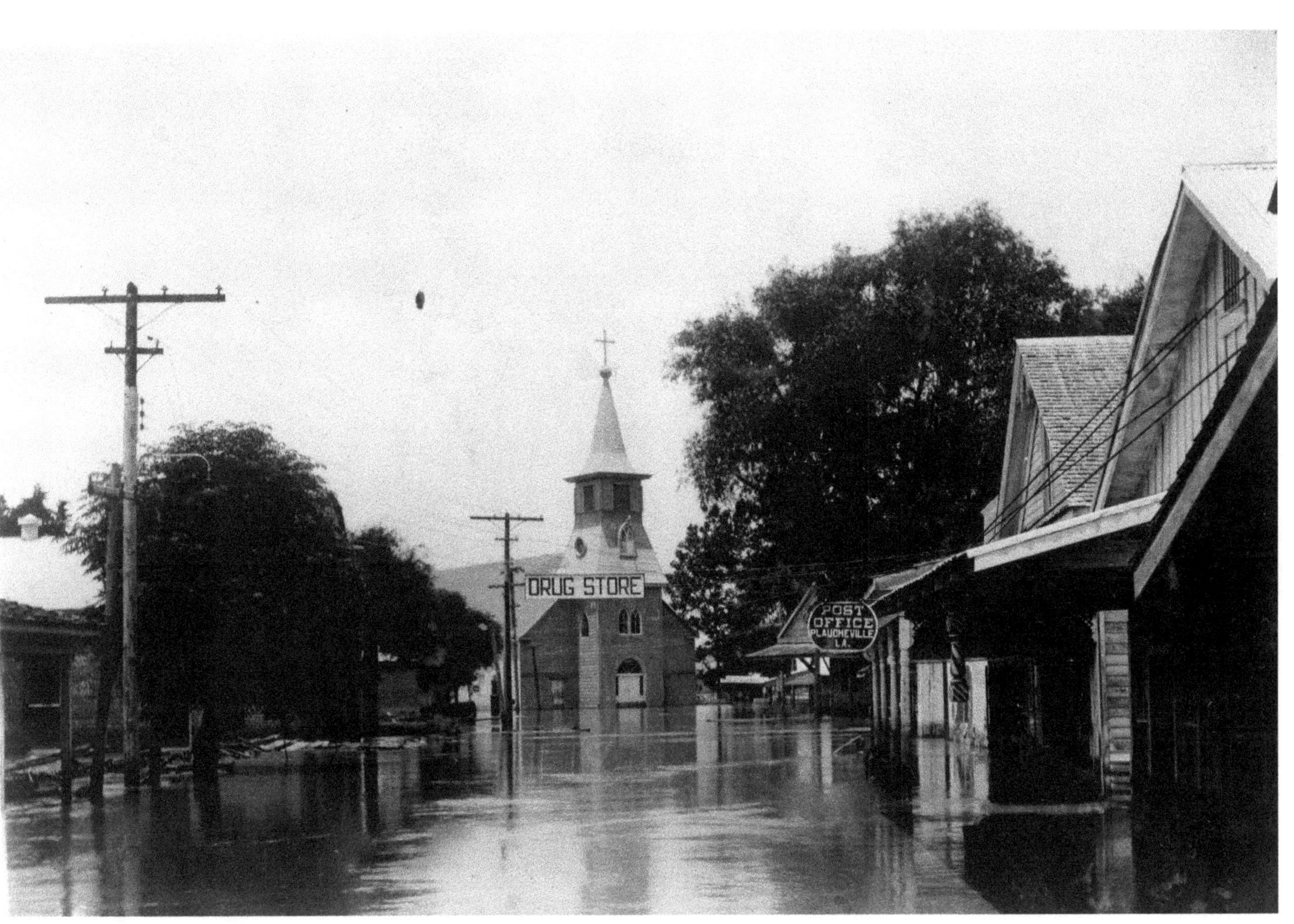

Rising waters flood a street in Plaucheville in Avoyelles Parish in May 1927. The Mississippi River broke out of its levees in 145 places and flooded 27,000 square miles, inundating some places up to 30 feet deep. The flood caused more than $400 million in damages and killed 246 people in seven states. By May 1927, the river below Memphis had reached a width of 60 miles, flooding towns like Plaucheville earlier thought to be safely inland.

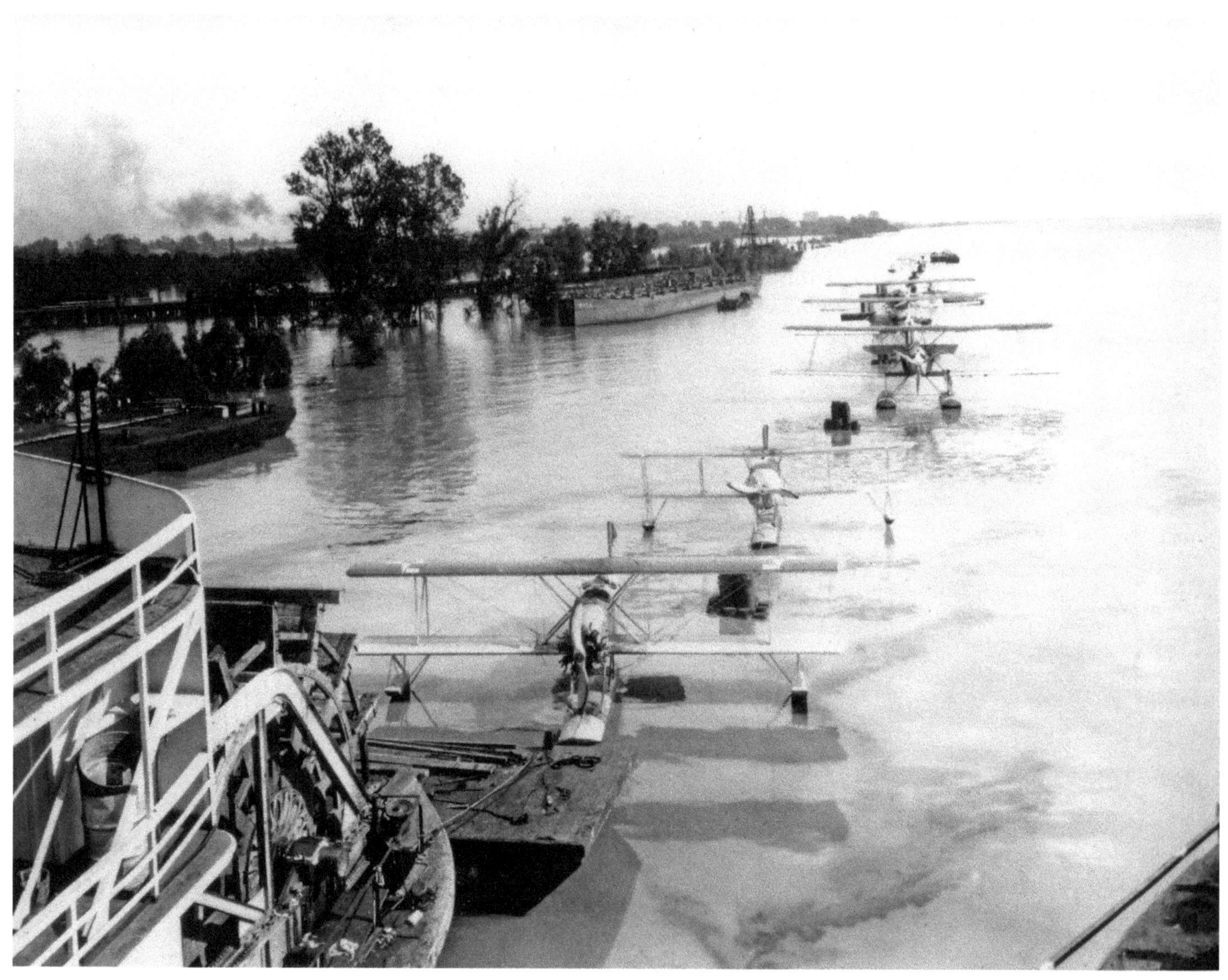

A paddlewheel steamboat heads up a flotilla of seaplanes in the Mississippi River during the flood of May 1927. The aftermath of the flood led to a landmark federal decision to elevate and strengthen the levees along both banks of the lowest-lying sections of the Mississippi and to build two giant spillways to divert high water from the major population centers of Baton Rouge and New Orleans.

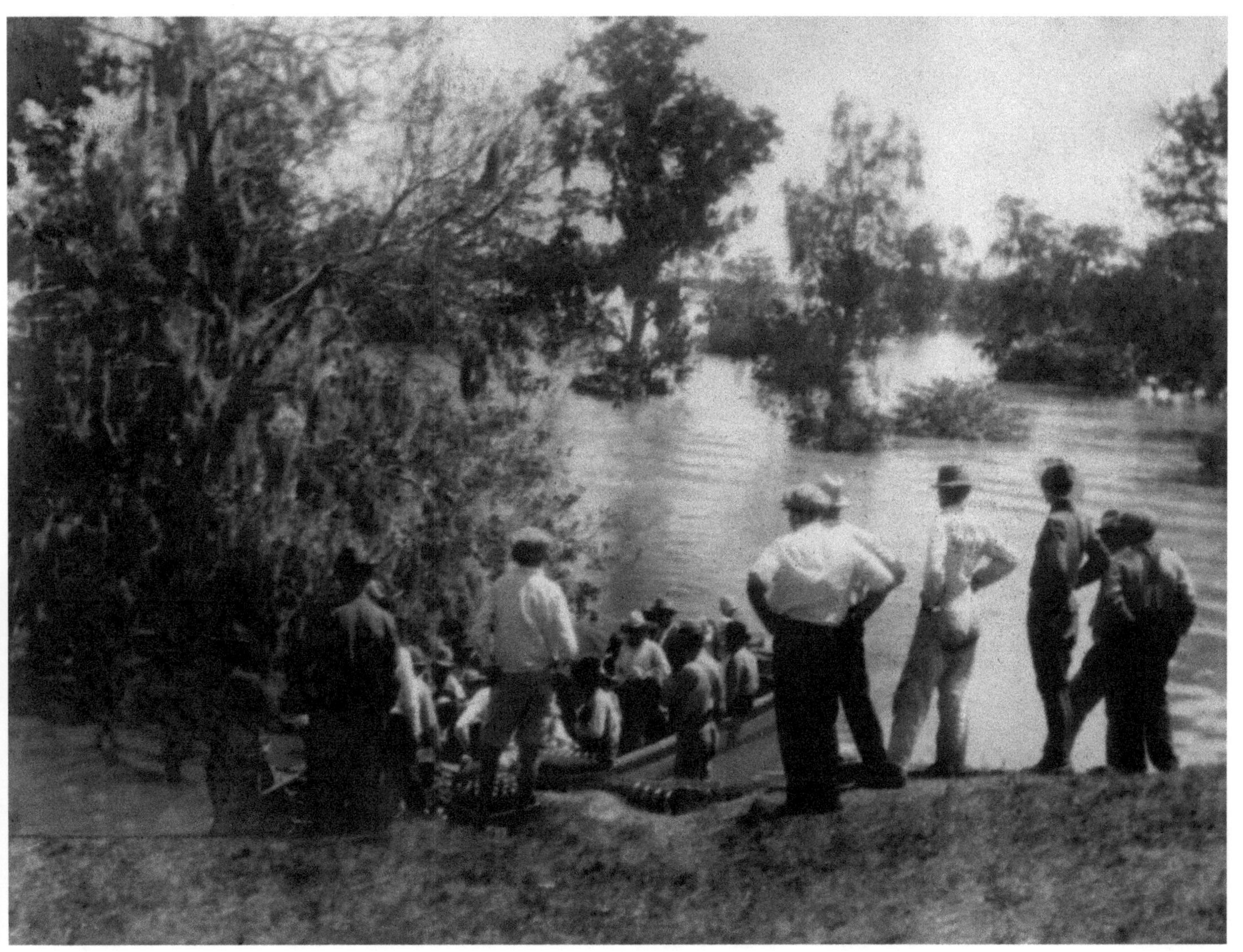

Residents displaced by the May 1927 flood are removed by boat from Junction Landing in this photograph taken on May 20, 1927. It was the most destructive flood in U.S. history, displacing more than 700,000 people including 330,000 African-Americans, who were moved to relief camps on high ground.

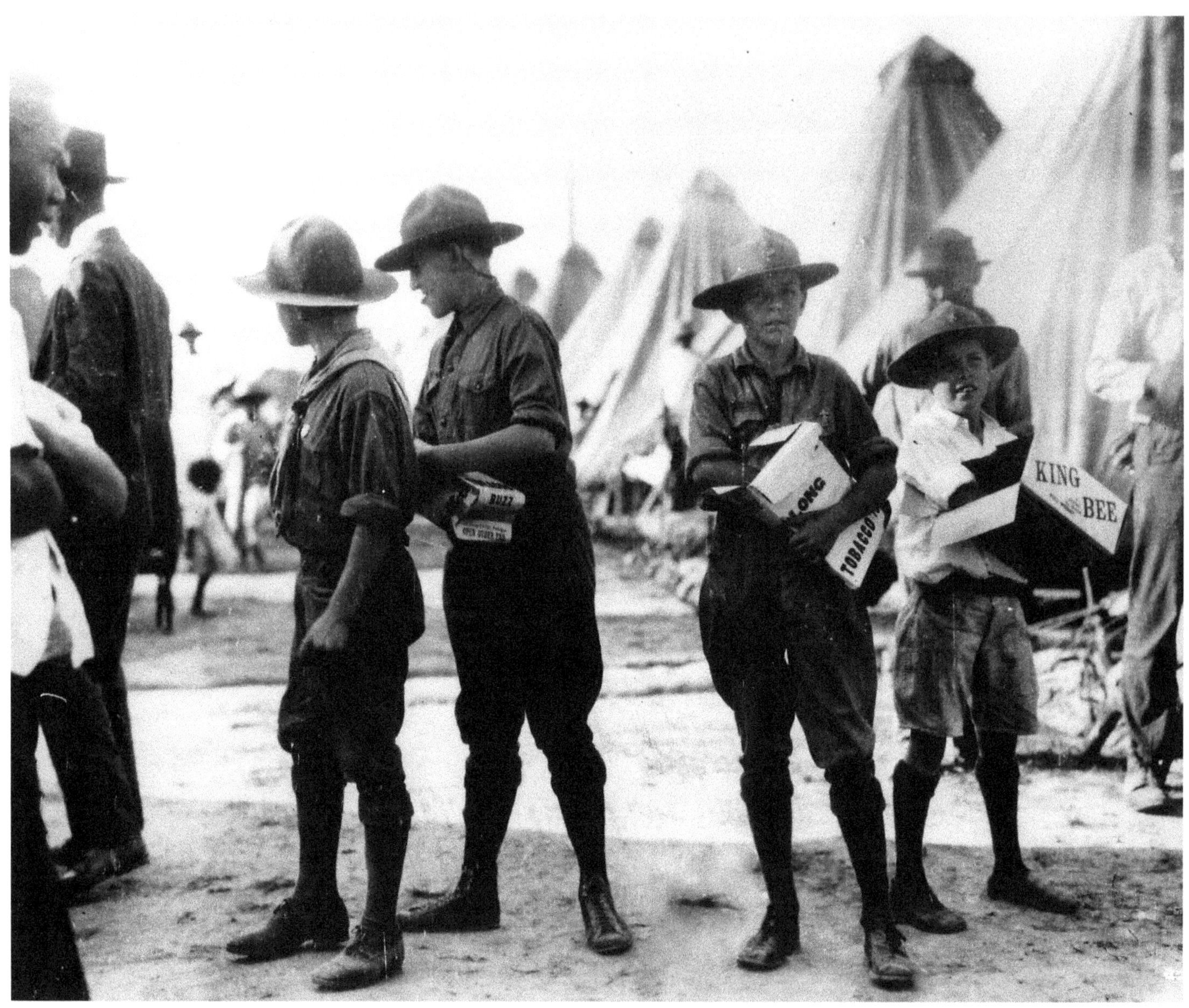

A troop of Boy Scouts distribute tobacco to African-American evacuees in a camp near Baton Rouge in May 1927. The Great Flood of 1927 had a strong sociological impact on American life. Many blacks who had lost their small farms to the flooding and were displaced migrated to northern cities in order to find work to support their families. Over the decades that followed, African-Americans gradually became the majority of the population in many northern cities.

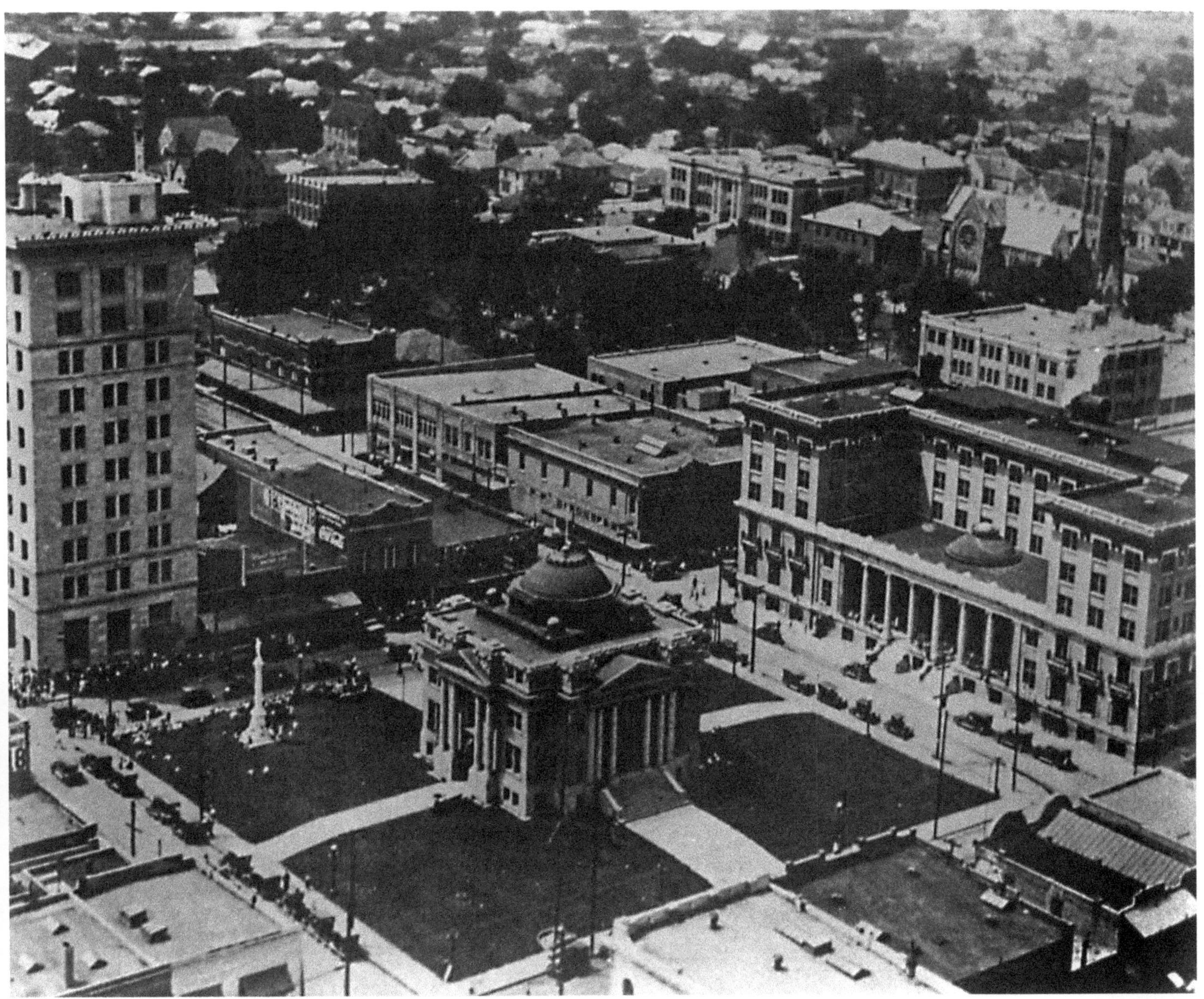

This aerial shot of Alexandria in 1929 shows the domed City Hall in the center and the stately Hotel Bentley to the right. With a population of around 50,000, Alexandria (nicknamed "Alec" by the locals) is the commercial hub of the central Louisiana region. It was named for Alexander Fulton, a Pennsylvania businessman who received a land grant from Spain in 1785 and organized the settlement there, platting the town twenty years later.

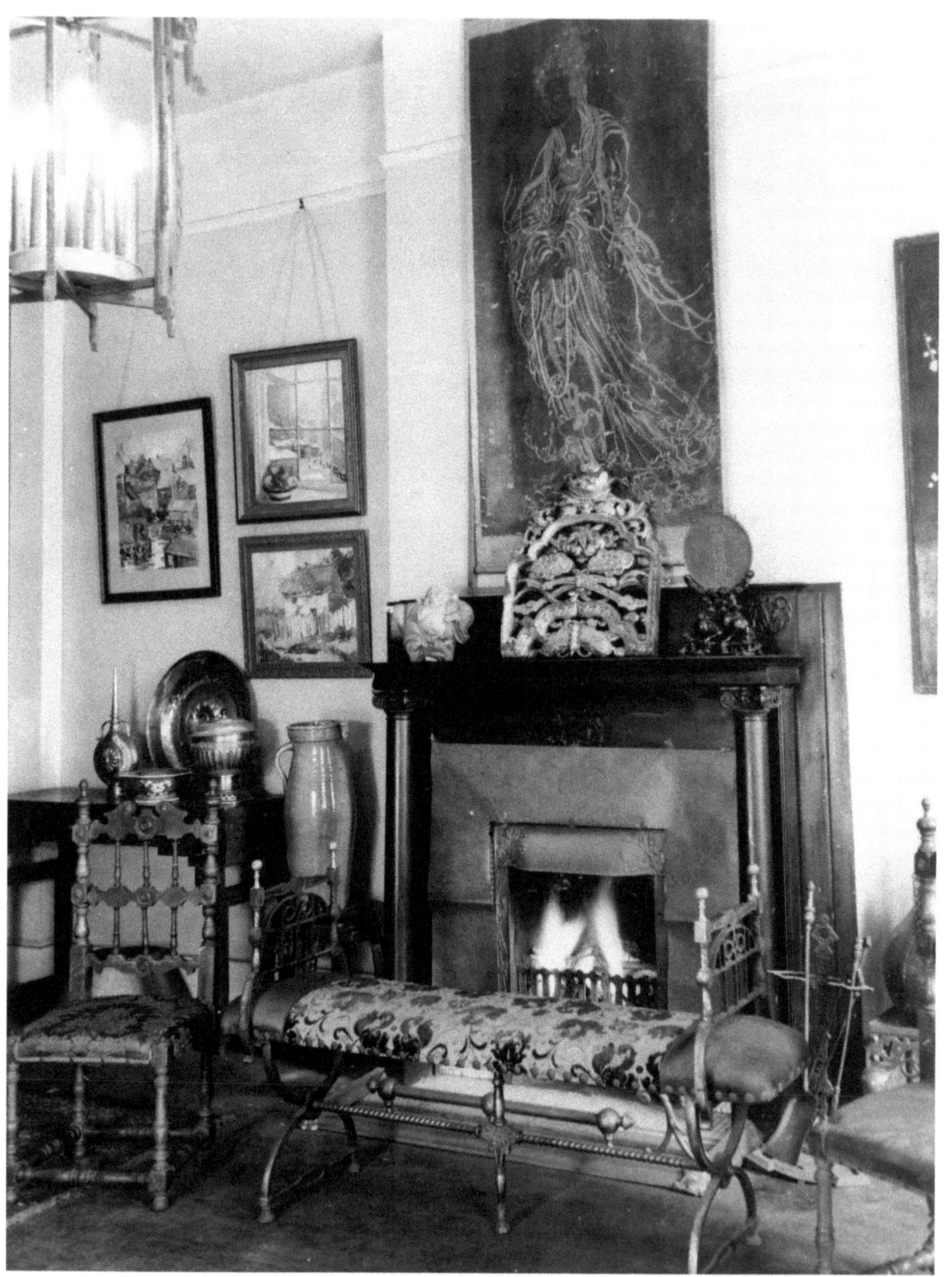

The interior of the Frances Benjamin Johnston home at 1132 Bourbon Street, New Orleans, is seen in this example of her work. Johnston became a prominent early American photographer after receiving her first camera from photography pioneer George Eastman. During her long career she captured many famous people on film and was the official photographer for five presidents—Benjamin Harrison, Grover Cleveland, William McKinley, Theodore Roosevelt, and William Taft. She died in New Orleans in 1952 at the age of 88.

The State Capitol in Baton Rouge is seen lit up at night several months after it opened in 1932. At 450 feet, it is the tallest state capitol in the United States. Baton Rouge replaced New Orleans as the capital of Louisiana in 1849, the same year Zachary Taylor, a Baton Rouge citizen, became President of the United States. Huey P. Long, the governor and later a U.S. senator, commissioned the building and was assassinated there on September 8, 1935.

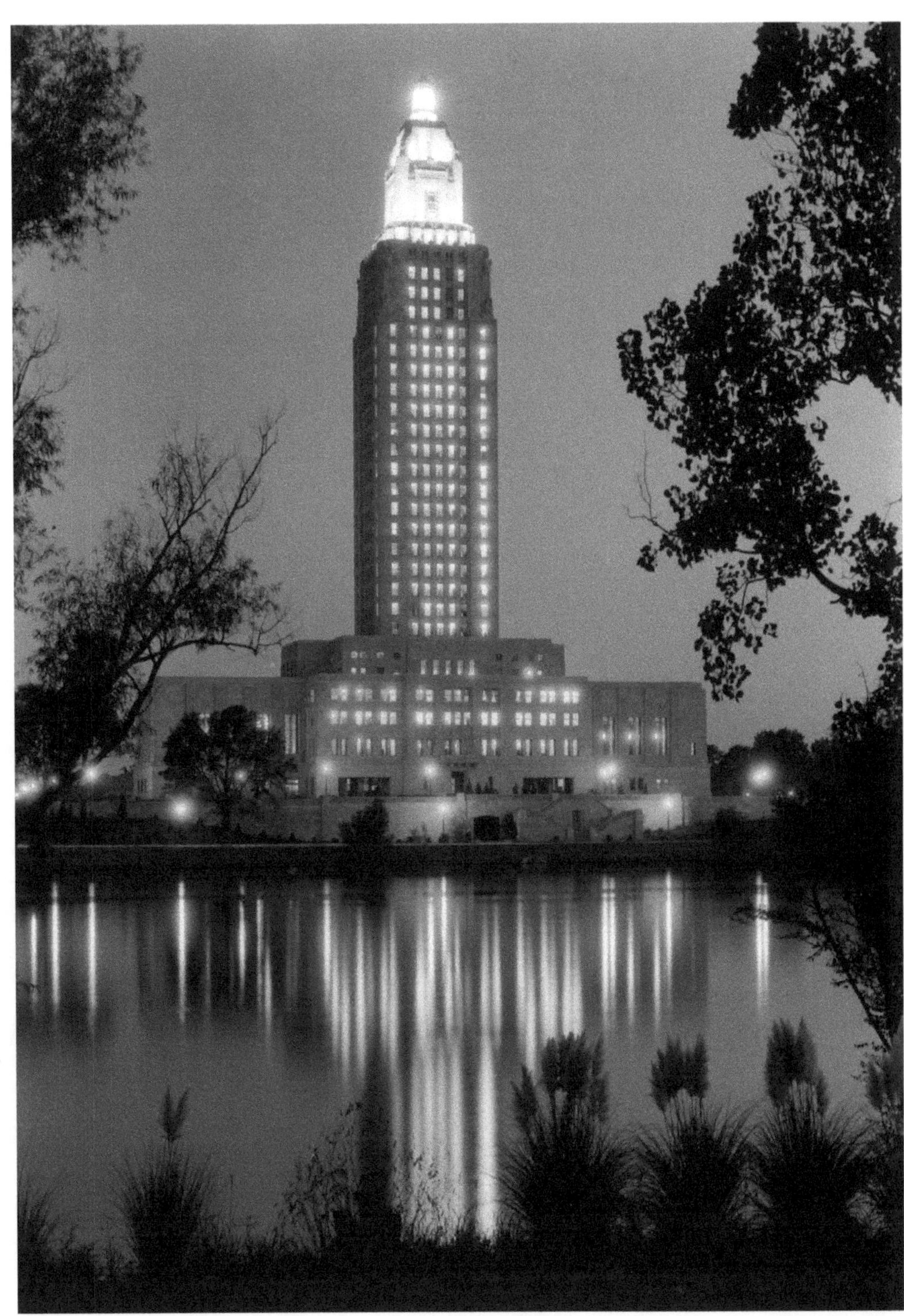

A group of Cajun singers sit on the steps of a building in southwestern Louisiana during the summer of 1934. Cajun singers and songwriters, whose lyrics were mostly in French, helped keep the language and Cajun culture alive through twentieth-century government attempts to force them to assimilate. Today only the most elderly Cajuns still speak French as their primary language, but French is again being taught in schools in the Acadiana parishes.

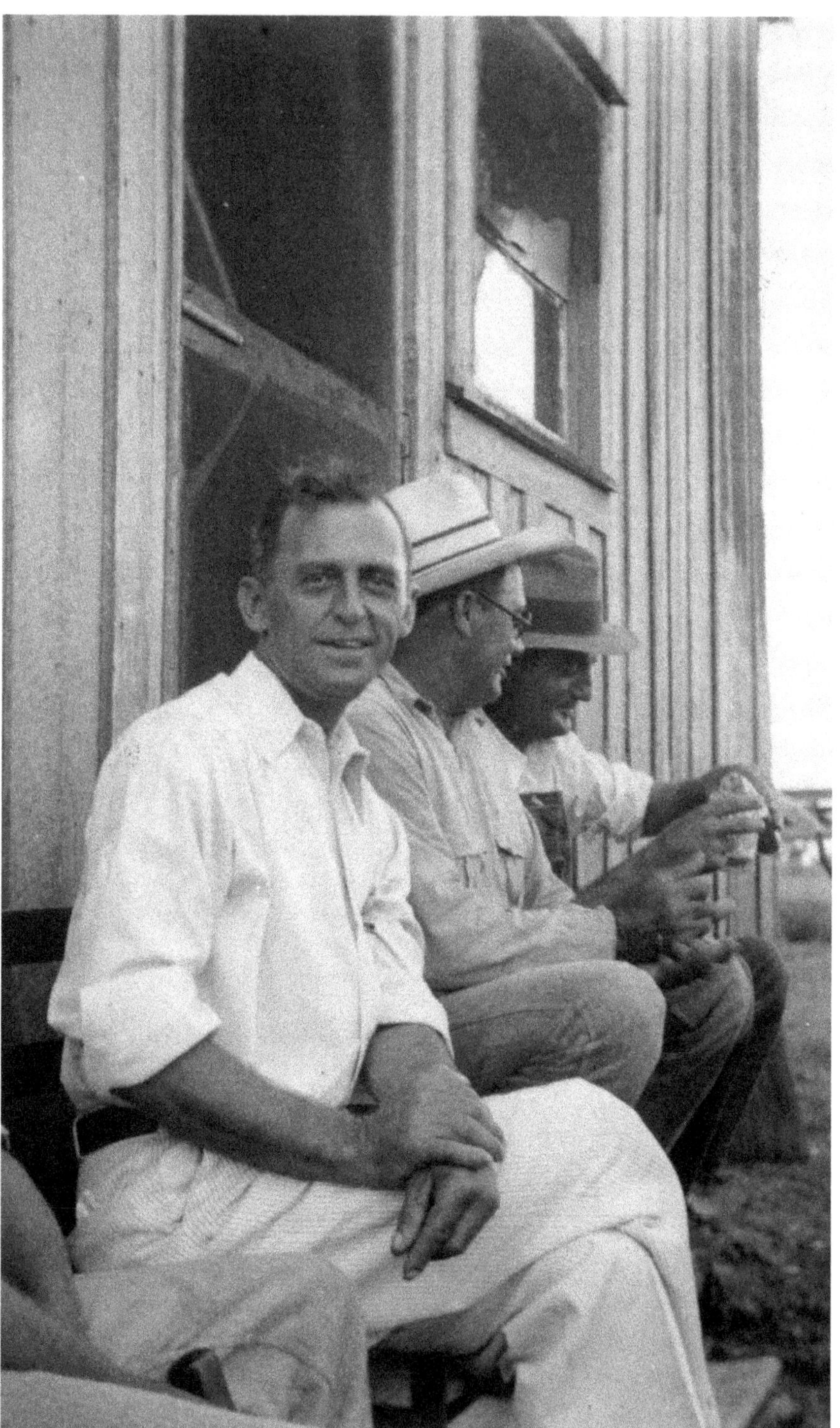

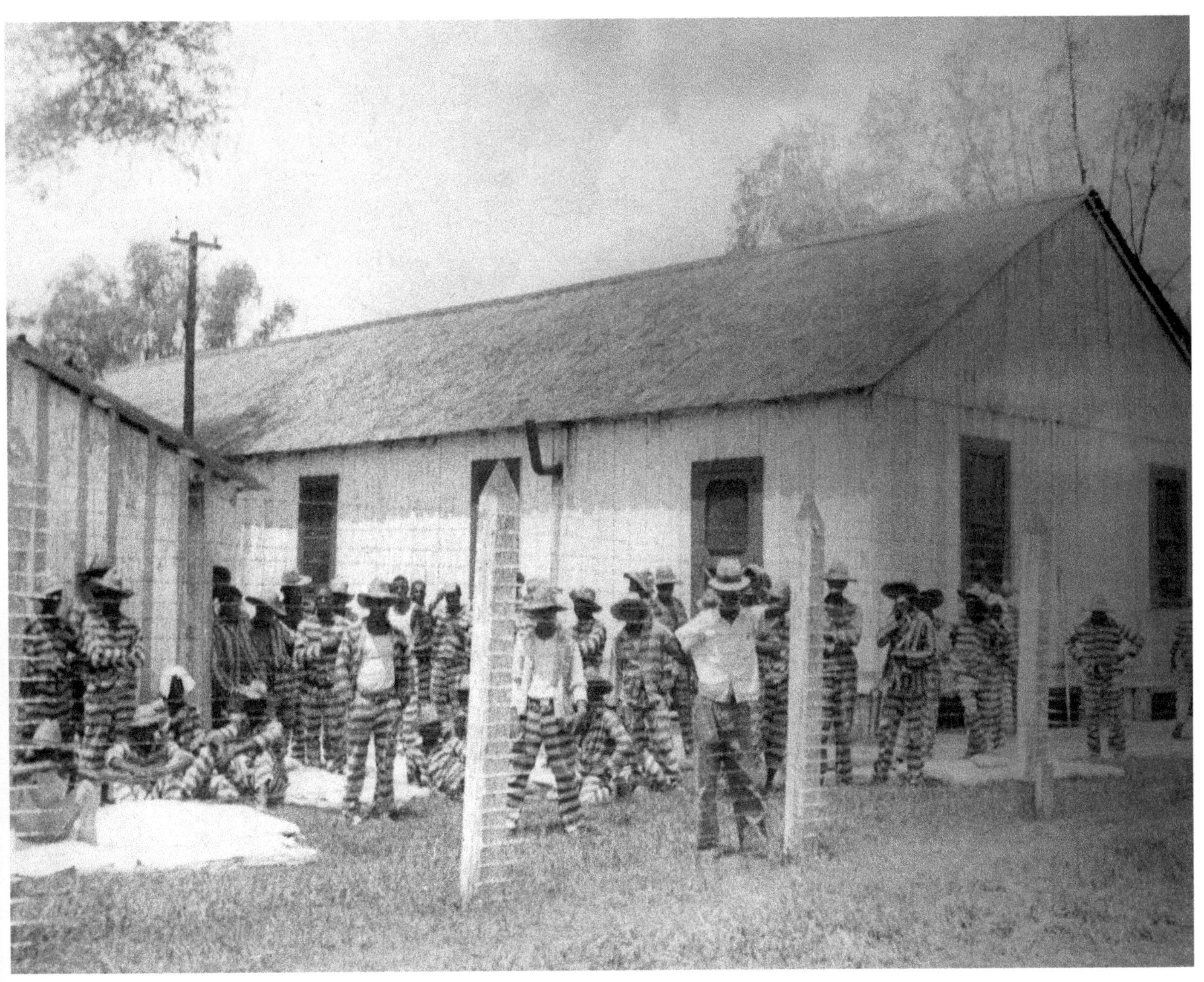

Huddie Ledbetter is visible in the foreground of Prison Compound Number 1 at Angola State Penitentiary in July 1934. Better known as "Lead Belly," he became famous as a blues singer and guitarist after his musical talents were discovered during his years in prison. Born in Mooringsport in 1888, Lead Belly had a volatile temper and spent time behind bars more than once for murder and attempted murder. His most famous songs include "Goodnight Irene" and "Midnight Special."

A prisoner plays a guitar alongside a wagon on the grounds of Angola State Penitentiary in this photograph taken by Alan Lomax in the 1930s. Lomax, a New York record company executive, is credited with discovering the talents of Lead Belly, who was incarcerated at Angola from 1930 to 1934. Prisons like Angola were incubators for musical talent and a number of famous singers "did time" before achieving fame onstage.

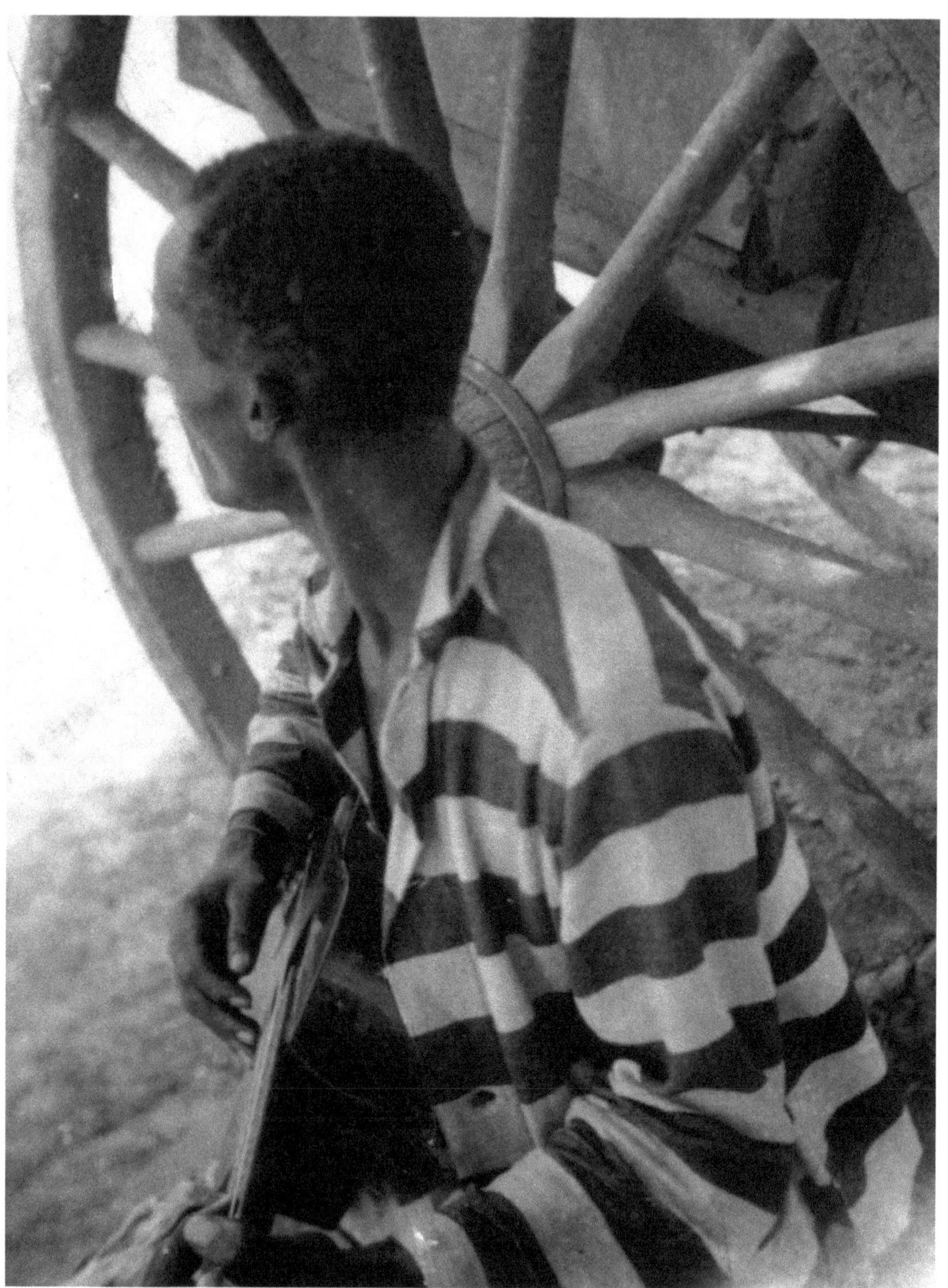

Hard Times, War, and Return to Prosperity (1936–1949)

Despite the rigors of day-to-day living and the harsh economic realities of the Great Depression, life went on as usual in southern Louisiana, as documented in a series of 1938 photographs by Russell Lee. Cajun customs of music, dancing, festivals, and private social events continued to be enjoyed. In the northern regions of the state, Marion Post Wolcott traveled around with her camera, documenting the daily lives of African-American rural dwellers.

With the death of Huey P. Long in 1935, his brother Earl took the reins of power in the family, serving three non-consecutive terms as governor and dominating politics in the state for nearly three decades. Huey Long's son Russell was elected to the U.S. Senate in 1948 and became a powerful figure there for the next 39 years. The political clout exercised by the Longs during much of this time brought key projects and dollars to the people and industries of Louisiana.

The annual celebration of Mardi Gras went on in New Orleans, despite a challenging economic climate. Members of the city's Carnival krewes (clubs) still managed to find the money needed to put on their parades. Several new krewes were added to the rolls of parading organizations during this time.

With the clouds of war hanging over and finally descending on Europe in the late 1930s and early 1940s, Louisiana began gearing up for what would eventually become America's entry into the conflict. Military bases that had been dormant since the end of World War I were reactivated. Some of the largest training exercises in the nation took place over a large region in western Louisiana. When war finally came, bases like Camp Claiborne and Camp Beauregard became important hubs of military activity and training. Hundreds of thousands of soldiers stationed in the state were shipped to the European and Pacific theaters for service in the massive conflict.

Suspended during the war years, Mardi Gras returned immediately afterward, and large industries that had grown during the war, such as oil refining, continued to prosper into the peaceful postwar era. The state's industrial base continued to expand, attracting workers and new residents from all over the nation. By midcentury, the state's per capita income was among the nation's highest, and New Orleans' importance as a major world port remained unchallenged.

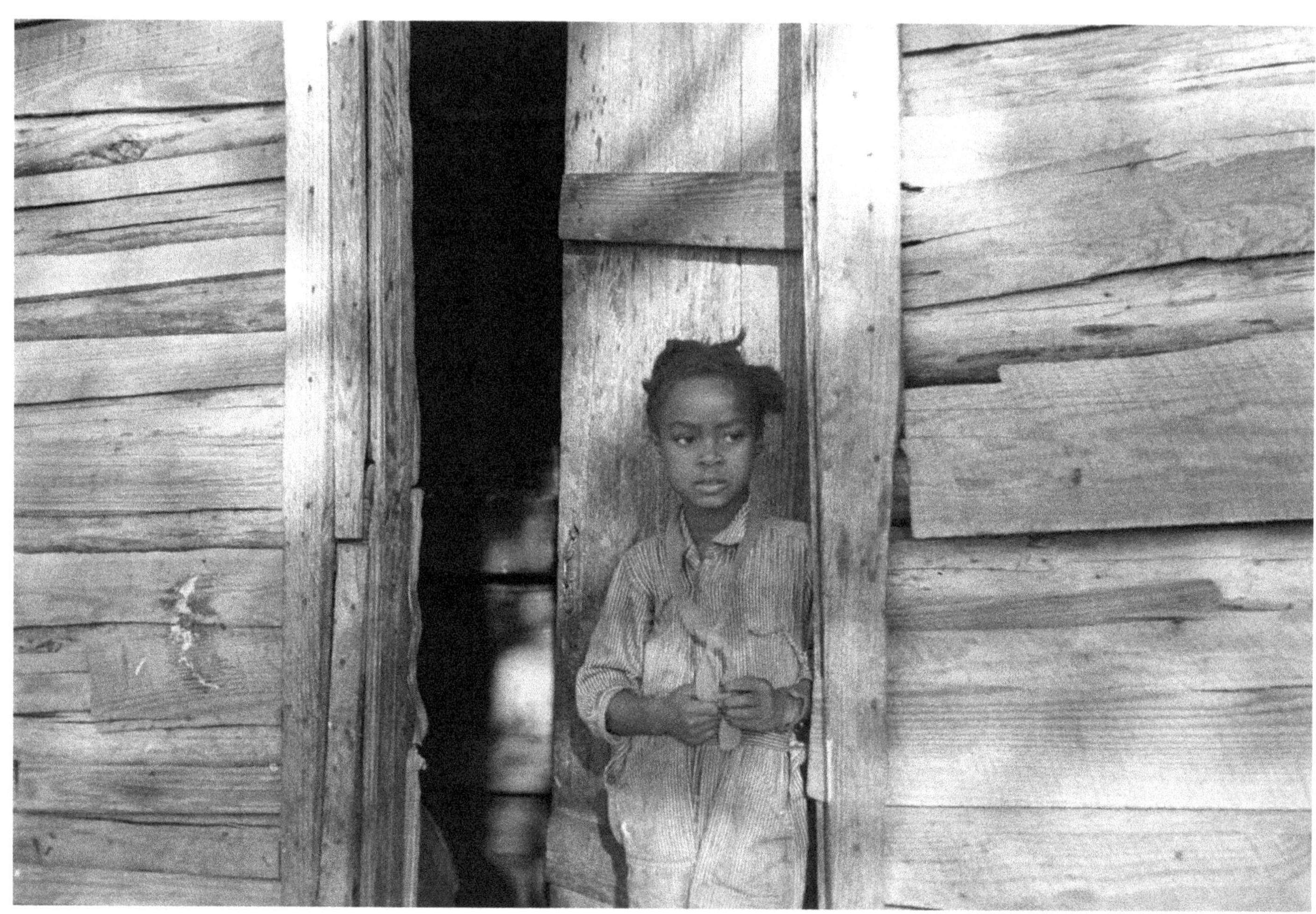

The child of a strawberry picker stands in the doorway of the family's shack near Hammond in this image by Ben Shahn. A celebrated painter, illustrator, photographer, and teacher, Shahn (1898–1969) was also a social reformer with strong views on human rights. During the Great Depression, Shahn traveled the South, documenting rural poverty with his camera and brushes for the Farm Security Administration and the Resettlement Administration.

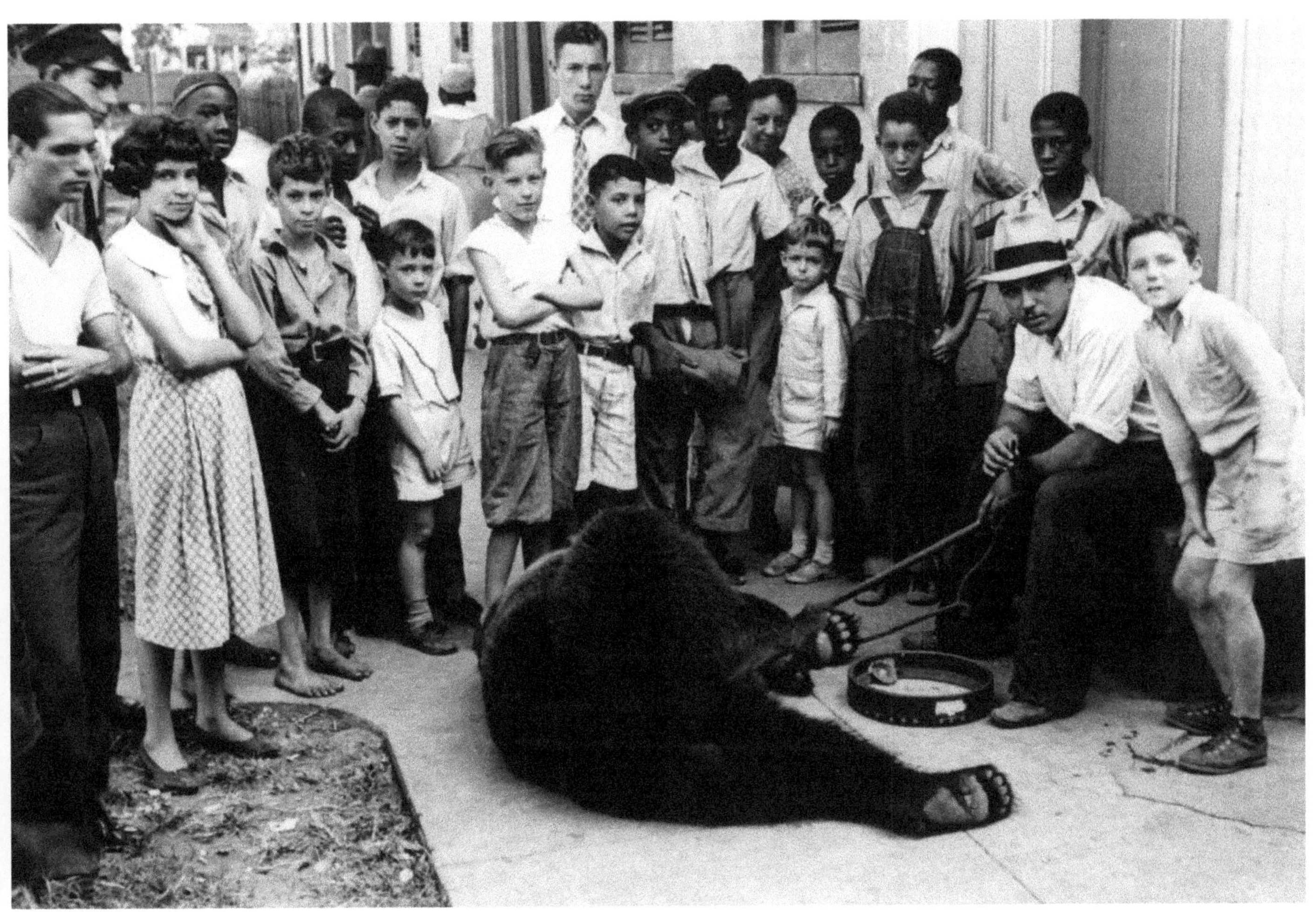

In this image by Ben Shahn, a group of young people gather on a New Orleans street around a man who has what appears to be a bear on a rope leash. During his photographic tour of the South, Shahn traveled with two other well-known photographers, Walker Evans and Dorothea Lange. A lifelong crusader for social justice, Shahn used his photographs as a way of attacking deplorable working conditions, bigotry, and other themes of the kind.

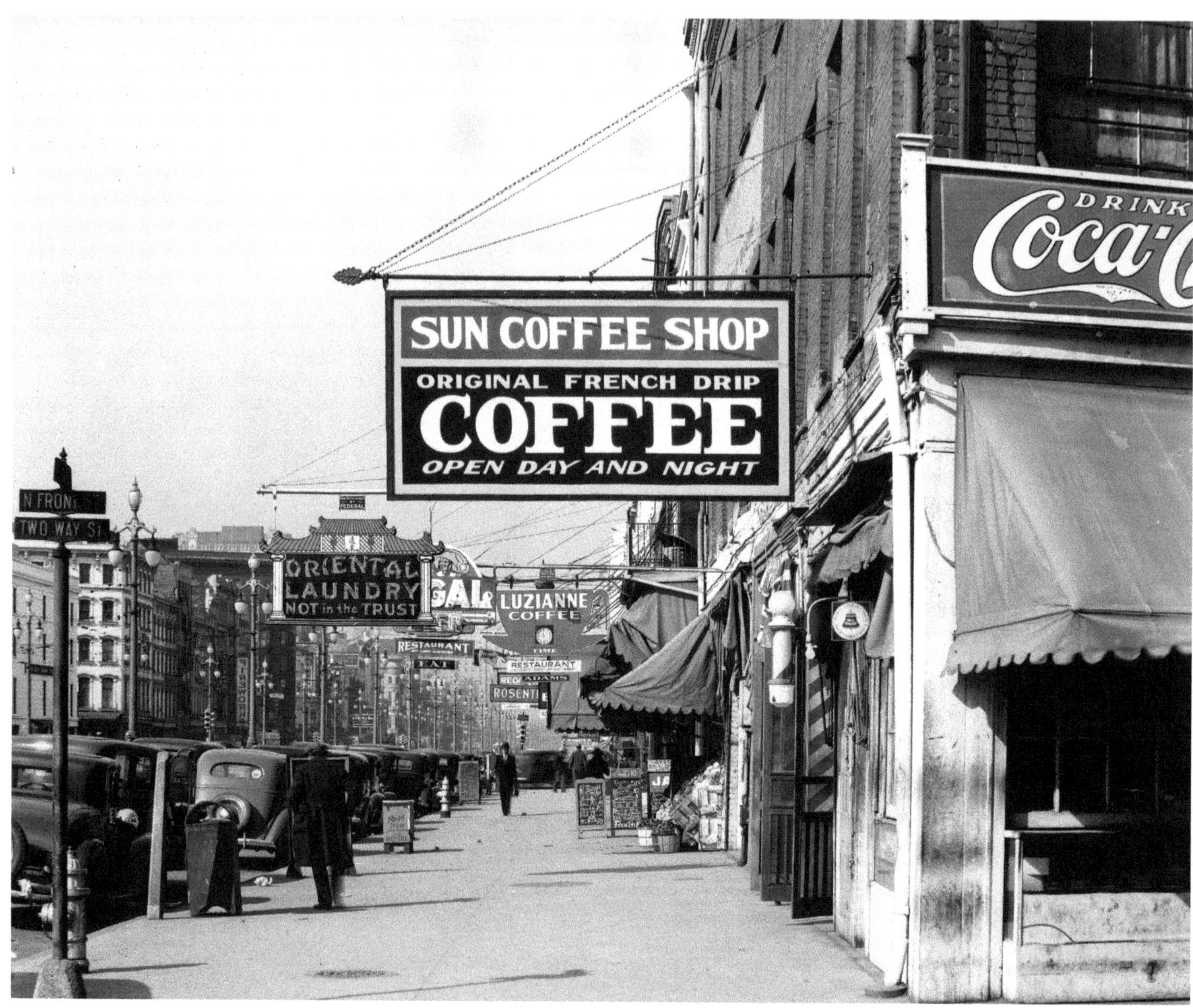

Following Ben Shahn in photographic documentation of the South was Walker Evans (1903–1975). Here in December in the mid-1930s, Evans captures a moment in time at Canal and North Front streets—a time when coffee shops, oriental laundries, barbershops, upscale department stores, and smaller retail shops were the dominant businesses in downtown New Orleans. Today Canal Street consists mostly of hotels, souvenir shops, and discount clothing and footwear shops.

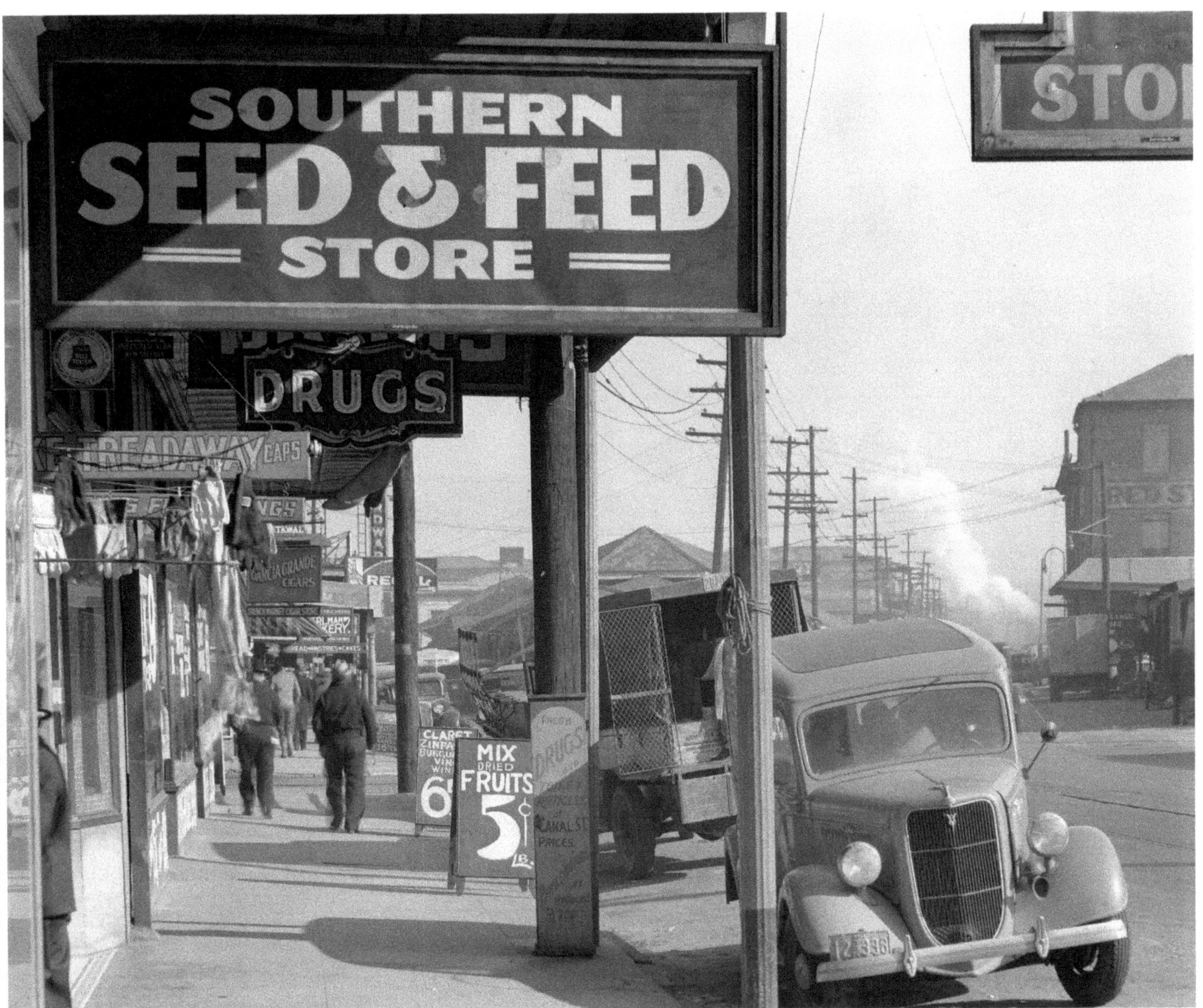

In this Walker Evans image, shops line Decatur Street in New Orleans in the vicinity of the French Market, the rooftops of which are seen at center in the background. Like Shahn, Evans is best known for documenting the conditions of rural poverty in the South, but he also photographed city life.

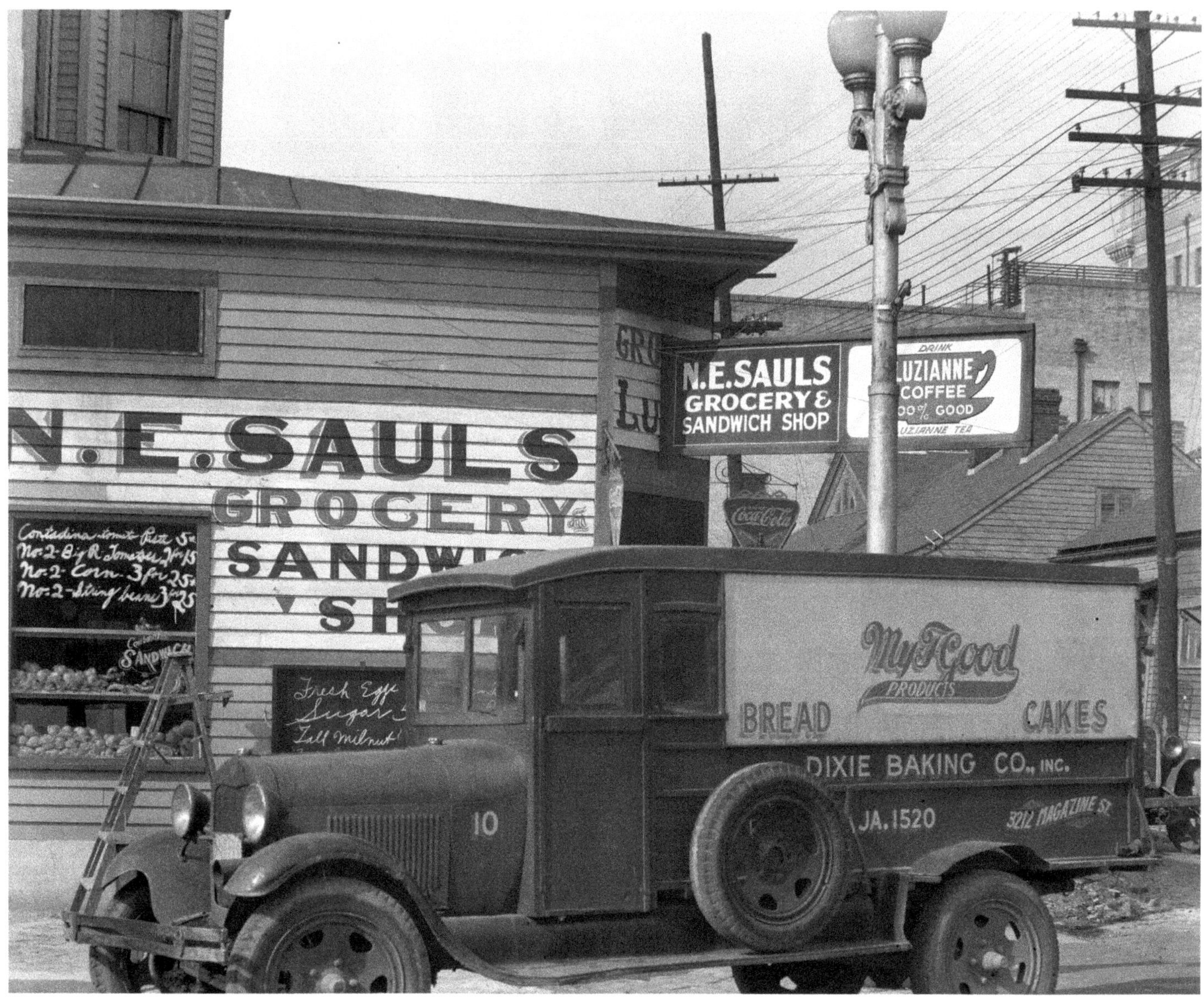

This image of a bakery delivery truck outside a grocery and sandwich shop in downtown New Orleans was part of another series of photographs shot by Walker Evans on his return to the city in August 1936. Small, family-owned-and-operated groceries selling "po' boy" sandwiches remain a popular feature of life in the neighborhoods of New Orleans today. The Luzianne coffee advertised on the grocery store sign is still manufactured and sold.

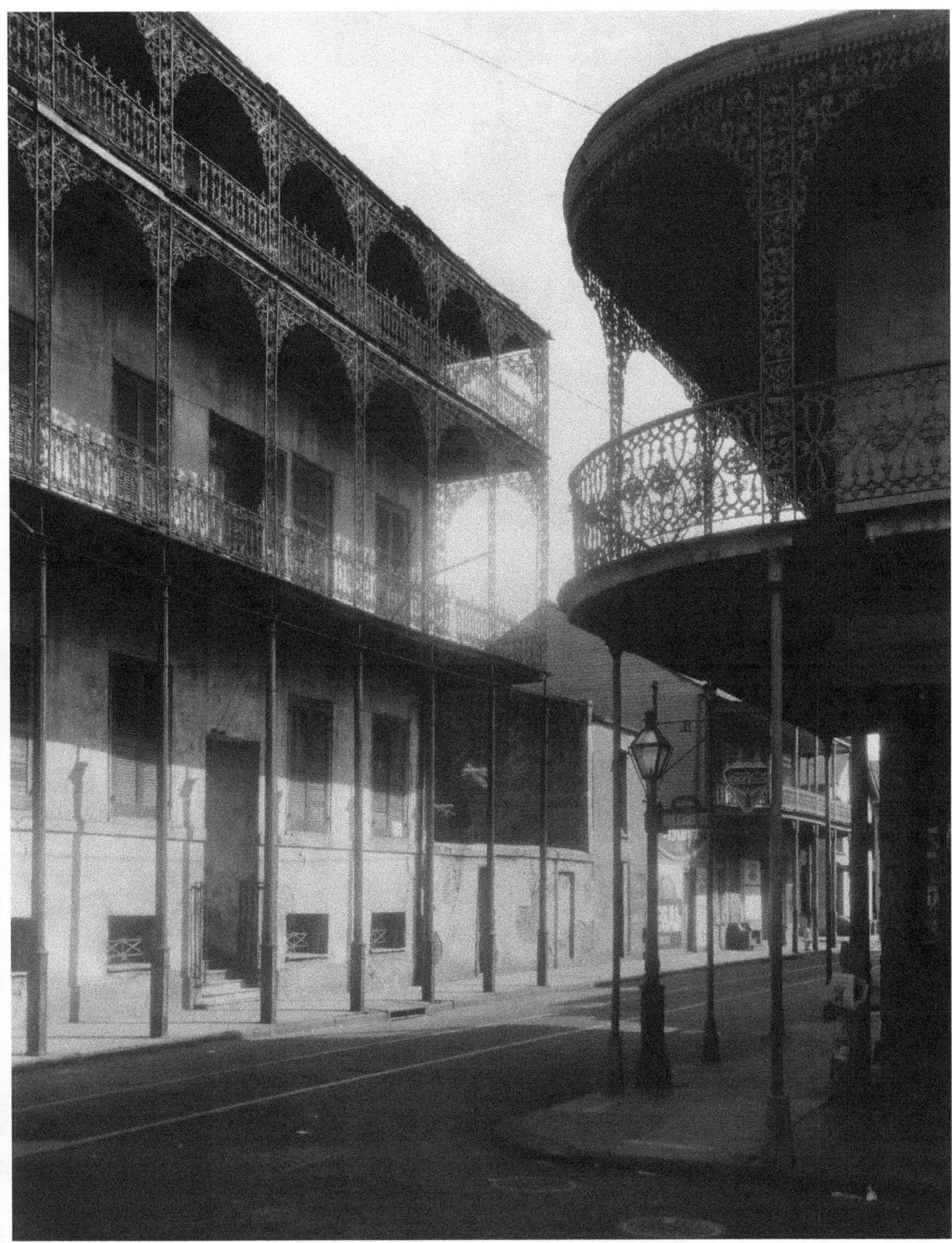

The three-story French Quarter structure at left, photographed by Frances Benjamin Johnston in the late 1930s, harbors an unfortunate history. Built in 1836, it was later leased to an exiled Turkish prince nicknamed "the Sultan," becoming the scene of secretive wild parties and orgies. One night in the 1870s, dozens of guests were brutally hacked to death with sabers, and the Sultan was buried alive in his garden. The house stands today, amid rumors of ghosts.

The La Branche House on Royal Street in the French Quarter was the subject of this image recorded in June 1938. Like many of the structures in the French Quarter, it dates from the first half of the nineteenth century. After New Orleans' capture by the Union during the Civil War, the house served as military headquarters for the occupation forces. Today it is one of the most photographed buildings in the French Quarter and is rumored to be haunted.

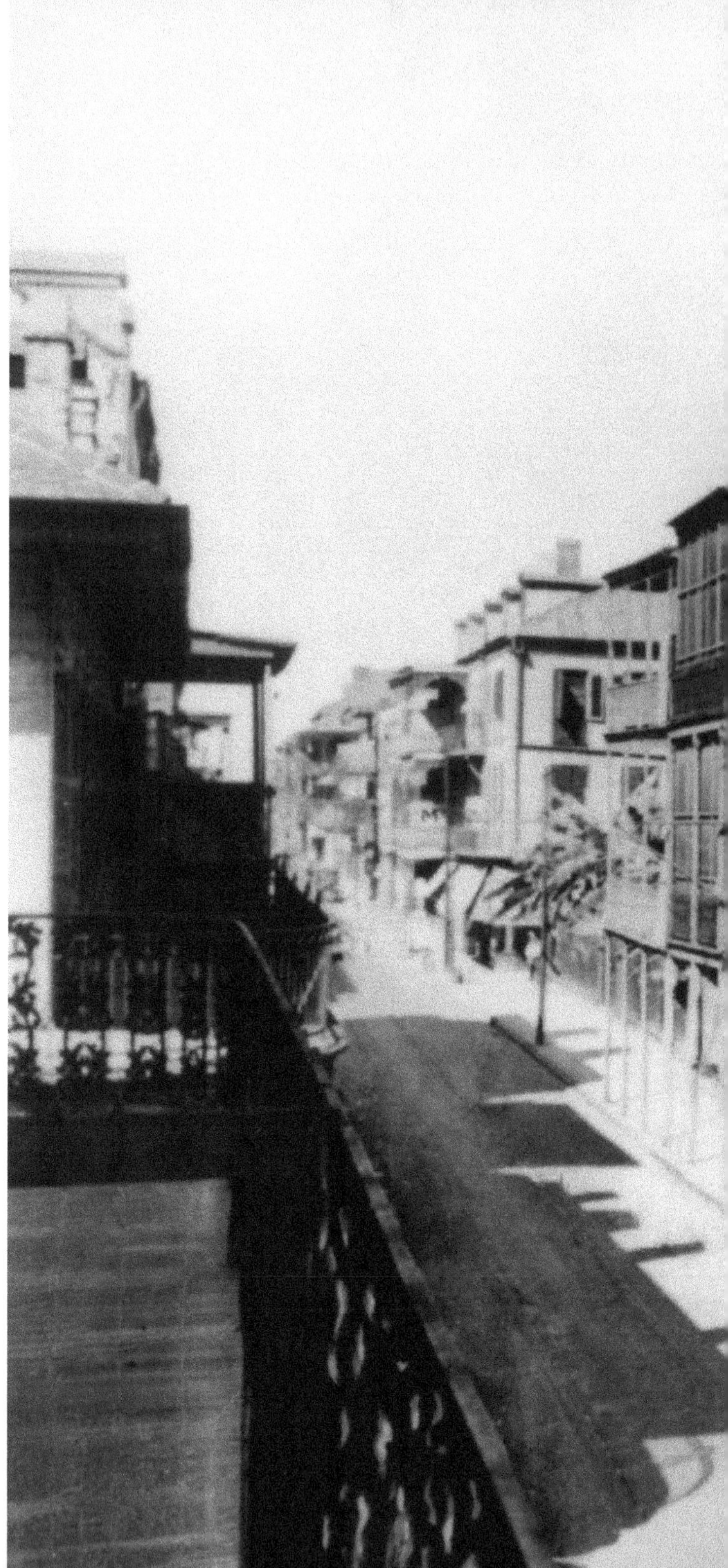

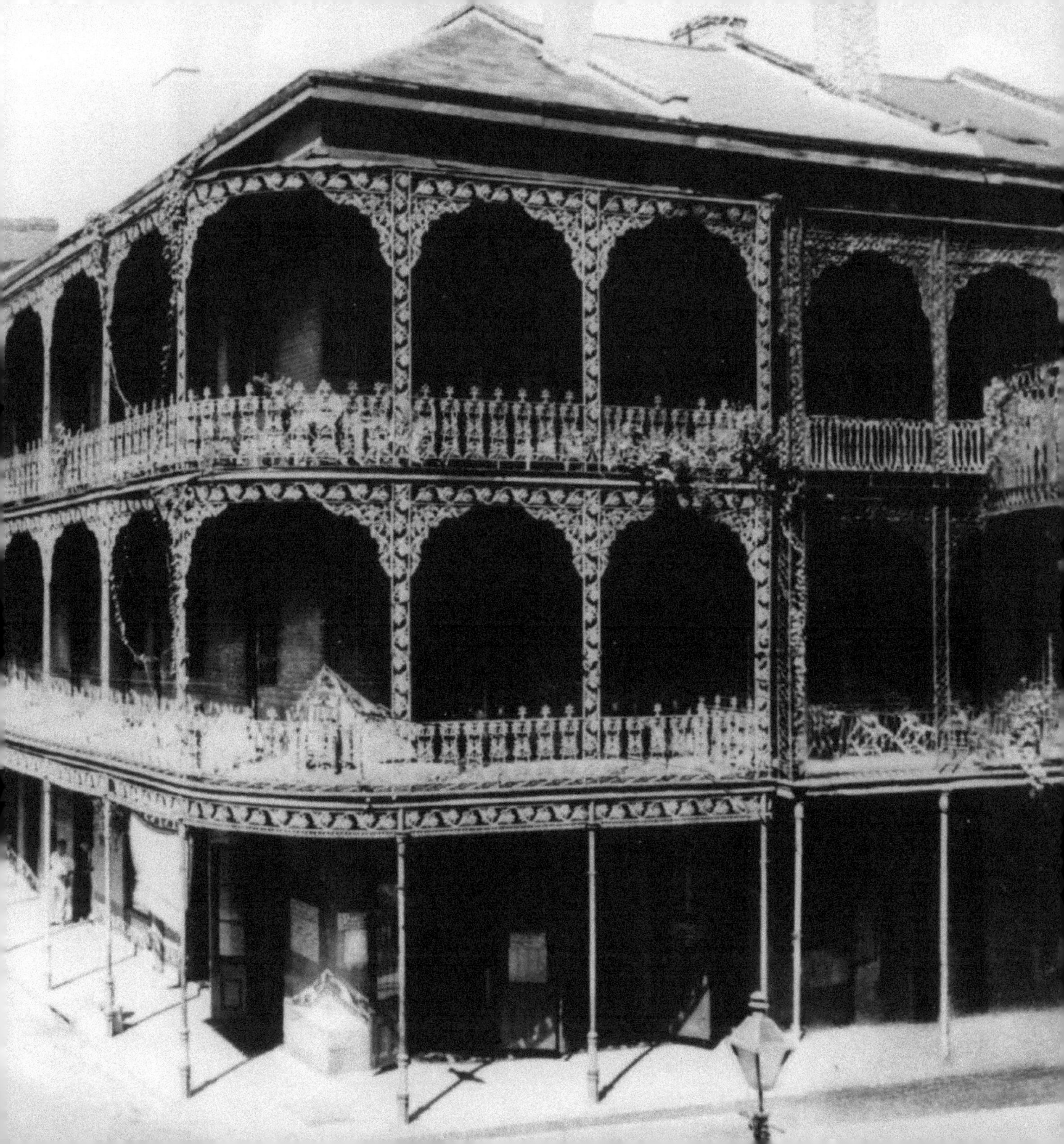

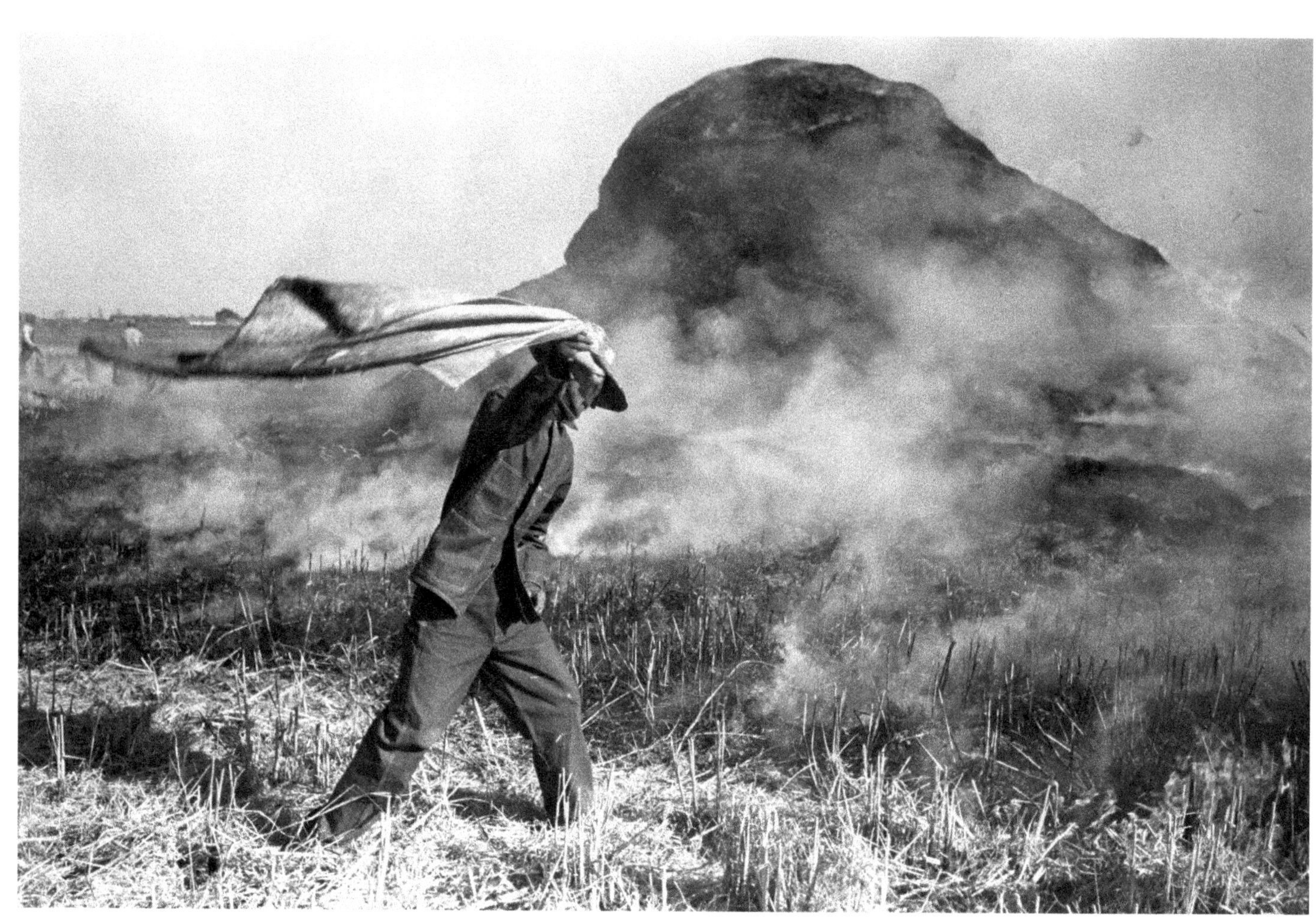

A Louisiana man attempts to put out a rice field fire near Crowley in Acadia Parish by beating it with a heavy cloth. This image and the 19 to follow were shot by noted photographer Russell Lee (1903–1986) between September 1938 and January 1939. Best known for his work with the Farm Security Administration during the Great Depression, Lee shot many iconic images of day-to-day life in the Cajun country of southern Louisiana.

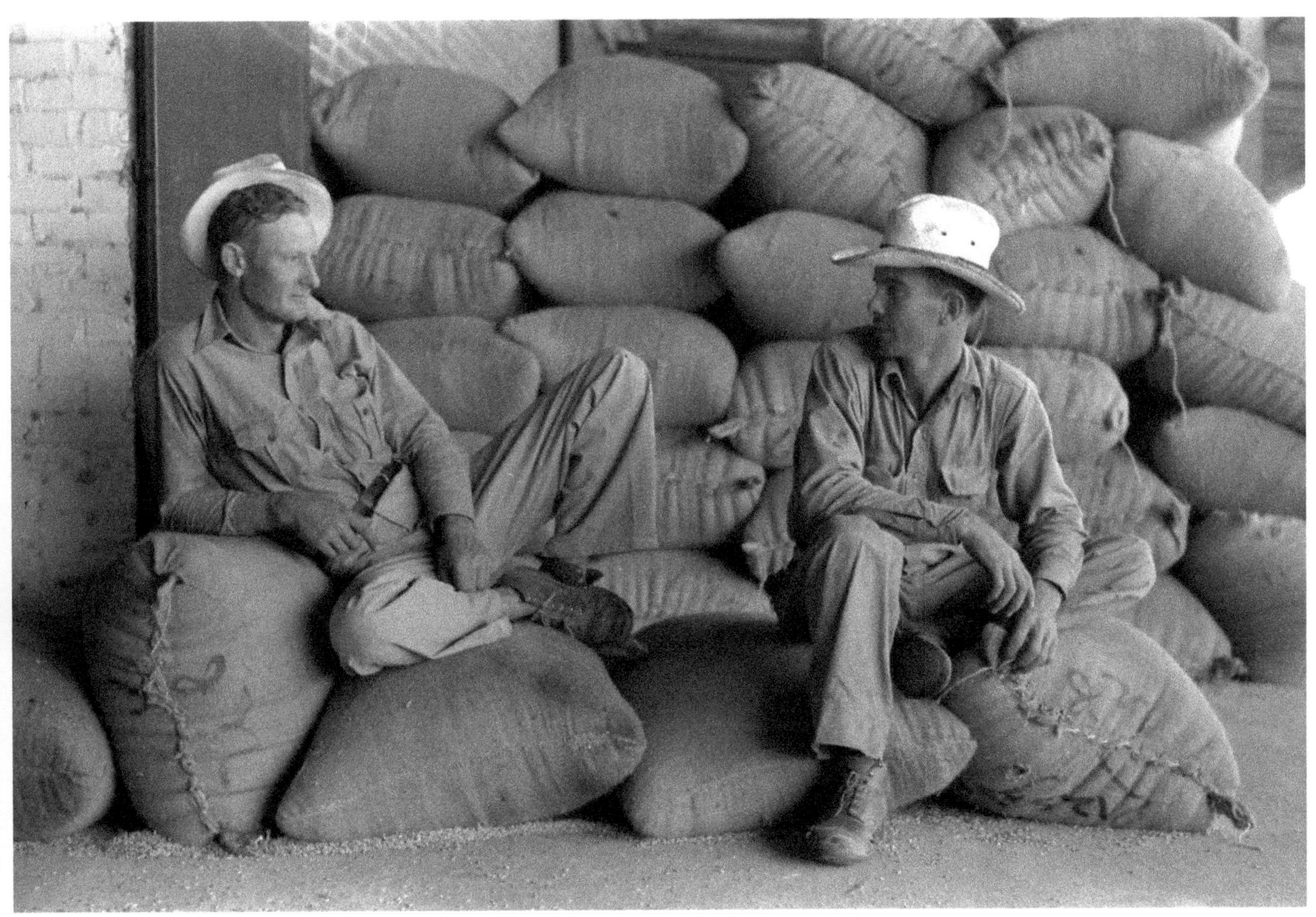

Two farmers take a break on sacks of rice outside a rice mill in Abbeville. The damp, swampy terrain of southern Louisiana around places like Abbeville, Crowley, and others made for ideal growing conditions for the crop, and dozens of mills worked year-round to refine the product.

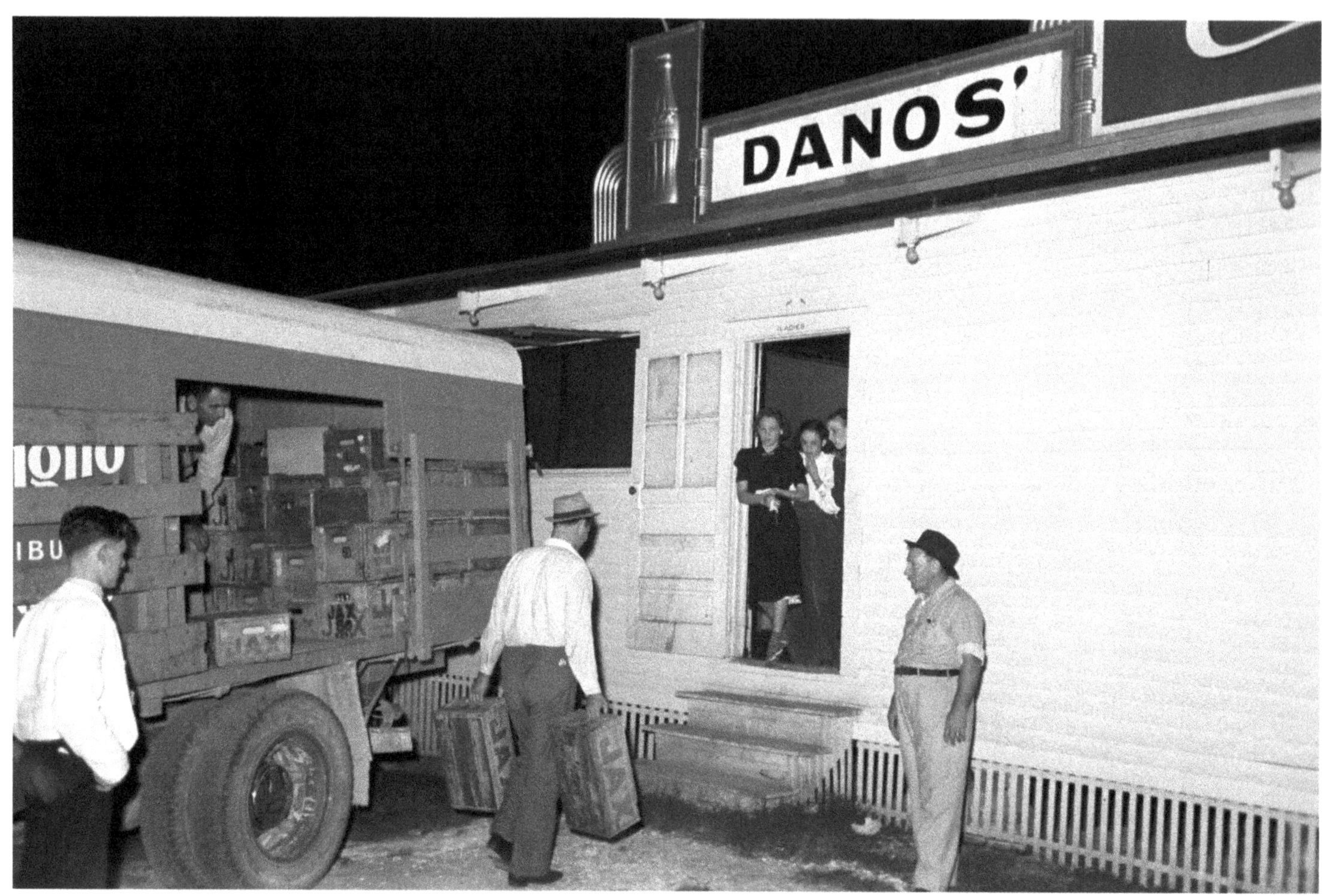

A truck delivers cases of Jax beer to a nightclub in Raceland as a group of young women watch from a doorway. Lying along scenic Bayou Lafourche in Lafourche Parish, about 40 miles west of New Orleans, Raceland is a community of about 5,000 people in the heart of the Cajun country.

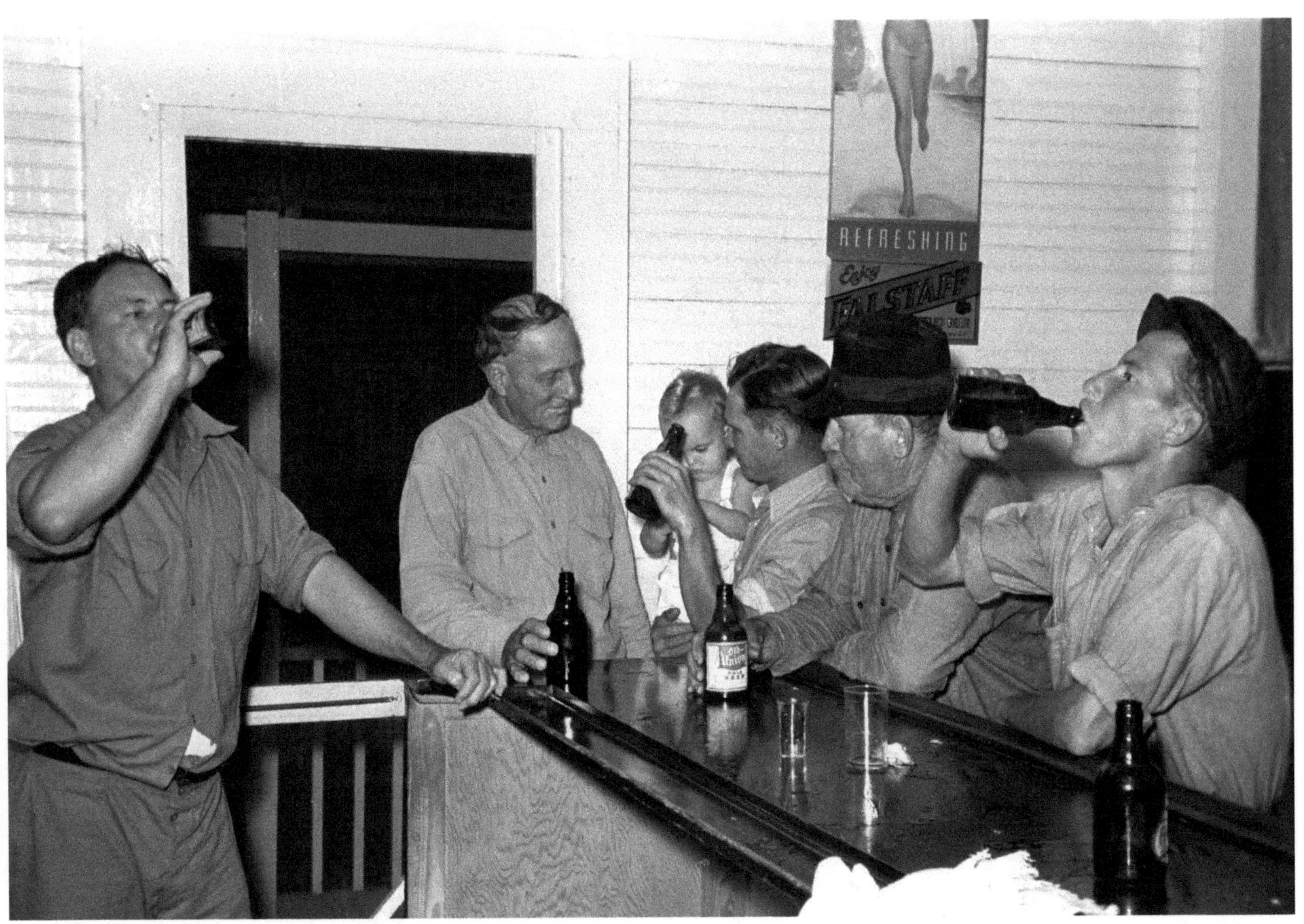

A group of men are seen drinking beer in a bar in Pilottown. Bars, rural nightclubs, and dance halls were popular subjects of Russell Lee's body of work during his three-month stay in Louisiana. Pilottown is the southernmost settlement in the state, located near the mouths of the Mississippi River, and is only accessible by boat. It was named for the river pilots who often assembled there to escort foreign cargo ships up and down the river.

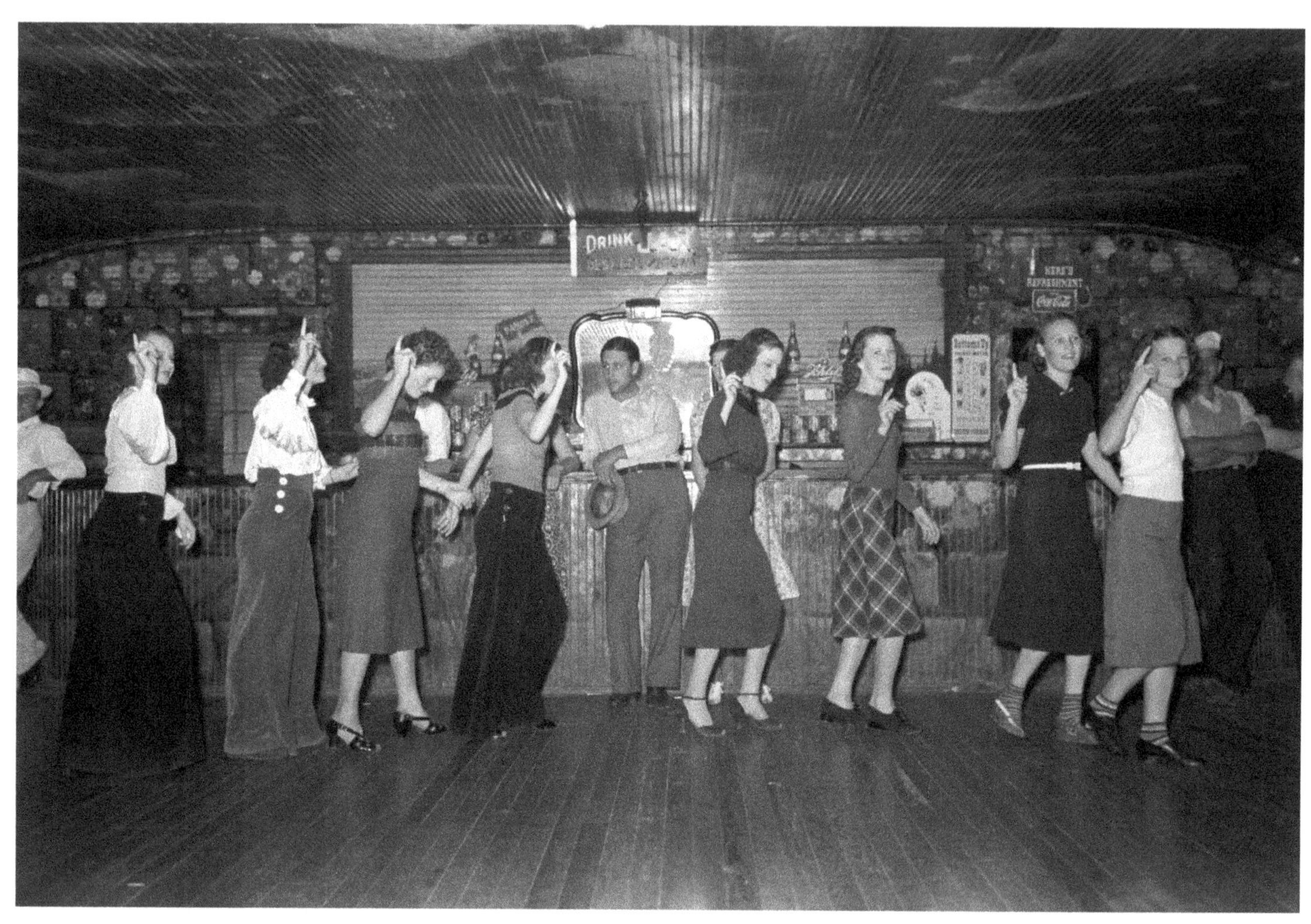

A group of young girls line dance across the wood floor of a roadhouse in Raceland as bemused male patrons look on.

Highway directional signs crowd the post at a busy intersection in Crowley. The place names on the signs all point to leading cities of southern and central Louisiana.

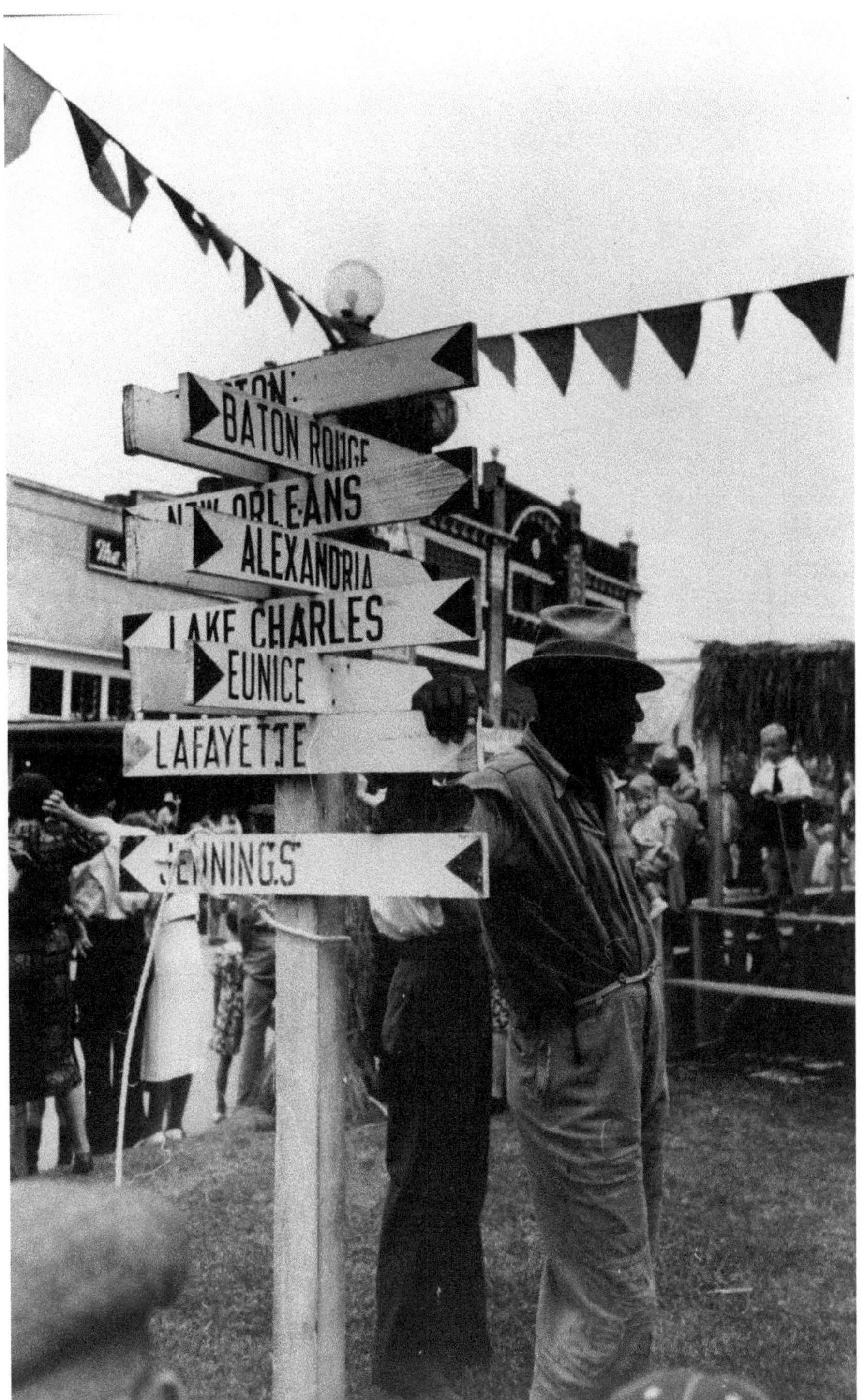

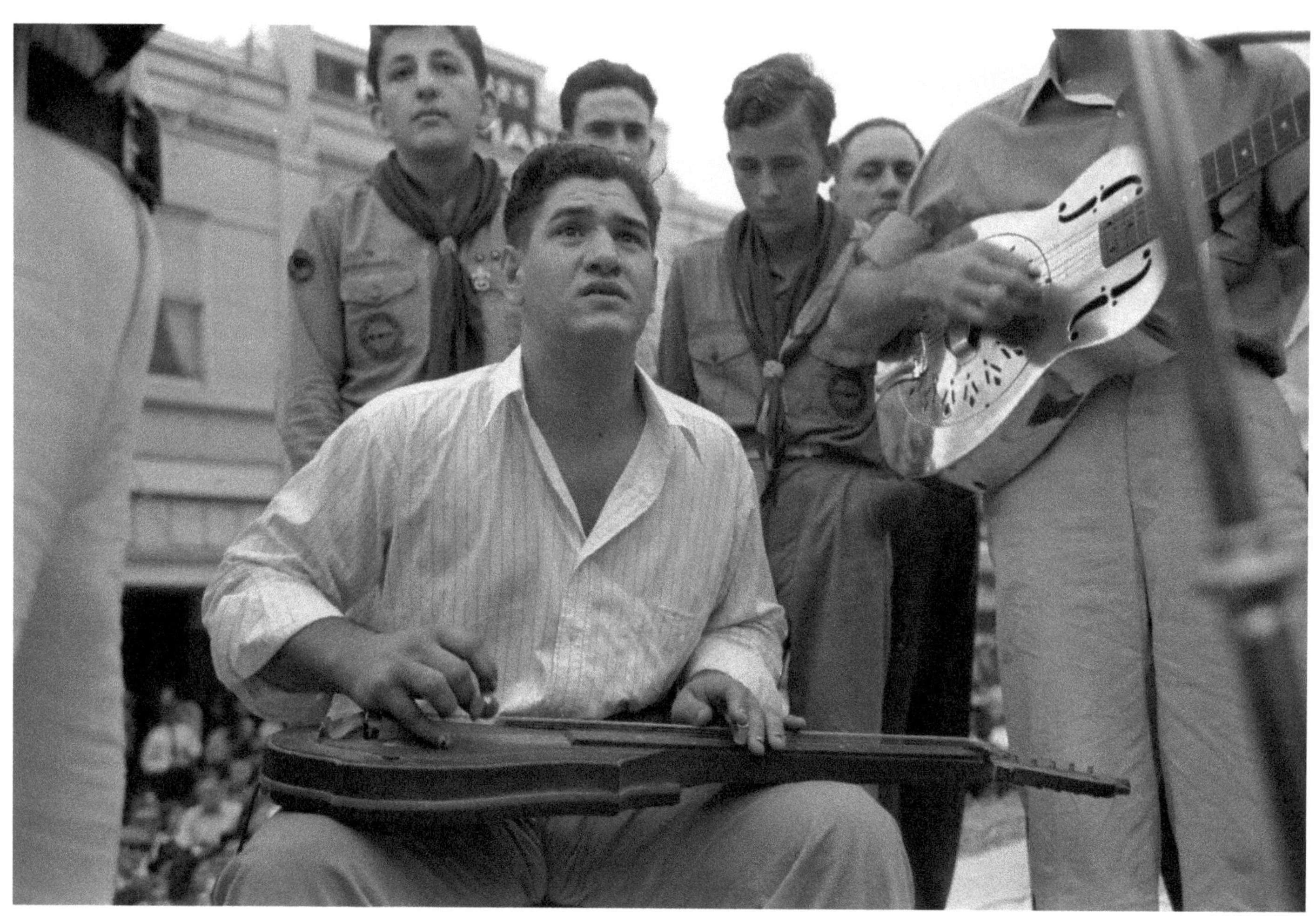

Two guitarists perform in front of a group of Boy Scouts at the Rice Festival in Crowley in October 1938. The man seated is playing a Hawaiian-style guitar and the man standing is playing a dobro.

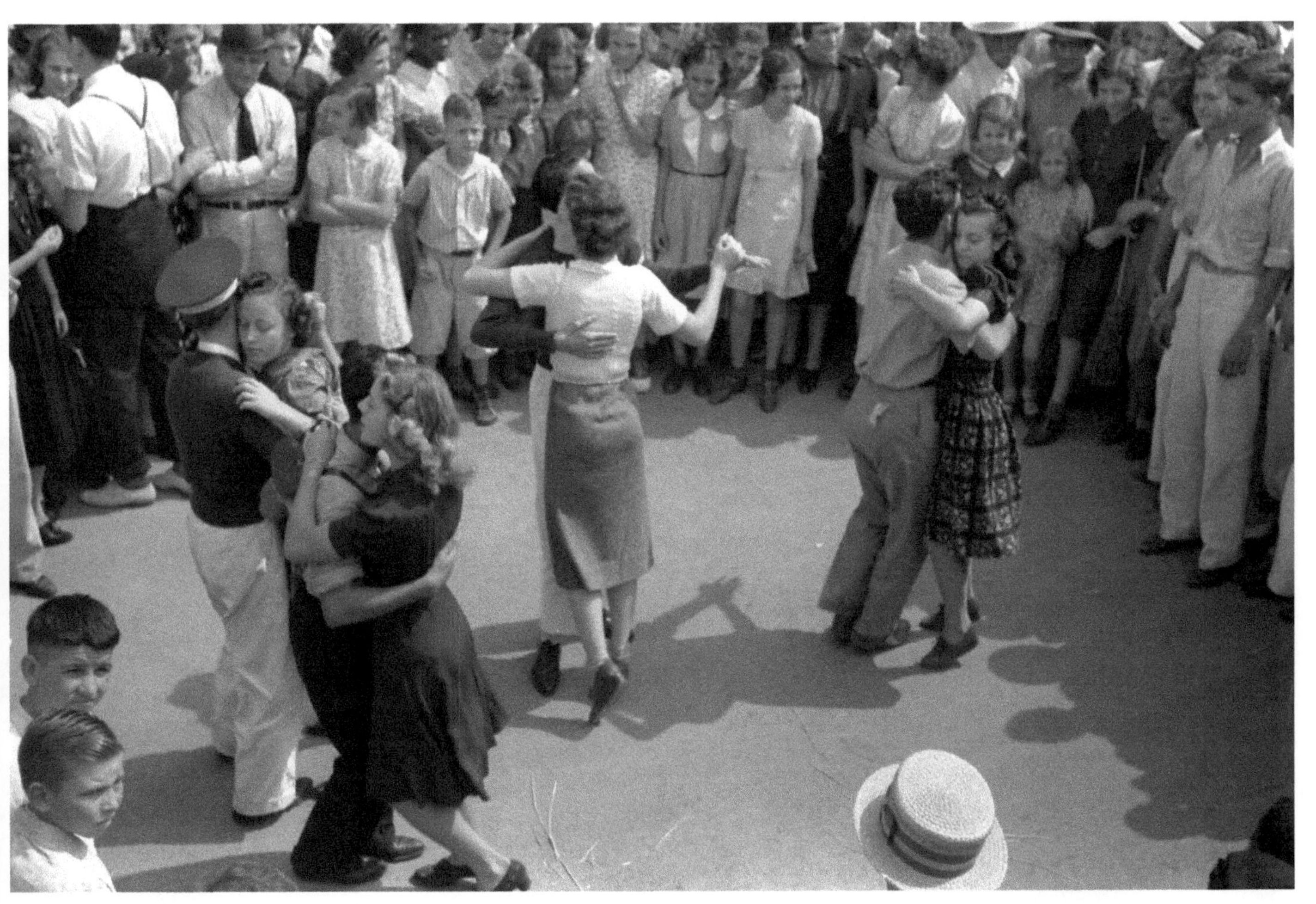

Young couples dance in the street at the Rice Festival as a crowd looks on.

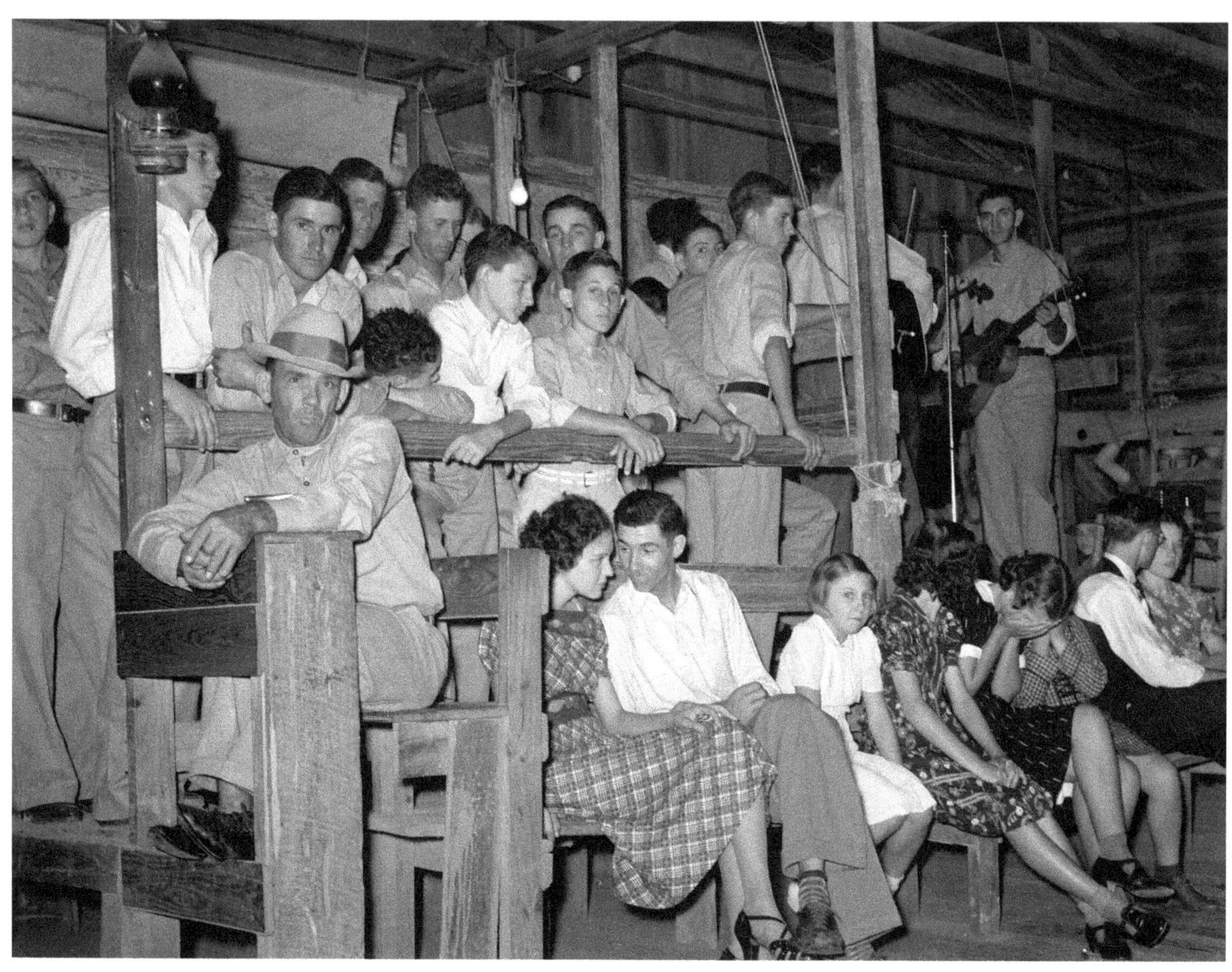

A wide range of age groups enjoy a *fais-do-do* near Crowley in 1938. Cajun French that is loosely translated as "go to bed," the fais-do-do is a Cajun custom in which families get together at someone's house or barn to hear music, eat, dance, and socialize. The youngest children are put to bed while the older kids and adults get to enjoy the party. A Cajun band is playing at upper-right.

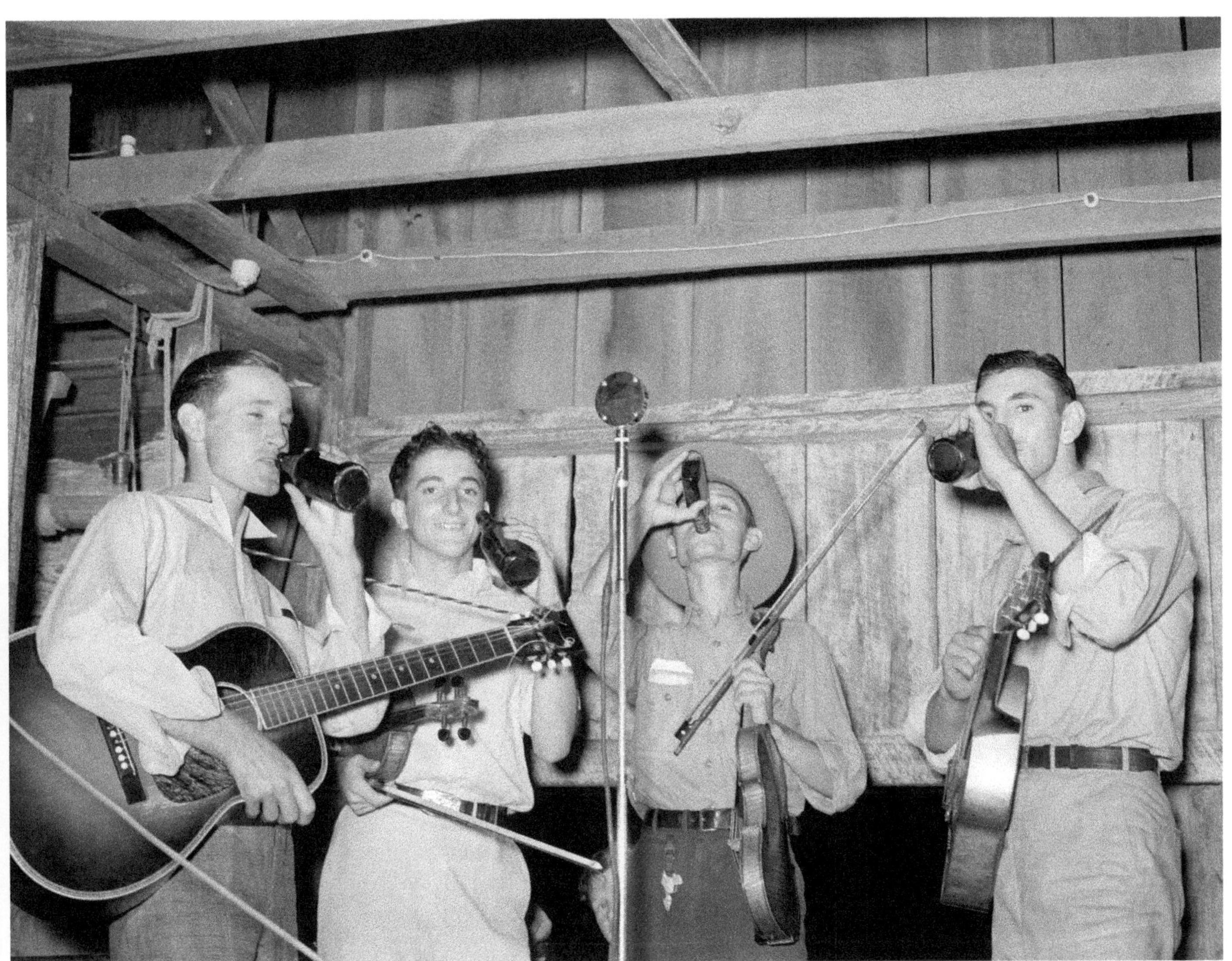

Cajun band members take a "beer break" between songs at the 1938 fais-do-do in Crowley. Traditional instruments in Cajun music include the accordion, fiddle, guitar, and a percussion instrument—often a washboard—but this particular band features two guitars and two fiddles. Cajun bands at that time usually sang in French, and most of them today do so as well, but with English translations. Today's Zydeco music evolved from the Cajun music style.

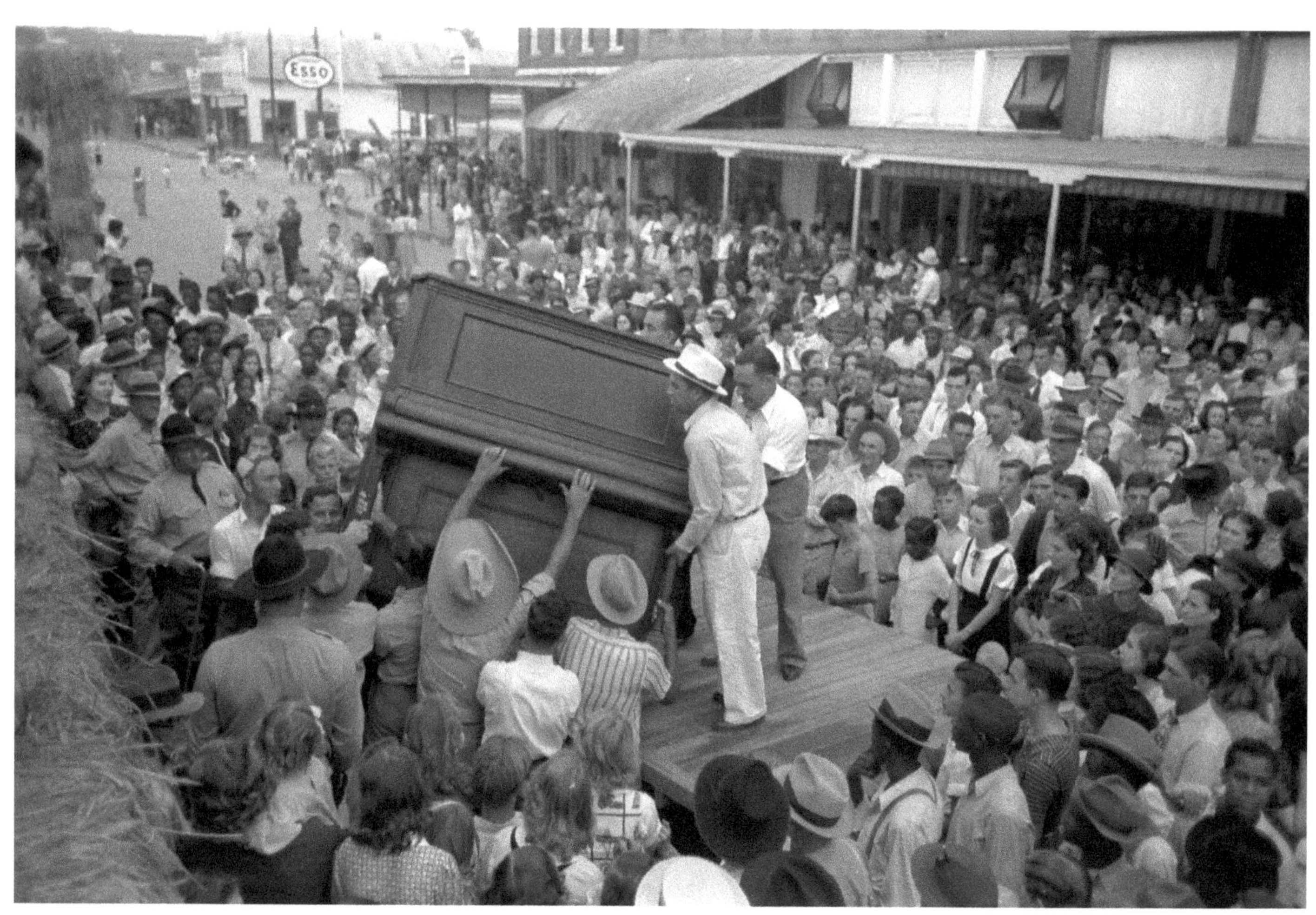

A group of men raise a piano up to an elevated platform for a Cajun band contest at the 1938 Rice Festival in Crowley. A crowd gathers in the street in anticipation of the lively musical event.

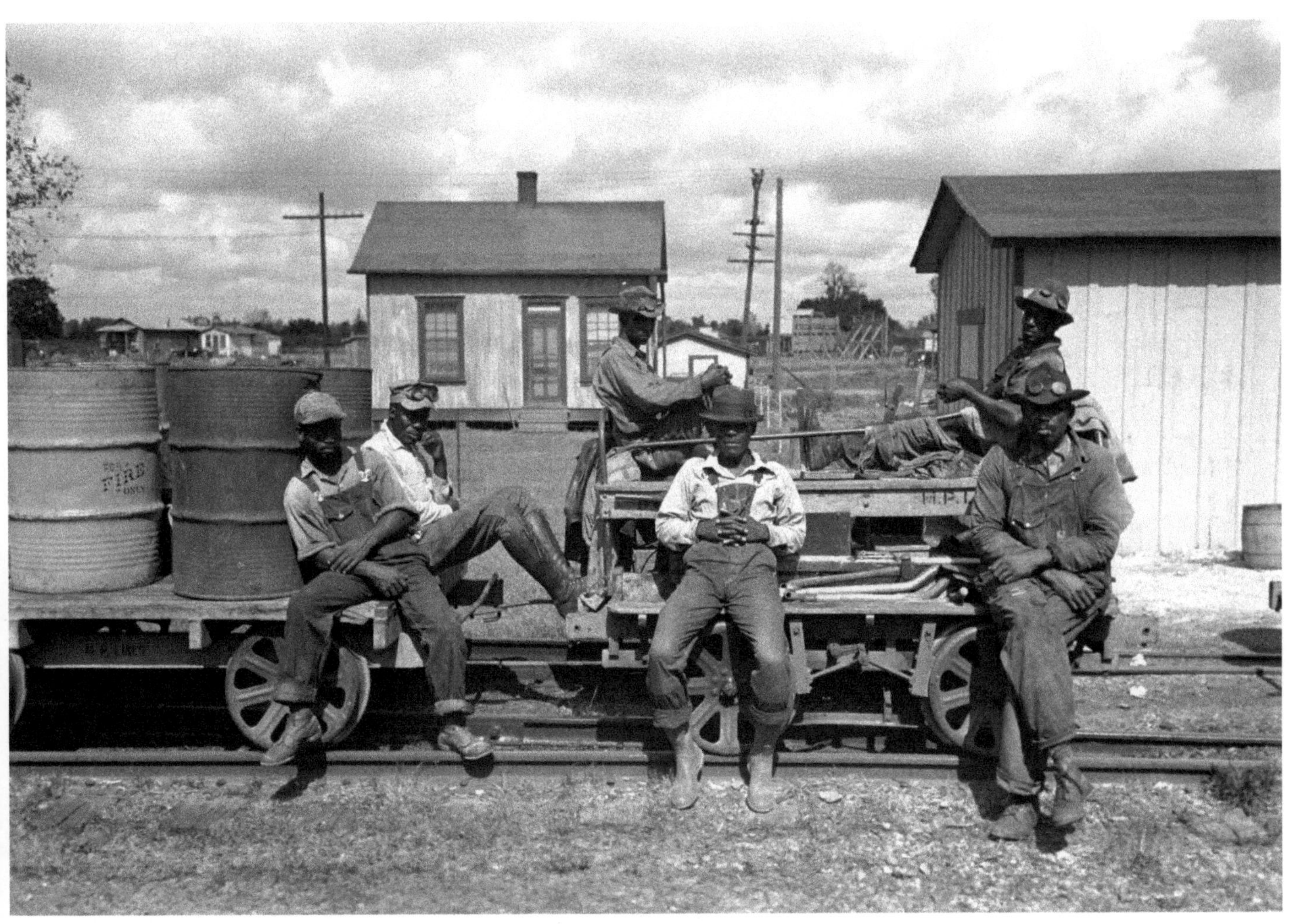

A railroad crew takes a break on a siding in Port Barre. Settled in 1820 by the Barre, Nezat, and Roy families, the town was named for the Barre family patriarch, Alex Charles Barre. The town, in St. Landry Parish, was originally serviced by the New Iberia & Northern Railroad, which was later absorbed by the Missouri Pacific, and then by the Union Pacific.

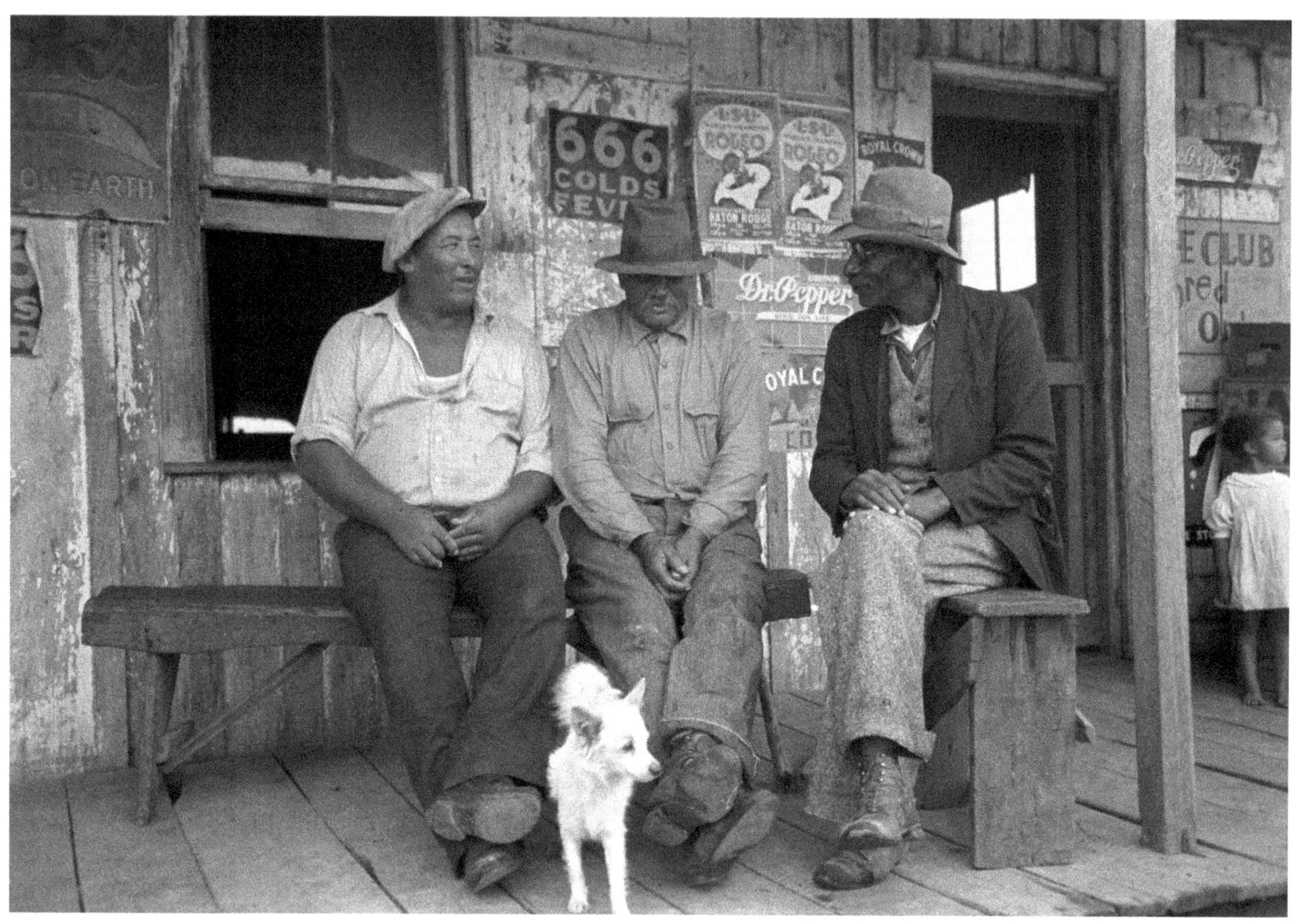

Three older men sit around chatting on crude benches on the porch of a small grocery store near Jeanerette, Iberia Parish. A brand of cold medicine very popular during the era was known as 666, seen on the ad behind the men.

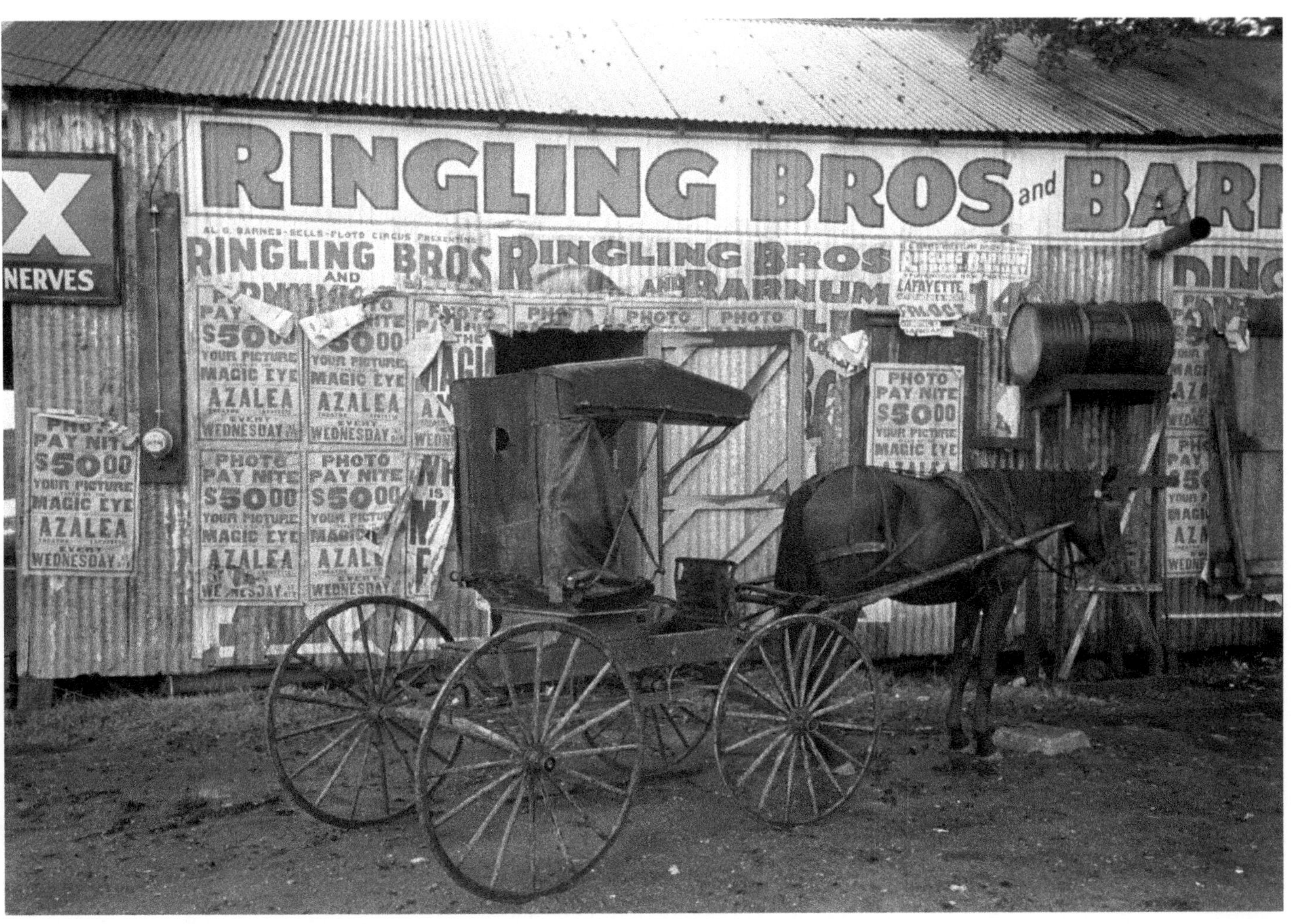

An aging horse and buggy idles outside a store in Lafayette almost completely covered with handbills advertising the Ringling Brothers Circus and a "Photo Pay Night." Because of the swampy terrain of much of southern Louisiana, modern paved roadways did not reach many small bayou communities until well into the twentieth century. Animal-drawn vehicles were still common sights in October 1938.

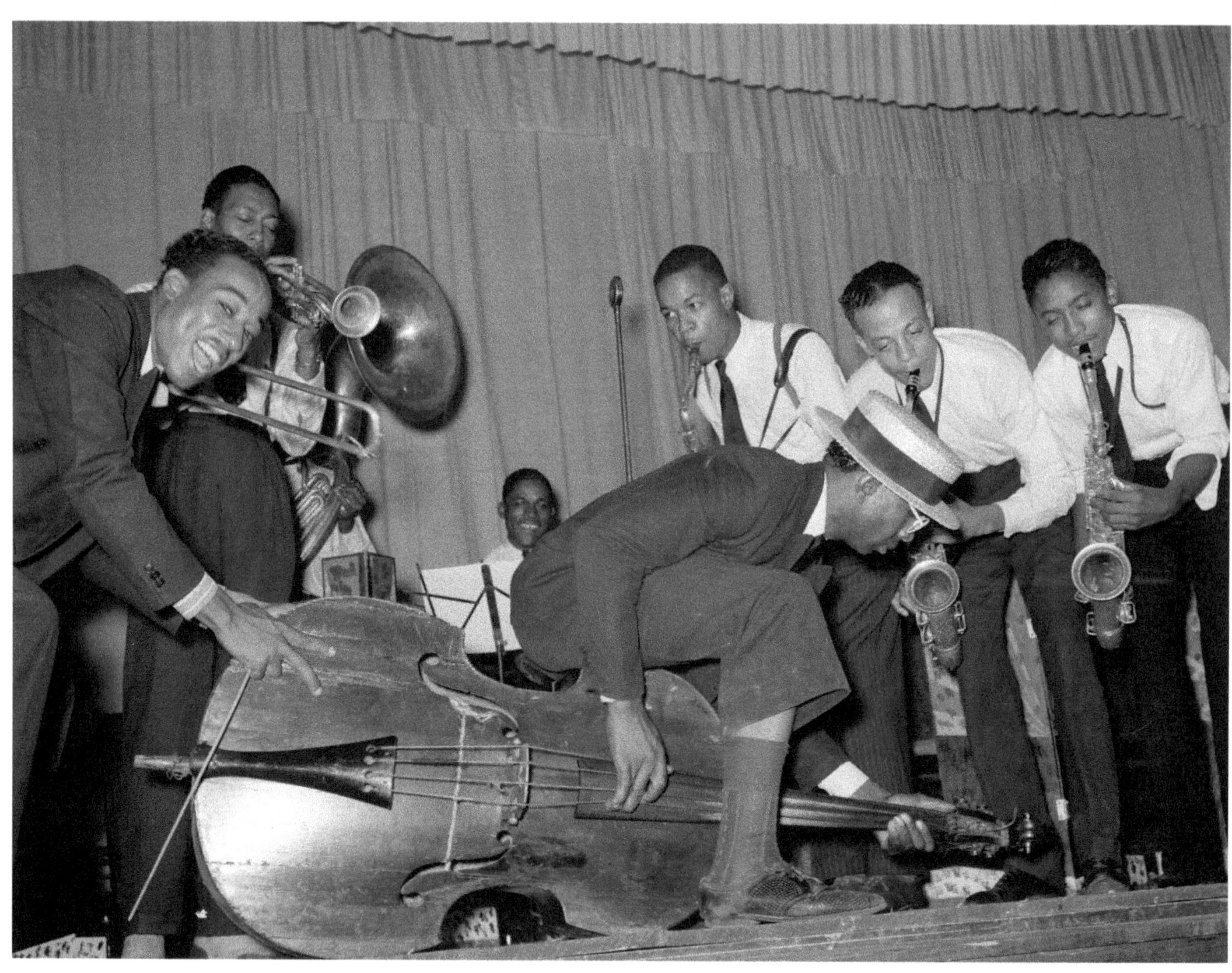

A brass band performs onstage during the 1938 Rice Festival in Crowley. Although Jim Crow laws at the time made segregation of the races a reality, all-black musical groups were allowed to perform in public places frequented by whites, and they were almost universally appreciated. Bands of mixed races, however, didn't come until many years later, after the Jim Crow laws were struck down by the court system.

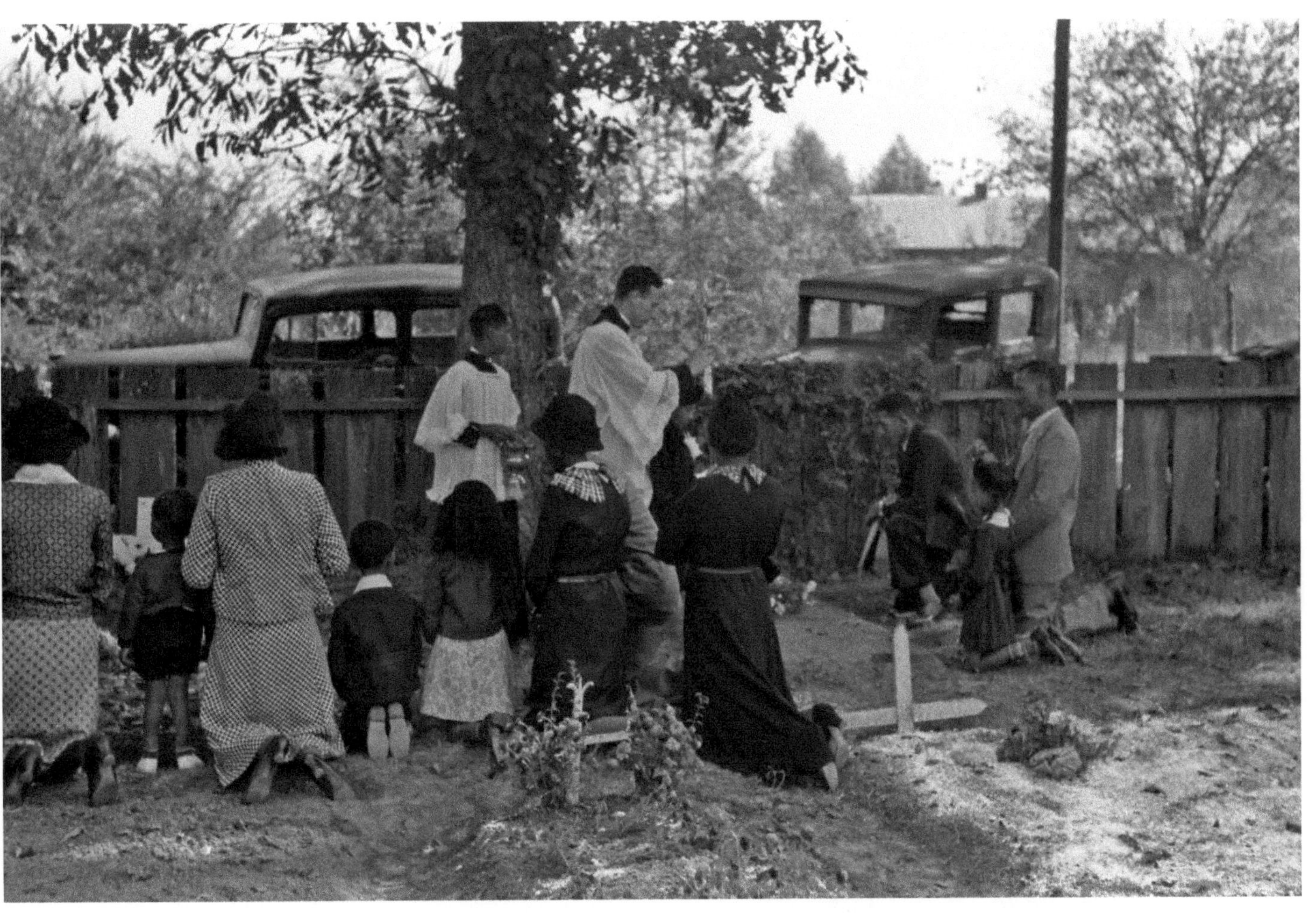

Family members offer prayers at the graves of their deceased relatives in New Roads on All Saints' Day 1938. Visiting the final resting places of loved ones and making offerings of flowers and prayers on All Saints' Day (November 1), is an ancient Catholic custom dating back to the 600s and brought to Louisiana by the earliest French settlers. The custom is still observed throughout southern Louisiana today.

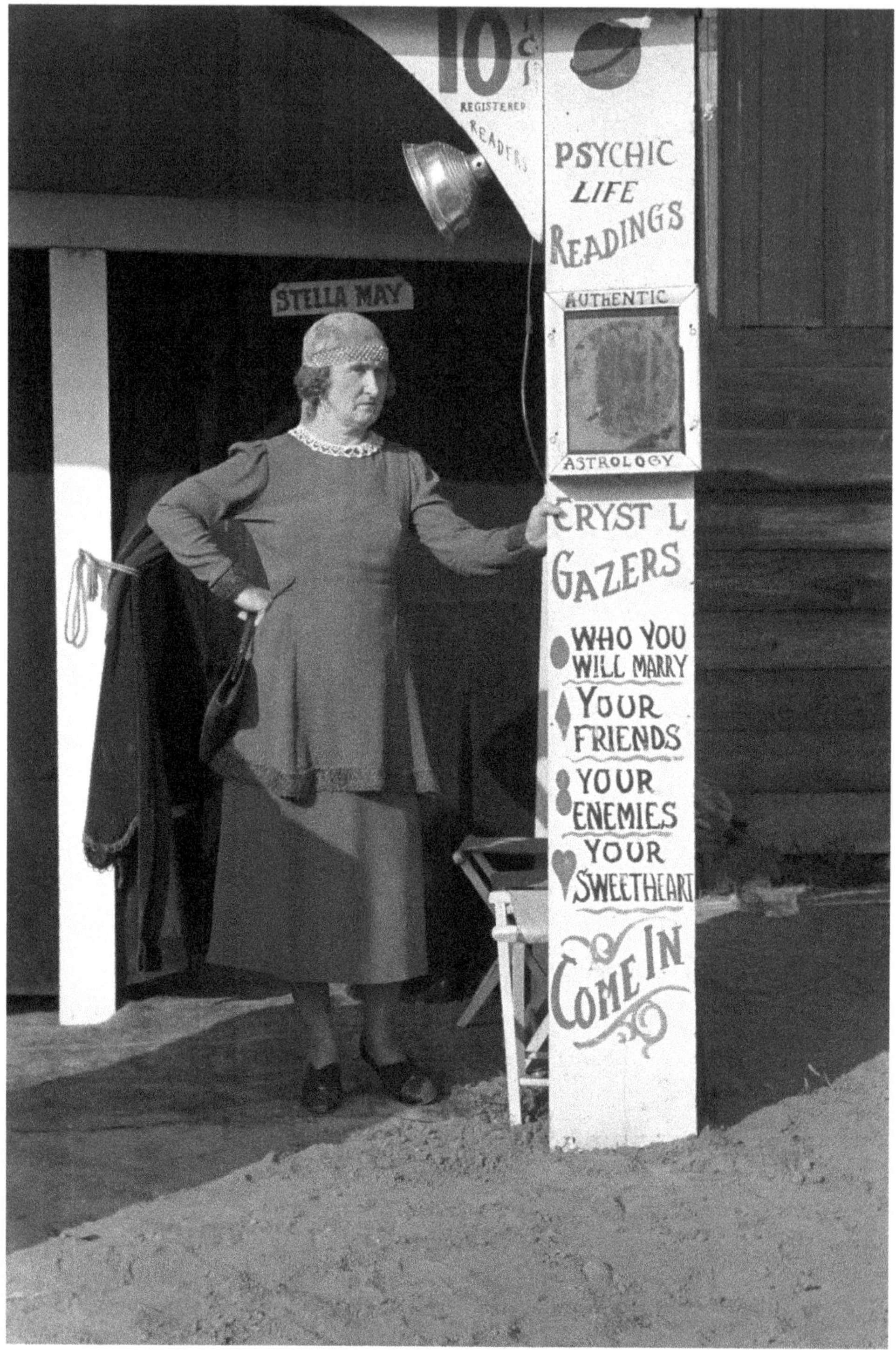

A fortune-teller named Stella May stands beside the sign that advertises her services at the South Louisiana State Fair in Donaldsonville. Fortune-tellers, mystics, mediums, voodoo priestesses, and others claiming to have psychic powers have been a part of the culture of southern Louisiana—especially New Orleans—for centuries. Today they make up a large group that sets up tables at Jackson Square, telling fortunes for visiting tourists and locals.

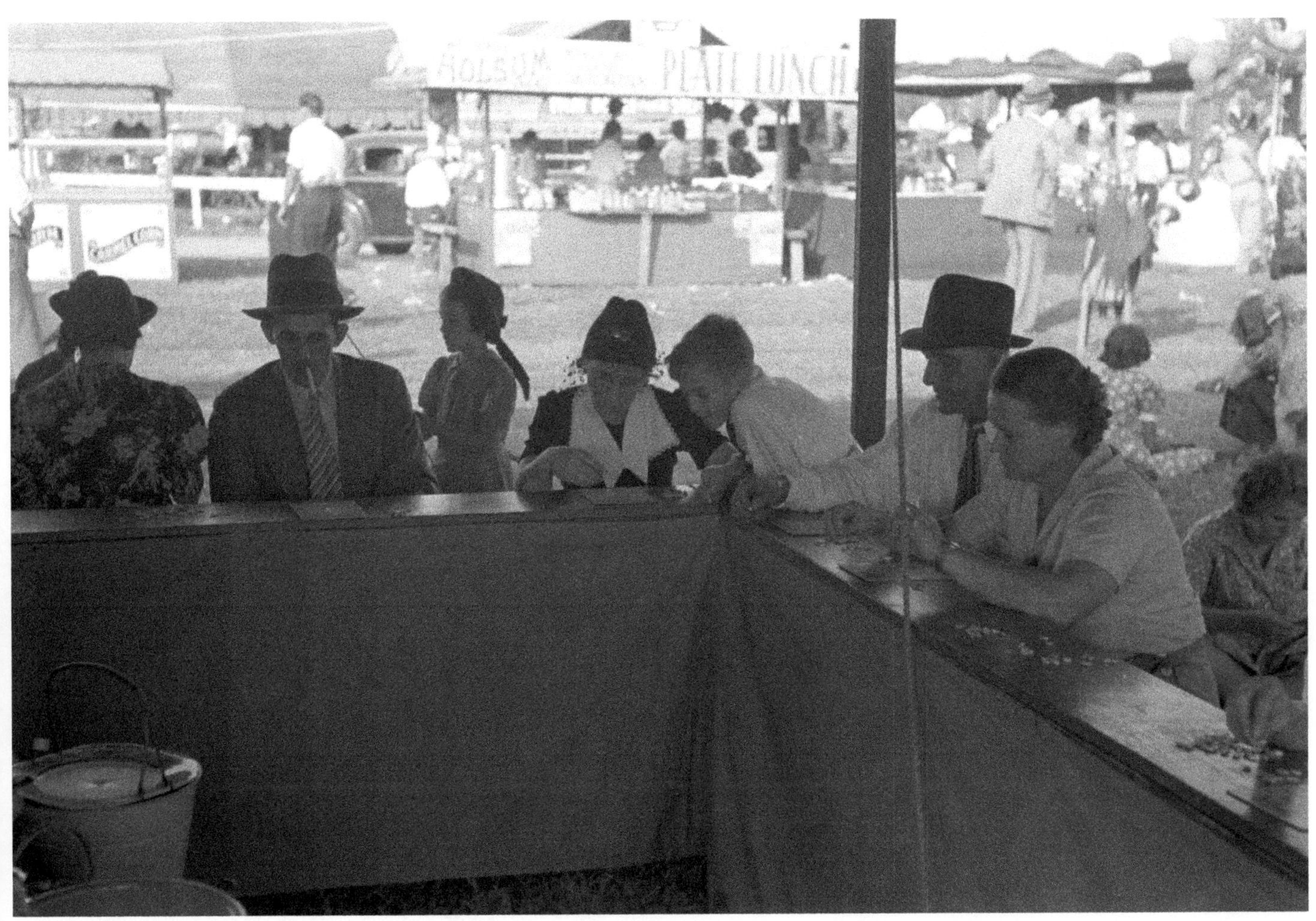

A group of men, women, and children gather around a booth at the South Louisiana State Fair to play Bingo. The South Louisiana State Fair was held in Donaldsonville, the parish seat of Ascension Parish, from 1913 to 1964. Today a scaled-down version of it is called the Sunshine Festival, after the nearby Sunshine Bridge over the Mississippi River. Concession stands in the background advertise caramel corn and plate lunches served on Holsum bread, which is still produced today.

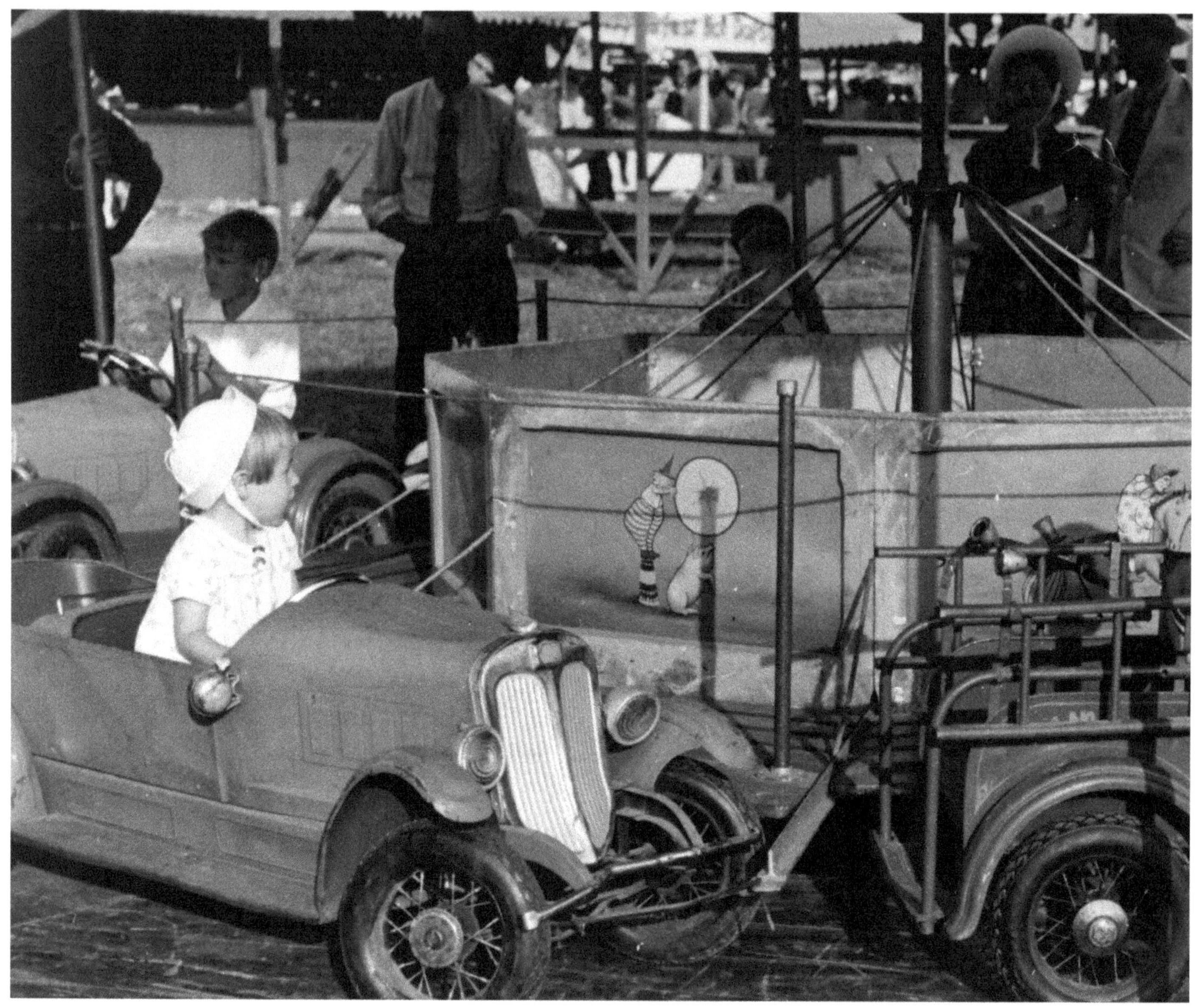

Children ride on models of automobiles and fire engines on a merry-go-round at the 1938 South Louisiana State Fair in Donaldsonville as their parents look on in the background.

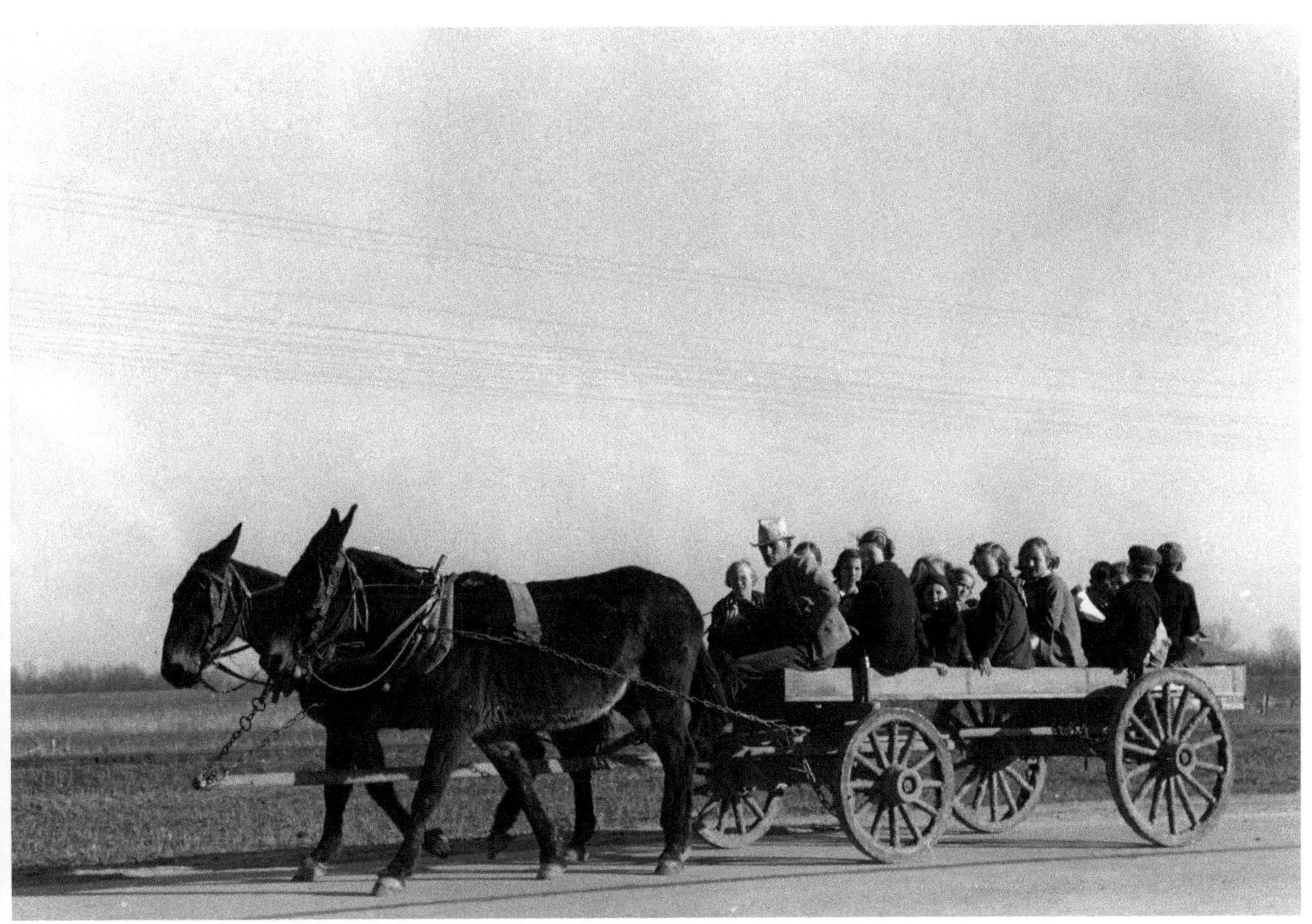

Children are transported home from school by a mule-drawn wagon near Transylvania in East Carroll Parish. In 1939, when this photograph was taken, motorized school buses had not fully replaced horsepower in this remote rural agricultural region. Taking advantage of its name, today the small town's general store sells vampire-related merchandise to tourists passing through on U.S. Highway 65, and the much-photographed Transylvania water tower has a vampire bat painted on it.

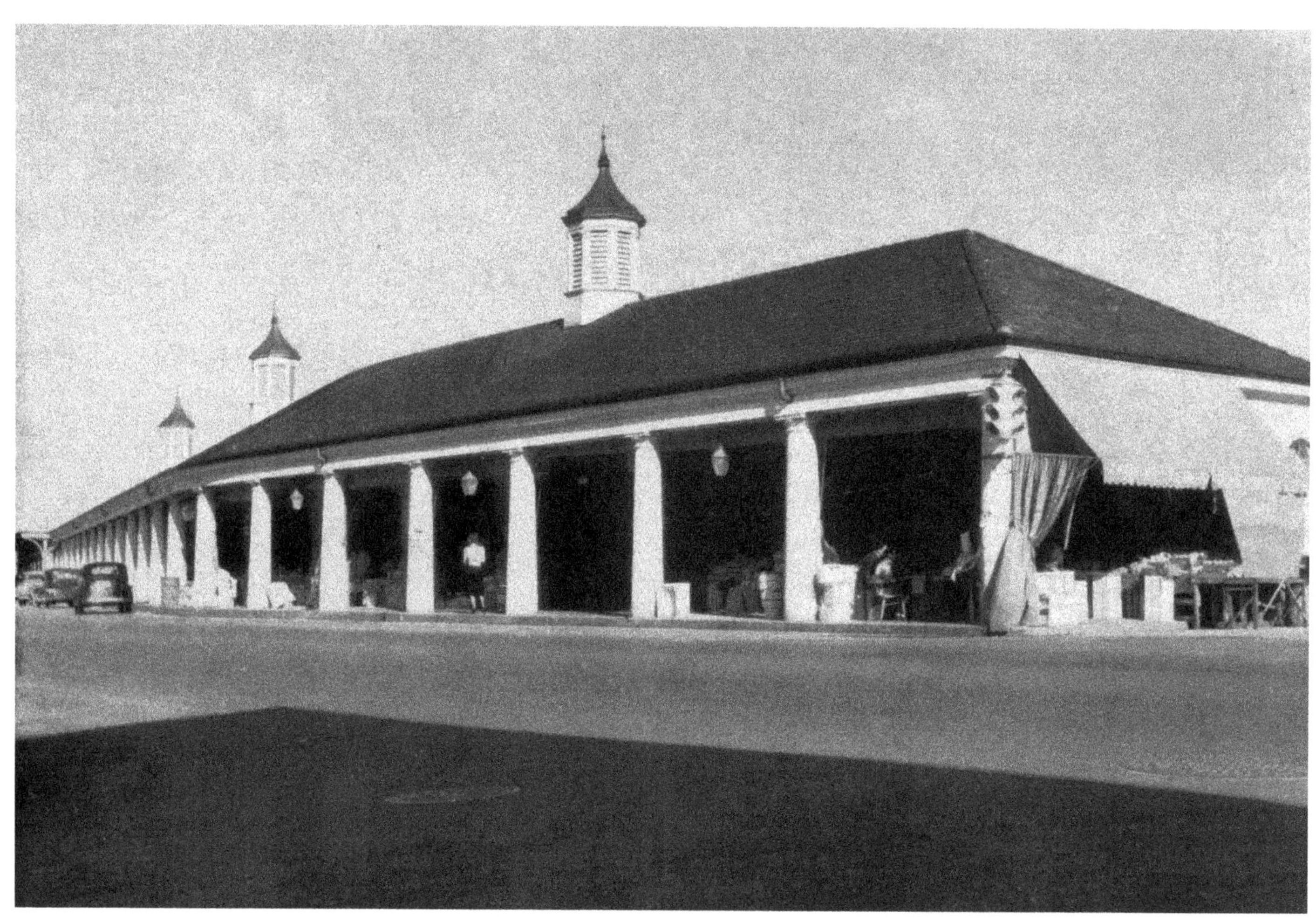

New Orleans' French Market is open for business in 1939, following extensive renovations by the Works Progress Administration. Sporting its new look, the market features a new roof and a series of cupolas in the style of the Spanish colonial era. The facility still stands today and is a popular tourist attraction featuring fresh produce and other indigenous foods, as well as crafts, collectibles, and just about everything else under the sun.

Belle Grove Plantation as photographed by Frances Benjamin Johnston. Designed by New Orleans architect Henry Howard and built in Greek Revival style in 1857, Belle Grove was located near White Castle in Iberville Parish. Known as the "Queen of the South," it was one of the South's largest plantation houses, but it was abandoned in the 1920s and burned to the ground on March 17, 1952.

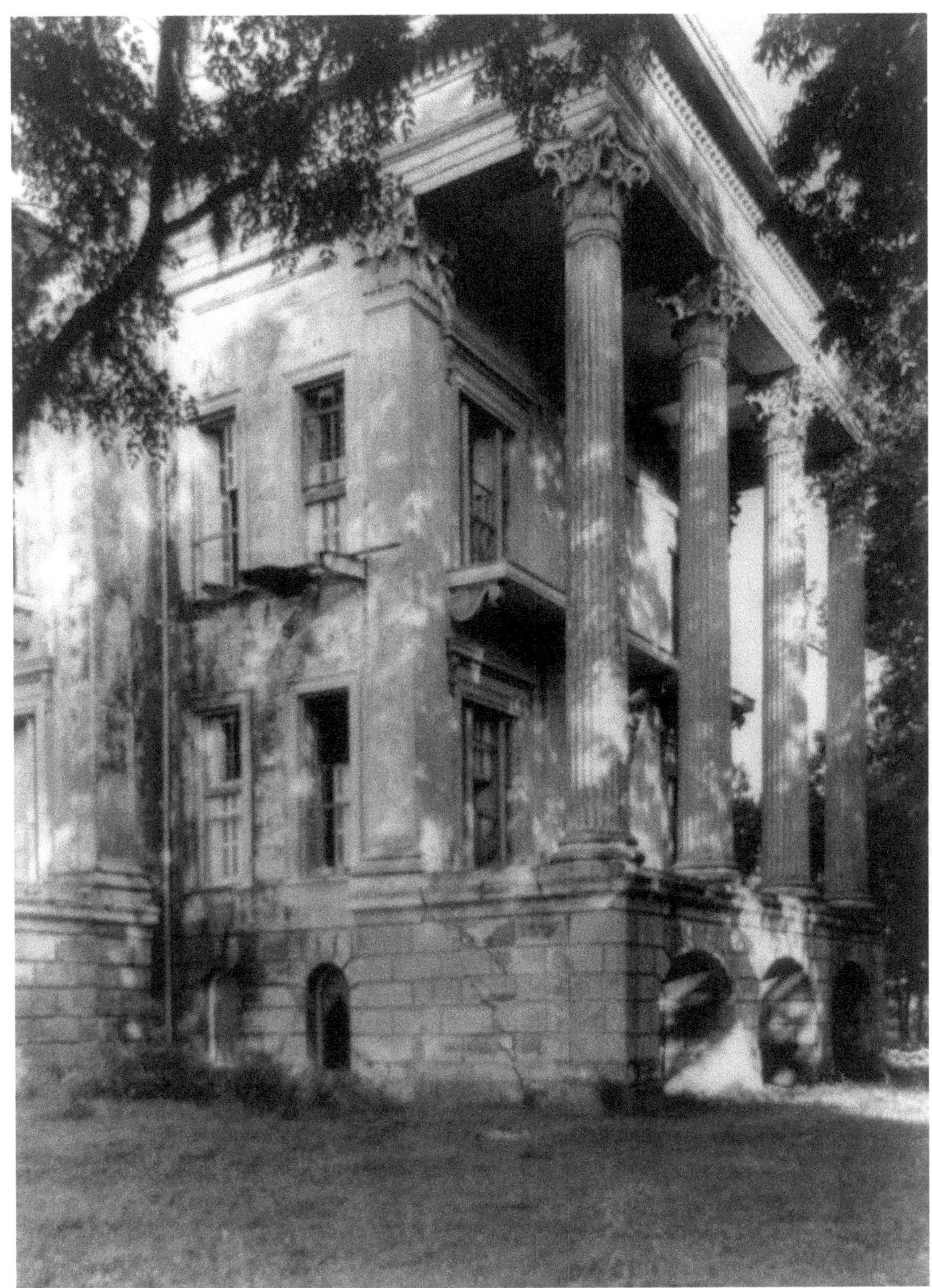

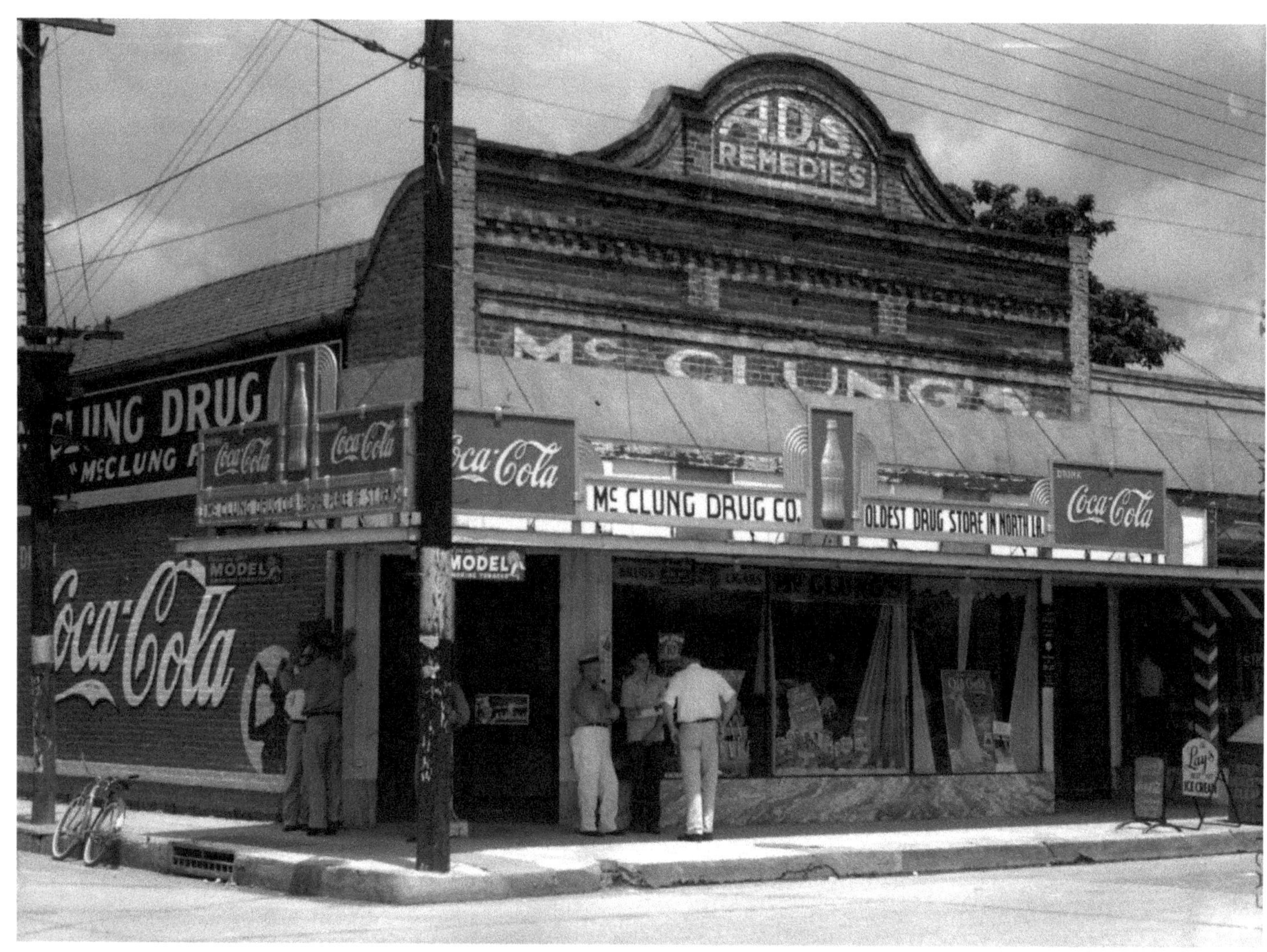

The McClung drugstore in Natchitoches is the subject of this June 1940 photograph by Marion Post Wolcott (1910–1990). As one of several photographers working under the auspices of the Farm Security Administration during the Great Depression, Wolcott pictorially documented day-to-day life and poverty in the rural South. FSA photographs influenced public opinion, boosting support for Roosevelt's New Deal policies and projects. Wolcott shot this image and the six that follow.

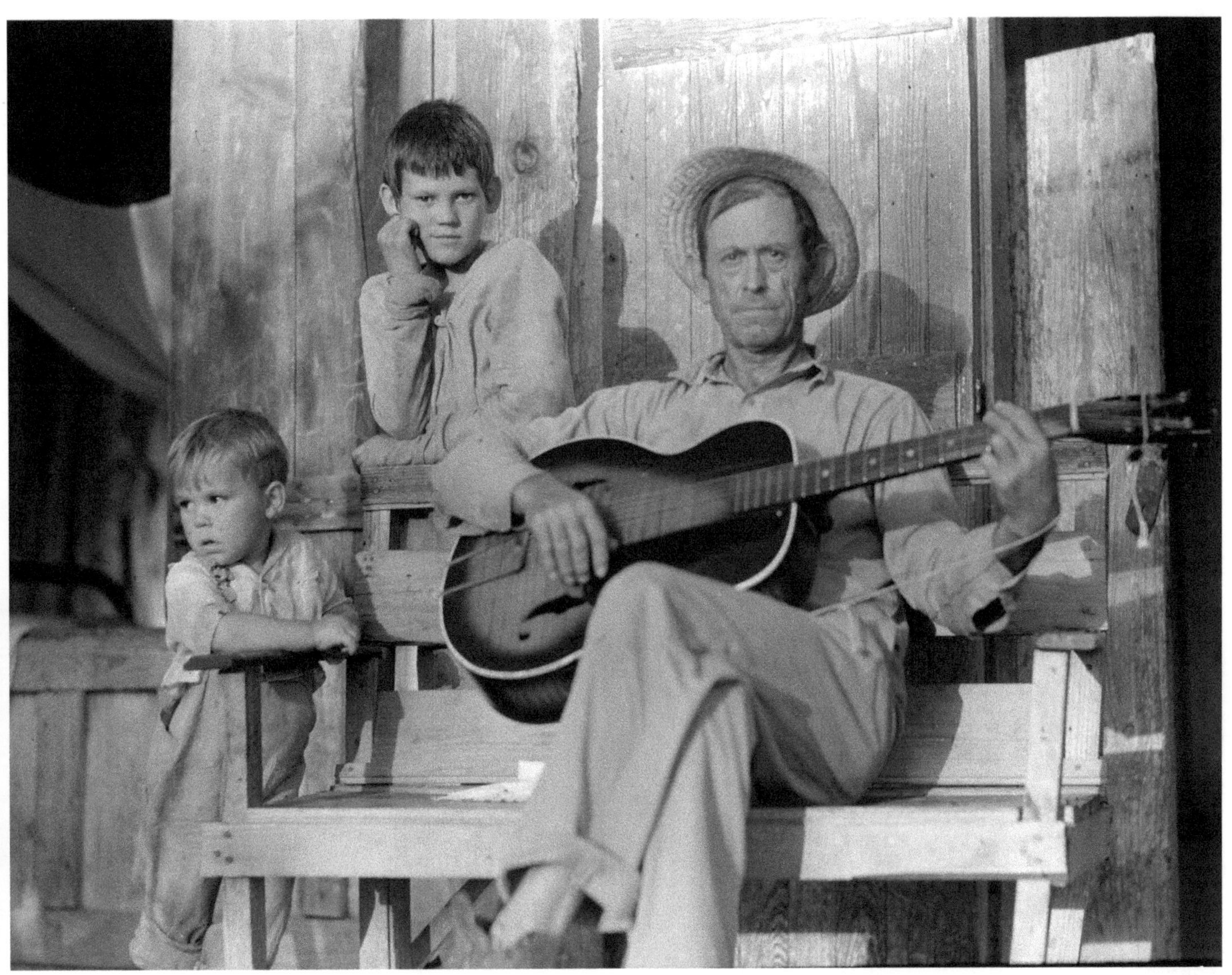

Locals in Natchitoches entertain themselves with guitar music. Natchitoches (pronounced nack-uh-tish) is the oldest permanent settlement in what was the Louisiana Purchase, founded on the Red River in 1714, four years before New Orleans. The Cane River plantations and many others sprang up in the area, which enjoyed an abundance of rich soil. The Red shifted course many years later, bypassing Natchitoches, but today the city's historic district is a mecca for tourism, thanks to the recently completed Interstate 49.

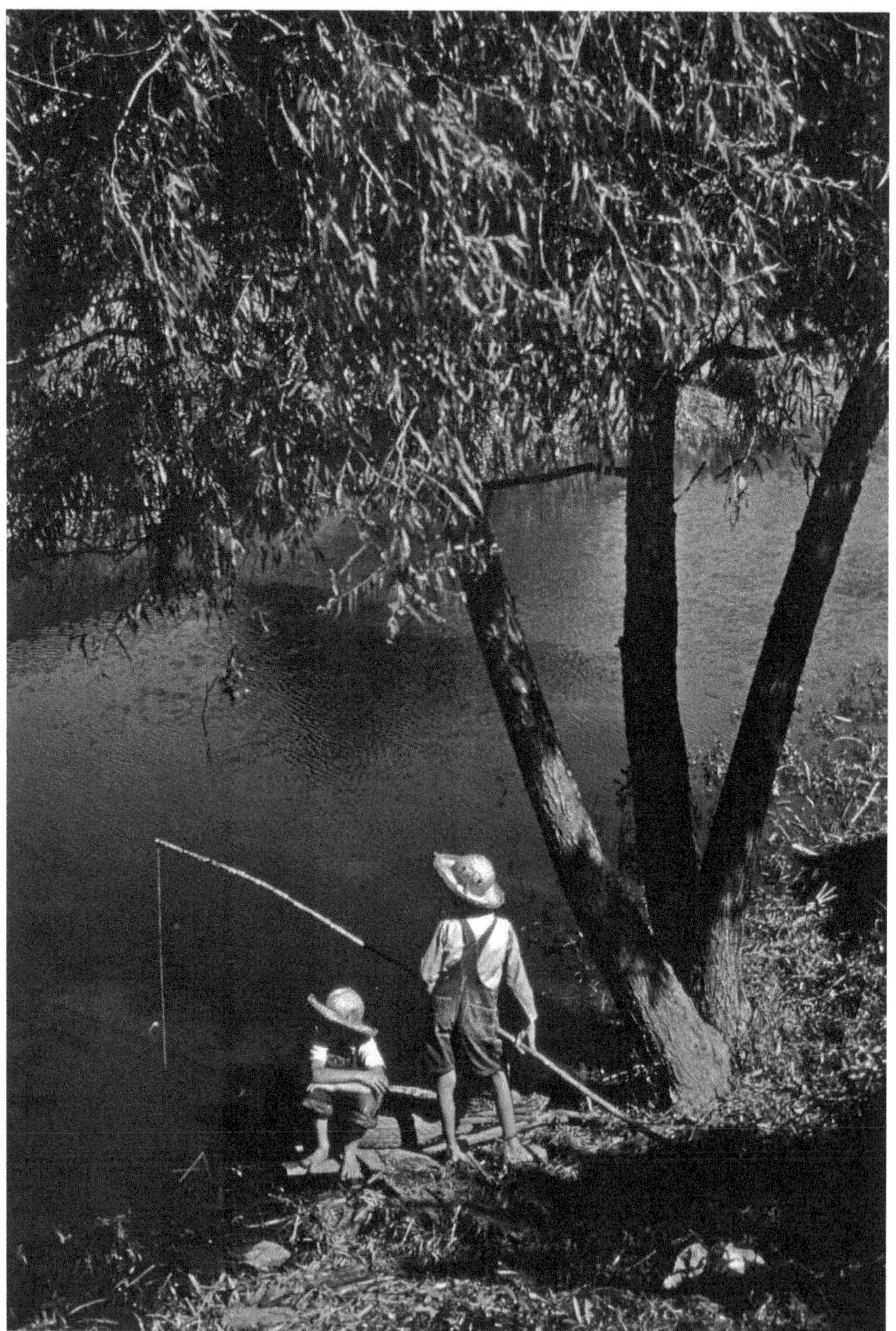

Two young Cajun boys fish with their cane poles in a bayou near Schriever in Terrebonne Parish. Their straw hats and denim overalls were standard apparel during a time when paved roadways were just beginning to connect many of the smaller, previously isolated bayou communities to other areas of the state.

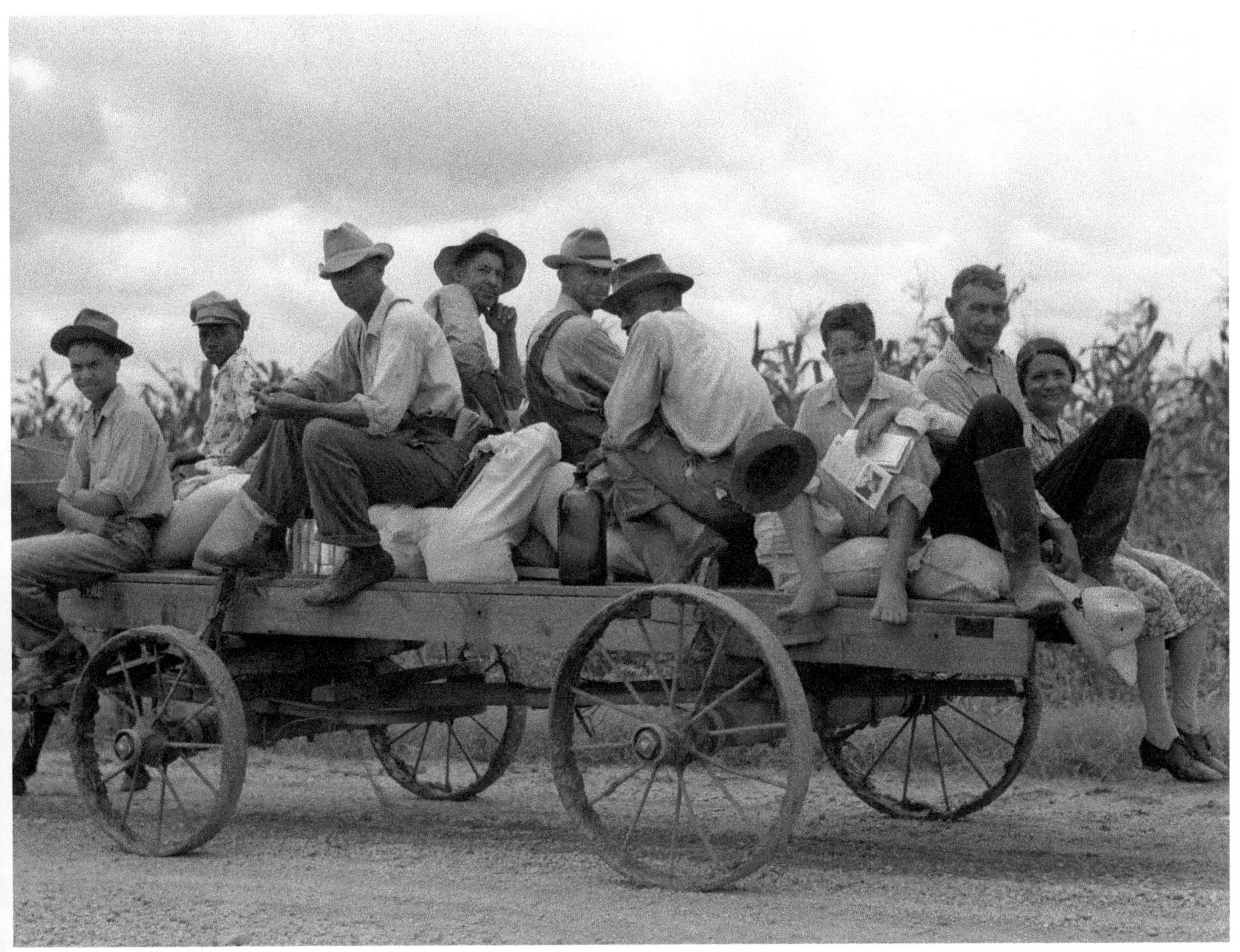

A wagon carrying young and older mulatto men and a lone woman returns from town with groceries and supplies near Melrose Plantation in Natchitoches Parish. One of half a dozen plantations along the Cane River, Melrose was the home for many years of noted folk painter Clementine Hunter (1886–1988). Hunter's primitive but colorful and expressive paintings of farm life in the region captured everyday scenes like the one shown in this Wolcott image.

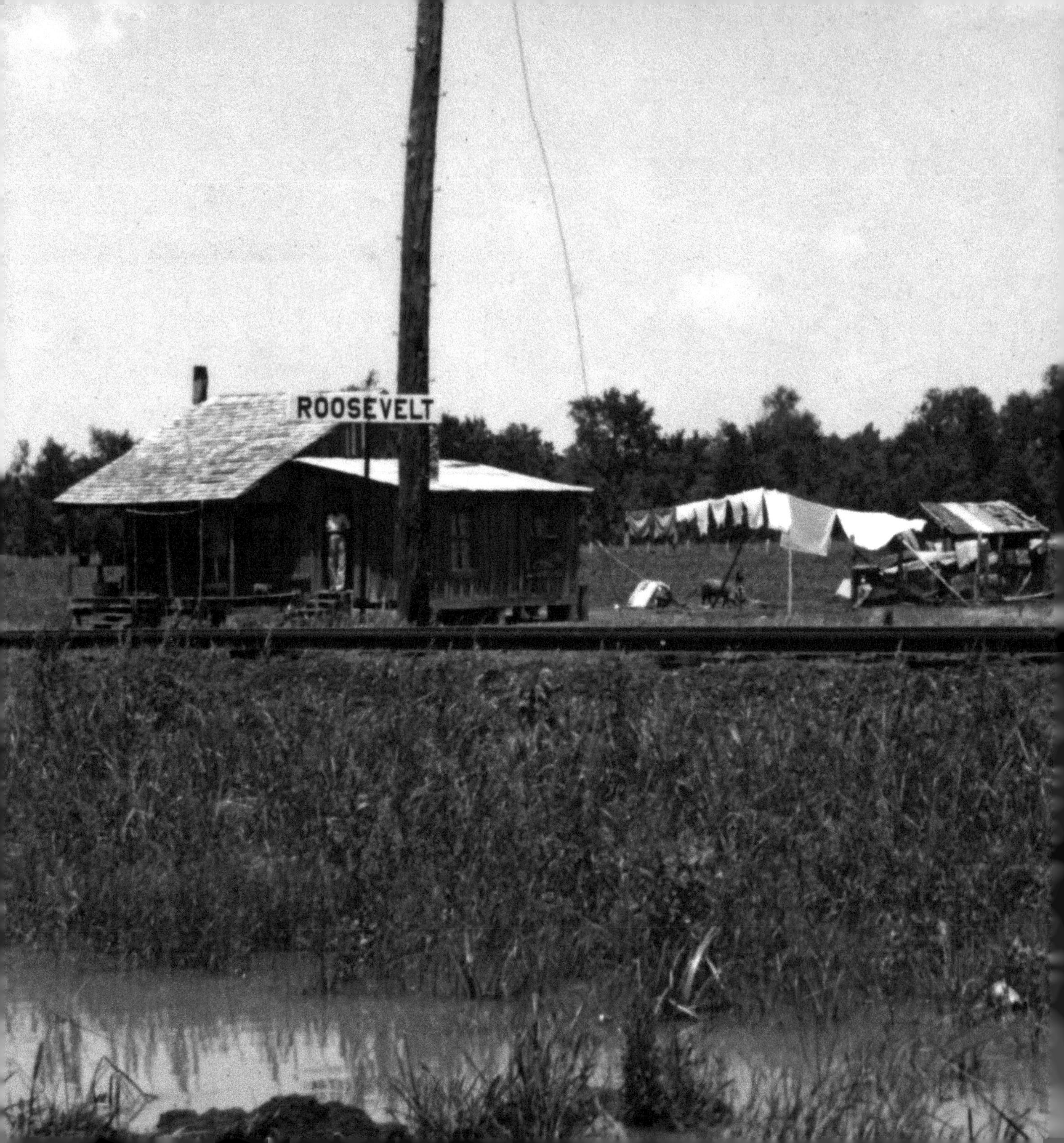
ROOSEVELT

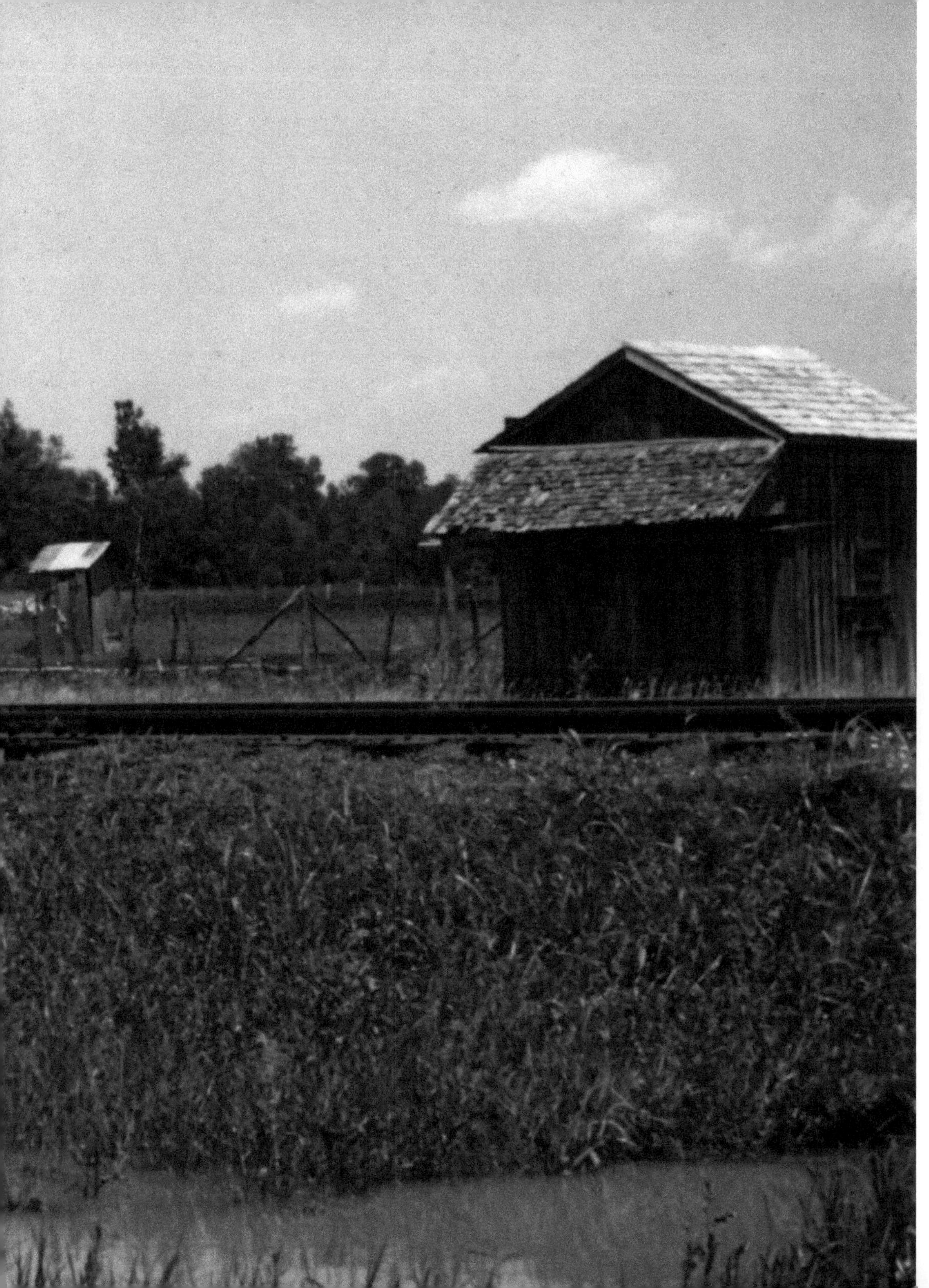

Two crude wooden shacks and several smaller structures (including what appears to be an outhouse) sit alongside the railroad tracks in Roosevelt, in East Carroll Parish. So small it doesn't appear on most state maps, Roosevelt was probably named for Theodore Roosevelt, who hunted bears in the region during his presidency in the early 1900s. His cousin, Franklin D. Roosevelt, was president when this photograph was taken in 1940.

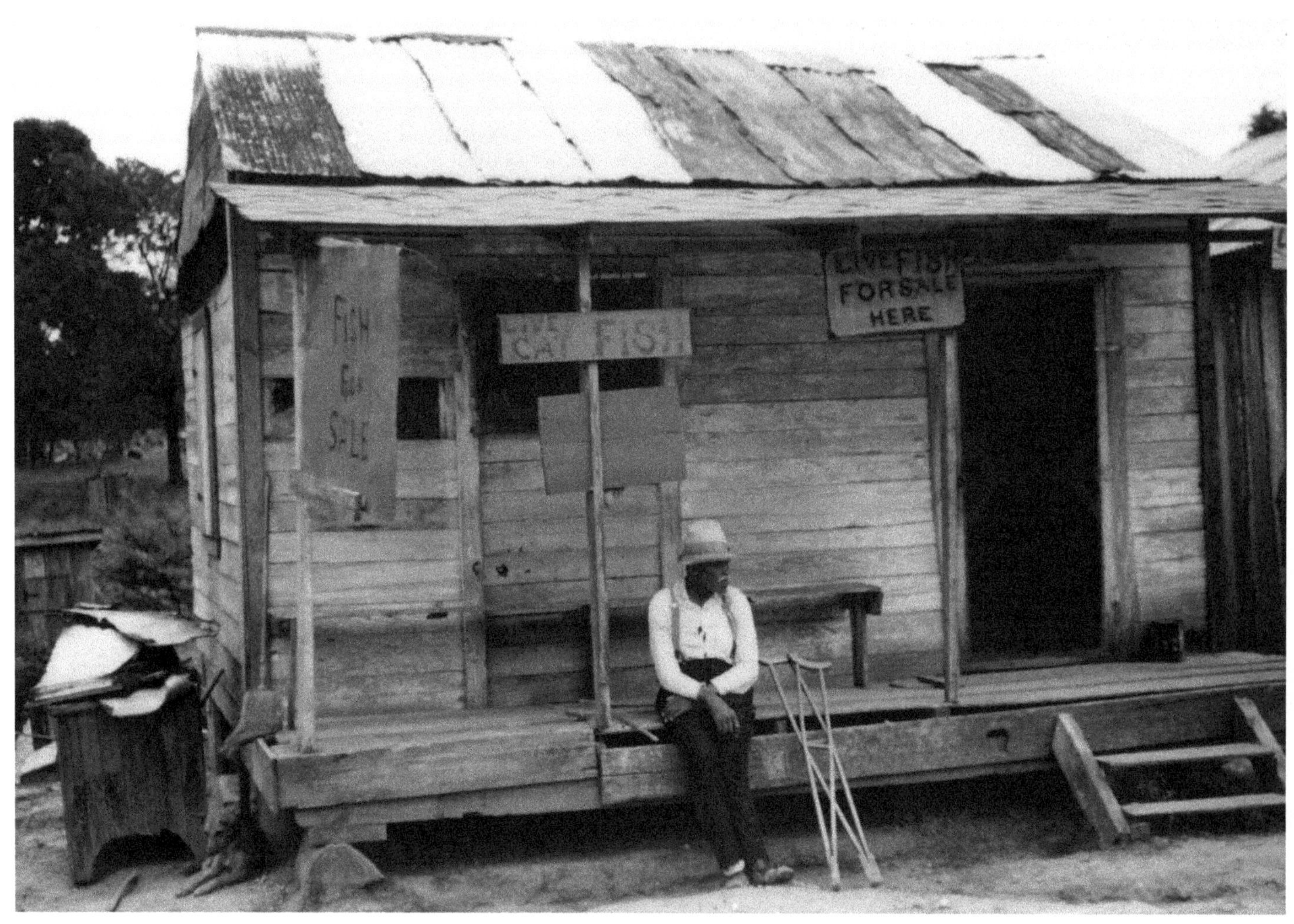

An elderly man with crutches rests on the front porch of a run-down shack near Natchitoches selling live fish, including catfish.

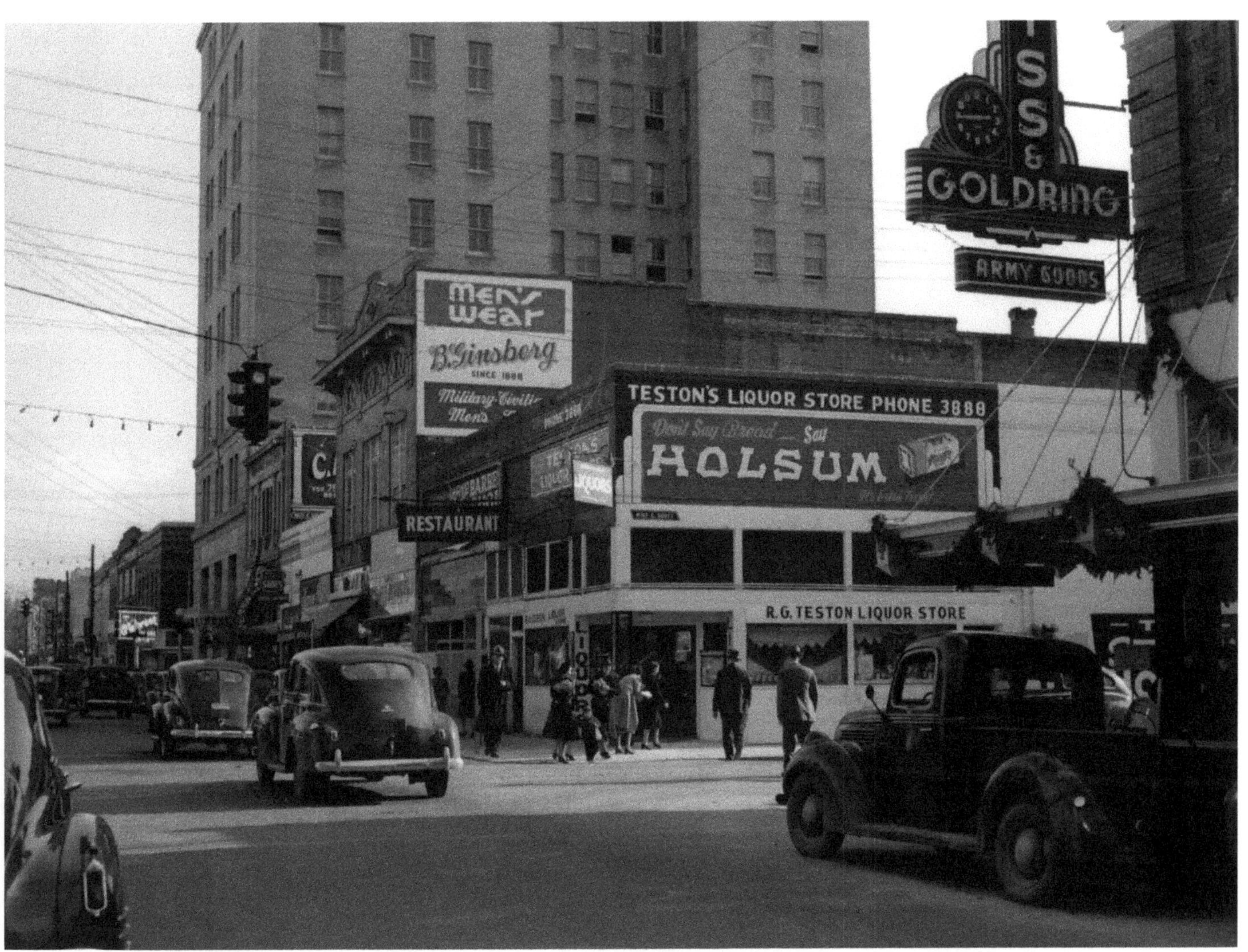

Cars and pedestrians take to the busy streets of downtown Alexandria. The store at right advertises "Army Goods," which were undoubtedly popular items at that time, owing to the proximity of camps Beauregard and Claiborne. Camp Beauregard, which saw activity during World War I, was reactivated the year this photograph was taken and used as a training base for soldiers who would be fighting in World War II a year later. Camp Claiborne was located about 10 miles south.

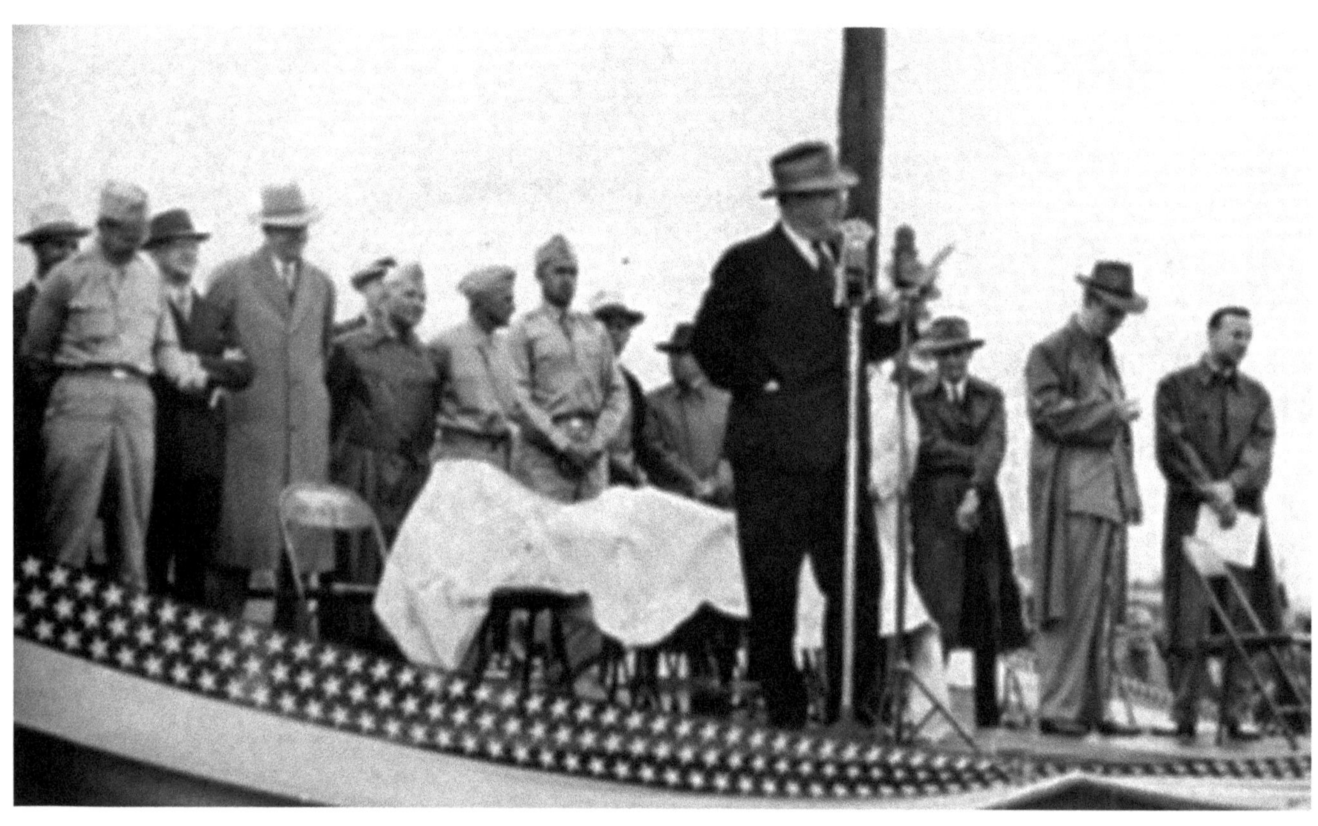

World War I hero Sergeant Alvin C. York of Tennessee (in the dark suit) addresses the 82nd Infantry Division at Camp Claiborne on May 7, 1942. Between 1939 and 1946 more than half a million soldiers trained at Camp Claiborne in Rapides Parish. Today the camp stands abandoned, and what remains is under the jurisdiction of the U.S. Forest Service.

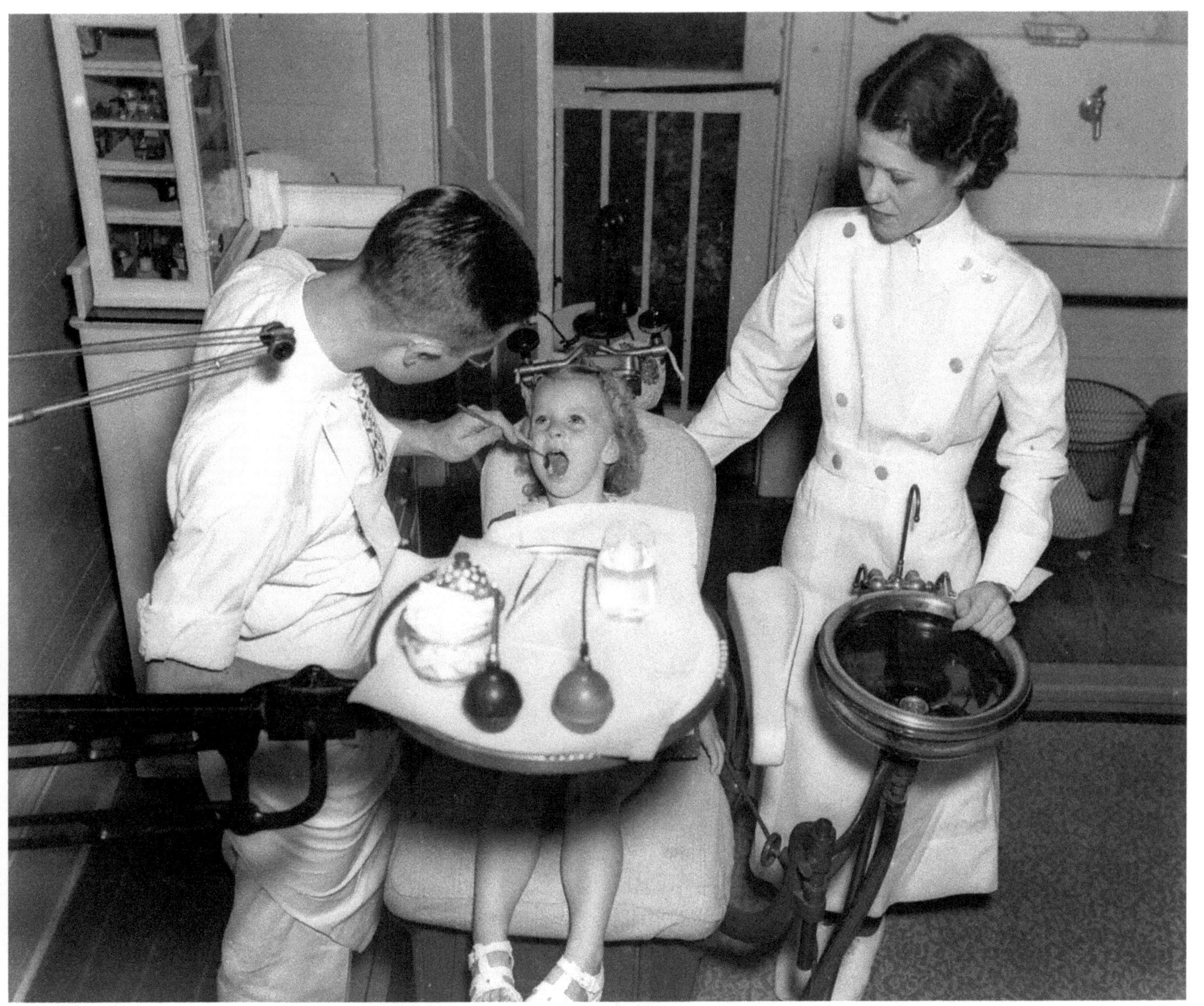

A young dentist, aided by an assistant, examines a child's teeth in a New Orleans dentistry office in the early 1940s.

Lieutenant General Lesley J. McNair, commanding general of U.S. Army ground forces in World War II, and an aide descend a slope while inspecting Third Army troop maneuvers in western Louisiana in 1942. McNair (1883–1944) served in the army for the last 40 years of his life, participating in the Mexican Expedition pursuing Pancho Villa in 1916 and in World War I.

He was accidentally killed during an Army Air Force bombing run in Normandy on July 25, 1944.

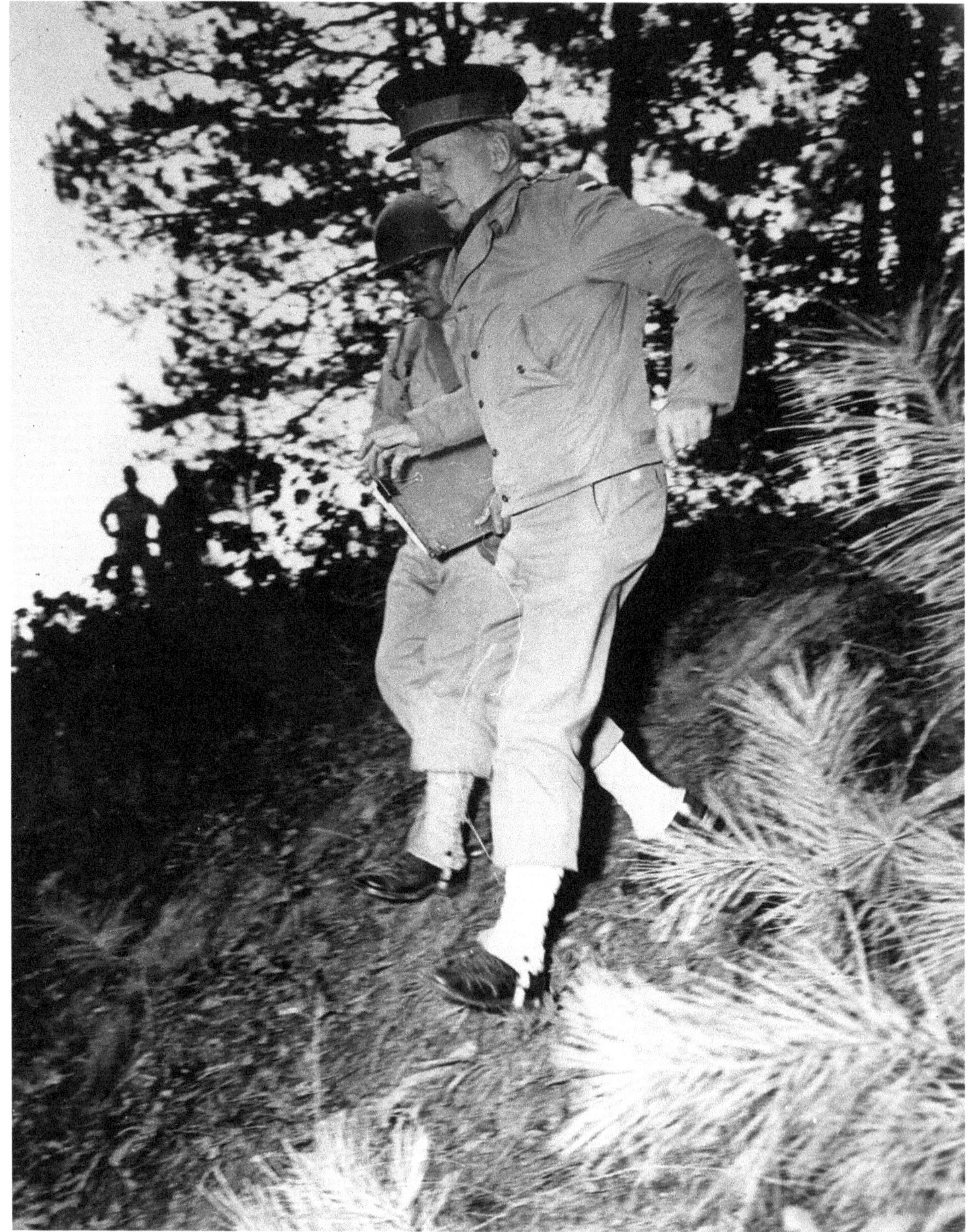

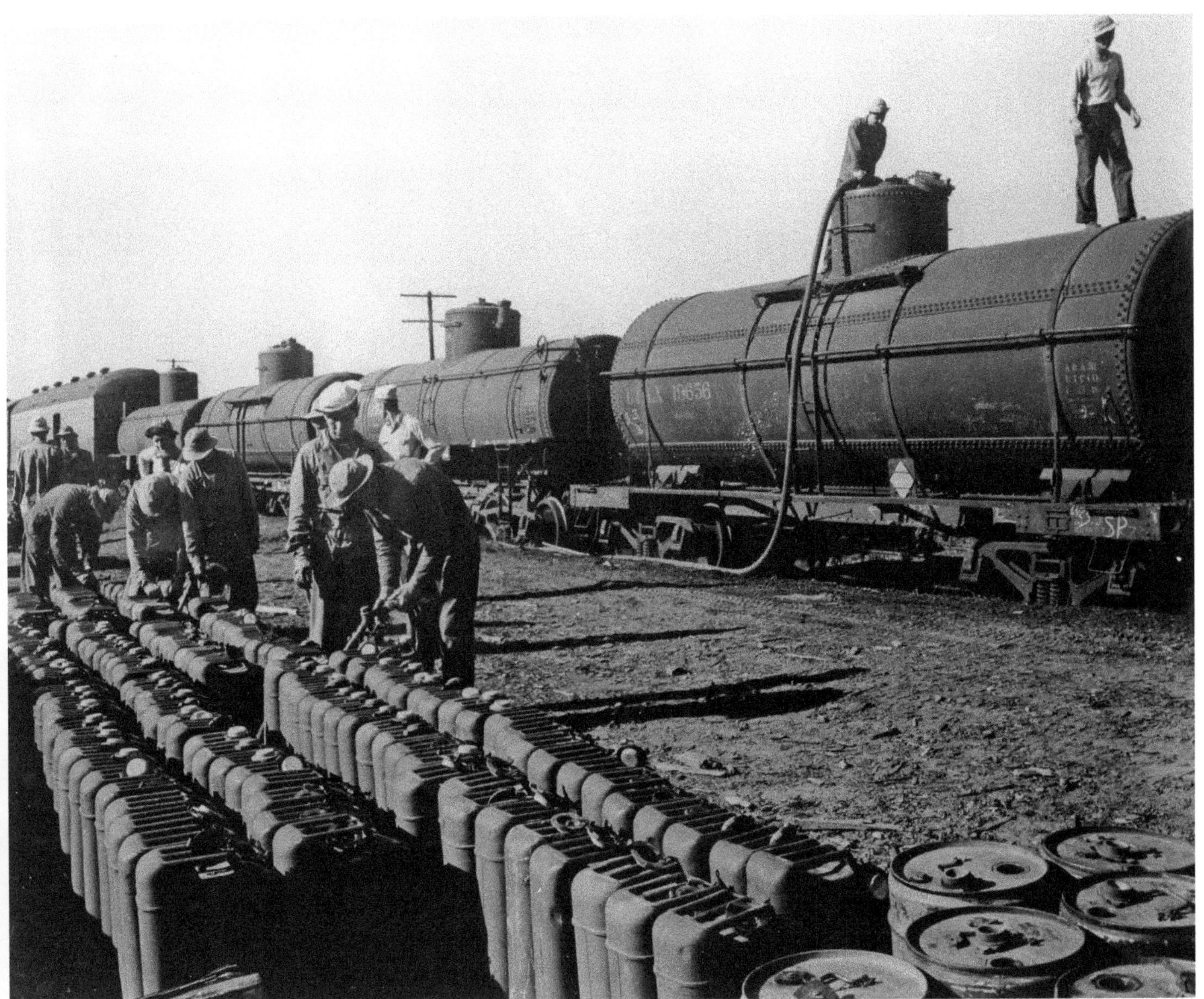

During Lieutenant General Walter Krueger's Third Army maneuvers in 1942, a group of civilian men supply the operations with gasoline directly from railroad tanker cars. The workers in the foreground fill up rows of five-gallon gasoline cans to be delivered to various field depots. The Third Army maneuvers began in summer 1941, before the U.S. entered World War II, and were held several times in subsequent years over a 3,400-square-mile area of western Louisiana.

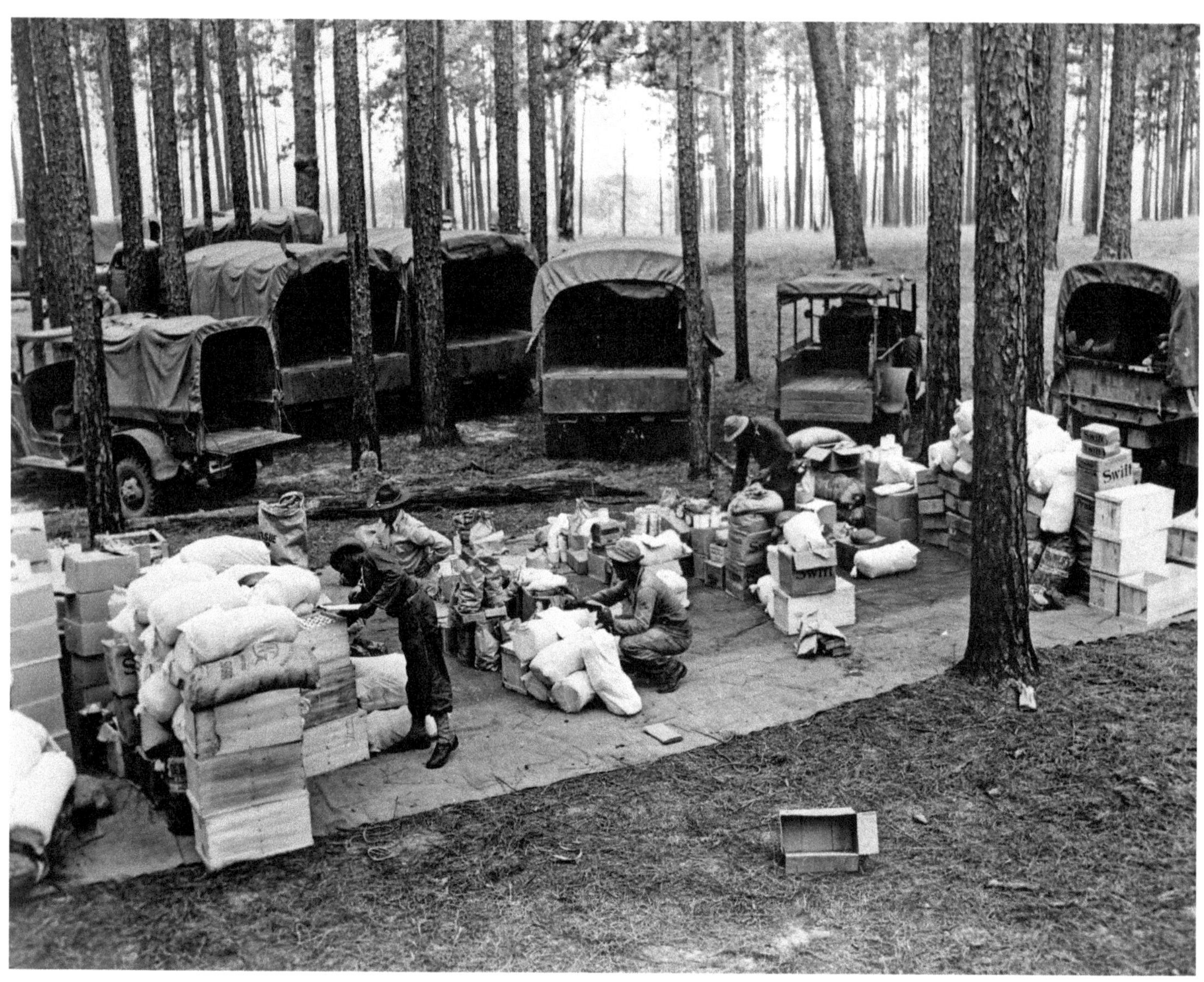

Food rations for the soldiers of the Third Army training in western Louisiana are sorted in a grove of pine trees. Among the rations are frozen beef, ham, potatoes, and fresh and canned vegetables. The open-backed, canvas-covered supply trucks are parked in the background. During the war nearly half a million men took part in army training exercises in western Louisiana.

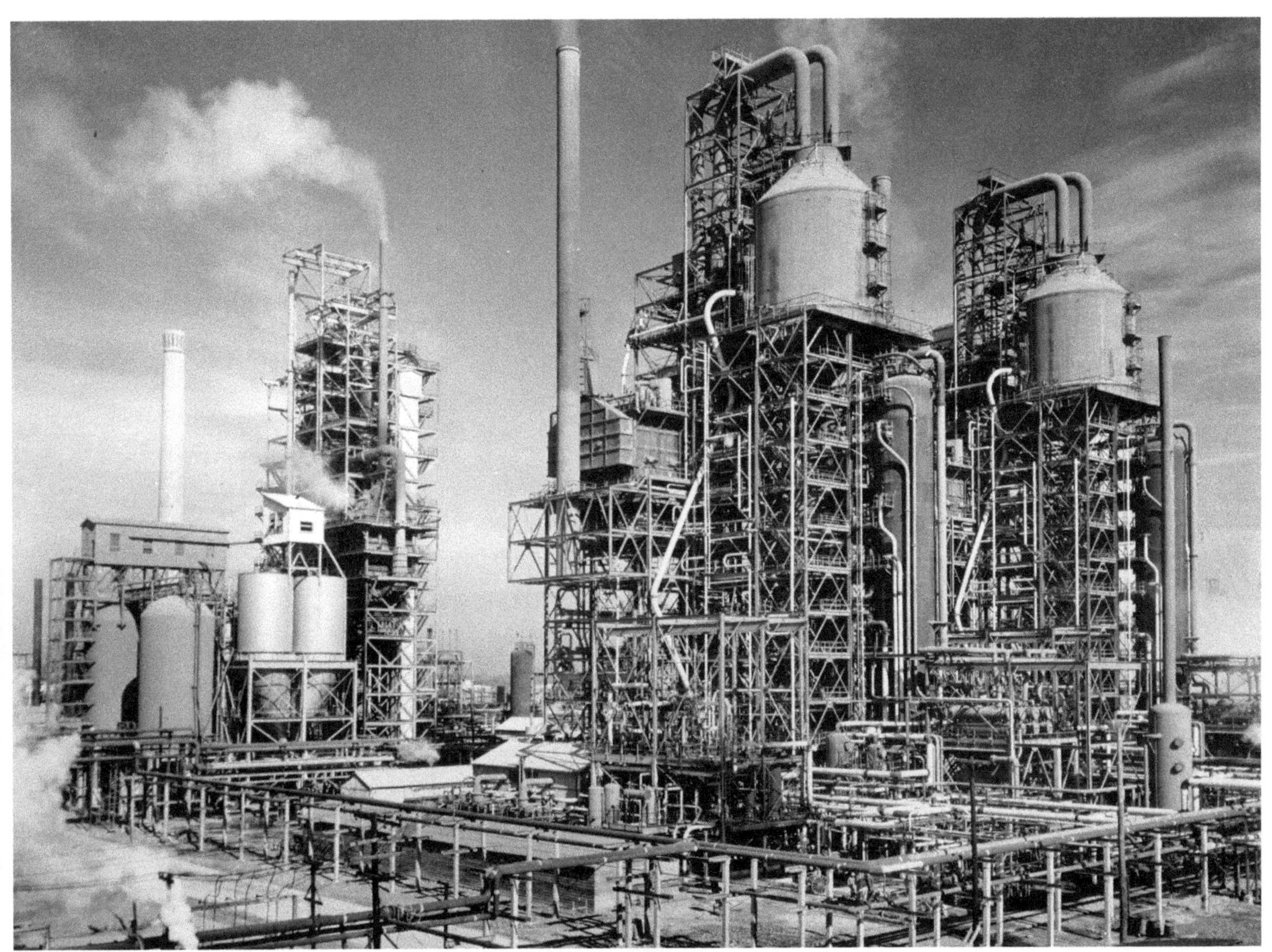

This massive oil refinery in south Louisiana in the mid-1940s was one of several in the state supplying fuel and lubricants to the Allied war effort. The refinery shown here featured three catalytic cracking units, better known as "cat crackers." The process breaks crude oil down into components that are refined into gasoline and other petroleum products. The American capacity to produce massive quantities of petroleum during the war is credited with helping hasten the Allied victory.

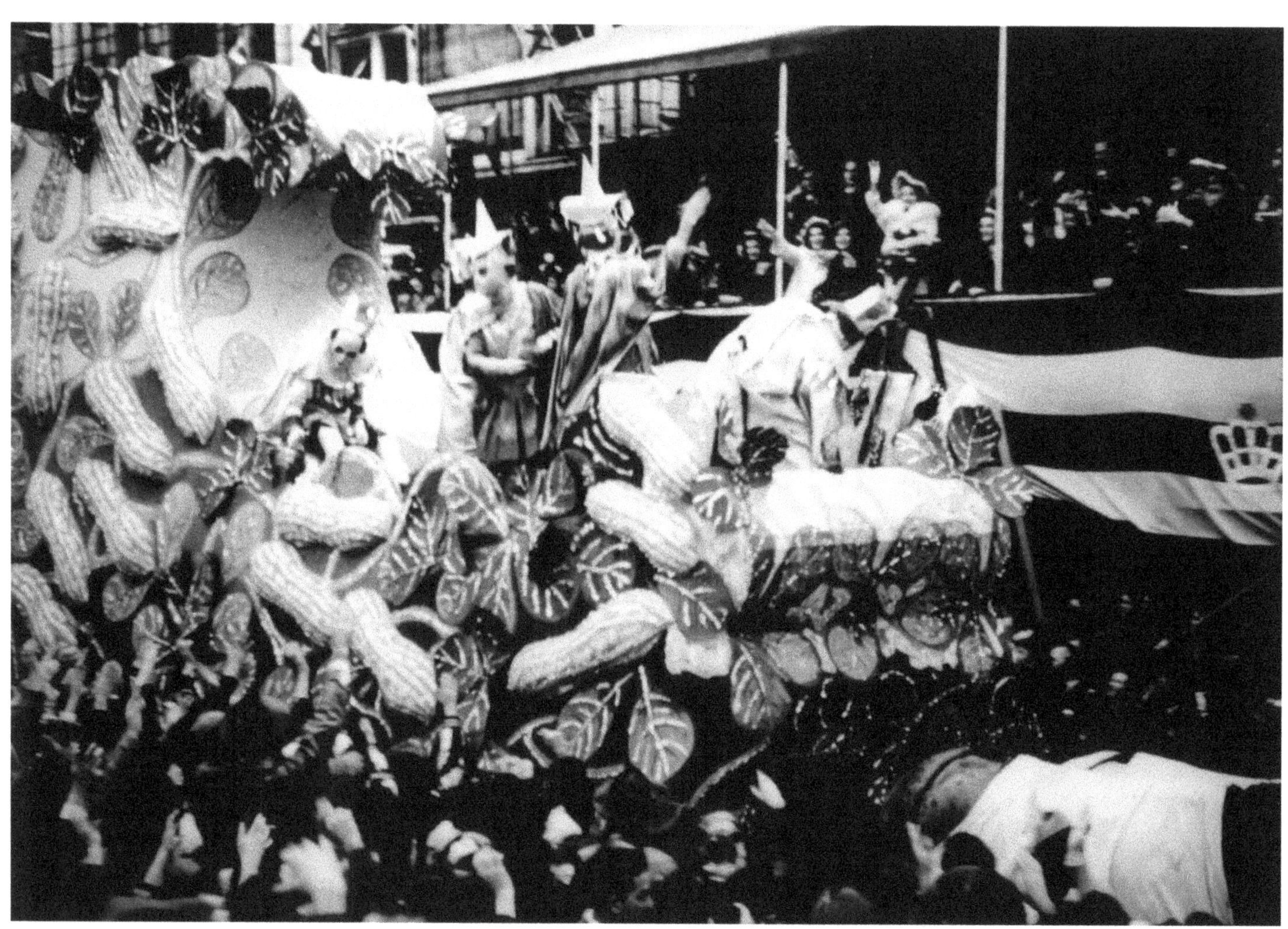

Spectators line the street in New Orleans during the 1949 Rex parade. The float in the foreground is decorated with large artificial peanuts. Mardi Gras celebrations were suspended for four years during World War II, resuming after the war in 1946. Also during Mardi Gras 1949, New Orleans native son Louis Armstrong reigned as king of the then-all-black Krewe of Zulu, providing one of the most memorable moments in the history of the annual celebration.

GROWING PAINS AT MIDCENTURY (1950–1969)

During the 1950s and 1960s, the oil industry remained Louisiana's economic mainstay. Newer and deeper wells were drilled offshore in the Gulf of Mexico, attracting thousands of laborers and pumping billions of dollars into the state's economy. To keep the operations as "local" as possible, massive refineries were constructed along a stretch of the Mississippi River from below New Orleans north to Baton Rouge. Other industries began to spring up along the river, as well. Grain elevators funneled thousands of tons of processed wheat into the holds of foreign vessels for shipment around the world. A thriving chemical industry developed, especially for petrochemicals relying on petroleum byproducts.

New Orleans reached the apex of its population growth in the 1960 census, with more than 600,000 people calling the city home. A steady decline would ensue in subsequent decades, but, for the moment, the city happily adapted to its growth with new downtown construction and transportation arteries. Much of the postwar prosperity was spread out fairly evenly around the state. New bridges were built over the Mississippi, speeding up travel and streamlining the flow of commerce. Improvements to infrastructure were undertaken, which included new buildings, better drainage, and better roads.

Attendance at the state's ever-expanding public university system grew, along with an increasing awareness of the importance of education in meeting the demands of a modern society. College athletics, especially LSU football, enjoyed wide popularity and support, bringing home more than a few winning and championship seasons. Festivals, always in abundance in Louisiana nearly year-round, continued to grow in number as more people found more things to celebrate. Whether it was crustaceans, crops, culinary delights, or some other product important to the state, there was a festival to tout it and an economic impact to be gained.

Not all of the state's progress was rosy. Oil and natural gas drilling and shipping in the state's coastal wetlands began contributing to marsh erosion and disruptions to the vital commercial fishing industry. Large population centers like New Orleans became more vulnerable to destructive hurricanes. Nonetheless, the state bravely soldiers on, in good times and bad, all with the same basic attitude often seen on today's souvenir T-shirts: *Laissez le bon temps rouler.* "Let the good times roll."

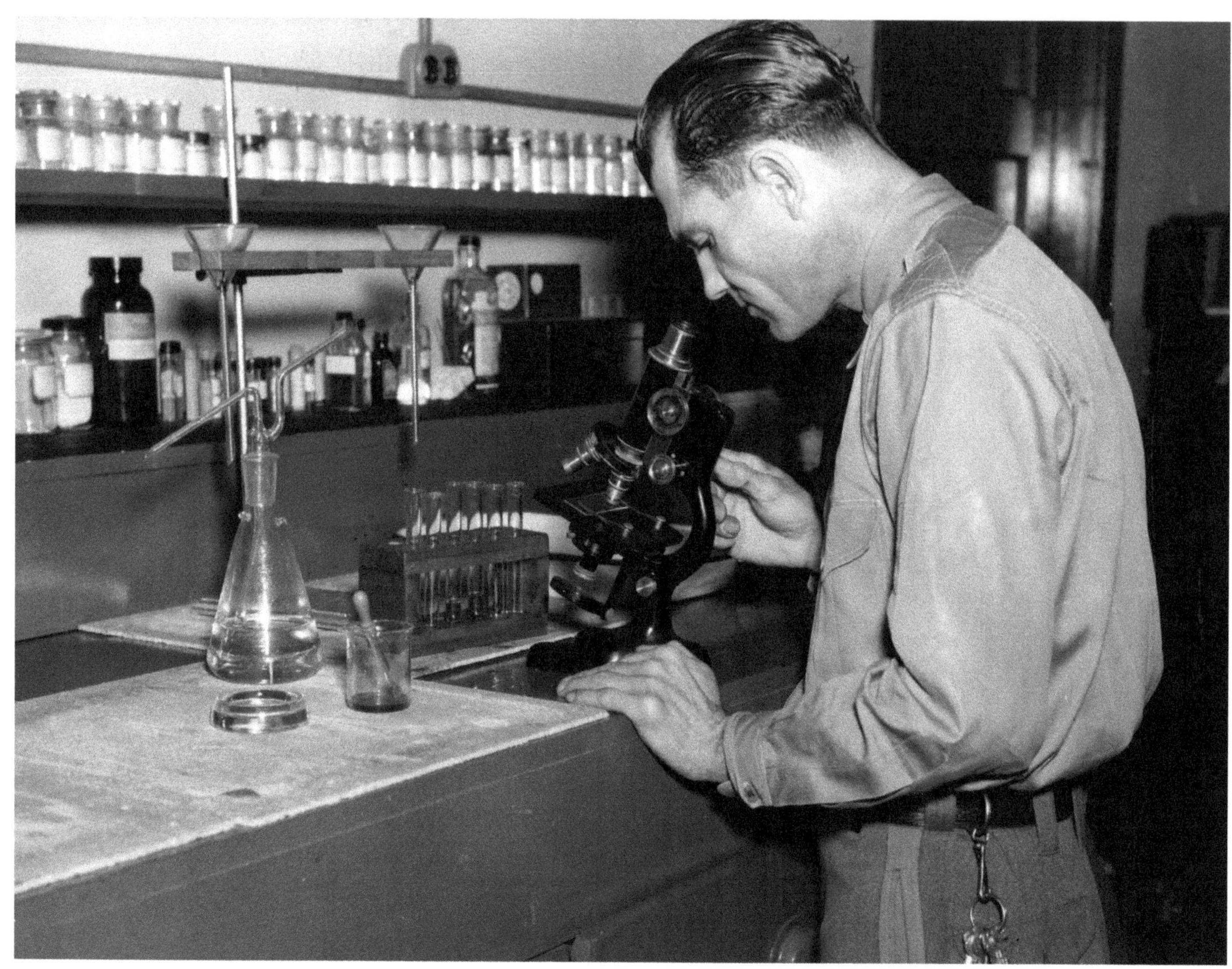

A law enforcement officer examines crime scene clues under a microscope in the Louisiana State Police Crime Lab in Baton Rouge around 1950.

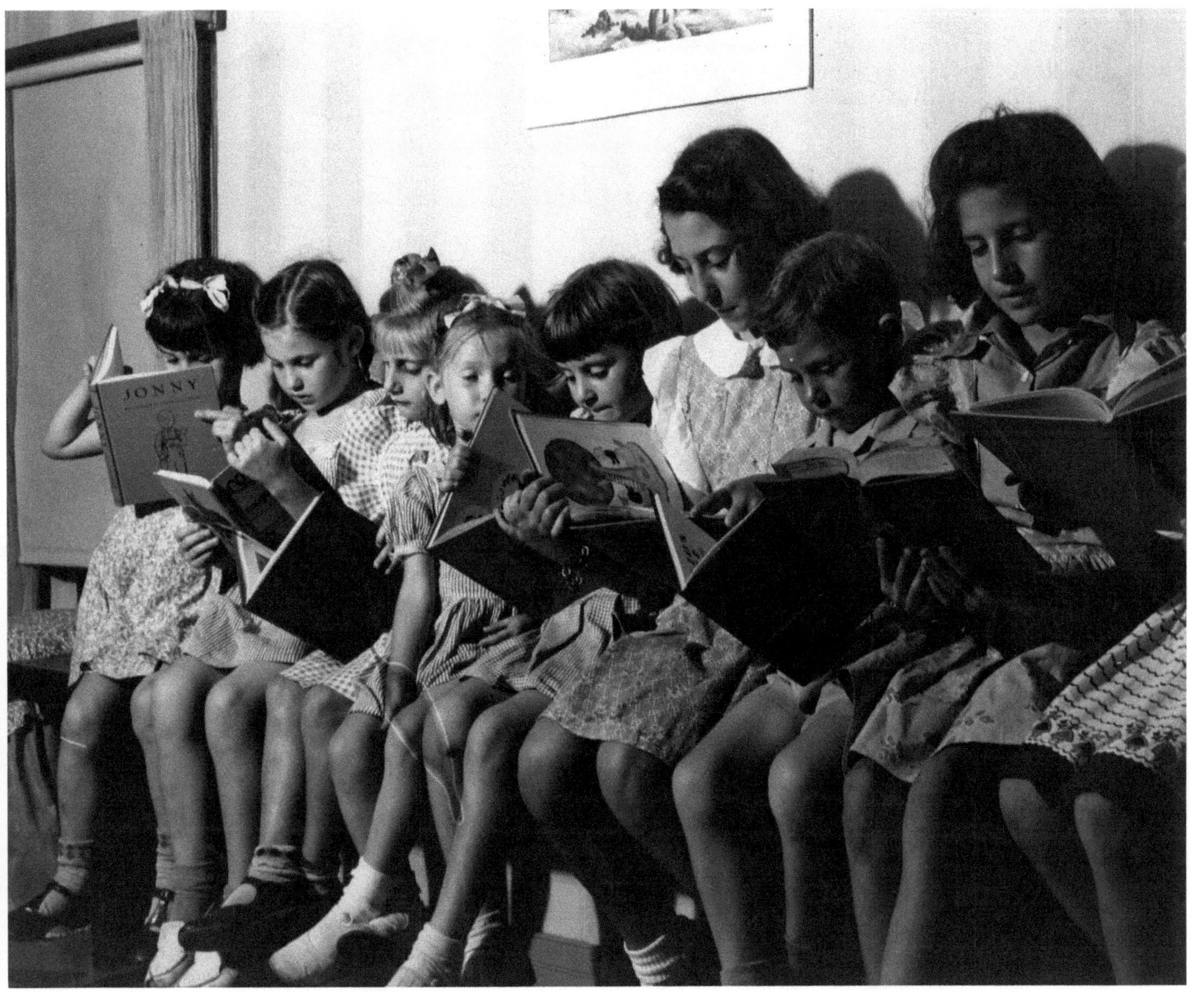

Around 1950, a group of children of varying ages sit on a bench reading books in the Bell City branch of the Calcasieu Parish Library.

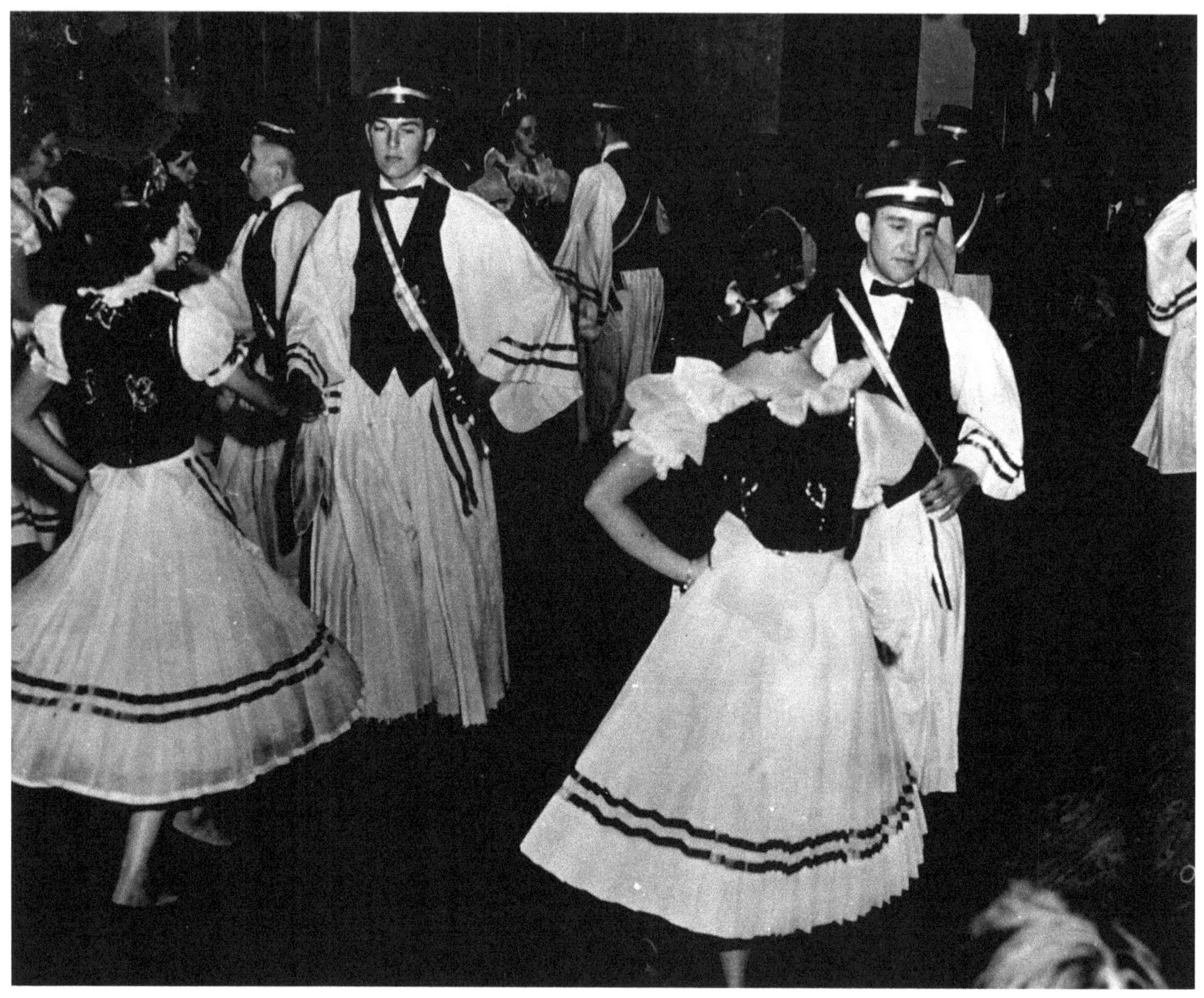

Louisianians of Hungarian descent in colorful folk dresses and military-style uniforms dance the Csardas, a traditional Magyar dance, at the 1950 Hungarian Harvest Festival in Albany, Livingston Parish. Reported to be the largest rural Hungarian settlement in the United States, it was established in 1896 under the name Árpádhon (for Árpád, a ninth-century Magyar tribal leader, and "hon" for home[land]). The festival is still held today, following the end of the strawberry harvesting season.

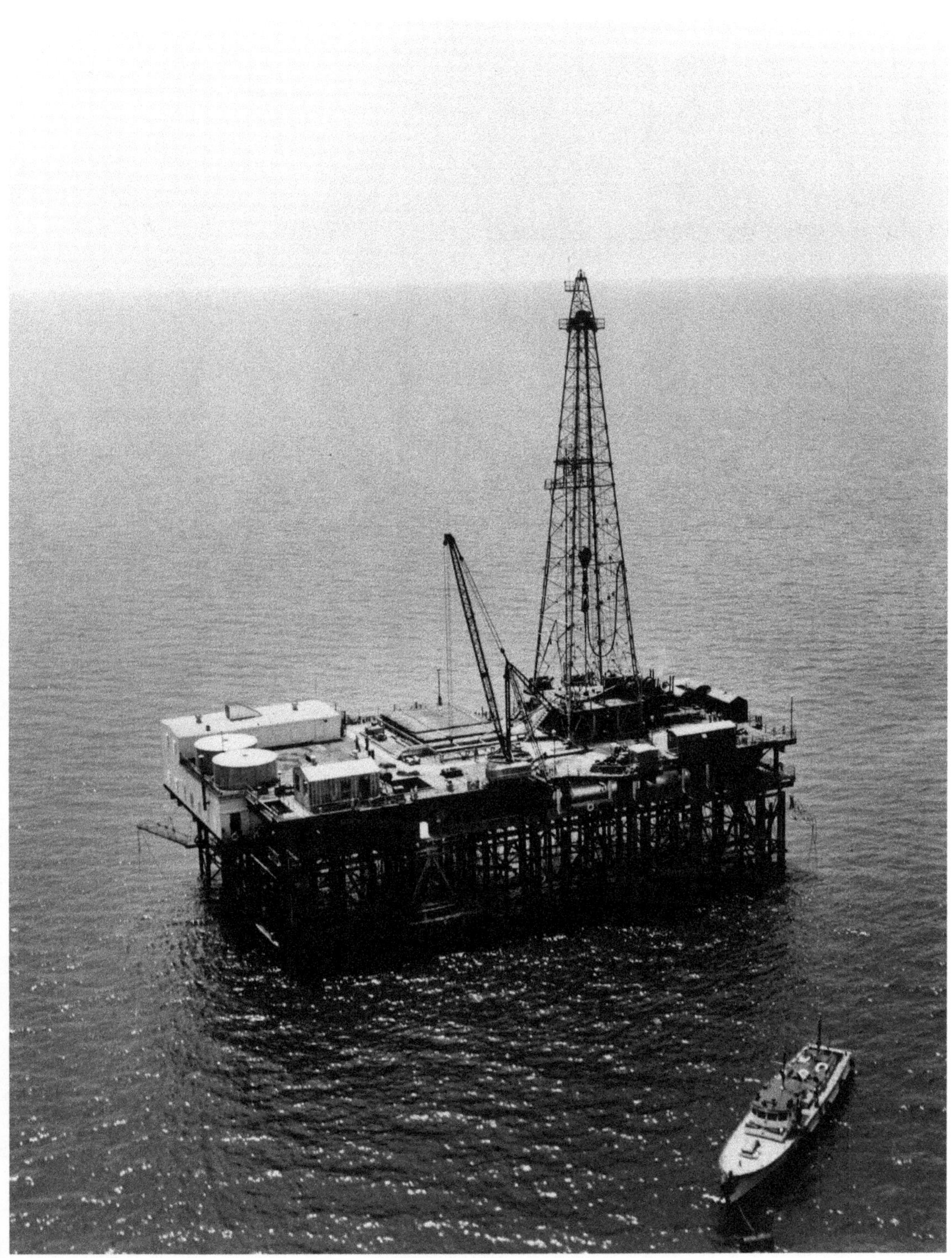

This photo of a Humble Oil & Refining Company drilling platform in the Gulf of Mexico was taken in 1950, the same year a U.S. Supreme Court decision gave dominion over offshore drilling operations to the federal government. After World War II, the demand for oil was so great that drilling operations in the Gulf were undertaken on a large scale. By 1949, 44 wells had been drilled there, many of which were off the coast of Louisiana.

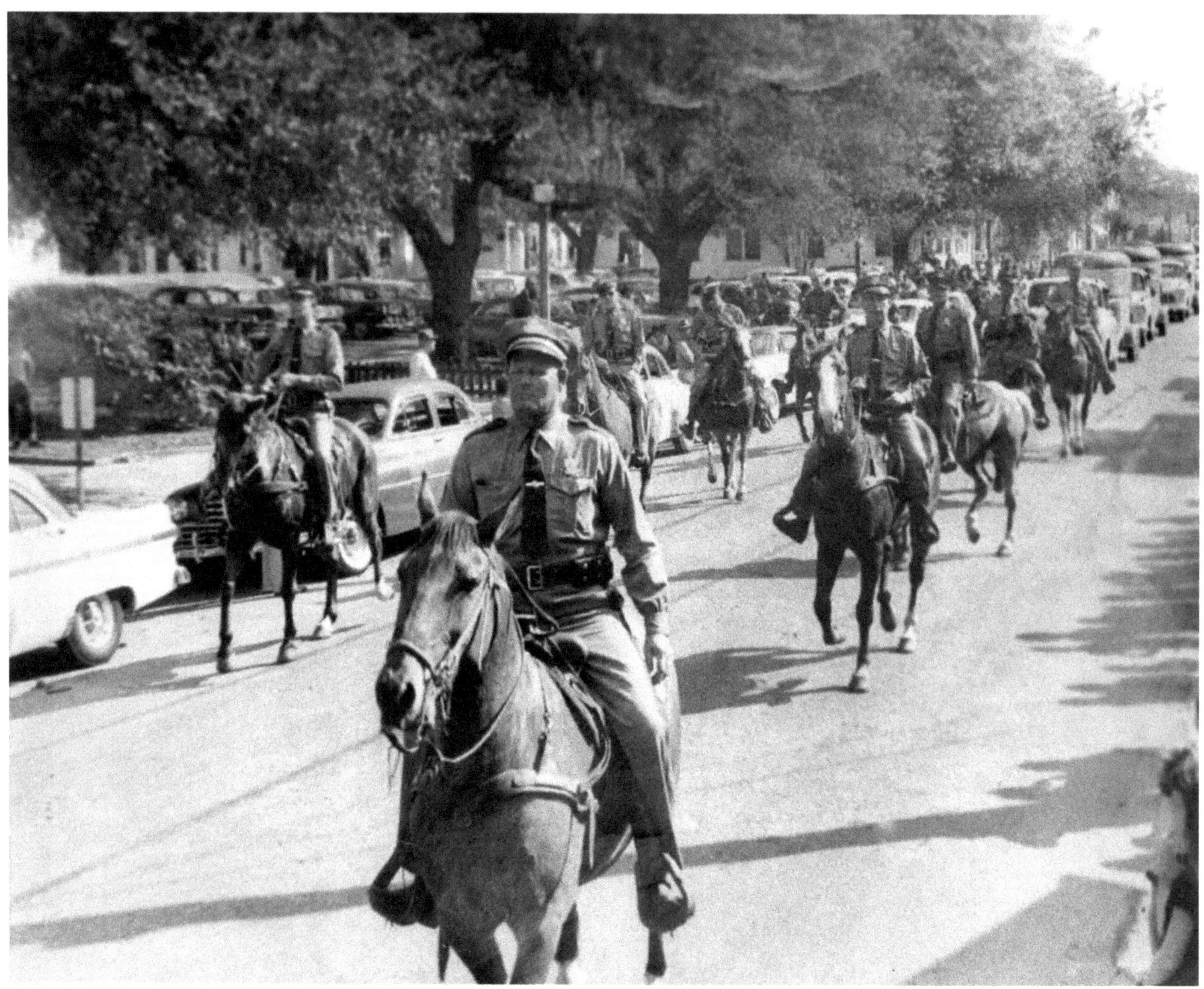

Louisiana State Police officers of the "Stock Patrol" ride their horses down the middle of a Baton Rouge street in 1951. The Stock Patrol was started that year to remove livestock from highways, but their role expanded to assist as security during civil rights marches and live music concerts. State and local mounted police are still relied on today, especially during large-scale events like Mardi Gras, where their position high in the saddle gives them a better view of crowds.

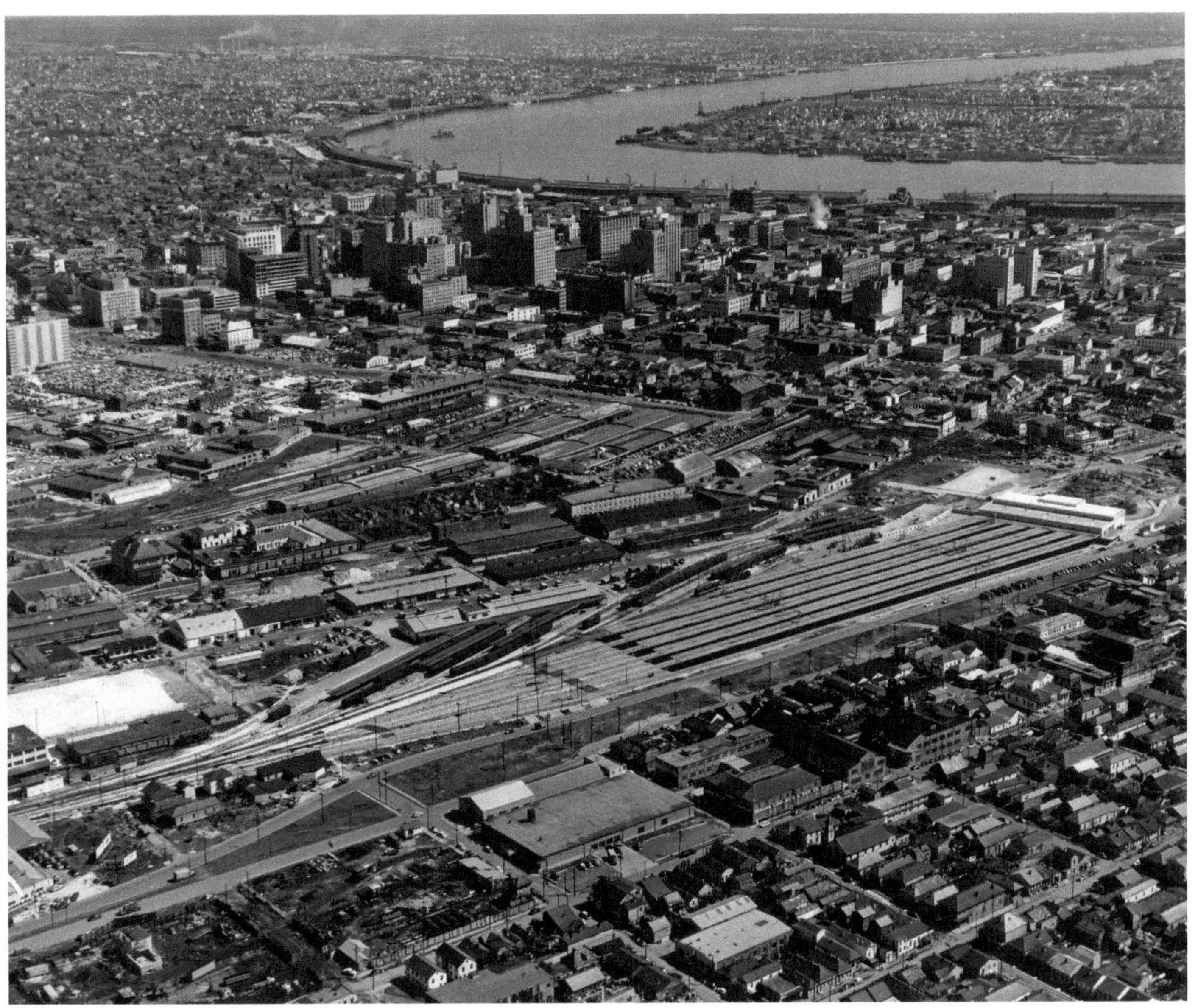

This aerial photo taken in 1954 shows the newly completed Union Passenger Terminal in downtown New Orleans. The new station centralized passenger train operations, which had been scattered throughout the city. The UPT, which operates today as both an Amtrak and Greyhound Bus terminal, was built for a cost of $54 million and eliminated 144 track crossings from the city. The New Orleans skyline and the hairpin bend of the Mississippi River are visible in the background.

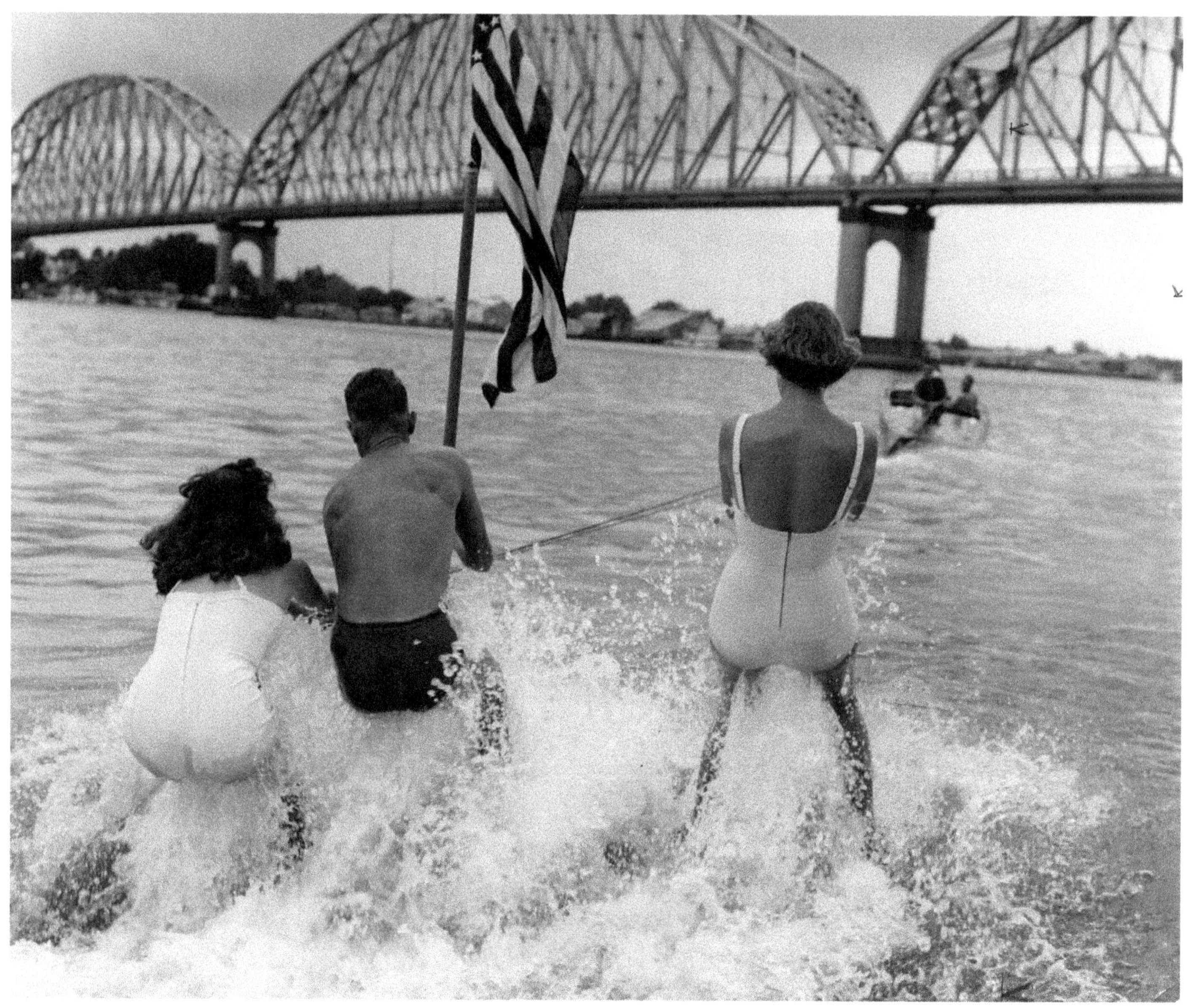

Water-skiers hang onto their tow ropes as they prepare to pass under a bridge during the 1955 Delcambre Shrimp Festival. Locally pronounced "Del-cum," this village of about 2,000 residents is 20 miles south of Lafayette and lies within both Vermilion and Iberia parishes. It is the hub of a large shrimping industry, and the Delcambre Shrimp Festival is held the third weekend in August each year to commemorate this heritage.

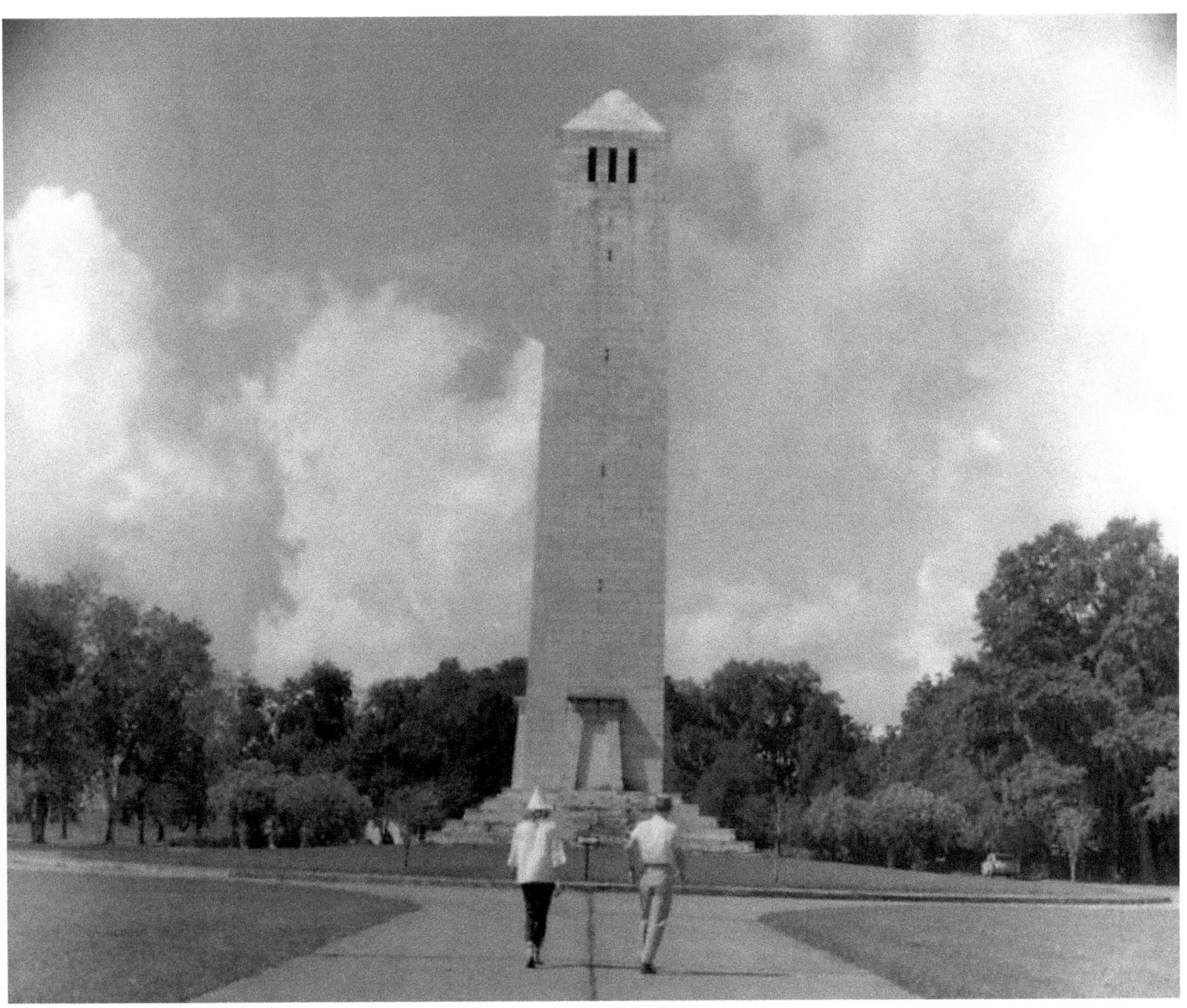

Here in 1959, two visitors approach the obelisk of the Battle of New Orleans monument on the grounds of the Chalmette Battlefield Unit of Jean Lafitte National Historical Park in Chalmette. It was on this site that a ragtag army under General Andrew Jackson soundly defeated seasoned British troops in the final engagement of the War of 1812. The January 8, 1815, battle ended the last invasion on American soil by a hostile foreign army and helped propel Jackson into the presidency in 1828.

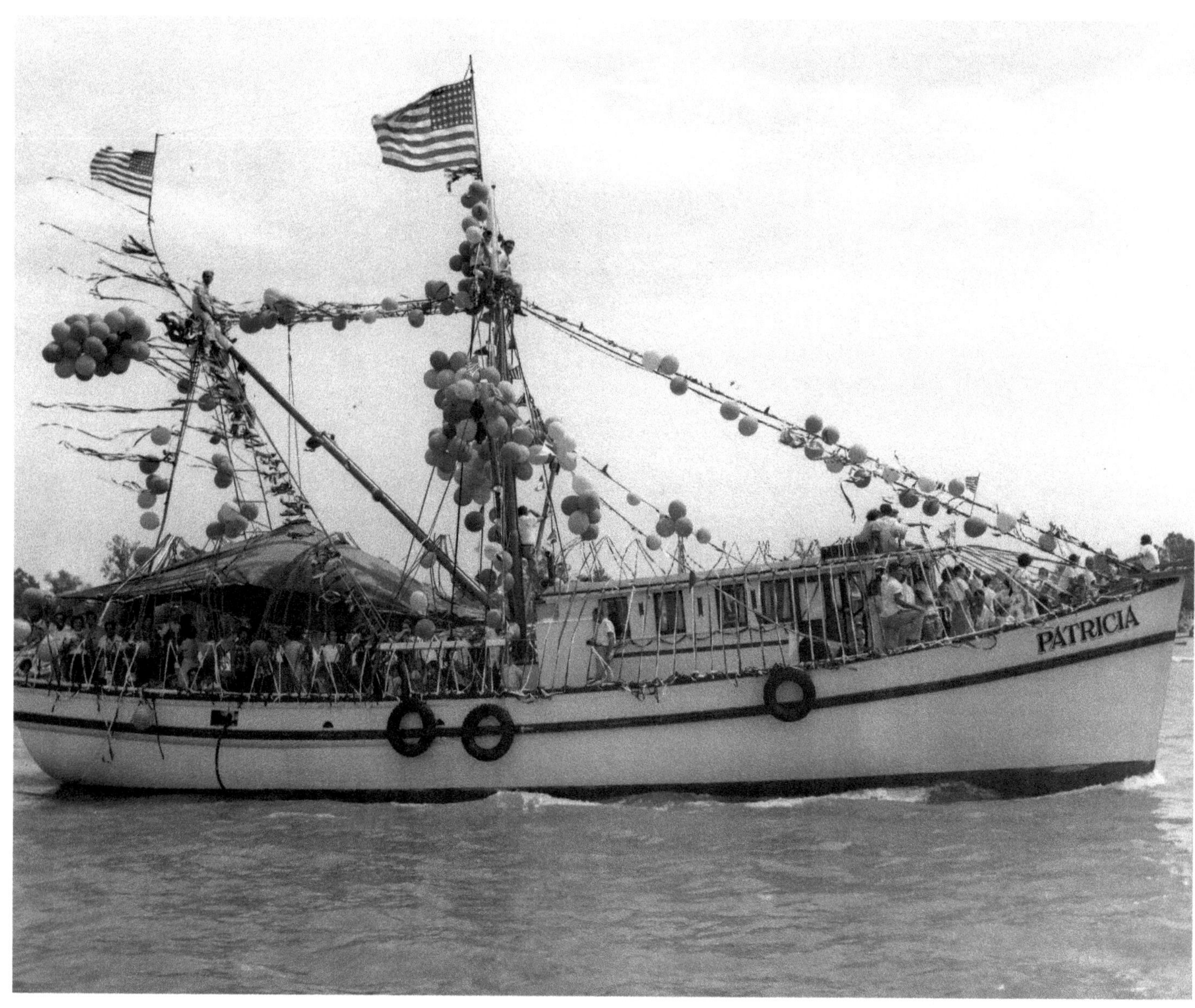

A festively decorated shrimp trawler bearing the name *Patricia* takes part in the annual Blessing of the Fleet at the Morgan City Shrimp Festival around 1960. A colorful ritual dating back several centuries to predominantly Catholic regions along the Mediterranean Sea, the tradition took root in the southern U.S. in the 1800s. A priest would come aboard a fishing vessel and bless it, offering a prayer for the safety of those aboard and for a bountiful harvest.

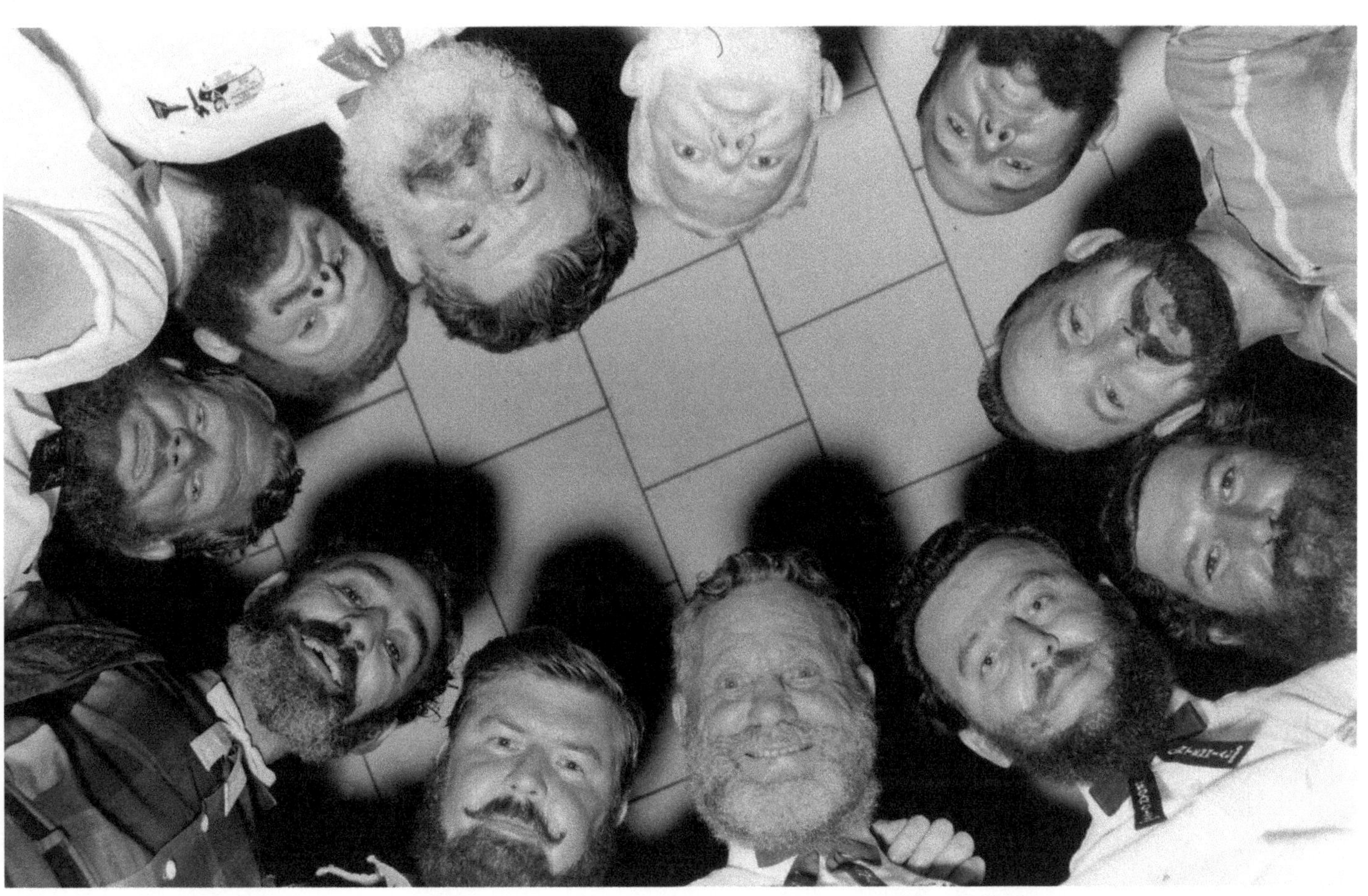

A group of bearded men take part in the 1960 Centennial celebration at the Morgan City Shrimp Festival. Incorporated in 1860 as Brashear City after early settler Walter Brashear, the name was changed to Morgan City to honor rail and steamship magnate Charles Morgan, who first dredged the Atchafalaya Bay Ship Channel to accommodate oceangoing vessels. Held annually on Labor Day weekend, today's Shrimp and Petroleum Festival honors Morgan City's two leading industries.

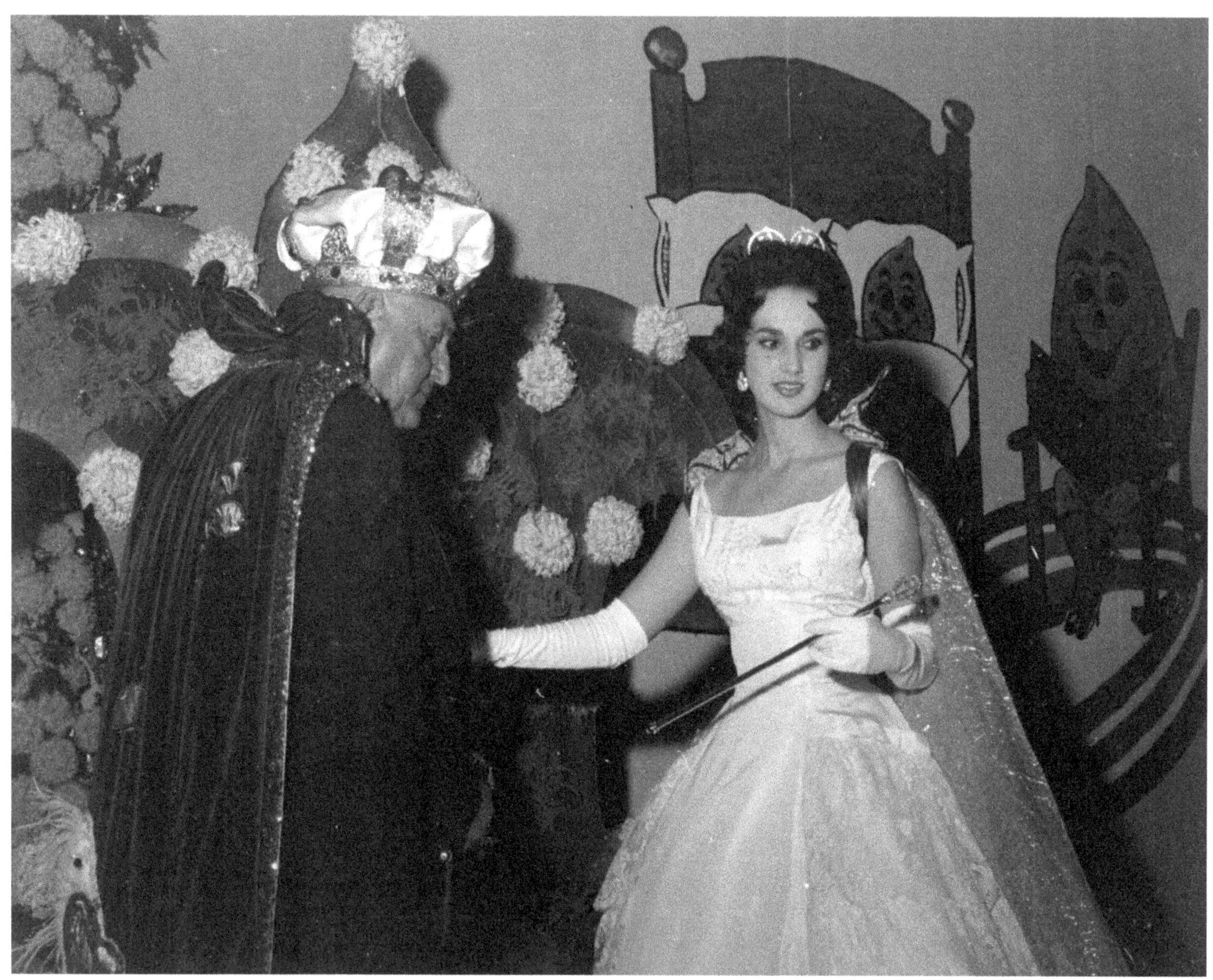

The King of the Yambilee Festival in Opelousas greets his Queen. Opelousas, the seat of St. Landry Parish, lies in the heart of a productive sweet potato region, and the Yambilee Festival is held the final weekend of October, around the time the yams are harvested. The festival was first held in 1946; the one shown here, some years later.

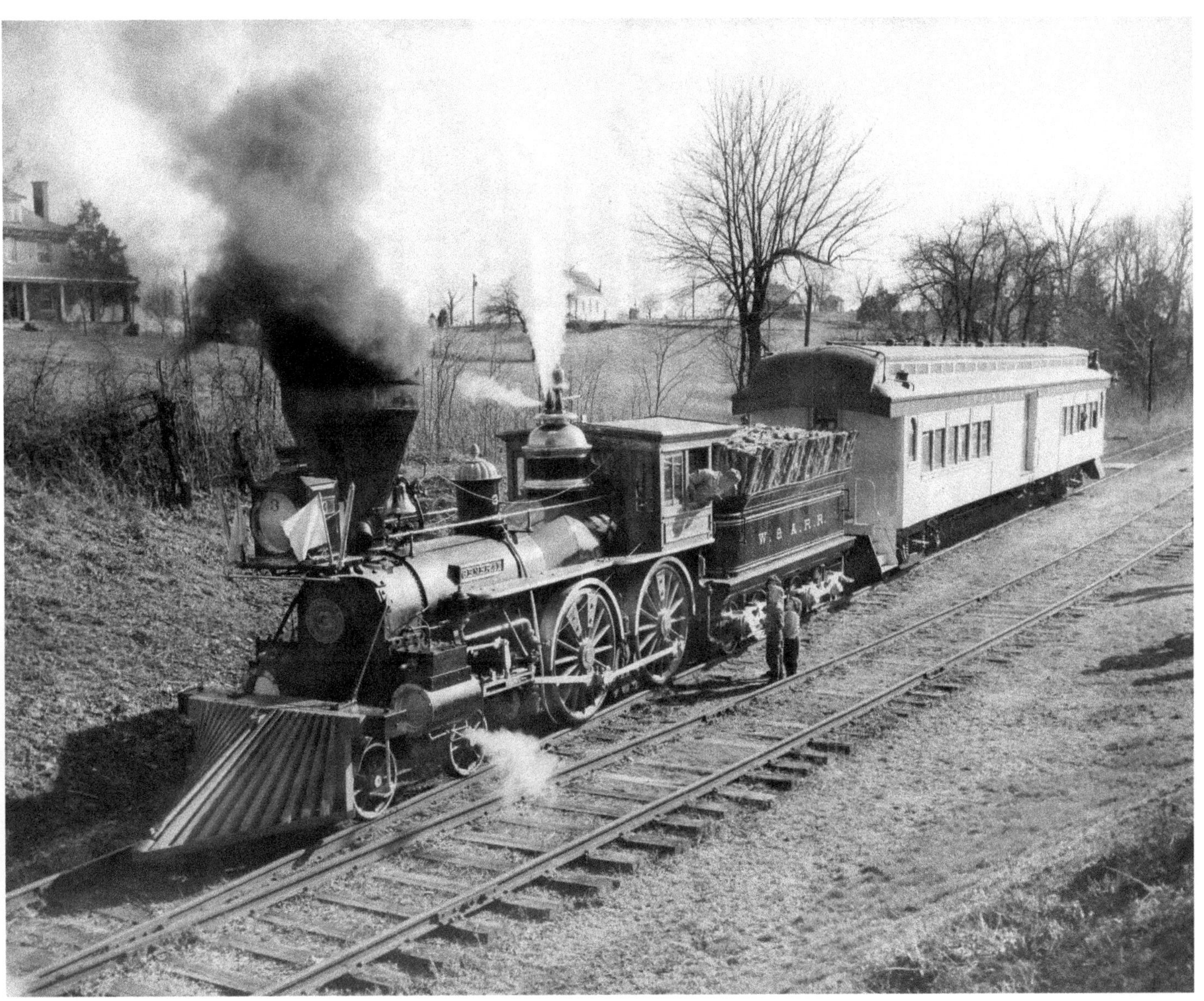

The historic steam locomotive *General* makes a stop in an unspecified rural location in 1962 during its Centennial tour through parts of the nation. The *General* figured prominently in the Civil War when a group of Northerners led by James Andrews commandeered the engine at Big Shanty, Georgia. Formerly the famous engine was preserved at Chattanooga, Tennessee, the northern terminus of its route between Atlanta. Today the engine and tender are on display at the Southern Museum of Civil War and Locomotive History at Kennesaw, Georgia.

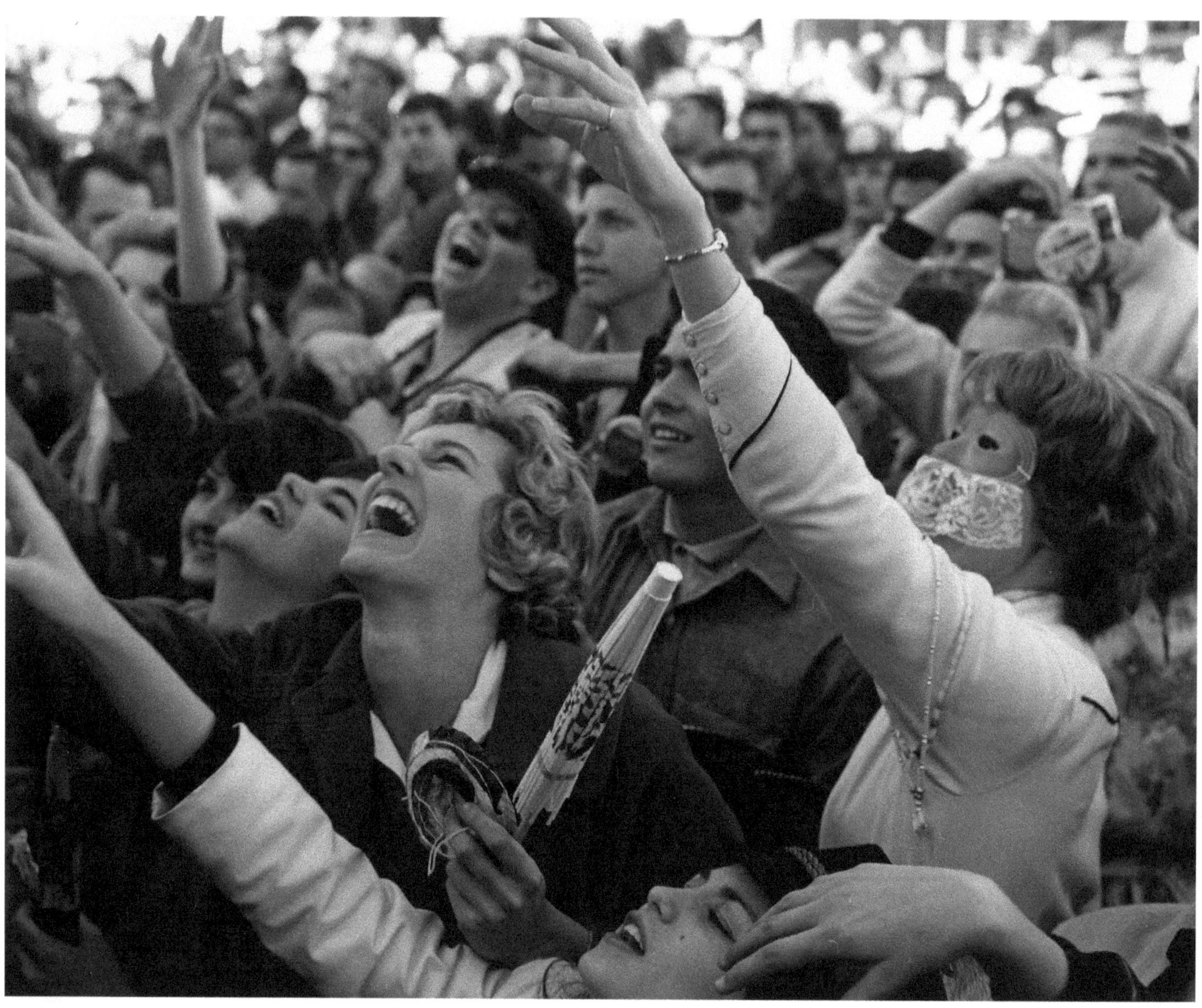

Mardi Gras parade-goers wave their hands in the air, trying to catch "throws" from passing floats in 1962. The tradition of float riders throwing trinkets to the crowds along the parade route dates back to around the 1920s. Originally, glass beads were thrown but were replaced with plastic beads in the 1960s. Today there are hundreds of different throws, ranging from aluminum coins (doubloons) and plastic cups to stuffed animals and much more.

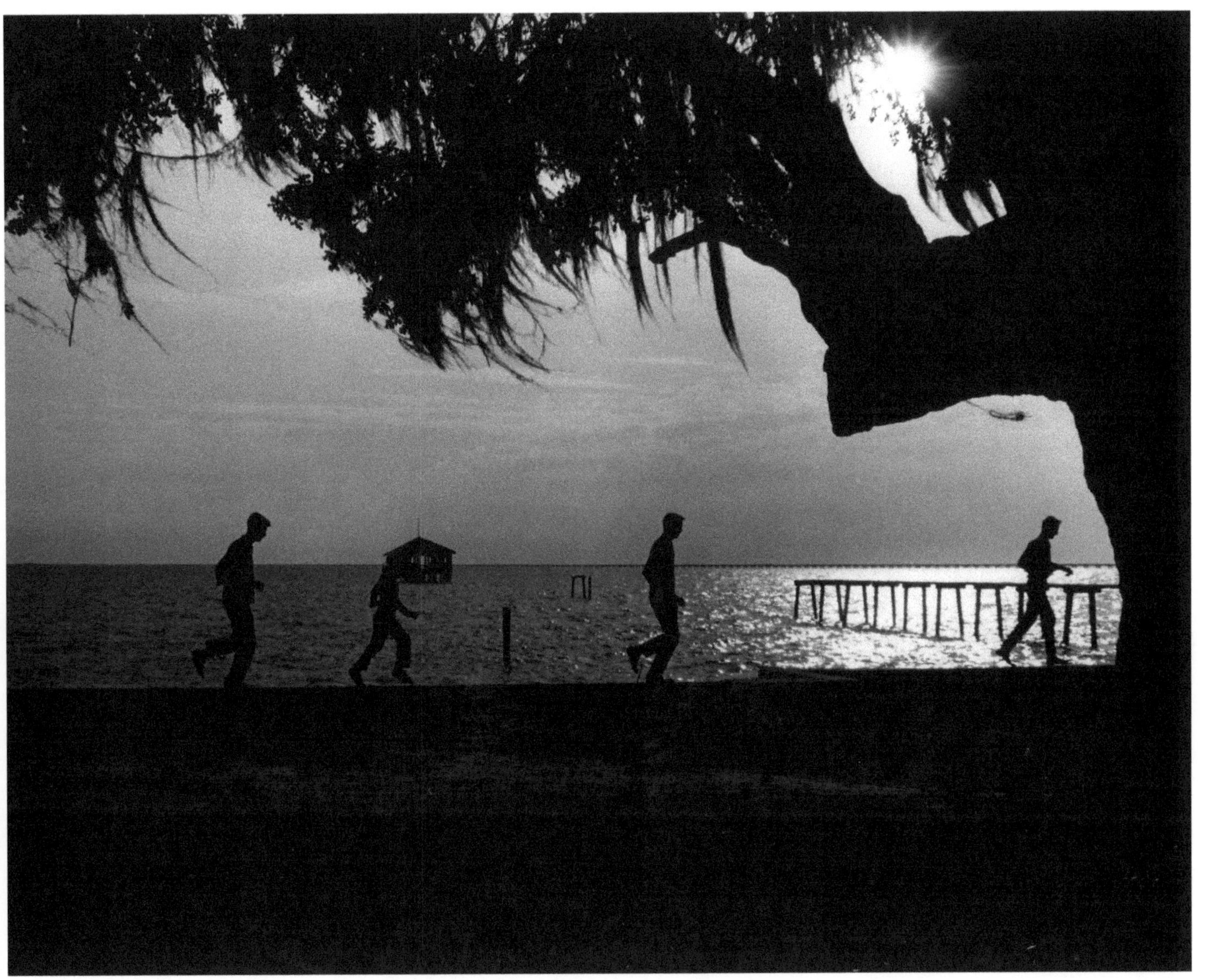

Four young men jog along the shore of Lake Pontchartrain in Mandeville at sunset in 1963. The placid scene along the Mandeville lakefront looks much the same today, but the surrounding area in St. Tammany Parish has experienced explosive growth since the 1980s, made possible in large part by the 24-mile-long Lake Pontchartrain Causeway, which connects Mandeville to the New Orleans area. Barely visible in the background, the causeway is the longest continuous overwater span in the world.

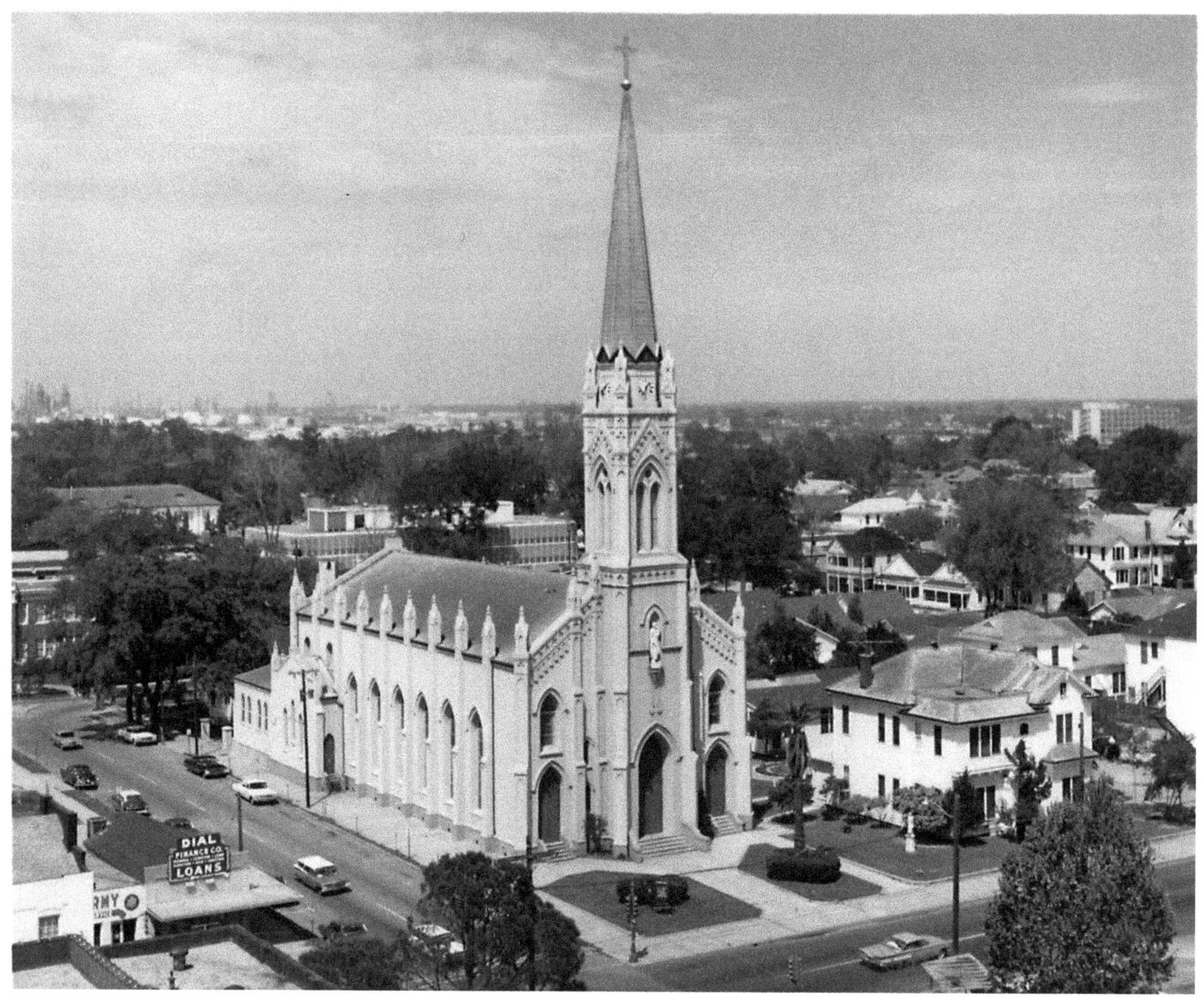

St. Joseph Cathedral and its rectory in Baton Rouge as they appeared in 1964. Built in 1853 in the classic Gothic style and consecrated as a cathedral in 1970, St. Joseph's is the home church of the Bishop of the Baton Rouge Diocese.

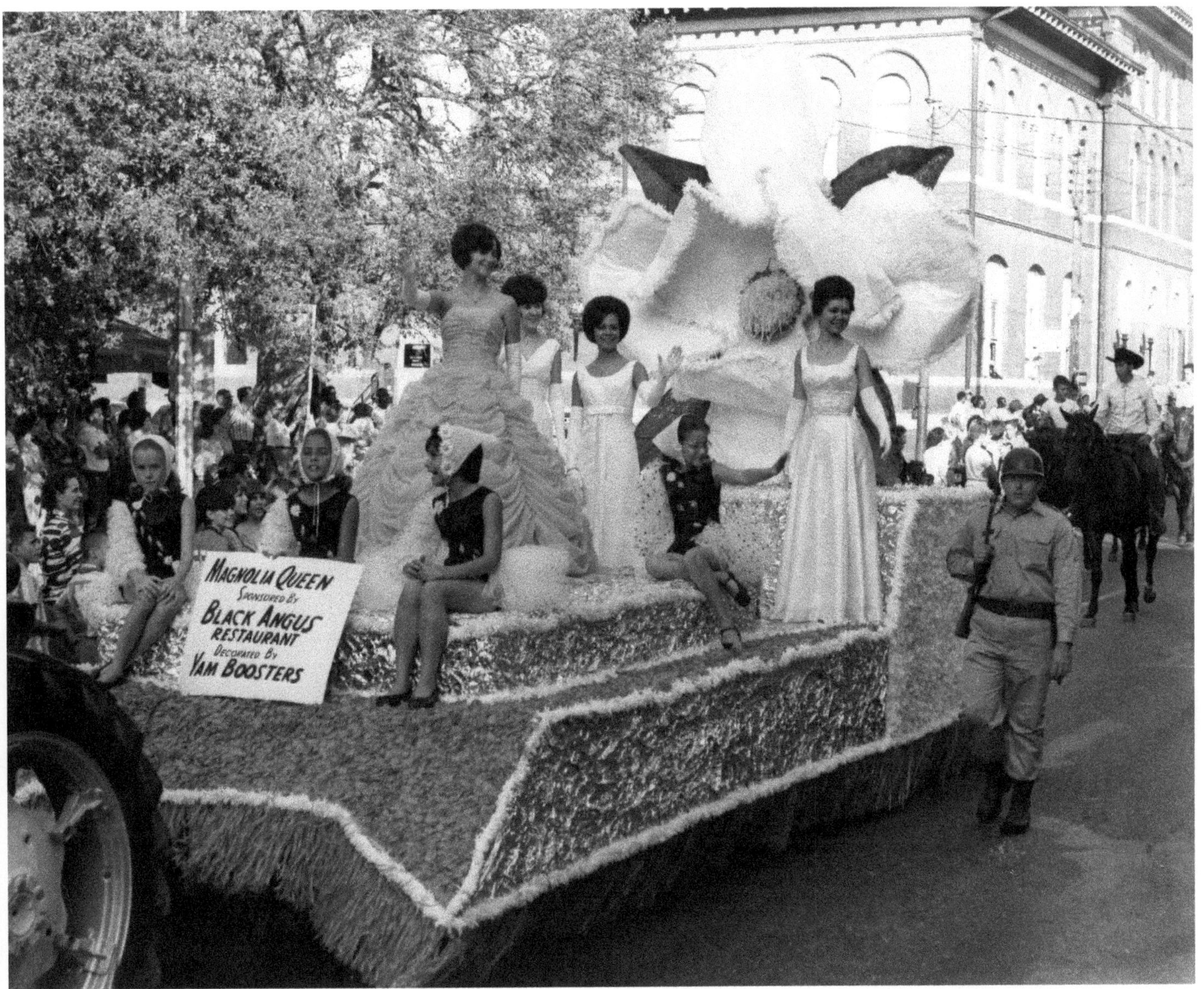

The 1965 Magnolia Queen of the Yambilee Festival and members of her court ride through the streets of Opelousas in the "Grand Louisyam" parade. The award-winning float in the parade, it was sponsored by the Black Angus Restaurant and decorated by Yam Boosters. A uniformed soldier walks alongside the float and men on horseback ride behind it.

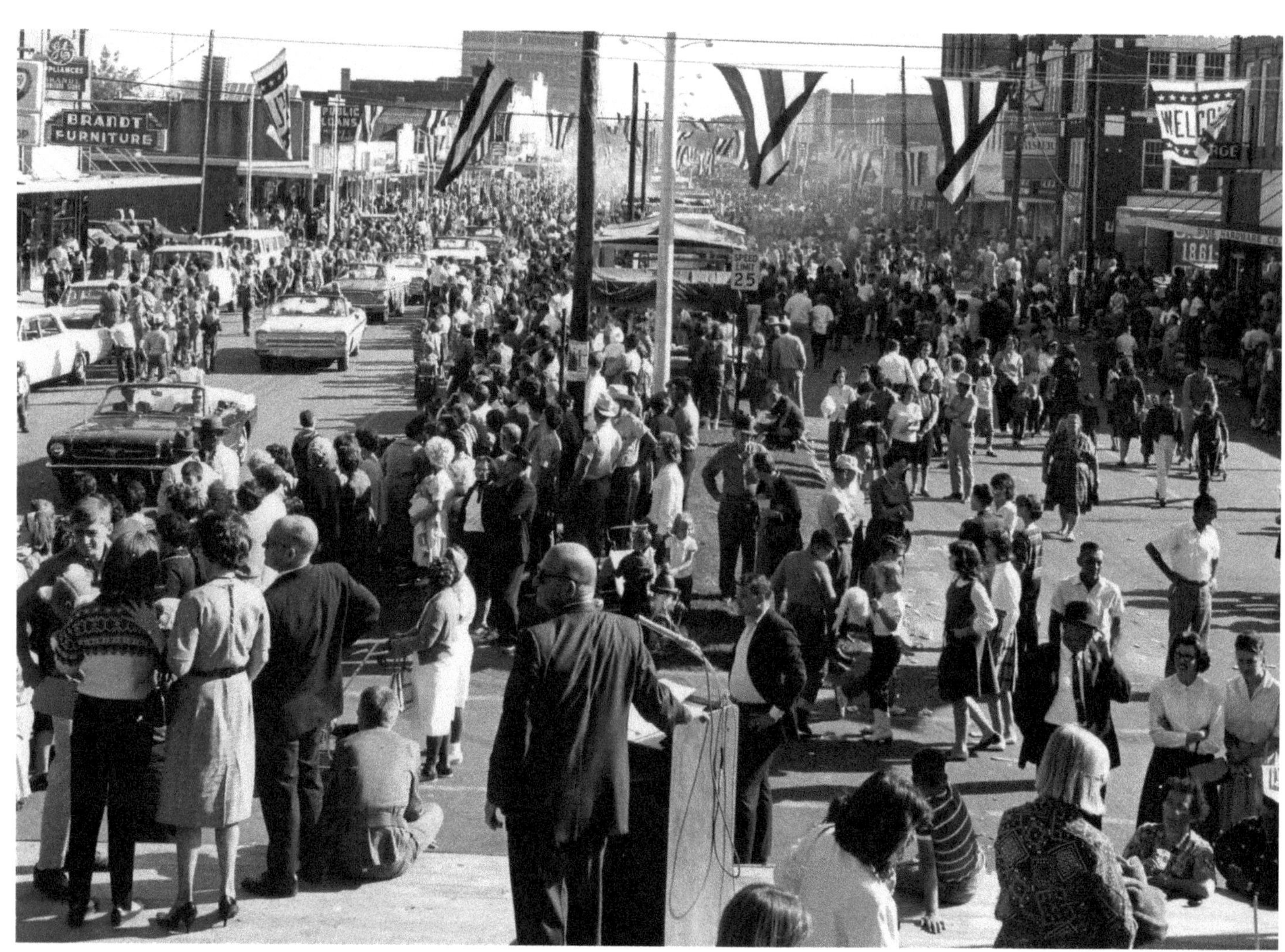

Spectators gather along a main street in Crowley to watch the 1965 Rice Festival parade.

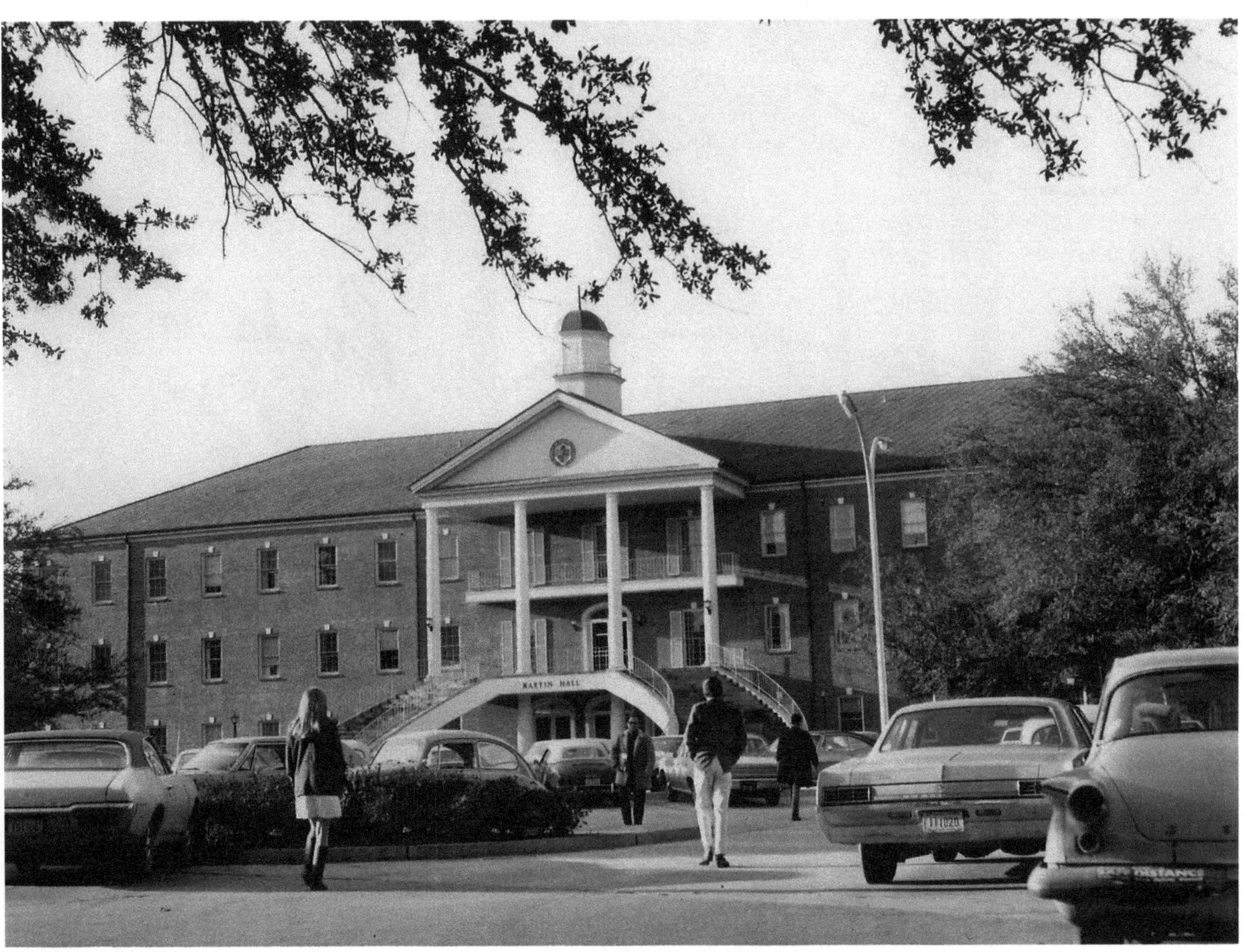

Students approach the front of Martin Hall on the campus of the University of Southwestern Louisiana sometime in the 1960s. Founded in 1900 as the Southwestern Louisiana Industrial Institute, USL went through several name changes before becoming the University of Louisiana at Lafayette in 1999. Today it is the home of the colorfully named "Ragin' Cajuns" NCAA athletic teams and counted a student body of nearly 20,000 in 2008.

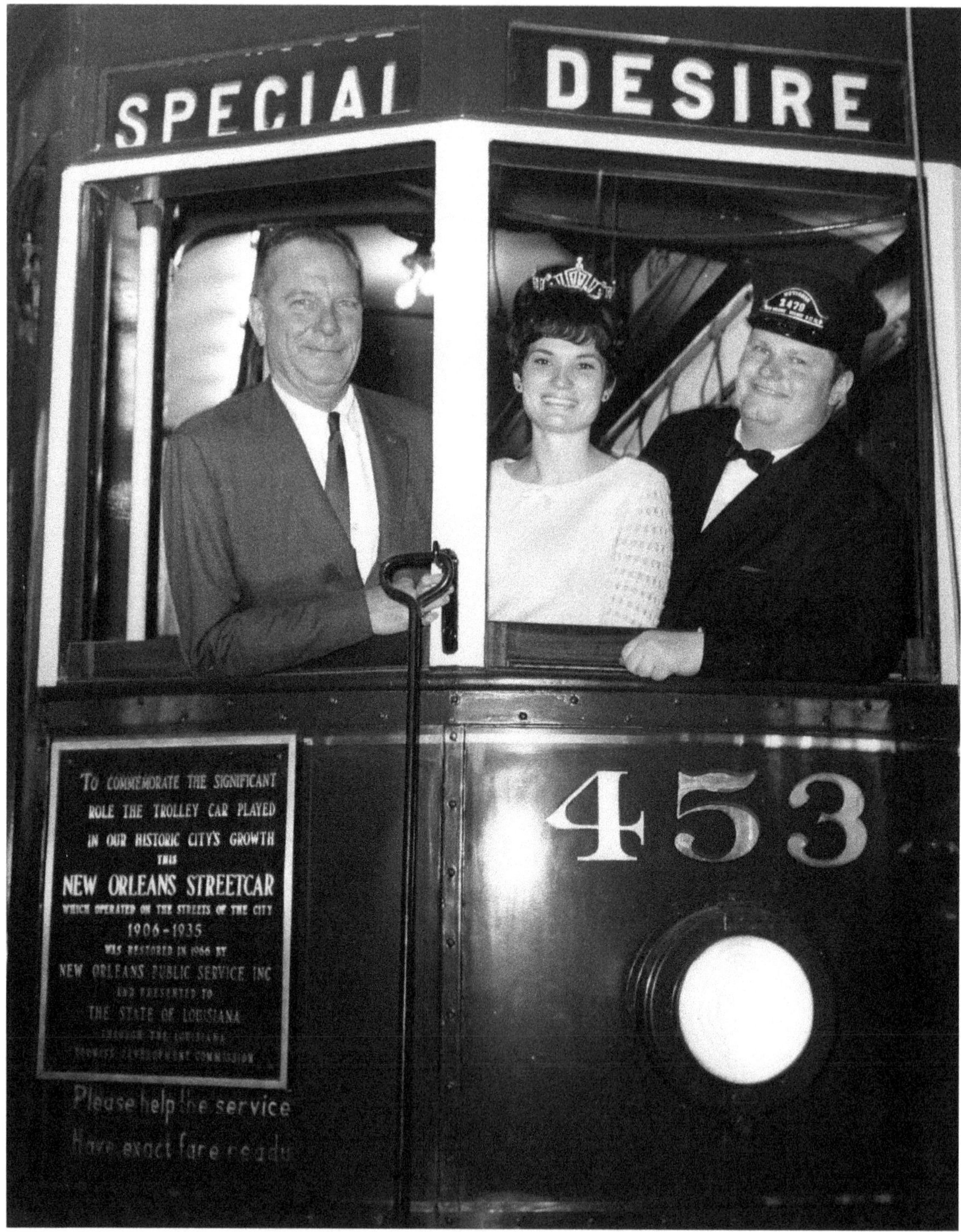

Three happy individuals pose inside a restored "Desire" streetcar in New Orleans in 1966. Made famous by the Tennessee Williams play (and later movie) *A Streetcar Named Desire,* the Desire Street line ceased operation in 1948. The Perley Thomas Series 400 car seen here never ran along the Desire line but was used in the movie and later placed on display near the French Market. It now rests in the Carrollton Avenue streetcar barn in need of further restoration, and streetcar buffs are trying to raise the necessary funds to complete the work.

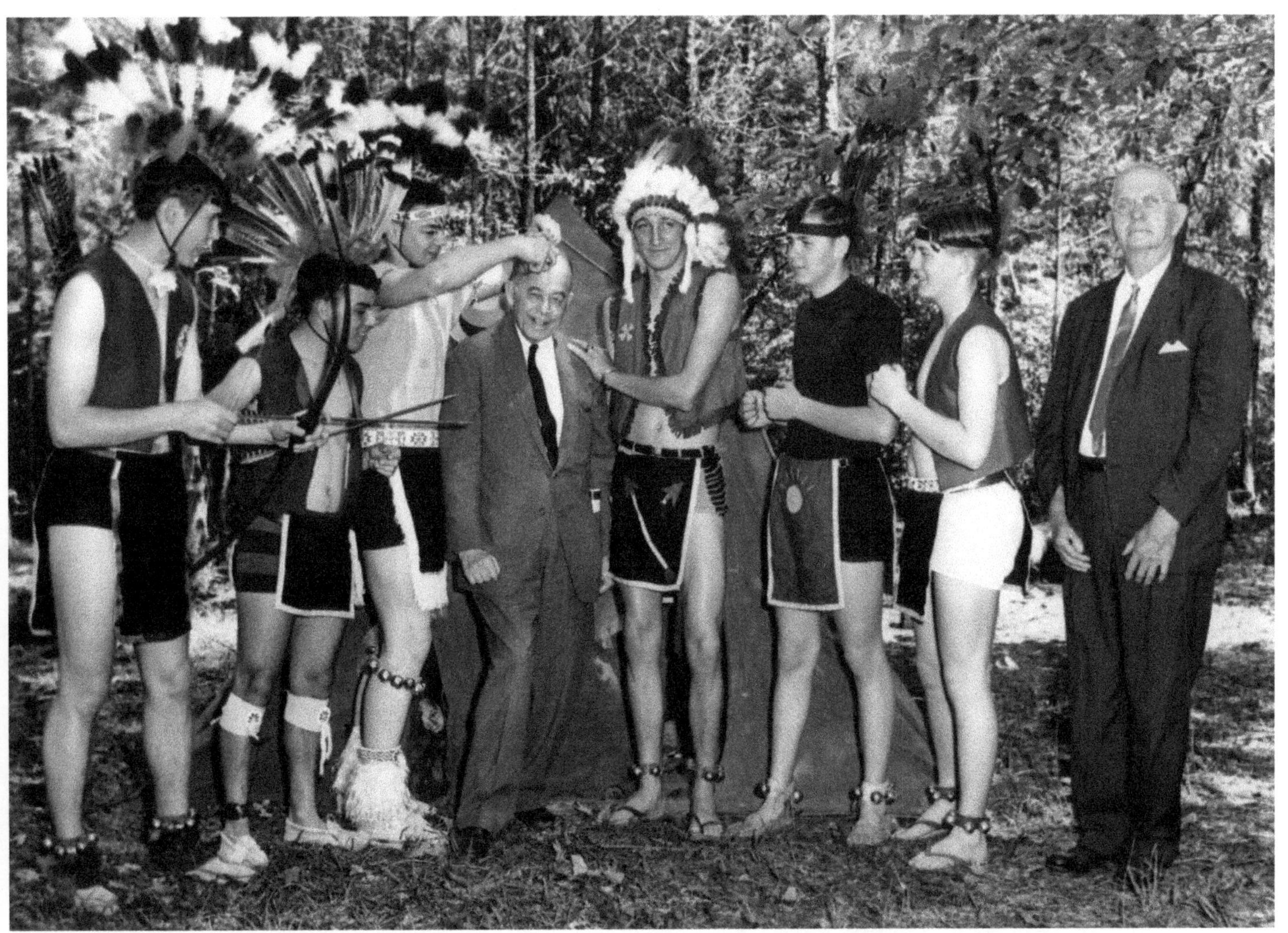

Former Louisiana governor Sam Houston Jones (1897–1978) poses with a group of young people wearing costumes representative of ancient Americans at the 1966 dedication of a historical marker at the Old Camp Ground Cemetery near Sugartown, Beauregard Parish. Jones was from Beauregard Parish and his grandfather is buried in the Old Camp Ground Cemetery. Running as a reform candidate in 1940, Jones defeated the powerful Earl K. Long for the governorship but lost to him in 1948.

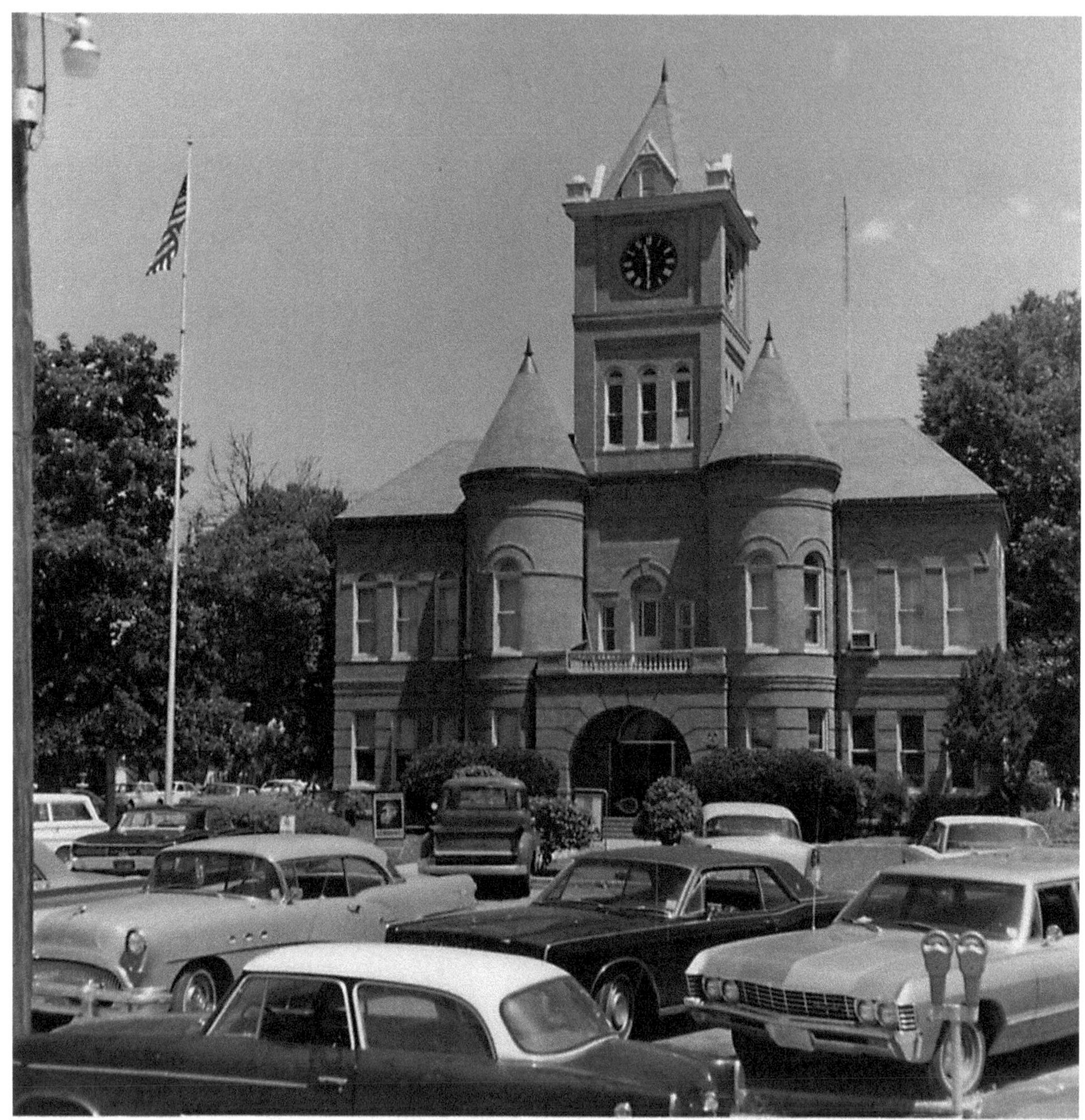

The Pointe Coupee Parish Court House in New Roads as it appeared in 1967. Built in 1902, it still stands today. Meaning "cut point" in French, Pointe Coupee Parish was given its name by early French explorers to describe a sharp bend in the adjacent Mississippi River. New Roads is situated on a curved oxbow lake named False River that was once part of the river's main channel. It has served as the parish seat since 1847.

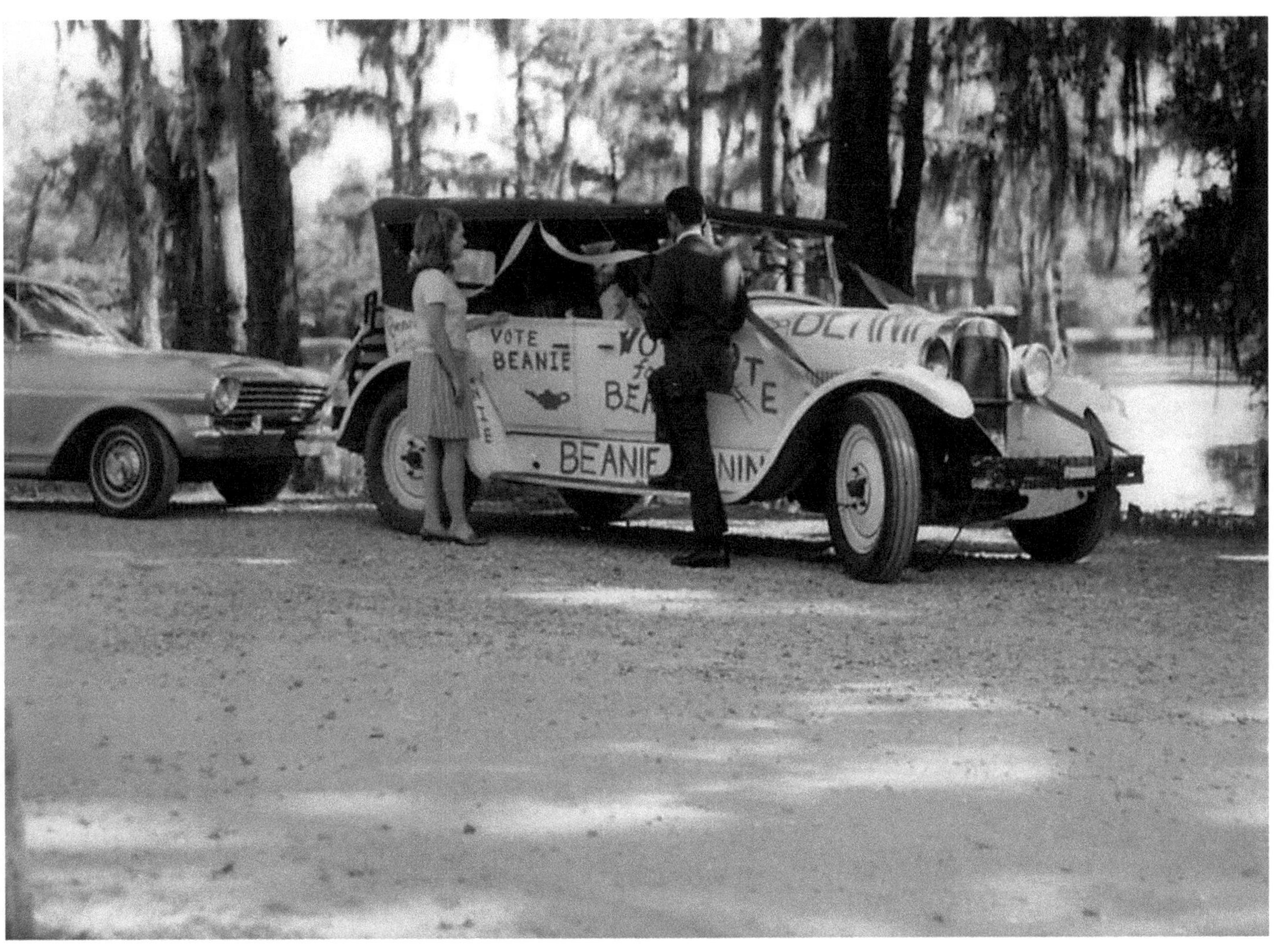

An antique car with campaign slogans saying "Vote Beanie" is parked alongside Cypress Lake on the campus of the University of Southwestern Louisiana in Lafayette. The occasion was probably an on-campus election in 1968. USL is now known as the University of Louisiana at Lafayette.

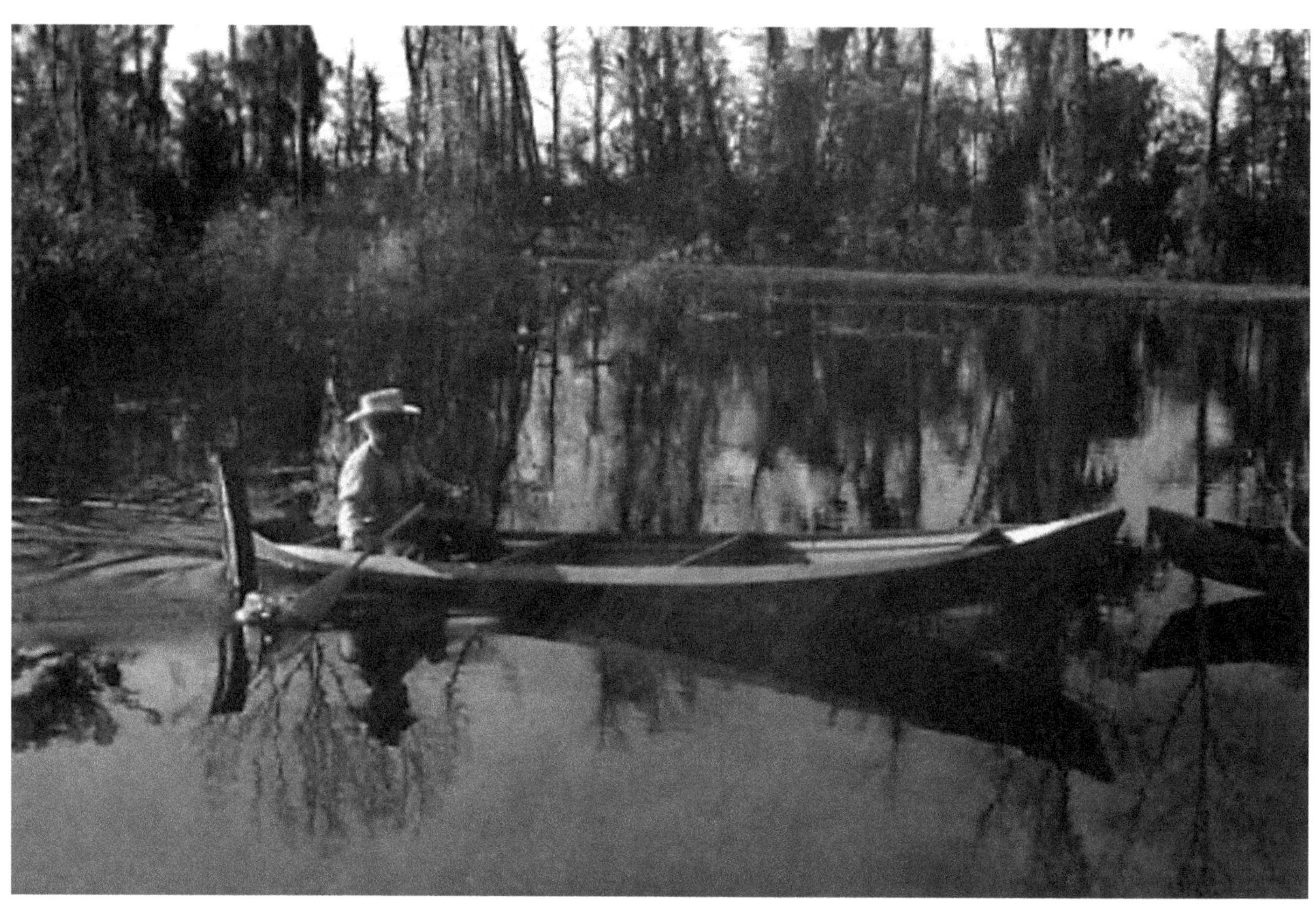

Paddling a pirogue down a bayou in southwestern Louisiana. The picture was shot as part of a documentary titled "Cajun Country," which focused on the Guidry family of Delcambre and cinematically depicted life among the descendants of the original Acadian settlers of the region. The film was produced with the cooperation of the Louisiana Department of Tourism, written by Joe Hurley, and narrated by Virginia Gibson. It aired on ABC TV on January 14, 1968.

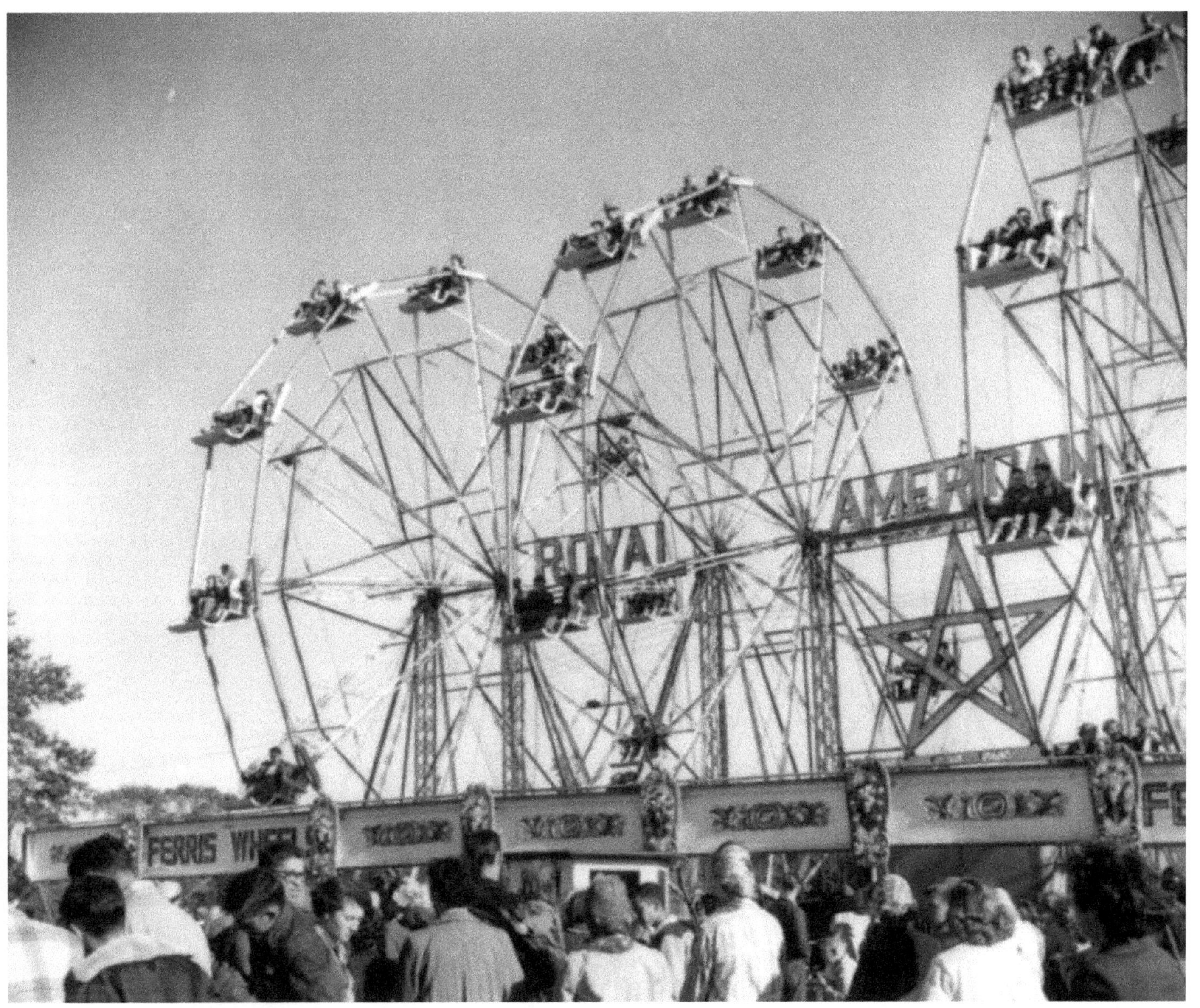

A trio of Ferris wheels take riders around in high, wide circles while others on the ground await their turn. The scene was the 1968 Louisiana State Fair in Shreveport.

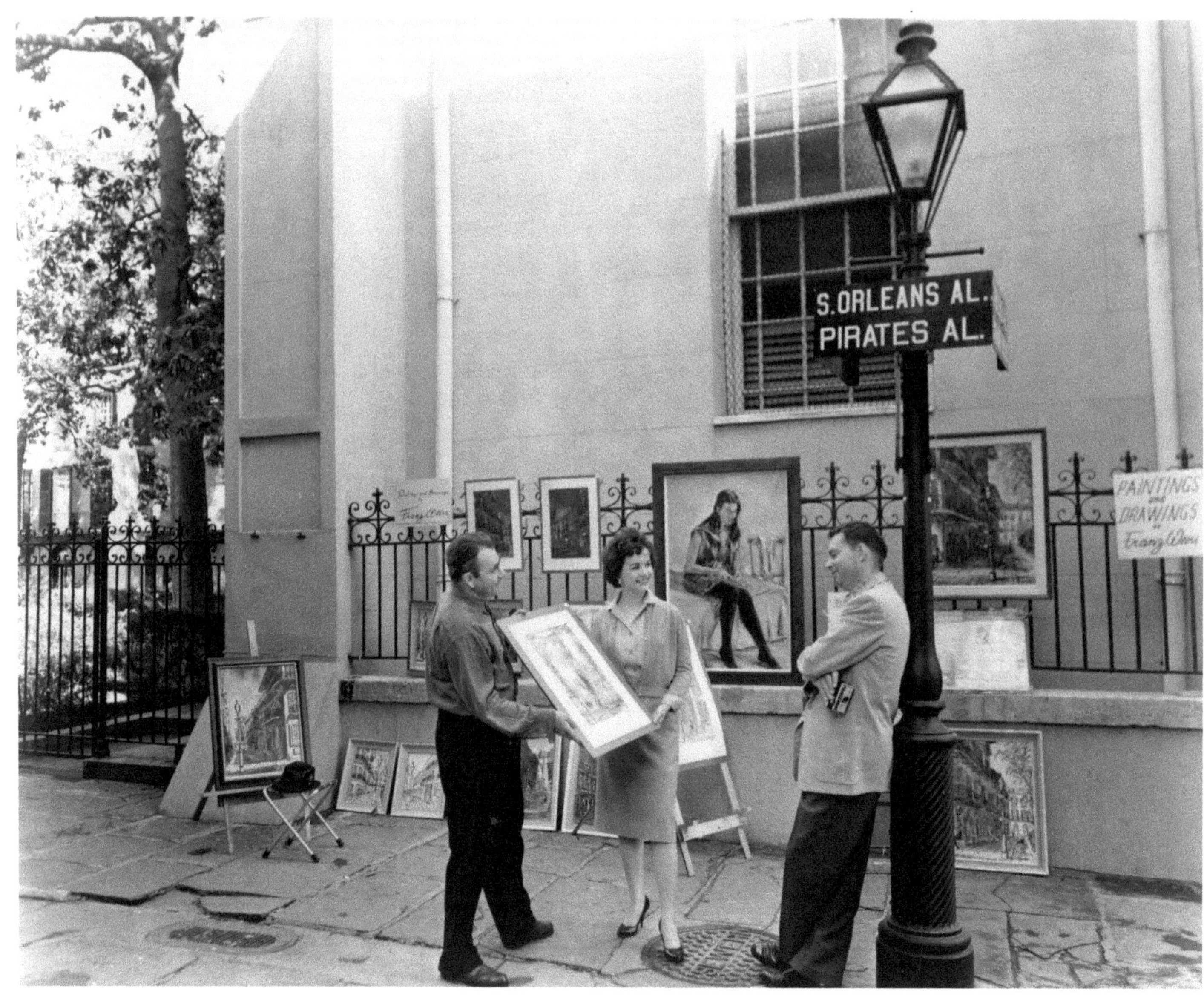

Tourists peruse a selection of paintings by a French Quarter artist in Pirate's Alley alongside St. Louis Cathedral in 1969. The narrow passageway's colorful name owes to New Orleans' history as a haven for pirates, most notably Jean and Pierre Lafitte, in the early 1800s. In 1925, writer William Faulkner lived in a small house on the one-block-long Pirate's Alley and wrote his first book there, *Soldier's Pay.* The house is preserved today as a bookstore and museum.

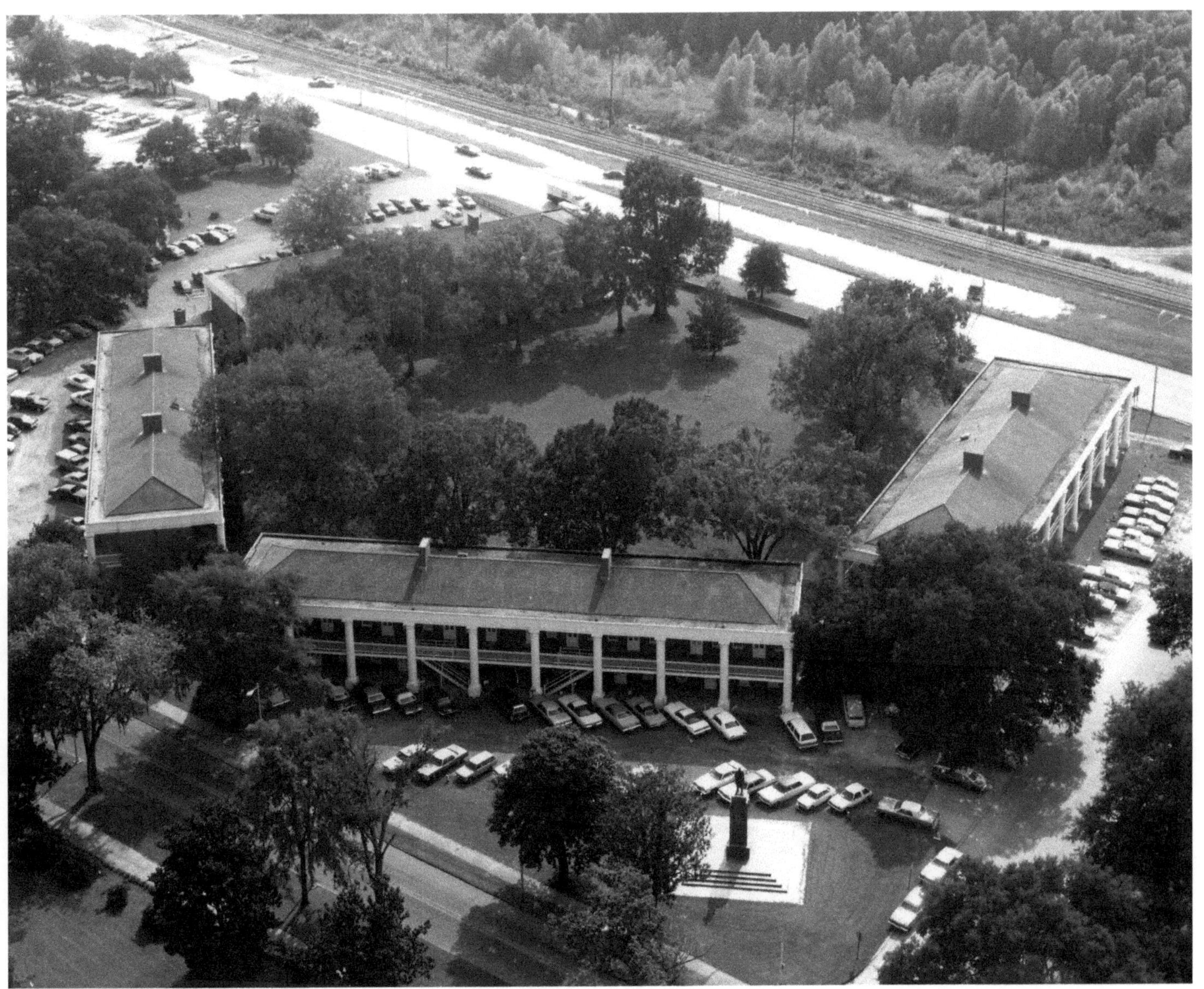

An aerial view of the Pentagon Barracks in Baton Rouge. The barracks, a military complex on the grounds of the State Capitol, stands on the site of a fort first built in 1779. The armies of Spain, France, Great Britain, the U.S., and the Confederacy have all had a presence there at one point in time. In 1976 the barracks were placed on the National Historic Register.

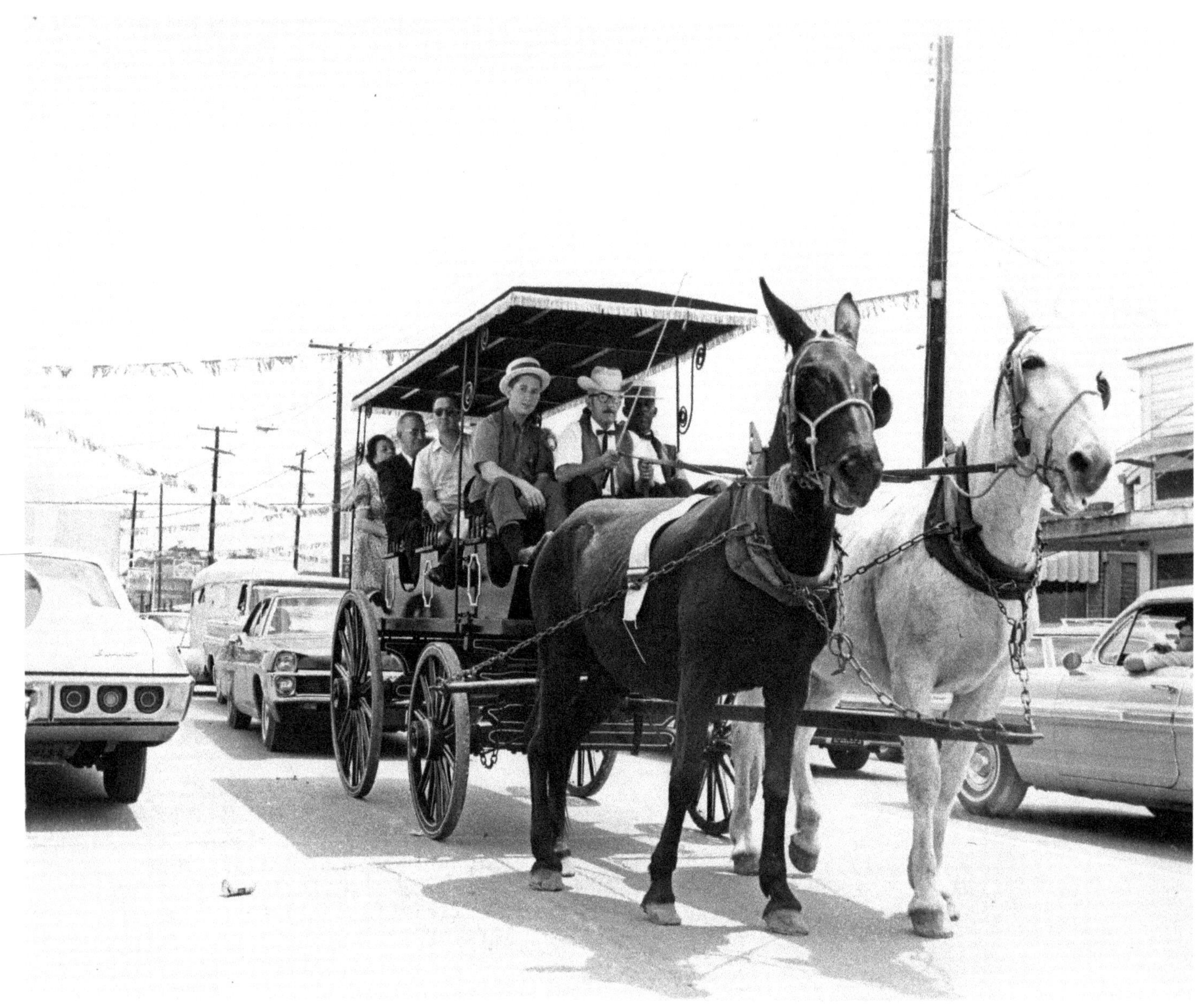

A mule-drawn surrey takes riders through the streets of Breaux Bridge during the 1968 Crawfish Festival. Proclaiming itself the "Crawfish Capital of the World," Breaux Bridge, in St. Martin Parish, draws many more people than its population of 8,000 during the popular festival celebrating the state's "Official Crustacean." The festival is held annually during the height of the crawfish season in late April and early May.

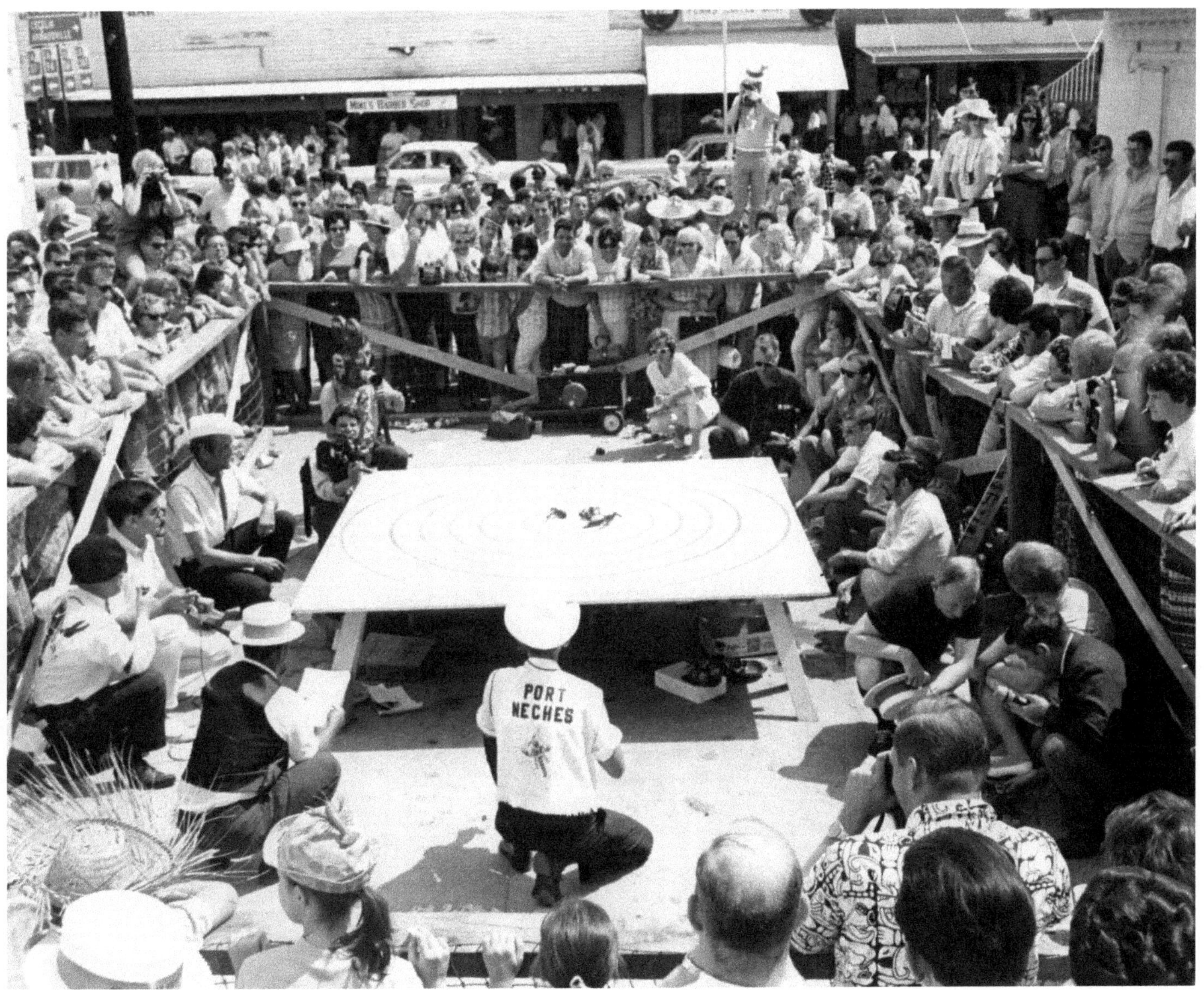

Among the most popular activities at the Breaux Bridge Crawfish Festival are the crawfish races. Bettors gather around the table during the 1969 festival, putting money down on the crustacean they think is going to win while spectators gather on the outer ring to cheer them on.

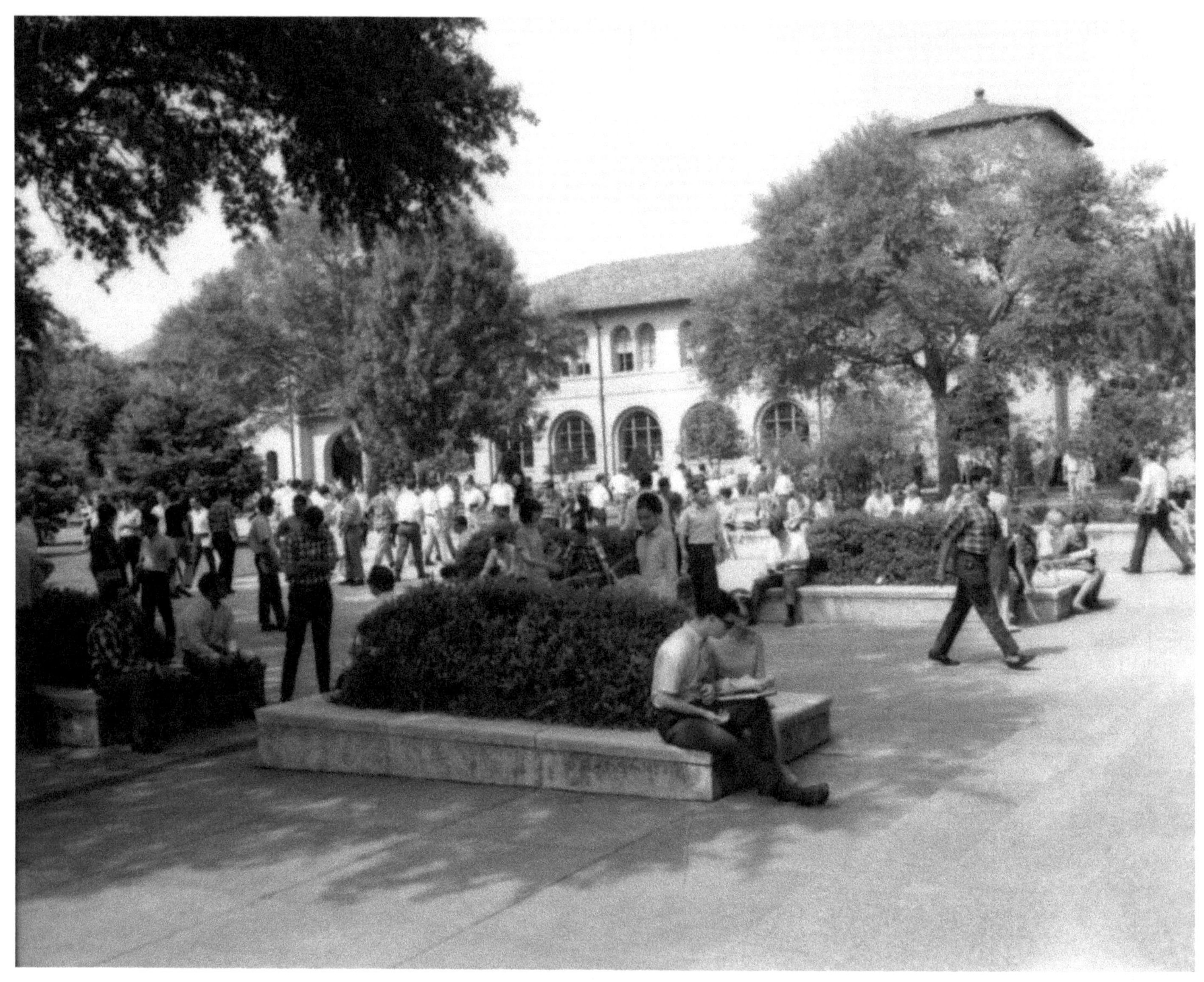

Students gather around the Quadrangle at Louisiana State University in Baton Rouge in 1969. Like most colleges and universities around the United States during this time, LSU experienced its share of on-campus radical political activity. Sports—especially football—still reigned supreme. The Tigers played in eight major bowl games between 1961 and 1970, winning six of them.

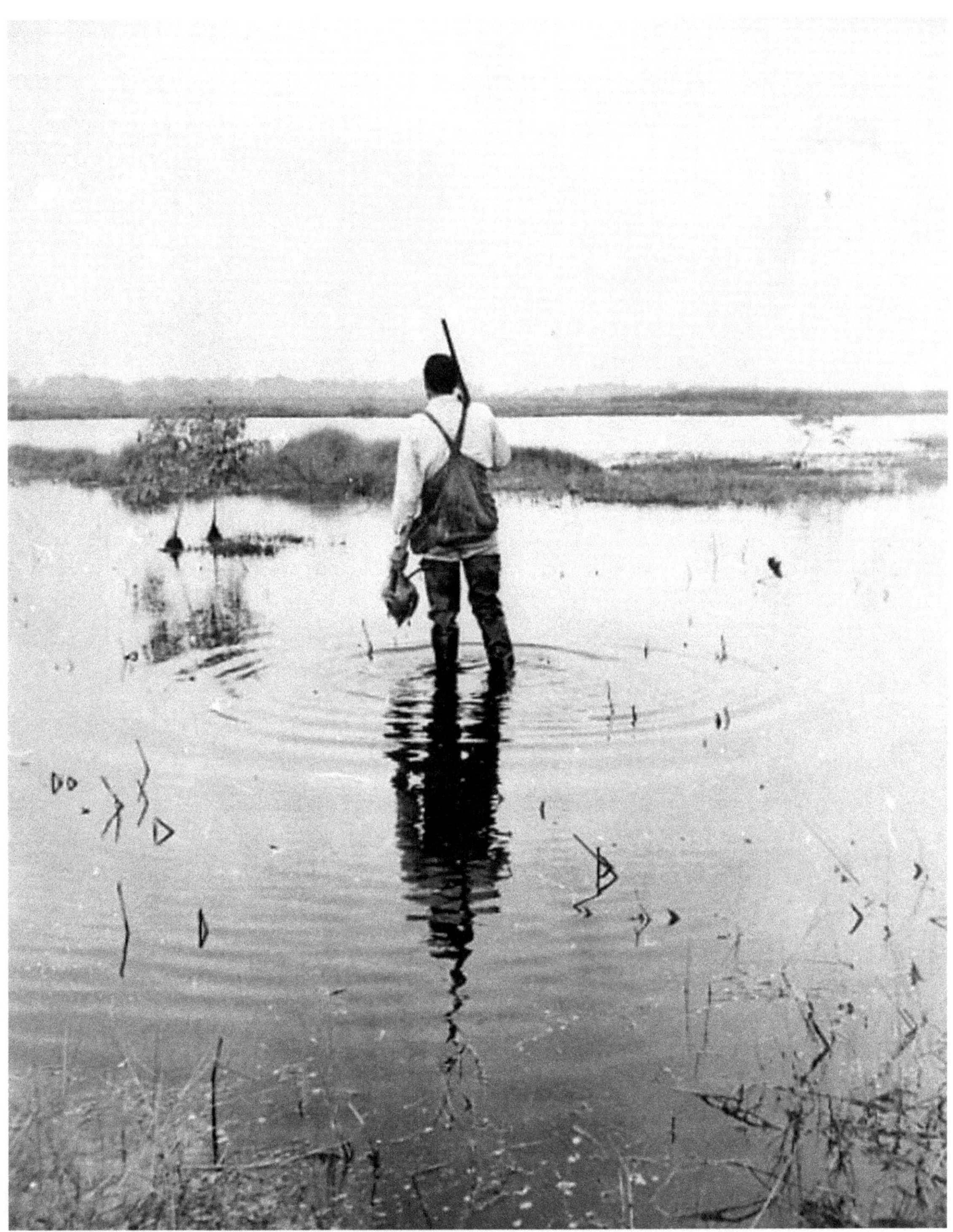

A duck hunter wades through a marsh in southern Louisiana in 1969, holding a shotgun in one hand and what appears to be a duck in the other. Duck hunting is still a popular sport in Louisiana, which advertises itself as "Sportsman's Paradise," although some areas are less than perfect. Many wetlands and barrier islands, hit hard by unchecked coastal erosion and the relentless force of recent hurricanes, have begun to disappear.

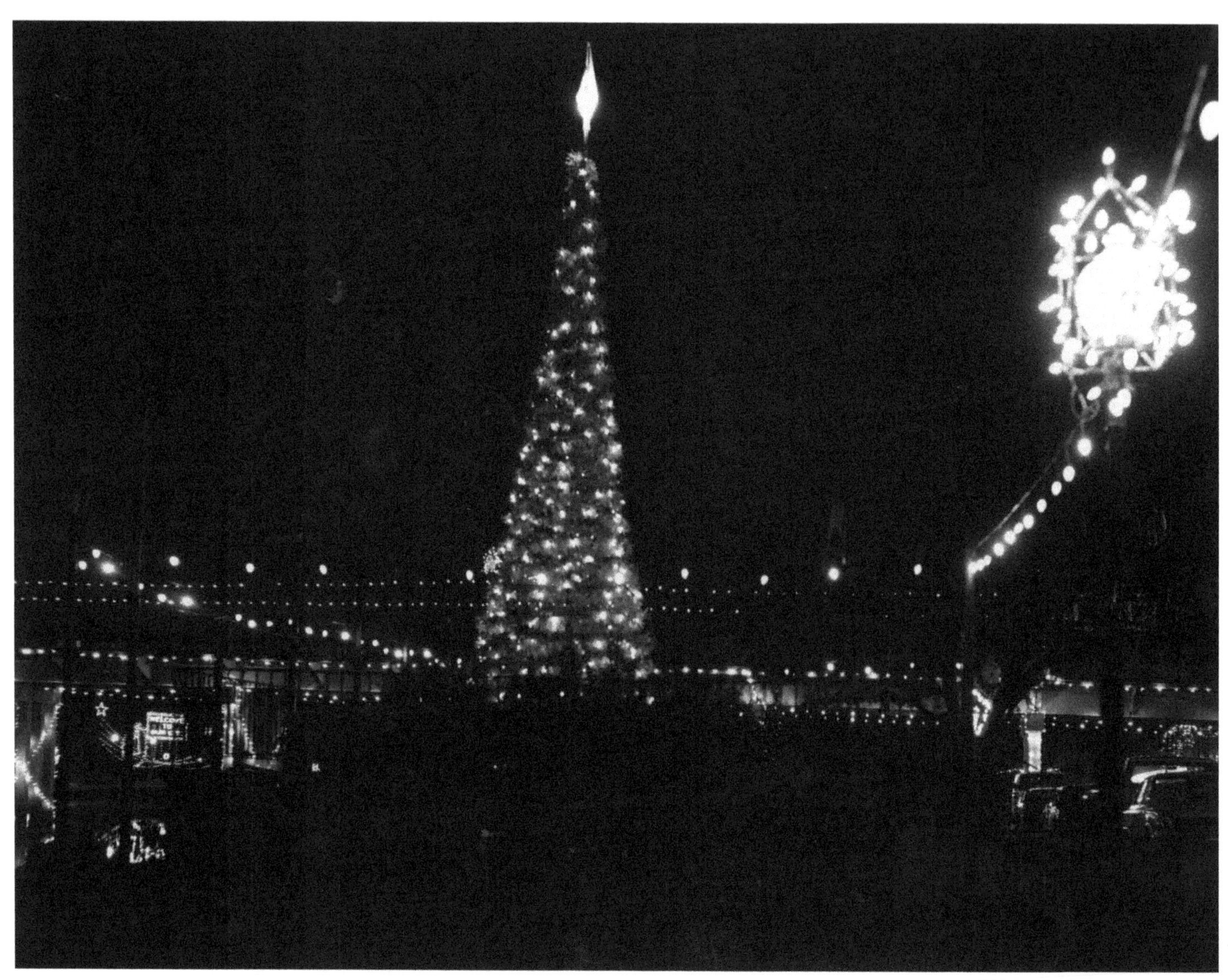

The "Singing Christmas Tree" lights up the night sky in Natchitoches in December 1969.

Notes on the Photographs

These notes, listed by page number, attempt to include all aspects known of the photographs. Each of the photographs is identified by the page number, photograph's title or description, photographer and collection, archive, and call or box number when applicable. Although every attempt was made to collect all data, in some cases complete data may have been unavailable due to the age and condition of some of the photographs and records.

II **Front Street in Alexandria**
State Library of Louisiana
Front Street Alexandria
hp000706

VI **St. Paul's Episcopal Church, New Orleans**
Library of Congress
4a04327

X **Sandoz Store in Opelousas**
State Library of Louisiana
JB Sandoz Store
hp002049

2 **Henry Clay Monument**
State Library of Louisiana
Henry Clay Statue

3 **Lighthouse at Southwest Pass**
Library of Congress
09049

4 **Church on Jackson Avenue, 1872**
Library of Congress
10491

5 **New Orleans Jockey Club**
Library of Congress
4a04326a

6 **Sugarcane and Harvesters, 1880s**
Library of Congress
4a27001

7 **Pine Tar Gathering near Covington**
Library of Congress
LC-USZ62-075564

8 **French Market Delivery**
Library of Congress
4a26985

10 **Albert & Son Photographers**
State Library of Louisiana
A Albert and Sons
hp001858

11 **William Jackson Old French Market**
Library of Congress
4a26986

12 **Firemen's Parade in Thibodaux**
State Library of Louisiana
Firemen's Parade
hp001250

13 **Baton Rouge Fire Company, 1887**
State Library of Louisiana
No 3 Fire Co
hp002524

14 **Jefferson Davis Funeral Procession**
Library of Congress
3b47375

15 **Fourth Christ Church, New Orleans**
Library of Congress
4a04328

16 **Canal Street Crowd at Rex Parade**
Library of Congress
4a17909

17 **Ruins of Napoleonville**
State Library of Louisiana
Ruins of Napoleonville
hp000082

18 **Louisiana Sugar Exchange, 1890**
State Library of Louisiana
Sugar Exchange
hp001533

19 **Sugar Exchange Traders**
State Library of Louisiana
Sugar Exchange New Orleans hp001532

20 **First Electric Streetcars in Shreveport**
State Library of Louisiana
First Electric Streetcars
hp002212

21 **Red River Flood at Pineville**
State Library of Louisiana
Flood Waters in Pineville
hp000858

22 **Richardson Memorial Hospital, New Orleans, 1892**
Library of Congress
4a04322

23 **New Orleans Cotton Exchange**
Library of Congress
4a04318

24 **St. Charles Avenue Streetcar Line**
Library of Congress
4a04331

25 **St. Charles Street, New Orleans**
Library of Congress
4a04330

26 **Old State Capitol, Baton Rouge**
State Library of Louisiana
Old State Capitol
hp000401

27 **Old U.S. Mint on Barracks Street**
Library of Congress
4a04317a

28 **U.S. Mint Employees**
Library of Congress
3b39820

30 **State Constitutional Convention, 1898**
State Library of Louisiana
Louisiana Const Convention
hp009081

31 **Interior of Teacher's Home**
Library of Congress
3a51598

32 **Sisters of the Holy Family**
Library of Congress
3b01479

33 **Water Tower Construction at Thibodaux**
State Library of Louisiana
Thibodaux Water Tower
hp001258

34 **Lafourche Parish Courthouse**
State Library of Louisiana
Thibodaux Courthouse
hp001254

36 **Old New Orleans French Opera House**
Library of Congress
4a04320

37 **Old New Orleans Customs House**
Library of Congress
4a04316

38 **Royal Street in the French Quarter**
Library of Congress
4a28933

39 **Old New Orleans City Hall**
Library of Congress
4a04314

40 **The Cabildo at New Orleans**
Library of Congress
4a04319

41 **A Busy Canal Street**
Library of Congress
3c21543

42 **President McKinley at the Cabildo**
Library of Congress
3b44452

43 **French Market Mule Cart and Boys**
Library of Congress
4a19876

44 **Streetcars on St. Charles, 1901**
Library of Congress
3a00151

45 **Canal Street, 1902**
Library of Congress
3a49161

46 **Old New Orleans Carnegie Public Library**
Library of Congress
4a23117

47 **Morgan City Outdoor Market**
Library of Congress
LC-DIG-ppmsca-12323

48 **New Orleans Fruit Stand Vendors**
Library of Congress
LC-USZ62-90735

49 **Roosevelt Address at New Orleans Board of Trade Banquet**
Library of Congress
LC-USZ62-094395

50 **Scene on Canal Street**
Library of Congress
3c12759

51 **Mardi Gras Rex Parade, 1906**
Library of Congress
3c08139

52 **Houdini at New Orleans Riverfront**
Library of Congress
LC-USZ62-136533

53 **LSU Campus at Baton Rouge, 1909**
Library of Congress
6a05509

54 **New Orleans Rooftop Panorama**
Library of Congress
6a13296

56 **Courthouse Square in Shreveport**
Library of Congress
6a05538

57 **Modern Cooking in Crowley, 1910**
Library of Congress
3c00775

58 **Rex Parade Crowds**
Library of Congress
6a27991

59 **Lake Charles Fire Devastation**
Library of Congress
6a13192

60 **Steamboats on the Mississippi at New Orleans**
Library of Congress
6a27861

61 **The Old French Market, 1910**
Library of Congress
4a23693

62 **Louisiana & Arkansas Train near Minden**
Library of Congress
LC-USZ62-106094

63 **Scene at Dunbar**
Library of Congress
00916

64 **Oyster Shuckers**
Library of Congress
00920

65 **Oyster Shuckers no. 2**
Library of Congress
00911

66 **Bookkeeping Class at Ruston Institute**
Library of Congress
LC-USZ62-084357

67 **Machine Shop at Ruston Institute**
Library of Congress
LC-USZ62-060655

68 **Mississippi River Cargo Ship**
Library of Congress
4a04313

69 **Booker T. Washington at New Orleans**
Library of Congress
LC-USZ62-133988

70 **Scene at Shreveport**
Library of Congress
LC-USZ62-099296

71 **Flood at Alsatia, 1912**
Library of Congress
10514

72 **Flood Refugees**
Library of Congress
10509

73 **Flood Refugees no. 2**
Library of Congress
10512

74 **Governor Luther Hall and Louisiana Supreme Court**
Library of Congress
3d01852

75 **Oil Company Fire at Mooringsport**
Library of Congress
3c19264

76 **Mardi Gras Rex Parade, 1913**
Library of Congress
6a27381

77 **Messenger Boy on Bicycle**
Library of Congress
03921

78 **Old Caddo Parish Court House**
Library of Congress
6a05530

79 **Soldiers at Camp Beauregard, 1918, no. 2**
Library of Congress
LC-USZ62-088093

80 **Old French Opera House, 1919**
Library of Congress
LC-USZ62-112760

81 **Rooftop Panorama of Shreveport**
Library of Congress
6a05517

82 **Bull Bayou Oil Derricks**
Library of Congress
6a05565

83 **Navigation Lock near Mermenteau**
State Library of Louisiana
Mermentau Navigation
hp007081

84 **The New Basin Canal**
State Library of Louisiana
New Basin Canal
hp006352

86 **Oil Field Roughnecks at Derrick**
State Library of Louisiana
Oil Well and Workers
hp001627

87 **Sunshine Special in Northern Louisiana**
State Library of Louisiana
Sunshine Special Train
hp001964

88 **Haynesville's Main Street**
State Library of Louisiana
Main St. Haynesville
hp000599

89 **Oaks Hotel Croquet at Hammond**
Library of Congress
LC-USZ62-089839

90 **Minden High School and Students**
Library of Congress
LC-USZ62-097081

91 **Market Shoppers**
Library of Congress
LC-USZ62-112756

92 **Soldiers at City Hall in Baton Rouge**
State Library of Louisiana
City Hall Baton Rouge
hp002568

93 **Rooftop View of Crowley**
Library of Congress
6a16481

94 **Texas and Market Streets in Shreveport**
State Library of Louisiana
Texas St Shreveport
hp002135

96 **Lafayette Business District, 1921**
Library of Congress
LC-USZ62-068522

97 **Lafayette Business District, 1921, no. 2**
Library of Congress
LC-USZ62-068553

99 **Downtown Monroe**
Library of Congress
LC-USZ62-068556

100 **Royal Street from the Louisiana Supreme Court**
Library of Congress
LC-USZ62-112758

101 **LSU's Mike the Tiger Mascot**
State Library of Louisiana
Papier Mache Tiger
hp002331

102 **Cotton Bales on New Orleans Wharf**
Library of Congress
3b33683

103 **Lake Charles Panorama**
Library of Congress
3c36033

104 **School Buses at Plain Dealing High School, 1923**
State Library of Louisiana
High School and Transfer Busses
hp002195

105 **Patterson High School Students**
State Library of Louisiana
Female Students Patterson High
hp002197

106 **Snowfall at Alexandria**
State Library of Louisiana
Downtown Alexandria
hp000694

108 **Mobile Radio Telephone in Operation, 1924**
State Library of Louisiana
Mobile Radio Telephone
hp005656

109 **Third Street in Baton Rouge**
State Library of Louisiana
Third St Baton Rouge
hp000233

110 **Drexler's Ford Dealership Employees in Thibodaux**
State Library of Louisiana
Employees of Drexler's
hp001269

111 **Concordia Parish Bookmobile**
State Library of Louisiana
Bookmobile
hp009118

112 **Texas Street in Shreveport**
State Library of Louisiana
Texas Street Shreveport
hp002136

113 **Great Flood of 1927 at Plaucheville**
Library of Congress
LC-USZ62-129633

114 **Great Flood Seaplane Flotilla**
Library of Congress
LC-USZ62-075830

115 **Great Flood Relief at Junction Landing**
Library of Congress
LC-USZ62-129959

116 **Boy Scout Relief During Great Flood**
State Library of Louisiana
Boy Scouts
hp000855

117 **Alexandria from the Air**
State Library of Louisiana
Aerial View City Hall
hp000707

118 **Frances Benjamin Johnston Home**
Library of Congress
3c20462

119 **Baton Rouge State Capitol**
Library of Congress
LC-G612-19004

120 **Group of Cajun Singers**
Library of Congress
00338

121 **Lead Belly at Angola State Penitentiary**
Library of Congress
00346

122 **Prisoner with Guitar at Angola**
Library of Congress
00348

124 **Child of Strawberry Picker**
Library of Congress
8a17015

125 **Bear on a Leash**
Library of Congress
LC-SF3301-6097

126 **Canal and North Front Streets, 1930s**
Library of Congress
8c52104

127 **Decatur Street in New Orleans**
Library of Congress
8c52096

128 **Delivery Truck and Grocery**
Library of Congress
8c52270

129 **House of the Sultan**
Library of Congress
09508

130 **La Branche House on Royal Street**
Library of Congress
LC-USZ62-095394

132 **Rice Field Fire near Crowley**
Library of Congress
8a23613

133 **On Break at Abbeville Rice Mill**
Library of Congress
8a23731

134 **Night Delivery at Raceland Nightclub**
Library of Congress
8a23737

135 **Down the Hatch in Pilottown**
Library of Congress
8a24363

136 Dancing in Raceland Roadhouse
Library of Congress
8a23738

137 Crowley Directional Signs
Library of Congress
3c24415

138 Two Guitarists at Crowley Rice Festival
Library of Congress
8a24088

139 Rice Festival Dance
Library of Congress
8a24112

140 Fais-do-do near Crowley, 1938
Library of Congress
8b20704

141 Fais-do-do near Crowley, 1938, no. 2
Library of Congress
8b20671

142 Hoisting Piano at Crowley Rice Festival
Library of Congress
8a24081

143 Railroad Crew at Port Barre
Library of Congress
8a24699

144 Three Men at Jeanerette Grocery
Library of Congress
8a24610

145 Lafayette Store Circus Signage
Library of Congress
8a24658

146 Band Performance at Crowley Rice Festival
Library of Congress
8b20527

147 Prayers at Graveside on All Saints' Day
Library of Congress
8a24716

148 Fortune-teller at State Fair in Donaldsonville
Library of Congress
8a24308

149 Donaldsonville State Fair Bingo
Library of Congress
8a24307

150 Riders of the State Fair Merry-go-round
Library of Congress
3c25942

151 Mule-drawn Schoolbus near Transylvania, 1939
Library of Congress
18771

152 The French Market, Renovated
Library of Congress
12641

153 Belle Grove Plantation
Library of Congress
3b45333

154 McClung Drugstore in Natchitoches
Library of Congress
LC-F-34-054697-D

155 Natchitoches Musicians
Library of Congress
8c12548

156 Cane Pole Fishers near Schriever
Library of Congress
1a34360

157 Traveling by Wagon near Melrose Plantation
Library of Congress
8c12723

159 Roosevelt Shacks
Library of Congress
1a34364

160 Fish for Sale near Natchitoches
Library of Congress
1a34367

161 Downtown Alexandria, 1941
Library of Congress
LC-F34056575

162 Sergeant York at Camp Claiborne
Library of Congress
6a30227

163 A Visit to the Dentist
Library of Congress
LC-USZ62-112973

164 General McNair at Third Army Troop Maneuvers
Library of Congress
8e00231

165 Gasoline for Third Army Maneuvers, 1942
Library of Congress
8e00002

166 Food Rations for the Training Maneuvers
Library of Congress
8e00012

167 Refining Oil for the War Effort
Library of Congress
8e06335

168 Mardi Gras Rex Parade, 1949
Library of Congress
LC-USZ62-091272

170 At the State Police Crime Lab
State Library of Louisiana
Crime Lab
hp005469

171 Young Readers at Calcasieu Parish Library
State Library of Louisiana
Children Reading
hp005002

172 The Hungarian Harvest Festival in Albany
State Library of Louisiana
Hungarians Dancing
hp003652

173 Offshore Drilling Rig in the Gulf
Library of Congress
LC-USZ62-124119

174 Stock Patrol in Baton Rouge
State Library of Louisiana
State Police
hp005949

175 Aerial View of New Orleans and the New Union Terminal
State Library of Louisiana
Aerial View
hp010103

176 Delcambre Shrimp Festival Water-skiers
State Library of Louisiana
Water Skiers
hp002916

177 Battle of New Orleans Monument
State Library of Louisiana
Battle of New Orleans
hp007926

178 Trawler at Morgan City Shrimp Festival
State Library of Louisiana
Blessing of the Shrimp Fleet
hp007140

179 Beard Hijinks at the Morgan City Shrimp Festival
State Library of Louisiana
Centennial Celebration
hp005631

180 Yambilee Festival King and Queen
State Library of Louisiana
Yambilee King and Queen
hp007531

181 State Visit by the General
State Library of Louisiana
Centennial Tour
hp006071

182 Mardi Gras Throw Catchers
State Library of Louisiana
Crowd Lining Parade Route
hp001367

183 Lake Pontchartrain Joggers at Mandeville
State Library of Louisiana
lake Ponchartrain
hp001189

184 St. Joseph Cathedral at Baton Rouge, 1964
State Library of Louisiana
St Joseph Cthedral
hp000465

185 Opelousas Yambilee Festival Magnolia Queen and Court
State Library of Louisiana
Yambilee
hp002744

186 Crowley Rice Fesitval Parade-goers, 1965
State Library of Louisiana
Parade and Spectators
hp005454

187 Martin Hall at USL
State Library of Louisiana
Martin Hall
hp002351

188 The Streetcar Named Desire
State Library of Louisiana
Restored Streetcar
hp005856

189 Governor Sam Jones at Dedication near Sugartown
State Library of Louisiana
Dedication of Old Camp Ground
hp007382

190 Pointe Coupee Parish Court House at New Roads
State Library of Louisiana
Courthouse in New Roads
hp000649

191 "Vote Beanie" at Cypress Lake on USL Campus
State Library of Louisiana
Cypress Lake
hp010475

192 Pirogue in Cajun Country
State Library of Louisiana
Cajun Country
hp009798

193 Trio of Ferris Wheels
State Library of Louisiana
State Fair Shreveport
hp007546

194 Painter in Pirate's Alley
State Library of Louisiana
Tourists View Paintings
hp007466

195 The Pentagon Barracks
State Library of Louisiana
Aerial of Pentagon Barracks
hp004595

196 Surrey at Breaux Bridge Crawfish Festival, 1968
State Library of Louisiana
Horse Drawn Cart
hp008894

197 Breaux Bridge Festival Crawfish Races
State Library of Louisiana
Crawfish Races
hp008716

198 Scene at LSU Quadrangle, 1969
State Library of Louisiana
LSU Quad
hp009155

199 Duck Hunter with Duck
State Library of Louisiana
Duck Hunting
hp008486

200 Natchitoches Singing Christmas Tree
State Library of Louisiana
Christmas Tree
hp007470

HISTORIC PHOTOS OF LOUISIANA

For nearly 300 years, from its founding in the early 1700s to the present, Louisiana has been one of the most fascinating and culturally diverse geographical areas on the North American continent. To many people, the name calls to mind images of sleepy bayous with moss-draped cypresses and the hot sounds of New Orleans–style jazz, but there is much more to "the Bayou State" than what exists in the popular perception.

Louisiana holds a dimension seldom portrayed in the thousands of movies and television shows shot in the state. Across the state there exists a culture of hardworking people tilling the land, pulling fish and shrimp from the sea, staffing factories, and selling the fruits of their labors in the open marketplace.

Louisiana is also a place where the *joie de vivre*—the "joy of life"—is celebrated like nowhere else. Both sides of this captivating locale, the work and the play, the struggles and the pleasures, are seen in the diverse photographs showcased in this volume. Filled with nearly 200 images reproduced in vivid black-and-white, *Historic Photos of Louisiana* is an entrancing look at this unique state.

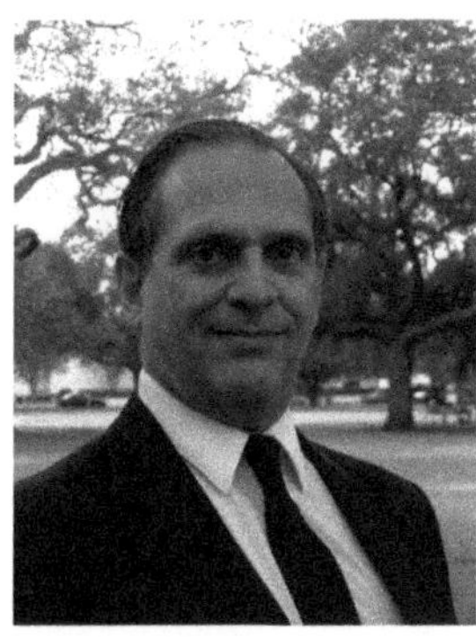

Dean M. Shapiro has lived in Louisiana since 1981 and has traveled widely throughout the state, writing about its attractions, culture, and heritage. He graduated Ramapo College of New Jersey with a B.A. in history and is the author of five other books, one of which became a made-for-TV movie *(Prophet of Evil: The Ervil LeBaron Story)* that aired on CBS in 1993. He also wrote the text and captions for *Historic Photographs of Steamboats on the Mississippi* for Turner Publishing Company in 2009. A journalist and freelance writer for 40 years, he has more than 1,500 published articles in newspapers, magazines, and Web sites to his credit. He currently writes for the New Orleans Tourism Marketing Corporation's Web site and monthly newsletter, *TravelHost* magazine, *Where Y'At* magazine, www.NewOrleans.com, and *Arthur Hardy's Mardi Gras Guide.* He is also a writer for world-renowned health and fitness guru Mackie Shilstone.

WWW.TURNERPUBLISHING.COM

www.ingramcontent.com/pod-product-compliance
Lightning Source LLC
LaVergne TN
LVHW060605110826
845154LV00003B/38

9781684421039